THE ROMAN CITY AND ITS PERIPHERY

Why did Roman cities develop an urban periphery? How was that space used, and how was it understood by contemporaries?

The Roman City and its Periphery explores the issue of periurban development outside the cities of the Roman world: the first time the issue has been treated in a comprehensive volume. Through a wide range of case studies, ranging from Rome itself to provincial cities across the western part of the empire, Penny Goodman explores contemporary views of periurban development, and compares them with the reality of archaeological remains. At the core of the work is a detailed case study of the cities of Roman Gaul, from well-known major cities such as Arles to small towns like Argentomagus, and from the Roman conquest to the end of antiquity.

This extensive study reveals that the development of an urban periphery was a widespread and characteristic feature of Roman cities everywhere, and shows that it could function as an important part of the urban fabric – a far cry from the low-grade artisanal suburbs of the medieval and early modern world. *The Roman City and its Periphery* shows the contributions which an understanding of periurban space can make to debates concerning the character of a Roman city, its relationship with the countryside, and the relationship of local elites with the power that was Rome.

Penelope J. Goodman is a lecturer in Roman history at the University of Leeds, where she specialises in the study of Roman urban space.

THE ROMAN CITY AND ITS PERIPHERY

From Rome to Gaul

Penelope J. Goodman

First published 2007
by Routledge
2 Park Square, Milton Park, Abingdon, Oxon OX14 4RN

Simultaneously published in the USA and Canada
by Routledge
711 Third Ave, New York, NY 10017

Routledge is an imprint of the Taylor & Francis Group, an informa business

First issued in paperback 2012

© 2007 Penelope J. Goodman

Typeset in Garamond 3 by
RefineCatch Limited, Bungay, Suffolk

All rights reserved. No part of this book may be reprinted or reproduced or utilised in any form or by any electronic, mechanical, or other means, now known or hereafterinvented, including photocopying and recording, or in any information storage or retrieval system, without permission in writing from the publishers.

British Library Cataloguing in Publication Data
A catalogue record for this book is available from the British Library

Library of Congress Cataloging-in-Publication Data
Goodman, Penelope J.
  The Roman City and its periphery : from Rome to Gaul / Penelope J. Goodman.
    p. cm.
Includes bibliographical references.
  ISBN-13: 978–0–415–33865–3 (hardback : alk. paper)
  1. Cities and towns, Ancient—Rome.   2. Cities and towns, Ancient—Gaul.   3. Suburbs—Italy—Rome—History.
4. Urbanization—Italy—Rome Metropolitan Area—History.
I. Title.
  HT114.G65 2007
  307.7609376—dc22

2006030519

ISBN13: 978–0–415–33865–3 (hbk)
ISBN13: 978–0–203–44625–6 (ebk)
ISBN13: 978–0–415–51844–4 (pbk)

FOR MY PARENTS

CONTENTS

	List of plates, figures and tables	viii
	Illustrations: sources and acknowledgements	x
	Preface	xii
	List of abbreviations	xiv
1	Exploring the edges of a Roman city	1
2	The urban periphery in Roman thought	7
3	The archaeology of the urban periphery	39
4	Gaul in the high empire: administrative cities	79
5	Gaul in the high empire: secondary agglomerations	167
6	Gaul in late antiquity	200
7	Some wider questions	232
	Notes	241
	Bibliography	273
	Index	299

LIST OF PLATES, FIGURES AND TABLES

Cover photograph
Temple 'of Janus', Autun.

Plates

2.1	Walled city vignette from the *Corpus Agrimensorum*, Arcerianus A manuscript.	30
2.2	Scene of the fall of Icarus including a walled city, from Pompeii: Blanckenhagen 1968, no. 10, unknown provenance.	31
2.3	'Open' city illustration from the *Corpus Agrimensorum*, Arcerianus A manuscript.	35
2.4	Personification of Rome and surrounding area, Peutinger Table.	36
4.1	East–west road and northern wall of the colonnaded enclosure at Saint-Romain-en-Gal, Vienne.	101
4.2	Part of the walled circuit at Autun.	109
4.3	Vats in the large fullery, Saint-Romain-en-Gal, Vienne.	114
4.4	Amphitheatre associated with the sanctuary of the Three Gauls, Condate, Lyon.	130
4.5	View from the amphitheatre at the sanctuary of the Three Gauls towards the urban centre on the Fourvière plateau, Lyon.	133
4.6	The amphitheatre at Saintes.	145
4.7	The 'Pyramide de Couhard' funerary monument, Autun.	153
5.1	Theatre of le Virou, Argentomagus.	180

Figures

2.1	Rome and its *suburbium*.	21
3.1	Lucus Feroniae.	53

LIST OF PLATES, FIGURES AND TABLES

3.2	Aosta (Augusta Praetoria).	61
3.3	Bologna (Bononia).	63
3.4	Verulamium (St Albans).	67
3.5	Timgad (Thamugadi).	70
4.1	Major Roman cities in Gaul.	84
4.2	Meaux (Iatinum).	87
4.3	Gallo-Roman variants on classical-type monumental public buildings.	88
4.4	Vienne (Vienna).	90
4.5	Paris (Lutetia).	94
4.6	The satellite agglomeration of Saint-Michel-du-Touch, with inset showing relationship with Toulouse (Tolosa).	95
4.7	Autun (Augustodunum).	97
4.8	Lisieux (Noviomagus), with inset showing relationship with Vieux-Lisieux.	99
4.9	Arles (Arelate).	100
4.10	Amiens (Samarobriva).	102
4.11	Sens (Agedincum).	104
4.12	Saintes (Mediolanum).	107
4.13	Fréjus (Forum Iulii).	110
4.14	Trier (Augusta Treverorum).	116
4.15	Lyon (Lugdunum).	120
4.16	Metz (Divodurum).	124
4.17	Narbonne (Narbo Martius).	132
4.18	Jublains (Noviodunum).	138
5.1	Mandeure (Epomanduorum).	168
5.2	Taden.	169
5.3	Glanum (Saint-Rémy-de-Provence).	177
5.4	Argentomagus (Argenton-sur-Creuse/Saint-Marcel).	182
5.5	Bliesbruck-Reinheim.	196
6.1	Périgueux (Vesunna).	208
6.2	Tours (Caesarodunum).	215
6.3	Bordeaux (Burdigala).	218
6.4	Saint-Bertrand-de-Comminges (Lugdunum Convenarum).	226

Tables

4.1	Types and locations of urban theatres in Gaul.	140
4.2	Types and locations of urban amphitheatres in Gaul.	143
4.3	Overall occurrence of periurban development at Gallo-Roman administrative cities.	158
4.4	Major periurban remains at Gallo-Roman administrative cities.	165

ILLUSTRATIONS: SOURCES AND ACKNOWLEDGEMENTS

Plates

2.1 Herzog August Bibliothek Wolfenbüttel: Cod. Guelf. 36.23 Aug. 2°, 56v.
2.2 © The British Museum.
2.3 Herzog August Bibliothek Wolfenbüttel: Cod. Guelf. 36.23 Aug. 2°, 72v.
2.4 Bildarchiv d. Österreichische Nationalbibliothek, Wien.

All other photographs by the author.

Figures

All line drawings by Maura Pringle, School of Geography, Archaeology and Palaeoecology, Queen's University Belfast.

2.1 Adapted from Talbert 2000.
3.1 Adapted from Potter 1979.
3.2 Adapted from Corni 1989.
3.3 Adapted from Bergonzoni and Bonova 1976 and Scagliarini 1991.
3.4 Adapted from Wacher 1995.
3.5 Adapted from Ballu 1911 and Lassus 1969.
4.1 Adapted from Petit *et al.* 1994b, Woolf 1998 and Bedon 2001.
4.2 Adapted from Laporte 1996.
4.3 Adapted from Golvin 1988, Dumasy 1992b, Pelletier 1982a and Fauduet 1993.
4.4 Adapted from Pelletier 1974 and Prisset 1999.
4.5 Adapted from Guyard 1998a.
4.6 Adapted from Baccrabère 1977, 1988 and 1996.
4.7 Adapted from Rebourg 1999 and Chardron-Picault and Pernot 1999.
4.8 Adapted from Lemaitre 1996 and 1998b.
4.9 Adapted from Sintès 1990.
4.10 Adapted from Roffin *et al.* 1966 and Bayard and Massy 1983.

ILLUSTRATIONS: SOURCES AND ACKNOWLEDGEMENTS

4.11 Adapted from Perrugot 1996.
4.12 Adapted from Maurin 1988.
4.13 Adapted from Béraud *et al.* 1998 and Rivet *et al.* 2000.
4.14 Adapted from Heinen 1985.
4.15 Adapted from Pelletier 1999.
4.16 Adapted from Schlemaire 1976 and 1978, Frézouls 1982 and Lefebvre and Wagner 1984.
4.17 Adapted from Rivet 1988.
4.18 Adapted from Naveau 1986.
5.1   Adapted from Petit *et al.* 1994b.
5.2   Adapted from Langouët 1985.
5.3   Adapted from Agusta-Boularot *et al.* 1998 and Bedon 2001.
5.4   Adapted from Dumasy 1992a.
5.5   Adapted from Petit and Schaub 1995.
6.1   Adapted from Garmy and Maurin 1996.
6.2   Adapted from Pietri 1983.
6.3   Adapted from Barraud and Régaldo-Saint Blancard 2000 and Bedon 2001.
6.4   Adapted from Guyon 1992.

PREFACE

This book began life as a D.Phil. thesis, accepted by the University of Oxford in 2002. Particular thanks, then, are of course owed to the supervisors of that thesis: Nicholas Purcell, and, in its early stages, the late John Lloyd. The debt to both is immeasurable, on a personal and an academic level. I am also immensely grateful to my examiners, Andrew Wilson and Greg Woolf, whose constructive criticisms have contributed much to the improvements made since submission. Like Nicholas Purcell, both have continued to offer generous support, advice, encouragement and scholarly guidance since my graduation. I, and the book, am the better for it.

In the process of writing the original thesis, I benefited from the assistance of numerous scholars who read and commented on my work, or shared their expertise in Gallo-Roman archaeology. In Oxford, Alan Bowman, Andrew Wilson, Amanda Claridge, Alison Cooley and the members of the Craven Committee for the academic year 1998–99 all offered valuable feedback on written work. In France, Robert Bedon was kind enough to read and comment on an early version of chapter 4. I also received warm welcomes and helpful information from Pascale Chardon-Picault, Jean-Luc Prisset, Ann Le Bot-Helly, L'Abbé Georges Baccrabère, Hugues Savay-Guerraz and Claude Sintès. Financial support came from the Arts and Humanities Research Board, which also provided a substantial grant towards travel in France and Germany. My travels were further assisted by awards from Oxford University's Craven Committee and Committee for Graduate Studies, as well as Christ Church college.

While revising the thesis for publication, my academic experience has been greatly extended by teaching positions at the Universities of Warwick, Reading, and Queen's, Belfast. My colleagues in all three institutions have been warmly supportive, but special thanks are due to Simon Swain for his consistent faith in me as both a scholar and a teacher. I am grateful, too, to Barry Cunliffe for offering advice on the publication process, Routledge's anonymous reader for encouraging and helpful comments on chapter 2, Janet DeLaine for guidance on baths, Marlies Wendowski and Andrew Wallace-Hadrill for sharing information on their unpublished research and Maura Pringle for her unparalleled professionalism as a map-drawer.

PREFACE

Finally, I would like to thank those closest to me. Friends too numerous to mention contributed both directly and indirectly. The kindness of all of them is greatly appreciated, but special mention must be made of Kate Walker's help with proof-reading and Charlotte Goodman's help with Spanish translation. But the greatest thanks of all is reserved for my parents, for their unfailing and unending encouragement, support and enthusiasm: not to mention further proof-reading services! To them, this book is gratefully dedicated.

LIST OF ABBREVIATIONS

AJAH:	American Journal of Ancient History
AnnÉp:	L'Année Épigraphique
ANRW:	Aufstieg und Niedergang der Römischen Welt
ArchAqui:	Archéologie en Aquitaine
ArchClass:	Archeologica Classica
ASHAL:	Annuaire de la Société d'Histoire et d'Archéologie de la Lorraine
AttiPontAcc:	Atti della Pontificia Accademia romana di archeologia
BCAR:	Bullettino della Commissione Archeologia Communale di Roma
BCPdC:	Bulletin de la Commission Départementale d'Histoire et d'Archéologie du Pas de Calais
BEAN:	Bulletin de l'École Antique de Nîmes
BMML:	Bulletin des Musées et Monuments Lyonnais
BMSAB:	Bulletin et Mémoires de la Société Archéologie de Bordeaux
BSAHCM:	Bulletin de Liaison de la Société d'Archéologie et d'Histoire de la Charente-Maritime
BSAS:	Bulletin de la Société Archéologique de Sens
BSAV:	Bulletin de la Société des Amis de Vienne
BTSAP:	Bulletin Trimestriel de la Société des Antiquaires de Picardie
CAG:	Carte Archéologique de la Gaule
CAHB:	Cahiers d'Archéologie et d'Histoire de Berry
CCGG:	Cahiers du Centre G. Glotz
CIL:	Corpus Inscriptionum Latinarum
CRAI:	Comptes Rendus de l'Académie des Inscriptions et Belles-Lettres
DossArch:	Dossiers d'Archéologie
JRA:	Journal of Roman Archaeology
JRS:	Journal of Roman Studies
LTUR(S):	Lexicon Topographicum Urbis Romae(: Suburbium)
MAAR:	Memoirs of the American Academy in Rome

LIST OF ABBREVIATIONS

MDAIR:	Mitteilungen des Deutschen Archäologischen Instituts, Römische Abteilung
MMPiot:	Monuments et Mémoires (Fondation Eugène Piot)
MSAM:	Mémoires de la Société Archéologique du Midi de la France
MSSNAC:	Mémoires de la Société des Sciences Naturelles et Archéologiques de la Creuse
NS:	Notizie degli scavi di antichità
OMRL:	Oudheidkundige Mededelingen uit het Rijksmuseum van Oudheiden te Leiden
PBSR:	Papers of the British School at Rome
PCPS:	Proceedings of the Cambridge Philological Society
PH:	Provence Historique
RAC:	Revue Archéologique du Centre
RAE:	Revue Archéologique de l'Est et du Centre-Est
RAN:	Revue Archéologique de Narbonnaise
RAO:	Revue Archéologique de l'Ouest
RAP:	Revue Archéologique de Picardie
RCRF:	Rei Cretariae Romanae Fautorum
RdN:	Revue du Nord
RevArch:	Revue Archéologique
RevLyon:	Revue du Lyonnaise
RIC:	The Roman Imperial Coinage
RivIstArch:	Rivista dell'Istituto Nazionale di Archeologia e Storia dell'Arte
RSaintonge:	Revue de la Saintonge et de l'Aunis
TAL:	Travaux d'Archéologie Limousine
TCCG:	Topographie Chrétienne des Cités de la Gaule des origines au milieu du VIIIe siècle.

1
EXPLORING THE EDGES OF A ROMAN CITY

A Roman city, like a text, a vase or a statue, is an artefact of the society which produced it. Its buildings, its infrastructure and its spatial organisation can therefore give us, as modern observers, an insight into the nature of that society. Working back from the material remains revealed by archaeology, and in the light of other forms of evidence such as art, literature, legal documents or coinage, we can seek to identify the social customs and processes which shaped the character and appearance of the urban fabric.[1] We may observe, for example, the effects of the efforts of the ruling elite to maintain their elevated social status through their use of public buildings, statues and inscriptions to impress and to court popularity.[2] Similarly, we may detect the desire of craftsmen and small traders to maximise trade in the clustering of shops and workshops along main roads.[3] We can also ask how the fabric of the city, once established, might in itself shape the day-to-day lives of its inhabitants.[4]

This book sets out to explore the organisation and use of a particular section of the Roman urban fabric – the urban periphery – as a means of better understanding the nature and workings of Roman urban society. Chapters 2 and 3 will offer a detailed exploration of what constituted the periphery of a Roman city, and how it might be identified. For the purposes of introducing the concept, however, a basic definition of an urban periphery may be offered here. A city's periphery can be taken to mean any occupation on the fringes of a city which is neither fully urban nor fully rural in character.[5] Although the urban periphery is intimately connected with the city, an observer familiar with Roman urbanism should be able to distinguish it not only from the centre of the city but also from the countryside beyond. Such an observer, of course, could be an ancient inhabitant of the Roman empire or a modern researcher.

To date, the Roman urban periphery has received relatively little attention from scholars. Yet it is clear that the concept of occupation which was neither fully urban nor fully rural did exist in the ancient world. Both literary texts and legal documents, for example, refer to such land-use with a variety of specialised words and phrases. Amongst the most common are the Latin adjective, '*suburbanus*', the adjectival phrases, '*extra urbem*', '*extra moenia*' and '*extra murum*', and the Greek noun, '*proast(e)ion*' and its related forms. The very use of these terms indicates that something which cannot be defined as either urban or rural is being described, while, as chapter 2 will show, the contexts in which they occur reveal much about ancient perceptions of periurban occupation. Meanwhile, archaeological evidence shows that the organisation of space and the use of land in the urban periphery was indeed different in certain respects from that in the urban centre or the countryside. Burials, for instance, were almost never made in the urban centre, while in the countryside they tended to be widely dispersed. Yet, on the periphery of the city, they were often concentrated into cemetery zones, or lined the edges of the main roads out of the urban centre. Thus, conventions differed between the city, the urban periphery and the countryside. This suggests that the people making the burials considered there to be a real distinction between the three.

It is clear, then, that the urban periphery was a widely recognised and meaningful feature of Roman urbanism in the past. If this was the case, it is of course important for us to examine and understand it, as an essential element in wider explorations of Roman urbanism and Roman urban society. This book offers such an investigation. It asks why periurban development arose at Roman cities; how, why and to what extent it differed from occupation and land-use in the city and in the countryside; what were its distinguishing characteristics; what factors and processes shaped those characteristics; and what it meant to choose to build a structure such as a house or a public building in the urban periphery. The goal of these questions will partly be to arrive at an understanding of the urban periphery in its own right. But the answers that they bring about will also be applied to wider debates. These include in particular the nature of the relationship between city and country in the Roman world, as well as the nature of the relationship between urban-based provincial elites and the metropolitan elite at Rome. The aim is to demonstrate the potential contribution of periurban evidence to the debates surrounding these issues, and to add fresh perspectives.

It will already have been noted that the terms used here to describe the intermediate zone between city and country are not the seemingly obvious choices: 'suburban' and 'suburbs'. Instead, throughout this book I use the phrase 'urban periphery' to describe the zone as a whole, and the adjective 'periurban' to describe individual features belonging to it. Although perhaps slightly cumbersome, there are two reasons for preferring these terms.

First, the Latin adjective, '*suburbanus*', and the rarer noun, '*suburbium*', carried specialised connotations in the ancient world, as chapter 2 reveals. Although both *could* be used in any context, in practice they are most frequently used to describe a specific landscape of private villa properties around the city of Rome. The goal of this book, however, is to explore the phenomenon of periurban development on a wider level than this. For this reason, the term '*suburbanus*' and its modern derivatives are reserved for discussing features around Rome itself, and alternative terms are used when discussing other cities. This approach is in keeping with an established modern convention of using the word '*suburbium*' as a technical term for the region around Rome.[6] Meanwhile, the other Latin terms which were used to describe the urban periphery either assume that it is distinguished from the urban centre by walls ('*extra murum*' and '*extra moenia*'), or define it only in relation to the city without necessarily implying that it is in any way different from the countryside ('*extra urbem*'). Although these have given rise to modern derivations such as extra-mural and extra-urban which could be used here, their roots again make them problematic. The cities of Roman Gaul, which are central to this book, amply demonstrate that walls were not necessary to create a clear distinction between the urban centre and its periphery. It is also crucial to the identity of the urban periphery that it was different from the countryside, and did not simply mean 'anything outside the city'.

The second major reason for rejecting the terms 'suburban' and 'suburbs' lies in their modern associations. For most westerners, these terms carry connotations derived from two related contexts: a knowledge of medieval and early modern urbanism in Europe, and an experience of modern European and American cities. Ideas of the suburban drawn from these contexts, however, are at odds with the reality of the Roman urban periphery in several important ways. First, the medieval or early modern city. 'Suburbs', wrote Braudel of fifteenth- to eighteenth-century Europe, 'housed the poor, artisans, watermen, noisy malodorous trades, cheap inns, posting-houses, stables for post-horses, porters' lodgings.'[7] The vision is of suburbs as a second-rate space, where people and activities expelled from the urban centre 'washed up' alongside one another. The Roman urban periphery was indeed home to traders and artisans, but it also featured monumental public buildings and wealthy elite housing. The idea of the suburb as a lower-class overspill zone is an anachronism for the Roman world: and, as we shall see, has arguably given rise to misinterpretations of its economic activity.

Medieval and early modern cities, though, did share with their Roman predecessors a tendency to have a distinct centre marked out by visible urban boundaries: either city walls, or, in the Roman period, other alternatives which will be introduced in chapter 3. The distinction between centre and suburbs in modern European and American cities is not usually so sharp. The transition from their centres to older, 'inner' suburbs,[8] and more recent 'outer' suburbs,[9] is usually detectable through changes in the character of the occupation and the age of the buildings, rather than because visible boundary markers are passed. Both inner and outer suburbs in Europe and America are also often the result of planned urban expansion, and as such tend to have a very homogeneous character. This gives rise to the endless landscape of identical houses and white picket-fences portrayed in films such as *American*

Beauty (and parodied in *Edward Scissorhands*), or, in a British context, a neighbourhood of cul-de-sacs and semi-detached houses satirised in sitcoms like *The Good Life* and *Birds of a Feather*. But Roman periurban development was rarely planned, and tended to be varied in character and appearance. Finally, land-use in the outer suburbs of modern cities is usually heavily 'zoned'. Outer suburbs are known for their commuter villages, industrial estates and, increasingly, retail parks. Although Roman periurban development could sometimes be dominated by a single type of land-use, this was not widespread. It was far more common for land outside a Roman urban centre to host a variety of structures and activities which existed side by side.

For all of these reasons, then, 'suburb' and 'suburban' are somewhat misleading terms to use in a Roman context, and especially of provincial cities. They evoke either the specific context of metropolitan Rome, or the suburbs of later cities, very different from their Roman equivalents. The words 'periurban' and 'urban periphery' are less loaded with existing connotations, and yet aptly describe occupation which is neither fully urban nor fully rural. Using these terms allows development on the fringes of Roman cities to be examined on its own terms, with less danger that the picture will be clouded by images drawn from elsewhere.

What is certain is that the need for such an examination is pressing, whatever term is employed to describe its subject. To date, the peripheries of Roman cities have received all too little attention. Past approaches to the study of Roman urbanism have frequently been based on the implicit assumption that the relationship between city and country was antithetical, with a sharp line dividing them both physically and conceptually. This is especially true of economic approaches: indeed, the polar division between city and country is an underlying principle of the 'consumer city' debate.[10] Such a viewpoint is not surprising, since it is in keeping with expressions of the same antithesis to be found in the ancient world (see chapter 2). But it leaves little scope for scholarly investigations of anything falling between the two poles. As a result, much work on Roman urbanism has overlooked the urban periphery, and the contribution which it can make to a richer understanding of the relationship between a Roman city and its rural surroundings.[11] Meanwhile, closer examinations of Roman literary texts and archaeological evidence reveal that the relationship between city and country was not as starkly opposed as it might at first appear. In fact, it was ambiguous and open to inversion: and the urban periphery is only a particularly vivid illustration of this.

This is not to say that no work at all has been done on Roman periurban development. Much has been written on the *suburbium* of Rome, partly because it is especially prominent in our literary sources, and partly because of the degree of archaeological attention which Rome in general has received.[12] The indispensable *Lexicon Topographicum Urbis Romae* is even now being supplemented by a second series devoted to the Roman *suburbium* under the title *Lexicon Topographicum Urbis Romae: Suburbium*.[13] There have also been studies of periurban occupation outside specific provincial cities, such as Lincoln or Bologna,[14] and some more detailed works aiming to review periurban development across a whole province. In 1987, Simon Esmonde Cleary published a monograph on the subject of extra-mural development at towns in Roman Britain,[15] while a conference held in France in 1997 focused on periurban occupation outside Gallo-Roman cities.[16]

These latter two publications have been particularly important steps forward in expanding the study of Roman urban peripheries into the provinces, and away from the special circumstances of Rome.[17] However, their scope could have been wider. Esmonde Cleary took a strictly archaeological approach to the towns of Roman Britain, employing textual evidence only when discussing the legal and administrative aspects of extra-mural occupation. He was able to produce an extremely comprehensive account of the physical form of extra-mural occupation in Roman Britain. But some conclusions which could have been drawn by comparing this account with evidence from other parts of the empire fell outside the scope of his work. He was unable to comment, for instance, on whether Romano-British cities were influenced by Roman literary treatments of the urban periphery. Meanwhile the papers of the French conference were written by many different authors, covering either specific periurban issues or individual sites. This encouraged a valuable range of ideas, approaches and regional studies. But it meant that the opportunities to draw comparisons between findings from different sites, or present an overall account of periurban development across Gaul, were limited.

Here, I shall again focus on one particular region – the four provinces of Gaul – but will seek explicitly to set the periurban development observed there into the wider context of urbanism throughout the western provinces of the Roman empire. My intention is to strike a balance between a detailed treatment of periurban development in a meaningful regional context, and an overview of the phenomenon of the Roman urban periphery as a whole. I shall examine both archaeological and non-archaeological evidence from a range of geographical contexts, and use this to draw direct comparisons between different cities within Gaul, and between Gallo-Roman cities and those in other parts of the empire.

Chapters 2 and 3 will begin by examining periurban development as an empire-wide phenomenon. Chapter 2 explores the 'thought-world' associated with this type of occupation: in Rome itself and in the places touched by Rome. Chapter 3 then goes on to look at the archaeology of the urban periphery, asking in particular how periurban occupation can be identified from a modern perspective. Chapters 4 to 6 will then move on to a detailed examination of the character and function of periurban development in the specific context of Roman Gaul. As these chapters will establish, Gallo-Roman cities have enough coherence as a group of related sites to allow meaningful comparisons to be drawn between them, and for an overall picture of periurban development in this region to be constructed. Finally, the concluding chapter considers the contribution of the periurban evidence from Gaul to our understanding of Roman urbanism as a whole, and especially to debates concerning the city–country relationship and the relationship between Rome and the provinces.

2

THE URBAN PERIPHERY IN ROMAN THOUGHT

Introduction

Much of the rationale behind setting out to study the Roman urban periphery rests on the fact that it was a recognised entity in the ancient world, and thus had meaning within Roman society. The evidence which indicates that this was so, however, can tell us much more than this. Legal documents, literary texts, and visual images provide an insight into the thought-world of the urban periphery, as well as the various means by which Roman observers distinguished the periurban from the urban or the rural.[1] This evidence comes primarily from an elite perspective: it was chiefly produced by and for individuals who held a dominant position within Roman society, and who were generally male, wealthy, well-educated and politically active. Specifically, much of it was produced by or for members of the unique metropolitan elite based at Rome. The view of the periurban which it preserves, then, is very much that of a select group. None the less, the very social dominance of those who belonged to this group makes their perspective of particular interest. These people were in a position to disseminate their understanding of the urban periphery to others via art, literature and the law. They were also able to affect the physical appearance of actual urban landscapes, both at Rome and elsewhere, through their control over land and wealth.

This chapter, then, aims to explore the attitudes towards and understanding of the urban periphery typically held by the elite of the Roman empire, through an examination of legal, literary and visual evidence. The legal status of the urban periphery, its importance as an element in Roman urbanism and the associations which it evoked will be investigated, while the issue of the extent to which these details were held to apply to provincial cities as well as Rome will also be raised. The conclusions drawn here will then provide a helpful context for the analysis of archaeological evidence from Gaul in chapters 4–6, and especially for establishing the extent to which the Gallo-Roman elite appear to have been influenced by the thought-world revealed in this chapter. Direct evidence for elite ideas about the urban periphery does not survive from the Gaul of the high empire, although some is available from late antique Gaul in the form of letters and poems, and will be treated in chapter 6. However, if the archaeological evidence for elite activity in the urban peripheries of Gaul can be viewed in the light of what is known about modes of thought constructed around such zones by elites elsewhere in the Roman world, this will at least allow us to ask whether the behaviour of the Gallo-Roman elite was consistent with such views. Was the thought-world of either Rome's urban periphery in particular, or periurban development more generally, part of the model of Roman urbanism that was transmitted to the Gallic elite, and did they seek to emulate it? This issue will be tackled in chapter 7, after the evidence from Gaul has been evaluated on its own terms.

The urban, the rural and the periurban

The urban periphery has already been defined as a zone which was neither entirely urban nor entirely rural, and could be recognised as such by an observer familiar with Roman urbanism. For the present, we will assume that an urban periphery could only exist when there was something recognisably urban against which to define it, although this assumption will be revisited and tested in chapter 5. If this is the case, then the concepts of 'the urban' and 'the rural' need to be reviewed before the thought-world of the urban periphery can be properly explored. Once again, the surviving evidence for Roman ideas about city and country comes from the elite, and especially the metropolitan elite at Rome. But since it is their concept of the urban periphery that we are seeking to understand, then it is their construction of the relationship between the city and the countryside which most needs to be examined here.

In order to understand the elite ideology of city and country in the Roman world, it is first important to consider the role which both played in the administration of the Roman empire, and the actual legal relationship between them. The basic administrative unit adopted or imposed across the Roman empire was not in fact the city *per se*, but rather a semi-autonomous civic community. Most of the empire was divided up into such communities,[2] and the leaders of each managed the day-to-day government of their land and people on Rome's behalf. The administration of each community usually centred on a single dominant city, where the local elite would meet, oversee local affairs and liaise directly with the central government in Rome. Other settlements within the community's territory were then administered from that city. Around this basic model, many varieties of civic community were recognised within the empire, and were distinguished by their different levels of status. In the western part of the empire, a hierarchy of communities developed, progressing upwards from a native or 'peregrine' community (including the *civitates* of Africa, Britain, Gaul and Spain), to a *municipium* and finally a *colonia*.³ In the east, *coloniae* also existed, but most communities were interested only in attaining or maintaining the status of a Greek *polis*.⁴

The laws governing individual Roman civic communities varied according to their status, their cultural background and the period when they had come under Roman influence.⁵ *Coloniae* and *municipia* were granted charters, establishing constitutions which broadly reflected the administrative system at Rome itself. Direct constitutional intervention was less common in established Greek *poleis*, but Greek civic constitutions could be revised at Roman discretion, and newly created *poleis* did receive charters from Rome.⁶ *Civitates* were technically allowed to govern themselves using their own laws, but when agreements were drawn up to formalise the relationship between these communities and Rome, measures were probably taken to ensure that these laws were consistent with Rome's interests.⁷ Significant differences could therefore exist between local legal systems, but all were liable to some degree of modification from Rome. It can be assumed that this was used to ensure conformity to the basic model of a population governed from an administrative city which Rome required to manage the empire.

In constitutional charters, very little distinction appears to have been made between urban and rural land or city- and country-dwellers. Where these charters use words such as '*colonia*' or '*municipium*' to define the scope of a law, this usually refers to the community as a whole, rather than its principal city. Thus both city and country were seen as the combined property of the community, and the same laws governed the population in any part of it.⁸ In this sense, city and country were complementary elements of a common unit. Within that unit, however, each served different functions. The city acted as a base for legal and political activity, and its structural and administrative links with Rome provided a means for interaction with the rest of the empire. It was also a convenient focus for other communal activities, such as social interaction, religious rituals and trade. Meanwhile, the community's rural land was dedicated primarily to agricultural exploitation, which formed the basis of the community's wealth. Thus two different spheres of action were defined. Significantly, the local elite would generally be active in both spheres, since they needed to spend time in the city in order to participate in local politics, but they also needed to own and oversee land in the country in order to generate and maintain the wealth which supported this. Meanwhile, Roman civil law, which applied to Roman citizens living in provincial communities alongside the laws written into constitutional charters,⁹ *could* distinguish between the urban and the rural. Thus the professional land-surveyors, whose job included investigating property disputes, recognised the potential for disagreements over land in two different spheres: the urban and the rural.¹⁰

Turning to literary portrayals of city and country, we find that one dominant theme is a desire to distinguish sharply between the two. Writers often portray city and country as an antithetical pair with opposing characteristics, especially on a moral level. A vivid example of such treatment occurs at the beginning of book 3 of Varro's *De Re Rustica*. Varro declares that there are two ways of life, *'rustica et urbana'* (the rural life and the urban life),[11] which he distinguishes on a historical, but also a moral level: 'the culture of the field is not only more ancient, but also more virtuous'.[12] For Varro, the rustic life is superior because country-dwelling Romans had always provided food and military aid to the state: by implication, city-dwellers have meanwhile contributed nothing. The theme Varro presents here is a literary commonplace, with which all well-educated Romans would have been familiar. The antithetical relationship between city and country, especially on a moral level, appears in literature of all genres,[13] and is even recommended by Quintilian as a suitable topic for mock classroom debates.[14] As Quintilian's recommendation implies, the subject was also capable of being inverted, so that an urban lifestyle could just as readily be presented as morally superior to a rural one. Both sides of the debate appear in Cicero's defence of Sextus Roscius of Ameria, where Cicero argues that Roscius' rural background makes him less likely than a city-dweller to have committed murder, while his opponents claim that it makes him 'savage and uncultivated' (*ferum atque agrestem*).[15]

The city itself was portrayed in elite literature as an important symbol of sophistication and civilisation, and especially of *romanitas* (essentially, 'Roman-ness'). Thus, Tacitus in his *Germania* is able to convey to his elite Roman audience just how barbarous and alien the Germans are by telling them, 'it is well known that no German people live in cities, indeed that they do not allow joined buildings amongst them'.[16] The same theme arises in Tacitus' *Histories*, when he has an embassy from the German tribe of the Tencteri offer an alliance to the people of the Colonia Agrippinensis (Köln) on the condition that they kill all Romans within their territory and pull down the walls of their city.[17] Thus the destruction of a major urban monument, described by the Tencteri as 'bulwarks of slavery' (*munimenta servitii*), would symbolise as complete a rejection of Roman rule as the slaughter of actual Romans.

From these passages, it is clear that evidence of *urbanitas* ('urban-ness') in a city was simultaneously a sign of *romanitas*. It indicated that the city, and by extension the community administered from it, was part of the privileged and civilised world of the Roman empire. *Urbanitas* itself sprang in part from a city's political status as the dominant administrative centre of a civic community. However, by the Roman period, urban identity had also come to be judged on the basis of the city's appearance, and particularly its public monuments. This attitude is well illustrated by the comments of Pausanias, writing in the second century AD, on the Greek city of Panopeus in Phocis.[18] Pausanias himself tells us that Panopeus is the centre of an independent city-state, since it sends delegates to the Phocian assembly, and has a territory defined by borders with neighbouring communities. The complete lack of government offices, gymnasium, theatre, *agora* or public fountains there, however, causes him to doubt whether Panopeus can really be called a *polis*. Clearly, then, public monuments could carry almost as much weight in judgements of *urbanitas* as the political role of the settlement in question. If a settlement failed to make a sufficient display of urban status through its public monuments, its identity as a 'true' city could be questioned, and, consequently, so could the semi-autonomous status of the community it administered.

The idea that urban status was contestable is also supported by other evidence. Strabo, for instance, argues against 'those who assert that there are more than one thousand cities [*poleis*] in Iberia' on the grounds that they 'seem to me to be led to do so by calling the big villages [*megalas komas*] cities'.[19] One consequence of this potential for questioning urban identity was that settlements with no political function, such as large towns within the territories of other dominant cities, could aspire to a form of urban identity through other means, such as the erection of public monuments. Sometimes, this could even result in the attainment of actual urban status. Inscriptions from the Greek east reveal that some secondary centres were promoted to the status of *polis* after convincing the emperor of their worthiness.[20]

A well-educated member of the metropolitan elite at Rome, then, or a provincial who was conscious of metropolitan Roman culture and wished to align himself with it, should have been familiar with an ideology of city and country which included several basic elements. First, he should have been aware of a sharp antithesis between city and country, particularly on moral grounds. Second, he should have understood that the cities used as administrative centres by Rome's subject communities were potent symbols of the status of those communities, and especially of their membership of the wider Roman world. And finally, he should have been aware of the importance of the physical fabric of the city, and especially its monumental public buildings, in expressing a community's *urbanitas* and, consequently, its *romanitas*. It is now possible to consider how these ideas related to actual elite behaviour in the city, and especially those aspects of elite behaviour which left their mark on the urban fabric.

A close connection can immediately be identified between the literary polarisation of city and country and the physical boundaries established around most Roman cities. The most obvious such boundaries are city walls: well-attested at Rome itself, and numerous provincial cities. Their very presence was a potent symbol of urban status in itself,[21] partly no doubt because of the command over resources and manpower which they demonstrated, but perhaps also because they displayed a commitment to the ideology of the city as a distinct and privileged space. As chapter 3 will demonstrate, however, even where walls were lacking, other types of visible marker were regularly used to define the edges of a Roman city, including monumental arches, the edges of an orthogonal street layout or natural features such as rivers.

These markers would make it clear to both residents and visitors when they were passing between rural and urban space, thus drawing attention to the differences between city and country.

The extent to which features such as city walls or orthogonal grid-plans in newly founded provincial cities were imposed by the central Roman administration or adopted voluntarily by local elites is somewhat uncertain. Two references in the *Digesta* suggest that by the second century AD at least, the construction of a walled circuit around any provincial city could be authorised only by the emperor.[22] This does not mean that the initiative for wall-building could not come from the provincial communities themselves, however, only that they would have to seek the emperor's permission to proceed. Meanwhile, Hanson argues that the relative lack of orthogonal grids in secondary settlements in the north-western provinces suggests that they were imposed on the sites of major administrative cities by Roman planners rather than initiated by the local elite.[23] Woolf, however, posits a greater level of provincial input, and explains the same pattern in terms of the immense cost to the community involved in establishing an orthogonal layout.[24] Whatever the circumstances of their initial creation, though, the subsequent maintenance of urban boundaries at any kind of provincial city must have been largely the responsibility of the local civic authorities. Archaeological evidence from across the empire suggests that these bodies were very interested in maintaining visual markers at the edges of their cities, even where actual occupation had expanded beyond them (see chapter 3). Thus provincial elites do appear to have wanted to distinguish between urban and rural space in their own right, even where Rome was no longer directly encouraging them to do so.

The Roman interest in distinguishing physically between the urban and the rural probably had its origins in defensive practicalities and a religious desire to ensure the favour of the gods by marking out sacred space.[25] However, in the context of the *pax Romana* of the high imperial period, it is also likely to have become linked with the two other major themes discussed above; the importance of *urbanitas* as a symbol of civilised and semi-autonomous status, and the role of the urban fabric in displaying it to others. The elite in any Roman city regularly made benefactions of public buildings, primarily in order to boost their own personal status.[26] A strong secondary motivation, however, is likely to have been an interest in enhancing the status of the community as a whole.[27] Their awareness of the contestability of urban status would have made this desirable, not least because their own standing would be greater if their city was widely recognised as highly urbane and sophisticated. By distinguishing sharply between city and country, local elites could potentially increase the effectiveness of such displays of status. The boundaries around a provincial city made it into a carefully defined arena, and ensured that the monuments erected within it would all be clearly understood as of and belonging to the city. Meanwhile, some of the features which helped to define this arena, such as city walls, monumental arches or a street-grid would also demonstrate *urbanitas* in themselves.

The antithesis between city and country, however, was not always as stark in reality as elite authors and town-planners might have wished. Archaeological evidence in fact points towards a very close relationship between most Roman cities and the surrounding countryside. This includes the farming of land immediately around the city by people resident within it,[28] as well as horticulture and even animal husbandry within the walls.[29] The elite themselves were also extremely capable of inverting the normal distinction between city and country, and making deliberate displays of *urbanitas* in the country or *rusticitas* in the city.[30] Perhaps the ultimate example of this is Nero's Golden House, the hostile reactions to which, Purcell argues, were provoked largely by the extravagance of Nero's attempt to bring landscapes properly belonging to the countryside into the centre of Rome.[31] Such elite inversions of city and country drew much of their effectiveness, and their notoriety, from the traditional interest in distinguishing between the two. However, the fact that they were made reveals that this interest was not universal.

The clearest indication of the gap between the elite ideology of the city and the reality of Roman urbanism, however, must be the persistent development of periurban occupation beyond the boundaries of urban centres. Not only is this type of occupation attested archaeologically at numerous cities, it was also recognised by the same authors who were interested in portraying city and country as polar opposites. Thus Horace, famous for his fable of the town mouse and the country mouse,[32] can be found in the same book of his *Satires* complaining about the washed-out flavour of cabbage grown in suburban market-gardens.[33] The widespread evidence for periurban occupation outside Roman urban centres suggests that, in spite of elite attempts to define their cities with clear visible boundaries, other forces at work in Roman society actually encouraged a more gradual transition from city to countryside. The tension between these social forces and the elite ideology of the city may thus have helped to *create* a recognisable urban periphery, excluded from the urban centre by the elite interest in defining that centre with largely static boundaries, but differentiated from the countryside by its special relationship with the city. This hypothesis will be explored in further detail using the archaeological evidence from Gaul in chapters 4–6.

The urban periphery in Roman law

Our exploration of the evidence for Roman perceptions of the urban periphery begins with legal texts, which seek to define it for the purposes of legislation or property disputes, and to regulate land-use within it. The definitions they offer can help us to understand how Roman observers distinguished between urban, rural and periurban features, and to what extent it was actually possible for them to produce a rigid definition which would reliably tell them apart. Meanwhile, the fact that recognisable references to the urban periphery appear in legal documents at all also gives us some insight into attitudes towards it. It demonstrates, for instance, that periurban occupation was in some cases considered important enough to warrant special legal or administrative provisions. The documents discussed in this section include rulings from Roman civil law, colonial and municipal charters, and also inscribed prohibitions from various contexts. Some comparisons between the legal treatment of periurban occupation at Rome and elsewhere are therefore possible, although limited by the small total number of documents.

One major legal and administrative problem arising from the existence of periurban development was that of defining the city. Distinguishing the city from the countryside could be an important issue in defining the sphere of application of certain laws, as well as settling disputes over inherited property. At Rome, more than one jurist tackled the problem by drawing a distinction between the *urbs*, which technically meant only the area within the so-called 'Servian' wall, and the more inclusive term, *Roma*.[34] The following definition originally formulated by the Augustan jurist, P. Alfenus Varus, appears in the *Digesta* as a citation from the mid-second-century lawyer Ulpius Marcellus:

> As Alfenus said, '*urbs*' means '*Roma*' which was surrounded by a wall, but '*Roma*' also extends as far as there are continuous buildings: for it can be understood from daily use that Rome is not considered to extend only as far as the wall, since we say that we are going to Rome, even if we live outside the *urbs*.[35]

Alfenus included two distinct zones within his definition of *Roma*: not only the *urbs* itself, as defined by the Servian wall, but also the continuous occupation (*continentia aedificia*) lying beyond those walls.[36] His reference to the conventions of everyday speech reveals that the dense, urban-style occupation outside the Servian wall was normally considered a part of Rome by its inhabitants. However, the need to formulate such a definition shows that its identity as part of the city could also be contested. The extra-mural section of the *continentia aedificia* to which Alfenus refers was thus a part of Rome's urban periphery. It was considered to belong to the agglomeration of Rome, rather than to the countryside, but it was excluded from the urban centre marked out by the walls.

The concept of the *continentia aedificia* makes its first known appearance on the Tabula Heracleensis, in a law certainly predating 46–45 BC, and perhaps part of a Caesarian *lex Iulia municipalis*.[37] A clause of this law concerning road maintenance is said to apply 'in the city of Rome or nearer than one thousand paces to the city of Rome where it is continuously inhabited'.[38] The reference to continuously inhabited areas is equivalent to Alfenus' inclusion of built-up extra-mural regions in his definition of Rome, although here there is also a proviso that they must lie within a fixed distance of the city. The aims of the law include ensuring the maintenance of urban streets and preventing them from being blocked by wheeled traffic. The legislators appear to have considered that the built-up areas outside the Servian wall were urban enough in character to need such regulation, but to have recognised that they were not technically part of the *urbs*, and needed to be designated by a different phrase if the law was to be understood to apply to them. In later rulings, the concept of the entire *continentia aedificia* is used to define the areas affected by the *leges Iulia* and *Papia*,[39] as well as the places where a person could be said to be 'present at Rome'.[40] As in the Tabula Heracleensis, these definitions seem to have been rendered necessary by the mismatch between the actual extent of the urban-style occupation at Rome and the technical limits of the *urbs*.[41] However, it is important to note that they are not actually definitions of the urban periphery, but definitions of the city which seek to include periurban occupation. Only those parts of the *continentia aedificia* falling outside the Servian wall were actually periurban, while other periurban features which were not continuous with Rome, such as suburban villas or satellite settlements, would not be affected by these laws.

Rome was not the only city where the concept of the *continentia aedificia* was used in legislation. The *lex Irnitana*, a Flavian charter created for the otherwise unknown Spanish *municipium* of Irni or Irnium, includes a clause forbidding the de-roofing, demolition or dismantling of a building 'in the city [*oppidum*] of the Flavian *municipium* of Irni and where there are buildings continuous with that city'.[42] The word *oppidum* is used to show that the law is intended to apply to the city only, and not the whole territory of the *municipium*, but the legislators have then added a reference to the *continentia aedificia* in order not to exclude occupation which lay outside the actual urban centre but was, practically speaking, part of the city.[43] Significantly, this assumes that, as for the *urbs* at Rome, the word *oppidum* was understood to designate only a specific area marked out by urban boundaries, a practice explored further in chapter 3. It may be that occupation outside these boundaries already existed at Irni when the charter was granted, explaining the inclusive scope of the law, or that the drafters of the constitution were allowing for the development of periurban occupation in future. It is more likely, however, that the *continentia aedificia* was simply invoked at Irni in imitation of the precedents already established at Rome.[44]

A concept closely related to the *continentia aedificia* is the area less than one thousand paces (*passus mille*, or one Roman mile) from Rome. This appears as another means of ensuring that occupation outside the *urbs* proper is subject to laws intended to apply to the whole of the city of Rome.[45] The figure of one thousand paces was probably not to be taken literally, but rather as a round number certain to include all built-up occupation outside the Servian wall. Indeed, the method of counting the thousand paces seems to have been debated. The mid-second-century lawyer Gaius informs us that the judgements of the urban praetor are valid if made 'in the city of Rome or within the first milestone of the city of Rome',[46] yet the early third-century jurist Macer asserts that 'the one thousand paces are to be measured not from the milestone of the city but from the continuous buildings'.[47] The idea that what was really meant was not a literal radius, but all extra-mural occupation of urban character, is supported by the qualification of the *'passus mille'* on the Tabula Heracleensis by the phrase, *'ubei continente habitabitur'* (where it is continuously inhabited).[48] This law, then, applied not to the entire area within one mile's radius of the urban centre, but only to the parts of that zone which were densely built up. Later in the same text, the *'passus mille'* phrase appears without qualification,[49] but the reference to continuous habitation at its first appearance and the particular relevance of this law to built-up areas probably imply that this should be understood throughout the statute.[50]

Like the concept of the *continentia aedificia*, the *passus mille* clause could also be applied in a provincial context to extend the scope of legislation beyond a demarcated urban centre. The *lex Coloniae Genetivae*, a Caesarian charter granted to the Spanish *colonia* of Urso, stipulated that the community's decurions, augurs and pontiffs should have a house 'in the city [*oppidum*] or closer than one thousand paces to the city'.[51] The aim of the clause was probably to ensure personal interest in the community's principal city, and it would appear that the legislators considered the ownership of property within a mile's radius to be as sound a guarantee of this as property within the boundaries of the city proper. As at Irni, it is most likely that such provisions were made in the charter simply because the legislators were attempting to imitate similar institutions at Rome. However, we should not rule out the possibility that the legislators were allowing for the real development of built-up occupation beyond Urso's urban centre.

These examples of legislation reveal a need to manage the difference between areas technically defined as urban, and occupation which was urban in character but fell outside an area strictly designated as 'the city'. Such occupation, then, was ambiguous in status, since it could be considered to have or to lack an urban identity depending on the nature of the judgement: legal or quotidian. This same ambiguity could also be exploited in private property disputes. Two rulings in the *Digesta* express the opinion that legacies of property described in a will as being simply 'at Rome' should be held to include property technically outside the *urbs*.[52] Interestingly, a third ruling relating to the *municipium* of Gades (Cádiz) in Spain determines that the phrase *'quidquid in patria Gadibus possideo'* (whatever I possess in Gades, my home-town) can be extended to include the *'suburbanum adiacentem possessionem'* (adjacent suburban possession).[53] While the phrases *'continentia aedificia'* and *'passus mille'* may have been used in legislation at Irni and Urso simply in emulation of Rome, this appears to be a direct response to a specific periurban structure, and reinforces the idea that the same legal ambiguities did apply to such structures in the provinces.

Another group of rulings concerning private property approach periurban property from the opposite direction, revealing a concern for ensuring that suburban estates were subject to the same protection as rural ones. An entry in the *Digesta* cites a speech made by Septimius Severus in the senate, by which 'tutors and guardians are forbidden to sell up rural or suburban estates'.[54] The interest here seems to be to prevent the sale of family land where it is being administered on behalf of a ward. Several similar entries in the *Codex Iustinianus* suggest that this was an issue of ongoing concern to third-century emperors, perhaps aiming to protect the wealth of established aristocratic families.[55] The inclusion of *praedia suburbana* as well as *rustica* in all of the rulings suggests that suburban estates were seen as being just as essential to the income of a land-owning family as rural estates, while acknowledging that they needed specific mention to ensure their protection. Most of the rulings seem to concern Rome itself, since they allow for tutors and guardians to apply for exemption in special circumstances to the urban praetor. However, some evidently envisage a provincial situation: one ruling states that an estate may not be sold 'without a decree from the governor of the province in which it is situated'.[56]

The examples of legislation discussed so far have demonstrated the practical problems arising from the tension between the elite desire for a clearly defined urban centre and the reality of the urban periphery. A further body of law affected the urban periphery more directly by forbidding certain activities within the city. The most famous example is the law of the Twelve Tables forbidding burial within the *urbs*,[57] matched in a provincial context by the Urso charter, which forbids burial within the *pomerium*.[58] Another law often viewed in the same light is the restriction on tile-kilns also included in the Urso charter.[59] This is discussed in full in chapter 4, where the idea that it does not necessarily indicate a general interest in excluding industry from the urban centre is proposed. Where the activities forbidden by such laws were nevertheless important for maintaining the expected standards of urban life, the natural result would be for them to become concentrated in the urban periphery instead. The archaeological evidence for this will be discussed in the chapters which follow, but the principle may be demonstrated here through an inscription from Puteoli (Pozzuoli). Here, a *lex de munere publico libitinario* regulated the contractors charged with overseeing burials, punishments and executions in the city.[60] Their workers were forbidden to enter the town (*oppidum*) except in the course of their work, and were also not to live 'within the tower where the grove of Libitina is today': probably to be understood as meaning that they could not live on the Puteoli side of the grove.[61] The grove itself cannot now be identified, but it must have been closely connected with the work of the operatives, since Libitina was the goddess of burials.[62] Its equivalent on the Esquiline hill in Rome was certainly on the edge of the urban centre, and a similar arrangement is likely at Puteoli. The law thus reveals a tension between a desire to exclude workers involved in undesirable pursuits from the city,[63] and a need to allow them ready access to the city, where they will have performed the bulk of their work. The tension appears to have been resolved by allowing them to live in the urban periphery, beyond a clearly designated landmark.

The existence of these laws reveals much about relative attitudes towards the urban periphery and the urban centre. It implies a willingness to make use of periurban land for activities necessary to the smooth running of the city, but unwanted in its centre. Such relegations into the urban periphery relate to the elite ideology of the city seen in the previous section, supporting the suggestion that they were keen to make their urban centres into special showpieces of sophisticated and refined identity. Yet other laws reveal a concern for protecting the urban periphery itself from misuse. Examples include legislation to prevent the illegal burial or burning of corpses and the dumping of rubbish in paupers' burial grounds on the Esquiline hill at Rome and on a site which may or may not have been a sacred grove at Luceria.[64] Rubbish dumping was no doubt a problem throughout most Roman cities, but the disposal of corpses was an issue affecting the urban periphery in particular.[65] Doubtless part of the reason for the official concern was the income which properly enacted burials could generate for the civic authorities. Puteolan citizens seem to have been forbidden to employ anyone other than the official contractor to bury a corpse.[66] But a desire to protect the appearance of the city, even beyond its urban boundaries, was probably also at work.[67] The urban periphery may have been used for activities not wanted in the centre of the city. But it was also considered worthy of civic protection in its own right.

The urban periphery in Roman literature

The texts examined in the previous section revealed something of the practicalities involved in managing the urban periphery, and especially of the problems caused by its ambiguous status. Here, literary texts are analysed in order to reach a more complex understanding of the thought-world associated with the urban periphery. Literary authors do not generally provide definitions of the urban periphery, since they assume that their readers will be familiar with the concept. But they refer to it frequently, and in doing so provide insight into the many possible ways of understanding or representing this zone. Most of the authors discussed in this section can be considered part of the metropolitan Roman elite, in that they had significant experience of living amongst and interacting with the leading citizens of Rome. Unsurprisingly, then, many of their references to periurban development concern the area around Rome, and it is the thought-world of Rome's urban periphery in particular which they can reveal to us. However, these authors did sometimes write about periurban development at cities other than Rome, while a small number of references to the urban periphery also occur in works by authors whose main experience was of living in the provinces. Thus it is possible to explore the extent to which ideas associated with the periphery at Rome were also applied to other cities, or shared by provincial elites.

Most of the material discussed here was gathered using two searchable corpora of ancient texts: the Packard Humanities Institute CD-ROM of Latin texts and the *Thesaurus Linguae Graecae* online database.[68] The PHI CD is not a complete corpus of Latin texts, but it is extremely comprehensive up to around AD 250, and also includes selected texts from after that date. The *Thesaurus Linguae Graecae* database covers authors from Homer to the fall of Byzantium, and includes over 90 million words of text. Between them, then, these two collections offer an excellent cross-section of ancient literature, allowing the full range of literary references to the urban periphery to be identified and explored. Searches were run through these corpora for all forms of the Latin and Greek words *'suburbanus'/'suburbium'*, *'extra urbem'*, *'extra moenia'*, *'extra murum'* and *'proast(e)ion'/'proast(e)ios'*. The contexts in which these terms were used reveal that they fall into three broad groups, each with its own distinct connotations: *'suburbanus'* and its cognates, the various terms meaning 'outside the city' or 'outside the walls', and *'proast-(e)ion'* and related forms. Each group will therefore be discussed separately, so that the precise meaning of each can be explored, and comparisons drawn between them. The search-terms described above, however, cannot be relied upon to identify all passages of relevance to the urban periphery in Roman literature. An author may describe part of a city or a particular feature in terms which indicate to his readers that it is periurban without using any of these specific words. In order to help compensate for this, a number of other passages of relevance to the thought-world of the urban periphery have also been examined: notably descriptions of the city of Rome and particular villas in the area around it.

Descriptions of Rome are in fact a useful starting point for this investigation, because of the city's dominance amongst our evidence. Strabo, Dionysius of Halicarnassus and the Elder Pliny were all clearly struck when describing Augustan and early imperial Rome by its sheer size. Dionysius in particular states that the extent of the built-up area makes it difficult to discern where the city ends and the countryside begins.[69] Attempting to measure the size of the city by looking at the Servian wall is no easier, he adds, since this has become engulfed by buildings in many places: an observation confirmed by Livy.[70] These comments reveal that elite authors in the early imperial period were still keen to distinguish between the city of Rome and the surrounding countryside. However, the extent of the city's periphery also prompted them to make a somewhat ironic observation about contemporary Rome: that the mother city was no longer proudly delineated by its walls, like so many of its *coloniae*, but had merged into a kind of continuum with the countryside. Meanwhile, Strabo adds a valuable perspective on the role of a particular periurban area, the Campus Martius, in expressing the grandeur and importance of Rome. His description of the monumental buildings of Rome, in fact, focuses almost entirely on the Campus Martius, and even includes the suggestion that builders here were actively seeking to make the rest of Rome appear a 'mere accessory' in comparison.[71] For Strabo, then, the Campus Martius, outstripped the *urbs* for monumental finery, despite falling outside both the Servian wall and the *pomerium*.

Literary uses of the term '*suburbanus*' and its cognates have already been closely investigated by both Champlin and Agusta-Boularot, and the discussion of their connotations offered here owes much to both of them.[72] The noun '*suburbium*' could be used in Latin, but it is found very rarely, and the descriptive adjective, '*suburbanus*', was the preferred form.[73] This adjective could be applied to features such as sanctuaries, tombs, funeral pyres or even small towns.[74] It could also be used to describe open land (e.g. *solum* or *terra*), or a whole region around Rome (*ager suburbanus*).[75] However, it is most frequently applied to private properties, as designated by words such as *villa, praedium, fundus* or even *rus*, in the sense of 'country place' or 'country seat':[76] this latter example highlighting the ambiguous position of the suburban in the wider antithesis between city and country.[77] In fact, private property is the context in which the word first appears: originally as a phrase, '*sub urbe*'. Already in the second century BC, Plautus and Cato were using this to describe a particular kind of agricultural property close to Rome.[78] By the late Republic, the commonest form was the substantive, '*suburbanum*', with '*praedium*' (estate) understood.[79] The conceptual landscape of the suburban was therefore above all a landscape of private properties, although it could include certain other features. Surviving uses of '*suburbanus*' and its cognates are also particularly strongly associated with the city of Rome.[80] Indeed, 'Rome' would have been understood by the *-urb-* element in the word.[81] The original suburbs were not just associated with *a* city. They were associated with *the* city: the *urbs* that was Rome.

We begin, then, by exploring the meaning of the term in its original context. Through compiling references which, directly or indirectly, refer to individual towns around Rome as suburban, both Champlin and Agusta-Boularot have concluded that the *ager suburbanus* (or the *suburbium*) was roughly equivalent in area to the modern Roman Campagna.[82] When plotted on a map, most of these towns fall into a radius of approximately 35 km around Rome, with Antium constituting an extreme at 50 km away, and a distinct emphasis on the Latin territory to the south-east of the Tiber (figure 2.1). However, although geography was of course a factor in helping to determine whether a particular feature was considered to be suburban or not, it was not the only one that counted. The designation *suburbanus*, especially when applied to a villa estate, also implied that the villa, and

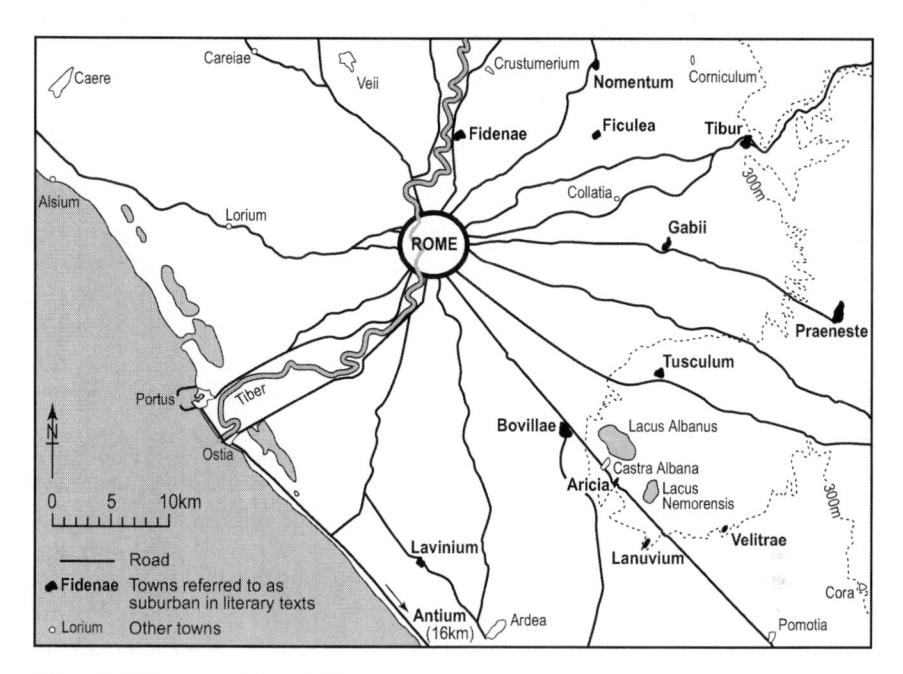

Figure 2.1 Rome and its *suburbium*.

hence its owner, was involved in a particular lifestyle enjoyed by the members of the Roman elite.[83] This is an idea played with by Catullus when describing his own 'farm':

> Oh my farm, whether Sabine or Tiburtine
> (for they swear that you are Tiburtine, those to whom it is not
> a pleasure to hurt Catullus: but those to whom it is
> vie to pledge anything that it is Sabine) . . .[84]

Tibur is referred to in other literary sources as suburban,[85] and so by telling Catullus that his farm is Tiburtine, his friends can suggest that he is a part of the sophisticated suburban 'set'. Indeed, Catullus reveals his own view only two lines later, when he describes the property as a '*suburbana villa*'. But the geographical location of the villa must have been ambiguous enough for Catullus to joke that his enemies could claim that it was Sabine, and therefore lay beyond suburban circles. Catullus recognises that the status of his property, and himself, is ultimately judged by its viewers. In similar vein, a ruling in the *Codex Iustinianus* states that a suburban estate is distinguishable from urban properties by its nature, not its position.[86]

We have already seen that, in the thought-world of the metropolitan elite, the Roman suburban landscape was dominated by the private villa estate.

Significantly, it did not include features such as kilns, quarries or small farms, all in fact present in the area around Rome (see chapter 3). This highlights the differences between literary constructions of Rome's urban periphery and the reality of the same zone. The thought-world of the suburban which emerges from literary texts, then, is really the thought-world of the suburban villa. By the late Republic, the suburban villa seems to have become part of the 'equipment' considered necessary for full participation in the metropolitan elite lifestyle, just like an urban *domus* or *horti* and a profitable country estate. This is clear from several letters and speeches of Cicero in which he refers (not always with approval, but never with surprise) to the sets of urban and suburban properties owned by various elite individuals, and from the encouragement which he gives to his brother Quintus in purchasing one.[87] It is equally clear that the suburban villa was a necessary investment first and foremost because it constituted a potent symbol of elite status. Land on the periphery of Rome was expensive, and only an individual who was both wealthy and active on a regular basis within the city would consider it worth paying for.[88] A telling epigram portrays the consuming jealousy of a friend of Martial's in the face of his new status symbols: his own mules and a suburban property. The satirical response plays on the lengths to which some individuals will go to maintain such assets: Martial wishes them as a curse on his friend, since financially they are more of a burden than a blessing.[89]

Besides demonstrating his elevated status, a suburban villa could also offer its owner leisure, privacy and the enjoyment of the countryside, without the need to sacrifice urbane comforts or easy access to the social and political life of the city. These aspects are clearly illustrated in Pliny the Younger's famous account of his villa on the Laurentine coast near Ostia.[90] Pliny's description of this property focuses on its sophisticated facilities, such as a gymnasium, heated baths, covered arcades and multiple dining rooms. Notably, the feature mentioned first is an atrium which leads into a D-shaped portico: an arrangement very similar to the axial atrium and peristyle found in fashionable urban *domus*.[91] Later, an arcade resembles that of a public monument: and, thus, of an urban building. The natural landscape, meanwhile, serves primarily as a tasteful backdrop for the villa, complementing the elegance of its rooms. Thus, one dining room has views of the sea on three sides, and through the house towards woods and mountains on the fourth: the ultimate in refined décor. Pliny also stresses the tranquillity which the villa affords him for his writing, implying that he does not enjoy such peace in the city. Another letter ironically contrasts the poor yields of Pliny's other two estates, at Tifernum in Tuscany and near Comum in north Italy,[92] with the rich literary 'crop' that he has produced on his Laurentine estate.[93] It is clear, then, that the purpose of the suburban villa is quite different from the other estates. While they are expected to generate wealth, the Laurentine estate is not: only to provide refined residential facilities impossible in an urban house.

Pliny's Laurentine estate, then, combines the advantages of both city and country, but avoids the disadvantages of either. In one sense, the suburban villa was the resolution of the city–country debate: the perfect compromise between the two.[94] Meanwhile, the location of the villa close to the city meant that its owner did not have to give up the social and political world of Rome in order to enjoy this. Thus Columella recommends a *suburbanum praedium* to his readers on the grounds that it can be reached on a daily journey ('*cotidianus excursus*') by its owner after completing his business in the forum, while Pliny notes the same quality in his Laurentine villa.[95] It is unlikely that many wealthy Romans actually performed a daily commute. Even Pliny's villa was in fact seventeen miles (25 km) from Rome, while the temporal concentration of activities such as the *salutatio*, court sessions and senate meetings into the morning would have made it sensible to start a day of serious public pursuits in the urban *domus*.[96] The suburban villa could then be retired to afterwards, when the following day did not require the owner's presence in the city. None the less, Columella's recommendation does suggest that a suburban villa owner expected to be *able* to reach his villa in less than a day's journey, and that he would travel between it and the city on a regular basis. Meanwhile, numerous texts describe visits to and from suburban villas between members of the elite, indicating that they functioned as nodes in an extended social network centred on the city of Rome.[97]

Crucial to the relationship between villa and city was of course the road network. Another letter of Pliny's, concerning the purchase of a small farm by Suetonius, describes the features likely to make it attractive to him.[98] These include not only the '*vicinitas urbis*' (proximity of the city), but also the '*opportunitas viae*' (convenience of its road). Many other literary references to suburban villas locate the properties specifically in relation to a major road. We encounter the suburban villa of Seneca on the road from Campania, that of Nero's freedman, Phaon, between the via Salaria and via Nomentana, that of Domitian's nurse, Phyllis, on the via Latina and that of the grammarian Remmius Palaemon on the via Nomentana.[99] The importance of the road was partly practical, since it provided easy access to the property for the villa's owner, as well as for other members of the elite who might visit him. However, the roads and the journeys made along them also created a more symbolic link with Rome, as well as with other suburban villas. A location on one of the major roads into the city indicated that a villa was intimately connected with the life of Rome, both physically and through the cultural values which its owner carried back and forth between the two.[100]

In certain circumstances, this picture of the suburban villa as a physical and cultural extension of Rome could be disturbed, and it could come to represent an exclusion, rather than a retreat, from the city. This is the situation described by Suetonius for Claudius, after he is refused any hope of political office under Tiberius: 'then at last, with his hopes of public status cast down, he gave himself over to leisure, sometimes in his garden estate and suburban house, sometimes taking refuge in a retreat in Campania'.[101] Here the suburban house of Claudius has become the geographical expression of his involuntary exclusion from the political life of Rome. Similarly, the younger Pliny paid a visit to the philosopher Artemidorus in his suburban villa, at a time when Domitian had expelled philosophers from the city.[102] Again, Artemidorus is situated both literally and metaphorically on the fringes of Roman society. Suetonius also uses the same motif of suburban exclusion to express the final rejection of 'bad' emperors by Roman society. Thus, the suicide of Nero and the obscure burial of Domitian both take place in suburban villas belonging to loyal, but low-class, members of their households.[103]

Literary texts also attest a complex set of views concerning agriculture and the suburban villa. It was essential to the identity of a suburban villa that it fell between city and country, and its value as a status symbol might be compromised if its owner was seen to use it for the serious agricultural production normally associated with a rural estate. In fact, some suburban villa owners made a special display of treating agriculture as a pastime, rather than a means to profit. The orator Hortensius was reputed to have shown great devotion to a particular plane-tree on his suburban estate, which he watered with wine. This was a pastiche of serious agriculture, demonstrating his ability to support a leisured lifestyle in the urban periphery thanks to real investments elsewhere.[104] Agriculture as an elite pastime, however, was not necessarily incompatible with profit-making. Thus Remmius Palaemon, although ostensibly only playing at being a farmer himself, quadrupled the value of his suburban estate by the shrewd employment of an expert in viticulture.[105] The most widespread approach was probably that of Pliny the Younger on his Laurentine estate. We have already seen that Pliny's description of this villa focuses on its urbanised amenities, and that he contrasts it elsewhere with his 'real' agricultural estates at Tifernum and Comum. However, he does mention one garden 'thickly planted with mulberry and fig', and another which is 'fertile and rural', as well as telling us that the villa provides all its own land-based products.[106] Thus the villa clearly *was* productive, even if Pliny chose not to present this as its chief interest for him.

The situation is summed up by Seneca, who recognises that the main reasons for buying a suburban villa are its healthiness and its privacy, but advises that, once bought, it should be looked after anyway, in order to maximise its profitability.[107] For those who wished to take Seneca's advice, a wealth of agricultural writings were available to guide the suburban villa owner in the efficient management of his estate. As early as the second century BC, Cato had devoted two chapters of his *De Agri Cultura* to describing the best way to lay out a suburban farm,[108] and similar advice could be found in the pages of Varro and Columella.[109] All three authors recommend the cultivation of luxury or perishable goods, such as flowers, fruit or young animals, on a suburban estate but not a rural one. This advice reflects the special nature of the market available in Rome, which was both wealthy and able to import staple goods over long distances. Suburban farmers could thus find a niche in the market by producing goods which could be transported only over short distances, as well as specialised products required by the fashionable urban elite.[110]

In the references discussed so far, the word *'suburbanus'* and its cognates are used to evoke a refined and privileged lifestyle led by the metropolitan elite at Rome, and centring around their villa estates. But the word is also applied in an Italian or provincial context.[111] Notably, all such occurrences without exception concern private properties, confirming that the literary suburban landscape, wherever it was set, was dominated by elite residences. Pliny, writing to a friend living near Comum in north Italy, enquires after his *'suburbanum amoenissimum'*,[112] while Suetonius ascribes to Tiberius on Rhodes the same set of properties encountered in Cicero's references to the metropolitan elite at Rome: 'a moderate house and a not much more spacious suburban estate'.[113] Similar references occur in Curtius Rufus, Pliny the Elder, Martial and the *Historia Augusta*,[114] while Aulus Gellius' descriptions of visits to and philosophical debates in the villas of Herodes Atticus near Athens clearly draw on the *topos* of the *suburbanum*, though without using the actual word.[115] With the possible exception of the enigmatic author(s) of the *Historia Augusta*, all of these writers spent the greater part of their lives in Rome. They must therefore have been familiar with the elite lifestyle centred around Rome which *'suburbanus'* and related terms evoked, as well as the range of other words which could be used in its place (see below). Their decision to apply the term to properties at cities other than Rome, then, implies that these authors felt its connotations *could* be transferred appropriately to a provincial context.

'Suburbanus' is also used three times of private properties in the works of Apuleius, a writer who lived most of his life in Africa. It is applied twice to his wife's villa in the *Apologia* and also appears in a story from the *Florida*.[116] Yet Apuleius was well-travelled, having been educated in Carthage, Athens and Rome,[117] and is noted for his inventive and cosmopolitan style. His use of the word *'suburbanus'* in an African context probably reflects this background. However, it does imply that Apuleius believed that properties in Africa, and particularly his own, could at least be compared with the suburban villas of Rome. Meanwhile, a funerary inscription found at Tarraco (Tarragona) in Spain records a donation of *'hortos coherentes sive suburbanum'* (conjoined gardens or a suburban estate) by a husband to four freedmen and freedwomen of his dead wife.[118] This example comes from outside the literary sphere, but confirms that the word could be used by provincial elites of their own properties. The practice is not attested for Gaul during the high empire, but it does appear in letters and poems of the late antique period, discussed in chapter 6.

In etymological terms, the phrases *'extra urbem'*, *'extra murum/muros'* and *'extra moenia'* do not necessarily evoke the periurban *per se*. They indicate that a particular feature or place fell outside a city or its walls, and hence was not urban, but they do not explicitly signal that it was not rural either. In practice, though, they were normally used to describe things or events located immediately outside the boundaries of a city and closely related to the city itself. The three phrases are largely synonymous, although authors are more likely to use *'extra murum'* and *'extra moenia'* when writing about military attacks, since walls and fortifications were defensive features as well as urban boundaries. For convenience, then, all three phrases will be designated here by the English term 'extra urban', unless otherwise indicated.

We have seen that the word *'suburbanus'* was mainly used in literature to denote a particular elite lifestyle, based around Rome. The extra urban, however, was a more generalised concept, which could be applied to features or events outside any city. The phrases in this group are most often used to describe armies camped outside cities, military sieges or attacks on citizens who have ventured outside their fortifications.[119] Within such descriptions, authors occasionally refer to specific features of the urban periphery, usually because they are directly involved in the action. Thus Tacitus describes the burning of an amphitheatre outside Placentia, or Frontinus that of a temple near a city in Caria.[120] Meanwhile, the dominant feature of the *ager suburbanus* – the villa estate – is significantly entirely absent from the extra urban landscape; at Rome or elsewhere. The only private dwellings described as extra urban seem to be houses outside Italian or provincial cities: the equivalent of the *continentia aedificia* at Rome.[121]

The extra urban landscape is thus markedly different from the *ager suburbanus*, both in terms of what could happen there, and what might be found there. When authors did apply the concept to Rome, they often appear to have done so in order to indicate aspects of Rome's urban periphery which did not fit into the refined elite world of the *suburbium*. This includes anything to do with the military sphere, at Rome largely personified by individuals who were forbidden to cross the *pomerium*. Rome's extra urban landscape is thus the proper place for holders of *imperium* who wished to consult with the senate or hoped to celebrate a triumph,[122] as well as for ambassadors from hostile nations.[123] Such figures are never situated in the *suburbium*, since they were not using the urban periphery as a place of leisured retreat from the city. The word *'suburbanus'* was, however, occasionally used in the context of the distant past to describe neighbouring towns and peoples who had once been enemies of Rome but had become part of her *suburbium*.[124] Here, the word is more effective than the phrase *'extra urbem'*, since it emphasises the change from a small warring city-state to the centre of a pacified subject territory, and hence carries with it a sense of the inevitability of Rome's success.

In Greek literature, the word most commonly used to refer to the urban periphery is the noun, *'proast(e)ion'*,[125] which denotes a geographical zone outside a city. An adjective, *'proast(e)ios'* also exists, as do related terms such as *'proastis'* (resident in a suburb), but the noun predominates. Authors of the classical period, such as Herodotus, Thucydides and Xenophon, use the term primarily in the context of military assaults, much as Latin authors do the *'extra . . .'* phrases discussed earlier.[126] The features of a classical Greek *proasteion* could include the groves, temples and public memorials which characterised the Kerameikos area outside the Dipylon Gate at Athens.[127] However, they might also consist of ordinary houses, such as those in Thucydides' description of an Athenian assault on the city of Nisaea.[128] The connotations of the classical Greek *proasteion* were thus much closer to a Roman extra urban landscape that to a suburban one. Yet the classical period had also generated the concept of the urban periphery as a refined intellectual retreat, thanks largely to the establishment outside Athens of Plato's Academy in the Kerameikos district and Aristotle's Lyceum in the eastern periphery. That the Roman elite sought to incorporate these precedents into their own suburban lifestyles is clear above all from Cicero, whose villa near Tusculum had its own 'Academy', and who begins a letter to Atticus in Athens with the words, 'When I was in my Tusculan property (that will do in return for your "When I was in Ceramicus") . . .'.[129]

In the Roman world of the late Republic and high empire, authors writing in Greek could still use the word *'proasteion'* in its classical sense. Frequently, it was used to describe places where military attacks and ambushes occurred, or, at Rome, military commanders met with the senate or awaited triumphs.[130] In addition, it could occur as a strictly geographical setting within descriptions of people's activities[131] or cities.[132] When applied to Rome itself, however, the word *'proasteion'* in this period took on some of the specific meanings of the Latin *'suburbanus'*. We find references to private villas in the *proasteion* of Rome which are closely comparable with Latin texts concerning suburban villas; for instance the 'pleasant villa in the *proasteion*' which Plutarch's Crassus attempts to buy.[133] Yet the Greek *proasteion* as a place of elite refinement was not as closely linked to the city of Rome as the Latin *suburbium*. Thus we find references to lavish private properties and pleasure gardens in the *proasteia* of several cities in the Greek east, including Ephesus,[134] Alexandria,[135] Sinope,[136] Aegae[137] and especially Athens.[138] The theme of death on the margins of society, which Suetonius situated in the *suburbium*, also crops up in the Greek *proasteion*. It appears in particular to have been a favourite *topos* of Herodian, who uses the *proasteion* as a covert dumping-ground for the body of Commodus outside Rome, and for the deaths of both Pescennius Niger at Antioch and Macrinus at Chalcedon.[139] It is worth noting that some of the authors who use the word *'proasteion'* to describe a landscape populated by a leisured elite, either at Rome or elsewhere, had largely provincial backgrounds. These include Flavius Philostratus, a prominent Athenian, and Plutarch, who spent most of his life at Chaeronea. Like '*suburbanus*', then, the word '*proasteion*' in its capacity as an indicator of a special elite lifestyle was capable of being adopted by well-educated provincials and applied to their own cities.

Finally, the *proasteion* provides us with another view of the urban periphery, not yet explicitly encountered: as a formal zone of transition between city and country. This concept is applied to Rome by Cassius Dio, who describes an excursion by Augustus into the *proasteion* to greet Tiberius, returning from his suppression of the revolt in Illyricum in AD 9, and to accompany him back into Rome.[140] Here, the *proasteion* functions as the symbolic meeting place between the domestic world of the city, embodied in Augustus, and the external world of military activity personified by Tiberius. This symbolic function was not unique to Rome, however, as shown by Plutarch's comparable description of a Spartan woman, who, having sent her sons to war, waits anxiously in the *proasteion* for news of battle.[141] Meanwhile, the symbolism is extended into a full-blown metaphor by Philo Judaeus and Lucian, who both use the transition from the country and through the *proasteion* into the city as an analogy for moral advancement.[142]

Images of the urban periphery

It is by now clear that the urban periphery was a widely recognised concept in Roman law and literature, and that it had a range of distinct connotations in the elite mind, often evoked by the use of different descriptive terms. The final stage in our exploration of the thought-world of the Roman urban periphery is to examine visual representations of cities. The discussion that follows will ask how common it was for city representations to include periurban development at all, and this information will help to indicate how much such features could contribute to conveying general notions of *urbanitas* or identifying a specific city. It will also examine the character of such development when depicted. This will illuminate attitudes towards the urban periphery in itself, and provide a basis for comparison with the picture emerging from the literary texts.

The images discussed in this section vary widely in terms of provenance, medium, purpose and audience. This means that they can offer insight into the perceptions of a number of different groups; for instance, provincial elites as well as the metropolitan elite at Rome, and working professionals as well as the imperial authorities. The cities depicted also vary, from Rome itself and several Italian or provincial cities to what appear to be imaginary or generic cities. These latter are in fact especially valuable, since they can be used to explore ancient constructions of 'the city' in the abstract sense. Meanwhile, even where specific cities were portrayed, most artists were clearly not aiming to produce what we would recognise today as accurate or photo-realistic representations of them. Instead, cities were usually idealised or schematised, with only a selection of features shown, and some of these being given special prominence over others. Even the Severan-period *Forma Urbis*, ostensibly a cartographically accurate map of Rome, in fact varies in scale between extremes of 1:189 and 1:413, possibly in order to give special emphasis to public buildings.[143] Such devices can be very helpful in the present context, since they reveal much about the attitudes towards or perceptions of cities which an artist hoped to convey or expected amongst his audience.

Perhaps the most common means of depicting a city in the Roman world was to show a prominent walled circuit, enclosing a collection of buildings. Walls, as noted earlier, were closely connected with *urbanitas* in the Roman mind, and hence could represent a city clearly and effectively, especially where space was limited. A vivid example is provided by local coin issues from the eastern part of the empire which expressed civic pride through representations of their cities of origin.[144] On these coins, the city is usually represented by a walled circuit seen from a bird's-eye perspective, with especially spectacular or recognisable monuments shown within. This style of depiction was probably favoured on coins largely for practical reasons. The rounded shape of a walled circuit suits the circular field of the coin, meaning that the space can be all but filled with a recognisable symbol of *urbanitas*. Meanwhile, the monuments inside help to identify the city intended. The absence of any periurban features thus probably reflects the die-cutters' concern for maximising the visual impact of the walled circuit. However, it also implies that monuments outside the walls of such cities were not generally considered important enough as symbols of local identity to be included on their coins.

Bird's-eye views with prominent walled circuits were also used to represent cities clearly and concisely when information was being conveyed in diagram form. This is the case in the *Corpus Agrimensorum*, a collection of land-surveying texts. The texts of the *Corpus Agrimensorum* were compiled between the fourth and sixth centuries AD, and a number of medieval manuscripts contain illustrations which were probably inserted at this point and copied later on.[145] The two earliest surviving documents are known as the 'Arcerianus A' and 'Palatinus' manuscripts, and these include a total of twenty diagrams featuring pictorial vignettes of cities.[146] Like the coin depictions, most show bird's-eye views of walled cities, with no periurban features (plate 2.1): two exceptions to this rule, however, will be discussed later. The aim was probably to clarify surveying problems discussed in the text without taking up undue amounts of space.

On the Peutinger Table, a twelfth- or early thirteenth-century copy of a map originating in the fourth century, similar principles apply. This map represents the Roman empire not cartographically, but as an elongated strip, and is perhaps best thought of as a diagrammatic equivalent of text-based road itineraries.[147] The great majority of the towns featured on it are indicated simply by a labelled kink in the road, but some are represented by

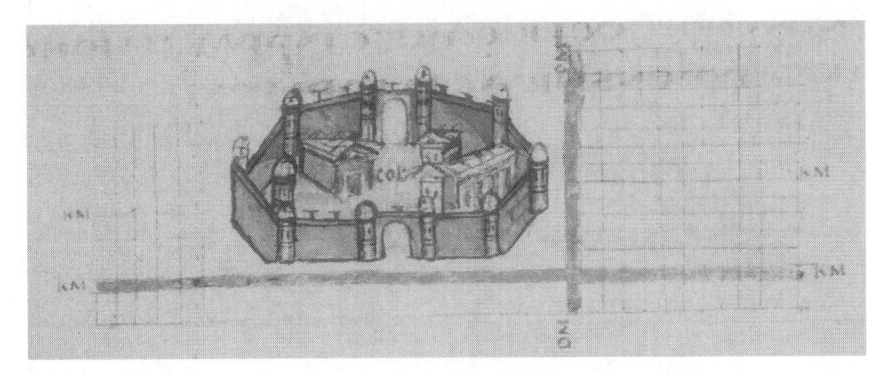

Plate 2.1 Walled city vignette from the *Corpus Agrimensorum*, Arcerianus A manuscript.

pictorial symbols. These include stylised temples, baths and pairs of towers[148] (see examples around Rome in plate 2.4, p. 36), while six towns are represented by bird's-eye views of hexagonal walled circuits, with some monuments shown within them, but none outside. All of these symbols have the advantage of indicating a town or city clearly within a small space, while the hexagonal fortifications, and probably also the double towers, again attest the popularity of the uncluttered walled circuit as a visual shorthand for the city. Three more lavish city depictions from this map will again be discussed later.

Finally, the same device of a compact walled city with no periurban monuments also occurs in a more decorative context. A small walled city can be seen in the background of four out of a corpus of ten related Pompeian wall-paintings depicting the story of Daedalus and Icarus (plate 2.2).[149] Here, the cities act as part of the setting for the myth, probably standing for Knossos in Crete.[150] Thus, they are not the focal point of the scene, and were probably depicted in a concise and simplistic manner in order to enhance the overall meaning of the painting without distracting attention from the main subject.

Where space was at a premium, then, Roman visual artists in a range of genres and contexts tended strongly towards representing cities as compact entities, clearly defined by prominent walls, and with no outlying periurban features. This certainly lent clarity to the images, but the prominence of the walls in particular probably also reflects the ideological association between walls and cities already noted in this chapter. In images such as these, the walled circuits evoke the same city–country antithesis observed above in elite literature. They indicate a sharp division between the surrounding landscape or diagrammatic ground and the buildings within the circuit, and thus act as a guarantee for the *urbanitas* of those buildings. A viewer could not mistake them for a scatter of unrelated, individual structures: surrounded by their

THE URBAN PERIPHERY IN ROMAN THOUGHT

Plate 2.2 Scene of the fall of Icarus including a walled city, from Pompeii: Blanckenhagen 1968, no. 10, unknown provenance.

walls, they are bound together into a recognisable city. In fact, this capacity for walls to convey *urbanitas* was so strong that in several contexts they may be found representing cities on their own, without the need for any internal buildings. Examples include city personifications who wear crowns in the form of a city wall,[151] a number of illustrations from the *Corpus Agrimensorum* consisting simply of empty walled circuits,[152] and the use of the word '*moenia*' (fortifications) in literature to refer to a whole city.[153]

The absence of periurban features from the images discussed so far suggests, fairly unsurprisingly, that they were not seen as essential for conveying the notion of *urbanitas*. This does not mean that the urban periphery was never represented in the visual arts, however. We shall now turn to images which *do* include some kind of periurban development, and ask how it contributed to their meaning. We begin with works produced for a public audience, and specifically the sculpted reliefs on Trajan's column, erected to celebrate his victories in Dacia.[154] The military theme of this column means that although many camps and fortresses are shown, civilian settlements are rare. However, one city does appear close to the beginning of the column's scrolled relief, in Cichorius scenes III–IV.[155] These scenes show a city on the bank of the Danube, itself represented here as a personification. In the small space above the head of the river-god, the centre of the city is represented by a walled circuit with some buildings visible inside it. On either side of this circuit, however, are features shown at a much larger scale: a group of tall buildings and a portico to the left, and a single city gate through which Roman troops are setting out to the right. This difference in scale is probably intended to emphasise the two major functions of the city in the narrative structure of the column. First, it stands as a place for gathering war supplies, and second, it stands as a symbol of the civilised and well-ordered society from which Trajan's forces are setting out into barbarian territory.

The tall buildings to the left of the city are thus clearly of greater importance in the scene than the walled centre, and this is of interest since they can readily be interpreted as periurban buildings. They resemble a group of storehouses already featured in the previous scene on the column, where merchant ships were delivering goods to them as part of the Roman preparations for war.[156] However, several devices have been employed to associate the buildings in scene III specifically with the walled city. They share a common location on a rocky ridge, are physically linked by a portico, and apparently share the same system of infrastructure. A smooth line, probably a road, emerges from an opening at the left-hand end of the portico near to the tall buildings and joins a similar road emerging from the nearest city gate, which then leads down to the river. These roads, along with the storehouses and a merchant boat shown on the river below, all suggest that the city is intended to represent a river-port, to which goods delivered by boat are transported. Such a function would be difficult to convey without showing periurban features, since the storehouses would be less easily identifiable if enclosed within the walled circuit. At the same time, however, the notion of civilisation required for the next scene would not have been easily conveyed without the walled city to which the storehouses relate. Here, then, periurban buildings appear to have been depicted because this was the most effective way to convey both storage and *urbanitas* at once.

A walled city can also be seen in one of a group of fragmentary marble reliefs found in the 1870s during drainage works near the Fucine Lake, and subsequently housed in Avezzano. These reliefs were all found near to the entrance of the ancient *emissarium* (outlet tunnel) dug to drain the waters of the lake in the Claudian period.[157] We cannot now be certain what sort of monument they belonged to, or even whether they all came from the same structure. However, their style and scale suggested to Geffroy that they did,[158] while the appearance in fragment A of construction workers on the shore of a lake also caused him to wonder whether such a monument may have celebrated the Claudian drainage project.[159] The city appears on fragment B, and is represented with an unusual level of detail. A prominent walled circuit occupies the foreground, while streets, *insulae* and individual buildings are visible within. Beyond the walls to the right is a cultivated landscape, featuring a villa and a road running diagonally towards what may be a bridge leading over a stream and into the city. Along the road stand a number of structures. One resembles an altar, while the others are probably funerary monuments. All of these features are reminiscent of the literary *ager suburbanus*, with the villa in particular being extremely prominent. It is not possible to be certain whether further features on fragments C and D were also part of this scene, although fragment C does include a building which is closely comparable to the winged villa in fragment B. If indeed they come from a monument celebrating the draining of the Fucine Lake, all of these fragments may have been intended to represent the local benefits of the scheme, especially in terms of increasing the availability of land for villa-based exploitation. Meanwhile, if the city was intended to represent a specific local centre, such as Alba Fucens, its appearance as part of this idyllic scene may also have evoked the prosperity it would enjoy as more land was created.

Public depictions of the urban periphery also occur in scenes of imperial *profectio* (setting out) and *adventus* (arrival).[160] Such scenes are known from coin issues, as well as sculpted reliefs on monumental arches. The setting was often Rome itself, but scenes of arrival in Italian and provincial cities also occur. Most *profectio* and *adventus* scenes feature two distinct groups of figures: one static and one active. Thus a scene showing the departure of Marcus Aurelius from Rome, reused on the Arch of Constantine, depicts the active party of the emperor and his troops about to set out along the via Flaminia, and a static personification of the Roman senate seeing them off. In this example, the emperor and soldiers represent the external military sphere, while the senate represents the domestic world of the city. The setting, meanwhile, is the urban periphery, and this is made clear by the presence of a city gate, indicating the very edge of the urban centre. Such scenes, then, are the artistic equivalent of the meeting between Augustus and Tiberius in the *proasteion*, described by Cassius Dio.[161] The periurban setting is crucial to the meaning of the scene, since it reinforces the theme of the meeting between two worlds which the figures themselves convey.

A rather different kind of public relief, is the Severan map of Rome known as the *Forma Urbis*. This map, which showed the buildings of Rome in ground plan, was carved on marble slabs, and attached to the wall of a room adjoining Vespasian's *Templum Pacis*.[162] Its original size and shape have been reconstructed through analysis of both the wall and the surviving fragments, and the original locations of many of the pieces have been identified.[163] The coverage of the *Forma Urbis* clearly extended well beyond the circuit of the Servian wall on all sides, and indeed included much that was later left outside the wall of Aurelian. In fact, the map probably incorporated most of the contemporary *continentia aedificia*. This decision is extremely important for our understanding of the status of extramural areas in relation to the old walled *urbs*. Part of the purpose of the map was probably to draw attention to the glorious extent of the city of Rome, and particularly the public buildings provided by the state. Areas such as the Campus Martius, and even Transtiberim, then, were evidently considered just as fundamental for displaying Rome's magnificence as the areas within the Servian circuit. Regrettably, however, few slabs depicting extramural features have survived,[164] making it difficult to comment on the method of representation. The most that can be said is that the character of fragments known from Transtiberim and the Janiculum does not appear to differ markedly from that of fragments from within the walled circuit. Both show densely packed buildings lining open streets, although the nature of the development across the Tiber means that fragments from this area mainly show commercial buildings, *insulae* and occasional *domus*, rather than public buildings.[165]

A painted image of a city was found on the Oppian hill in Rome in 1998.[166] It probably came from a public building, perhaps part of the Flavian programme for eradicating Nero's hated Domus Aurea. Certainly, it has been dated on grounds of style to the second half of the first century.[167] Like several of the examples above, this city is shown from a bird's-eye view, and has a prominent fortified circuit. However, it is unusual in two respects. First, it takes a city as its primary subject, rather than as context for another subject, and second, it does not include human figures, which normally appear in generic landscape paintings.[168] This has led several scholars to suggest that it may be intended to represent a specific city, such as Rome, Ostia, London, Jerusalem or Lyon.[169] La Rocca, however, emphasises the importance of asking why such a painting was produced at all, rather than trying to identify which city was intended.[170] For the time being, it is probably best to treat the painting as an idealised type of the Roman city, possibly produced to express the glory of Roman civilisation.

Much of the ground visible beyond the walls in this painting consists of green colouring, probably intended to represent agricultural land. However, some specific features are also included. To the top left of the circuit is a covered bridge, leading to what van der Meer describes as '*un alto edificio grigio*', but too little of this remains for it to be commented upon. Meanwhile, at the bottom, a harbour surrounded by moles is shown. Thus the city does not give way entirely to rural land at the walled circuit, but has some form of periphery. If a specific city was intended, the harbour in particular may have been a characteristic feature which would help it to be recognised. However, the central area within the walls clearly contains the city's most important monuments. The features outside the walls may have been depicted mainly in order to provide a realistic setting and prevent the city from hanging in an artistic vacuum, rather than because they were considered important in their own right.[171]

Finally, we return to the *Corpus Agrimensorum* and the Peutinger Table, to discuss the few city images from these documents which did not conform to the usual type of a walled circuit without periurban features. In the *Corpus Agrimensorum*, one unusual illustration appears to show an unwalled city (plate 2.3).[172] This is the only such example in the collection, and the text which it accompanies offers no special justification for depicting an open city. The drawing shows a centuriated grid crossed by a single road, at the centre of which is a group of buildings. Even here, however, the city is shown as a tightly packed nucleus, on an area of ground differentiated from the surrounding centuriation by its shading. There is also no sign of anything approaching an urban periphery. Possibly, having chosen to depict an open city, the artist aimed to show it as compactly as possible, in order to make it recognisable as a city, rather than a group of unrelated rural buildings. Another illustration from the *Corpus* shows a walled circuit with no buildings inside, but a variety of mausolea in the landscape around it.[173] This image accompanies an edict of Tiberius concerning the erection of funerary monuments, and was probably intended to depict examples in the general context where they might be encountered. In one sense, then, this *is* a generic representation of periurban land-use, created to convey information about a particular type of periurban monument.

The Peutinger Table, meanwhile, includes three city personifications, representing the major cities of Rome (plate 2.4), Constantinople and Antioch.[174] These personifications are all shown seated on thrones and accompanied by additional architectural features from the city. To the left of the representation of Constantinople is a column surmounted by a statue, which has been interpreted either as a lighthouse, or as the porphyry column and statue set up by Constantine in the city's forum.[175] The personification of Rome is

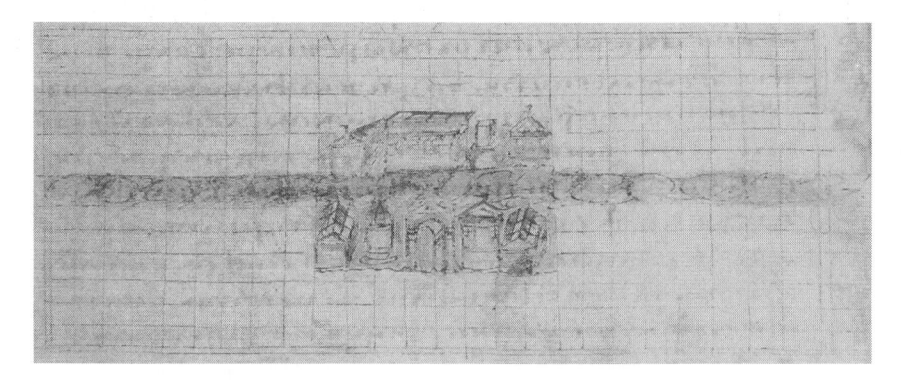

Plate 2.3 'Open' city illustration from the *Corpus Agrimensorum*, Arcerianus A manuscript.

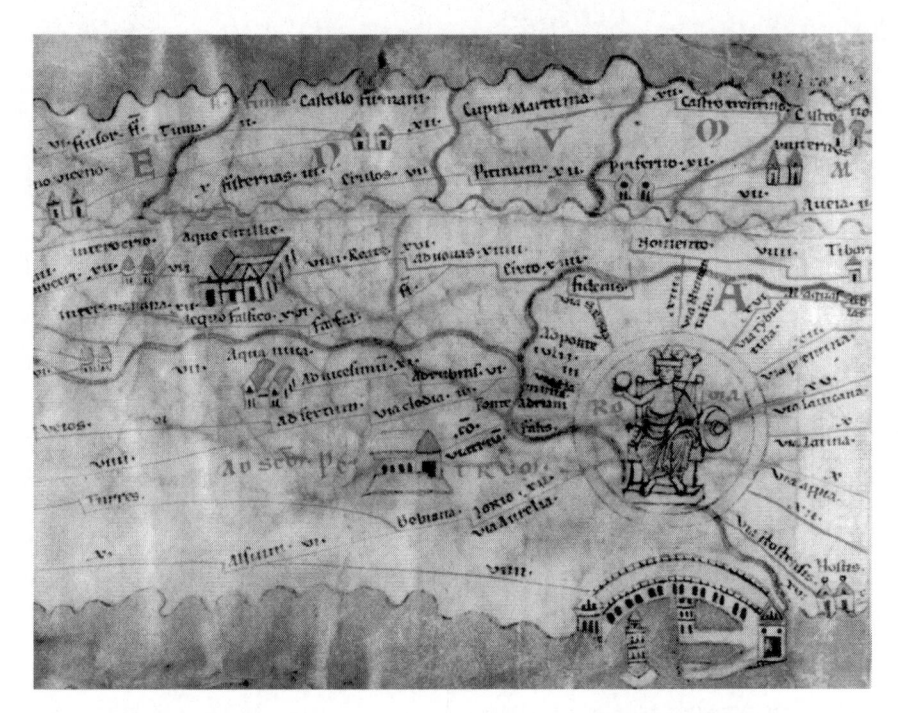

Plate 2.4 Personification of Rome and surrounding area, Peutinger Table.

shown within a double circle, perhaps representing the wall of Aurelian, from which the great consular roads radiate. Meanwhile, a representation of St Peter's is shown on the opposite side of the Tiber. That of Antioch is shown with a young boy, possibly a personification of the Orontes, resting his hand on a vase from which a river flows over a series of aqueduct arches to a temple surrounded by trees. Bosio has suggested that this may signify the Temple of Apollo at Daphne, a satellite of Antioch.[176] If this is the case, then the personifications of both Rome and Antioch on the Peutinger Table are represented with well-known contemporary features from their urban peripheries. We may surmise that the personifications were considered sufficient to represent the urban centres, while certain monuments from their peripheries were considered significant enough in their own right to warrant special representation on the map.

As a group, the periurban features shown in some of these images seem to have been included because they could make a specific contribution to their meaning or aesthetic value. Thus the bridge and harbour on the painting from the Oppian hill were probably included primarily for aesthetic reasons, while the storehouses outside the city on Trajan's column helped to bring out the narrative theme of preparations before a war. In certain cases, however, periurban features do appear to have been included in city representations because they were considered to be of interest or importance in their own right. This applies to the inclusion of extra-mural areas on the Severan *Forma Urbis* and the features accompanying Rome and Antioch on the Peutinger Table. Such inclusions could of course only have been relevant when the features of a specific city were being portrayed. Meanwhile, the copious examples of generic city images showing no periurban features of any kind make it clear that an urban periphery was not usually considered essential to abstract conceptions of the Roman city.

Conclusion

Various different attitudes to and perceptions of the urban periphery have been identified in this chapter, and can be summarised here. Legal texts revealed that the urban periphery could be seen as an ambiguous zone, considered to belong from some perspectives to the city and from others to the countryside. This ambiguity is of course an essential feature of the urban periphery, and is reflected also in the literary *topos* of the suburban villa as the meeting place of urban and rural comforts. The legal evidence also revealed that certain activities considered undesirable within the ideologically charged urban centre might be relegated instead to the urban periphery. At the same time, however, the periphery was not regarded simply as a convenient dumping-ground: periurban areas could themselves be subject to legal protections. Literary texts revealed that the term *'suburbanus'* in particular carried very specific connotations, evoking above all a refined landscape of private properties belonging to the metropolitan elite at Rome. Other texts also presented the urban periphery as a zone of exclusion, a place for military activity, and a formal zone of transition: an aspect matched in visual scenes of *profectio* and *adventus*. Finally, visual images made it clear that periurban development was not generally considered an essential indicator of *urbanitas*. They did reveal, however, that in some cases periurban features could help to express the identity of particular cities: a phenomenon mirrored in the prominence which Strabo gives to the Campus Martius in his description of Rome.

These themes chiefly reflect the interests and concerns of the metropolitan elite at Rome. However, the evidence does provide some indications of the extent to which their perceptions of the urban periphery were adopted by provincial elites. Legal texts can offer little illumination here, since Roman civil law and provincial charters were both normally formulated in a metropolitan context. With the exception of Apuleius, most of the authors who made use of Latin terms such as *'suburbanus'* or *'extra urbem'* had also lived most of their lives in Rome. More telling is the small number of provincial writers whose use of the Greek term *'proasteion'* suggests that they were familiar with the concept of the refined *ager suburbanus*, and felt it could be applied to cities in the Greek east. Visual images can also help to indicate the extent to which the thought-world of the metropolitan elite influenced provincials. In particular, Greek civic coinages clearly indicate the universality of the equation between walls and *urbanitas*, and the absence of a role for periurban development in conveying the notion of a city.

Such evidence suggests that provincial elites did absorb perceptions of 'the urban' and 'the periurban' presented to them by Rome. However, its scope is limited. It provides no detail about the application of these ideologies in provincial cities, and does not reveal whether alternative perceptions were *also* held by provincial elites. These issues must be investigated through evidence for periurban development drawn from the provinces themselves, and this can only be provided by archaeology. By examining archaeological evidence it will be possible, for instance, to determine whether provincial urban peripheries were actually used for idyllic elite residences or for activities which were not wanted within the urban centre. It will also be possible to see how else they may have been used, and whether or not they were sharply distinguished from the urban centre. These issues will all be addressed in chapters 4–6.

Finally, the conclusions drawn in this chapter can also be used to help interpret the archaeological evidence from actual Roman cities. Two findings in particular should be highlighted. First, all of the evidence discussed above made it clear that physical boundaries, and especially walls, held great significance in ideological terms, and were an expected feature of a Roman city. This is important for the identification of provincial urban peripheries, since it means that once the boundaries of a city have been recognised, they can be used from a modern perspective as a basic indication of the point where the urban ceded to the rural or the periurban. However, the second major conclusion to emerge from this chapter acts as a warning against assuming that periurban, or indeed urban or rural development, can ever be securely identified simply from its geographical position. This is the idea that periurban identity was subjective and contestable, illustrated most clearly by Catullus.[177] This issue is not likely to cause serious difficulties immediately outside an urban boundary, especially where features typically associated with a city, such as *domus*, theatres or market buildings are concerned. However, subjective perceptions become more important as features get further away from a city, especially when they are of a type which might equally be encountered in the countryside; for instance, villas, sanctuaries or kilns. The findings of this chapter indicate that in these cases, we must look for some positive evidence for a connection between the feature and the city before it can be assumed to have been seen as periurban, rather than rural, by the people who used it.

3

THE ARCHAEOLOGY OF THE URBAN PERIPHERY

Introduction

Chapter 2 concluded that archaeological evidence would be central to the study of periurban development in the provinces. It is now time to consider how such evidence may be approached, and in particular how features considered periurban in the Roman period can be identified in the archaeological record. As we have seen, periurban – and indeed urban or rural – status rested partly in the eye of the observer. It could be contested in the past, and can never be attributed conclusively in the present. Nevertheless, broad guidelines as to what sorts of features were typically considered periurban by Roman observers can be detected in the legal, literary and visual evidence already reviewed, and used to identify the most relevant archaeological evidence.

Clearly, the courses of urban boundaries such as city walls will be an important indicator of periurban status. Roman thinkers placed great emphasis on such boundaries for showing that an area was 'urban' in status, and their archaeological remains therefore constitute an important starting point for distinguishing between the urban and the periurban. Beyond the city boundaries, the traditional city–country antithesis held that the 'urban' ceded immediately to the 'rural'. However, as the previous chapter showed, Roman thinkers were also more than capable of conceiving of an urban periphery between the two. The challenge for modern observers, then, lies in attempting to decide whether individual features beyond a city's boundaries are likely to have been viewed as truly rural, or part of an urban periphery.

Where there is continuous, built-up occupation immediately outside the urban boundaries, this distinction should not be too problematic. The concept of the *continentia aedificia* shows that such occupation was generally seen as a part of the main agglomeration, despite falling beyond the urban boundaries. When identified archaeologically, it can thus be considered part of the city's periphery. Further from the urban centre, however, as structures become more isolated, it grows harder to differentiate neatly between the rural and the periurban. In part, we must accept that this is because there *was* no simple distinction between the two. Periurban land-use in Roman eyes was always ambiguous, and, falling as it did outside the urban boundaries, might always from some perspectives be considered rural. Yet if we are to use archaeological evidence in investigating the Roman urban periphery, some methods of identifying isolated periurban structures must be devised.

The conclusions of the previous chapter can help. The literary *topos* of the suburban villa emphasised the close social and cultural ties between such villas and the city of Rome, maintained especially through regular journeys between the two. Such a relationship, if it existed, may be expected to have left archaeologically identifiable traces. For example, the design and decorative themes of a villa might correspond with urban fashions and concerns, reflecting its role in an urban-centred lifestyle. Meanwhile, a good road link with the nearby city could at least confirm that frequent journeys between the two were possible, even if it cannot tell us who might have undertaken them and why. A combination of such indications might strongly suggest that a particular villa site would have been considered periurban in the past. Similarly, positive evidence for special, regular contact between a sanctuary, workshop or funerary monument and the nearby city may raise the same possibility.

Another approach is to draw upon economic and geographical models of the relationship between cities and their rural hinterlands. These can provide a framework of expectations concerning the land-use and occupation encountered outside a typical city, thus helping to distinguish between examples of expected rural land-use and development with a special, periurban function. One such model is central place theory, first formulated in the 1930s,[1] which proposes that a large city usually functions as the dominant economic centre for a surrounding hinterland. The city acts as a marketplace and redistribution centre for goods produced in that hinterland, and also provides centralised services for its population. Around it develops a hierarchical network of smaller, 'lower-order' settlements, which provide less specialised services for local sub-sections of the hinterland: their 'zones of influence'. Within the hierarchy, settlements of the same order should be more or less evenly distributed, with the zone of influence of each reflecting the distance that individuals are prepared to travel to obtain the services they offer.

Central place theory has been used to interpret settlement distributions and economic relationships in many societies, contemporary and historical.[2] Although factors such as political and administrative structures, communication routes and unevenly distributed economic resources mean that real urban systems are never perfect reflections of the idealised central place system, the model has proved to be a useful and relevant interpretative tool across a range of civilisations. For the Roman world, the theory has offered a way of understanding some urban systems, although not equally in all places or at all times. Morley has analysed networks of periodic markets in

Campania in terms of a dendritic central place system, affected by the special influence of Rome, while Woolf has suggested that settlement patterns in Gallia Narbonensis conform to the expectations of the model.[3] Yet Woolf has also demonstrated that some parts of Gaul did *not* develop the extensive hierarchical settlement networks which central place theory predicts, while Millett has argued that the administrative role of primary cities in late Roman Britain was not matched by an equivalent status as dominant economic centres.[4] The economic interactions at the centre of the theory, then, may not have been at the forefront of urban systems in all parts of the empire, particularly in the late antique era. None the less, Roman urbanism was clearly capable of developing in the manner which it predicts. The presence of networks of smaller settlements around a Roman city, then, would be in keeping with the expectations of the model, and should be understood as part of a typical rural landscape. They need not be considered to constitute periurban development unless a particularly close social and functional relationship with the city can be demonstrated.

Also of interest for the typical relationship between a city and its hinterland is von Thünen's model of land-use in an isolated city-state.[5] This model, formulated in the 1820s, attempts to describe the agricultural exploitation which will occur across a uniformly fertile and accessible plain around a city with no external trading contacts. The assumptions at its root are obviously unrealistic, and will never be met by any real example. However, they allowed von Thünen to highlight the economic effects of increasing distance from a city on decisions about what types of produce to grow. He concluded that land closest to the city would be farmed intensively for high-value perishable items such as fruit, vegetables and dairy produce, while more durable goods such as wood or lower value staples such as corn would be grown further afield. He also suggested that the intensity of cultivation would generally decrease with distance from the market. In any real situation, regional trade, transport routes and political structures disrupt the neat concentric rings of von Thünen's model. His predictions also take no account of smaller settlements within the hinterland, of the type covered by central place theory. Yet for any city whose day-to-day needs are supplied *primarily* from its hinterland – as most pre-industrial cities were – the basic principles of his theory should hold firm. Certainly, von Thünen's model suggests that, like networks of smaller settlements, intensive cultivation around the fringes of Roman cities should be expected. Thus, special signs of periurban status are again needed before individual agricultural establishments can be interpreted as anything other than the normal result of a city–country relationship.

In this chapter, the guidelines and expectations discussed above will be used to identify and explore archaeologically attested examples of periurban occupation: partly to establish a general sense of the character of Roman urban peripheries, and partly to provide context for the more detailed examination of the Gallo-Roman evidence which follows. As important determinants of periurban status, the discussion will also cover urban boundaries, asking how they may be identified archaeologically, what functions they actually performed, and what happened if they were moved. Geographically, the first half of the chapter will focus on the city of Rome, in its capacity as the cultural and political heart of the empire: a place capable of creating and disseminating to provincial communities a 'model' of city and periphery. The second half will examine a range of cities elsewhere in the empire, discovering what aspects of that 'model' were or were not widely applied. The evidence from Gaul can then be viewed in the light of both, allowing it be evaluated as an element of an empire-wide phenomenon.

Rome's urban boundaries

Rome possessed multiple urban boundaries, which developed at different times and served a range of different functions. One of the earliest, the so-called 'Servian' wall, has already been encountered in the context of juridical definitions of the city, and formed a continuous defensive circuit some 11 km long. Its construction date is still debated, although major work clearly took place after 396 BC, when the Roman defeat of Veii allowed access to the Grotta Oscura tufa from which much of it is built. Some sections, however, may already have been fortified as early as the sixth century BC.[6] At its origins, the function of the wall must have been primarily defensive, although it doubtless also conveyed messages of prestige and status, and much of its course seems to have been reinforced by the religious boundary of the *pomerium* (see below). By the early imperial period, the military function had become obsolete, the line of the *pomerium* had in several places shifted outwards, and the circuit itself was no longer completely intact. Livy and Dionysius of Halicarnassus report that parts had been engulfed by surrounding buildings,[7] while excavations have also revealed breaches.[8] However, the wall remained important. It continued to define the *urbs* proper, and must have remained traceable enough to do so. This gave it legal significance, as the references from the *Digesta* showed, as well as a continuing symbolic value; for example, Septimius Severus indicated his respect for Rome by walking through one of its gates on his first arrival as emperor.[9] Today, the wall survives only in short stretches. Parts of its course remain disputed, but its outline is generally well-established. The significance of this boundary is clear enough to conclude that any features known to have fallen outside it must be considered technically periurban, at least before the construction of Aurelian's wall in the AD 270s. The extent of the city by the imperial period, however, and the existence of other, more inclusive, urban boundaries, may mean that this distinction had little impact in everyday terms.

Aurelian's wall itself is a late feature, but worthy of comment, since it represents the culmination of several centuries' worth of topographical developments. Patterson has suggested that, as the centre of the city was increasingly taken up with monumental buildings, elite residences shifted outwards, and the Aurelianic wall may have been built partly to protect this housing.[10] Its construction, probably accompanied by an extension of the *pomerium*,[11] had a major impact on the urban fabric. Most significantly, burials ceased within all the newly enclosed areas, indicating that they had become subject to the ban on burials within the urban centre. These areas, then, appear to have had their identity transformed from periurban to fully urban by the construction of the new wall. It is also important to note that although Aurelian's wall enclosed a far larger area than the Servian wall, it did not enclose the full extent of Augustus' fourteen districts (see below), excluding most of the Janiculum.[12] By conferring urban status on some areas of the city, Aurelian's wall emphasised the periurban nature of those which remained outside.

The Tiber is seldom viewed as an urban boundary, especially since, unlike the other boundaries discussed here, its course could not be controlled.[13] Nevertheless, it could still be used to differentiate between parts of the city. It is important to note that the Tiber did not flow *through* Rome's urban centre, but past it, the original *urbs* having grown up on its left bank. By the imperial period, however, the right bank was also occupied, and the area included amongst Augustus' fourteen urban *regiones*.[14] Clearly, then, the area was part of Rome: it even received imperial benefactions, such as a set of baths built by Septimius Severus.[15] But it may not have been considered equivalent to extra-mural occupation on the left bank. It was defined by its very separation from the main city, as the use of the terms '*trans Tiberim*' and '*Transtiberim*' reveal.[16] Comments by Martial and Juvenal also suggest that it was seen as a downmarket area,[17] and Augustus' designation of it as his fourteenth *regio* may reflect a lesser status compared with the thirteen regions on the left bank.[18] Thus, while Transtiberim and, for example, the Campus Martius both fell outside the Servian wall, the Campus Martius was probably perceived as being 'more' urban, and certainly more prestigious, than the region beyond the Tiber.

From an early period, Rome's centre was also defined by a religious boundary, the *pomerium*.[19] During the Republic, its course probably followed the Servian wall,[20] but excluded the Aventine hill.[21] The *pomerium* protected the sacred space of the urban centre and defined the appropriate spheres for certain activities. Traditionally, it was only within the *pomerium* that the auspices of the city could be taken, and only outside it that burials could be made, military *imperium* held or ambassadors of hostile nations accommodated.[22] The restrictions on *imperium* became obsolete in the imperial period,[23] but the ban on burials remained in force until late antiquity.[24] An important characteristic of the *pomerium* is that it could be moved, traditionally by generals or emperors who had extended the empire's frontiers. Literary accounts of these extensions are contradictory, but the first certain extension, attested by a series of *cippi* which marked the *pomerium*'s new course, was by Claudius.[25] Further extension by Vespasian and Titus followed, as did a reaffirmation by Hadrian, and a probable extension by Aurelian, connected with his wall. All must have altered the status of the newly enclosed areas, if only by forbidding burial within them, but their courses are difficult to determine today from the limited number of surviving markers.[26] Rome's *pomerium*, then, is of limited use as a guide to the status of different parts of the city. Rather, the situation is inverted, with archaeological evidence for behaviour and land-use — particularly burial patterns — often being invoked in order to reconstruct the course of the *pomerium*.

Rome also developed boundaries with a legal or administrative significance. We have seen that the spheres of application for some laws were defined with reference to the edges of the *continentia aedificia*, for instance, or a line one thousand paces from the city (however measured). Since these boundaries were not formally marked out in themselves, they are difficult to identify archaeologically. However, they indicate an important ancient interest in differentiating between dense occupation immediately outside the Servian wall and the looser landscape beyond. A customs boundary, marked by gates and *cippi*, is also attested from the Vespasianic period, but may date back to Augustus.[27] This enclosed most of the urban agglomeration, and was probably followed in several places by the Aurelianic wall. Its wide circuit probably reflects a desire to ensure efficient taxation by surrounding as much of the *continentia aedificia* as possible, and this may have encouraged the concentration of trading warehouses just beyond it, causing a difference in character between the areas inside and out.[28] However, there is no evidence that the customs boundary in itself served to distinguish between areas which were 'more' or 'less' urban.

The outer edges of Augustus' fourteen *regiones*, probably created in stages between 7 BC and AD 6, constituted a more significant administrative boundary.[29] The limits of the *regiones* can be reconstructed with reasonable accuracy from sources such as the two fourth-century catalogues (the *Notitia* and the *Curiosum*) which describe Rome's monuments region by region. Together they enclosed a larger area than either the Servian or Aurelianic walls, probably including most of the Augustan *continentia aedificia*.[30] On a practical level, they defined arenas of magisterial responsibility, gave rise to seven fire-fighting districts, and were subdivided into *vici*: local neighbourhoods administered by *vicomagistri*.[31] But they also carried great symbolic significance. Reorganising Rome allowed Augustus to demonstrate his new influence over the city, and his intention to use it benevolently. The process also defined the new Rome: certainly, it demonstrated that Augustus' city was far larger than the Republican *urbs*.[32] The establishment of the *regiones* meant that the full extent of the *continentia aedificia*, including the important Campus Martius area, would now be seen as fundamental to the identity of the city.[33] Indeed, there is some evidence that the entire area included within the fourteen *regiones* came, after Augustus' reorganisation, to be seen as constituting the Roman *urbs*: hence the dedication of a statue base to Hadrian by *'vicomagistri* of the *urbs* of the fourteen *regiones*'.[34] Importantly, however, the qualification – 'of the fourteen *regiones*' – remained necessary, and references to the *urbs* alone were still taken by jurists of the second and early third centuries to mean only the area within the Servian wall.[35]

The visibility of Rome's boundaries within the urban fabric varied. Some, such as the Tiber or the city walls, were highly visible and indeed impassable at points other than bridges or gates. Others were marked with intermittent features such as *cippi* or gates, or perhaps simply recorded on administrative maps of the city. This makes some easier to identify than others today, but help may be gleaned in some cases from the positioning of monumental arches.[36] Arches in Rome did not have to be erected over urban boundaries: they often occurred at the entrances to monumental complexes. But it was common to find them at points of entrance into the city. An arch on the via Flaminia, erected in the reign of Claudius, probably marked the point where his *pomerium* crossed it.[37] Another on the via Appia, posthumously honouring Claudius' father, Drusus, was probably located very close to the Aurelianic porta Appia.[38] It may have been intended to mark the outer edge of the *continentia aedificia*, or, depending exactly when it was built, the entrance to Augustus' new *regio* I. Such arches would have helped an ancient observer to distinguish different stages in the nest of urban boundaries defining the city, and can play the same role today.

Of the many boundaries discussed here, some did more than others to distinguish between the 'urban' and the 'periurban'. The Servian wall and *pomerium* were of great importance under the Republic, and the former appears to have remained the literal delimiter of the 'urban' throughout the imperial period. It retained its juridical significance, while the *pomerium* continued to govern burial practices and was respected by triumphant emperors.[39] The development of the concept of the *continentia aedificia*, however, and especially the creation of Augustus' fourteen *regiones*, must have weakened the sense of difference between the intra-mural and the extra-mural, as must the separation of wall and *pomerium*. Instead, the correspondence between the outer edges of the Augustan regions and the approximate limits of the *continentia aedificia* probably lent a greater emphasis to the difference in character between the *continentia aedificia* as a whole and the looser landscape beyond. Meanwhile, within the fourteen regions, existing boundaries such as the Servian wall and the Tiber appear to have created a spectrum of zones with 'greater' and 'lesser' degrees of *urbanitas*, from the truly urban walled centre to the obviously periurban quarter of Transtiberim.

It is also notable that, once an urban boundary was established at Rome, it was unwillingly relinquished. This is clear in the continuing importance attached to the Servian wall, and also in the persistent commemoration of a supposed archaic circuit around the Palatine hill. This circuit, probably followed as part of the Lupercalia, could still be described by Tacitus in the early second century AD, and was traditionally attributed to Romulus.[40] Religious significance was also attached to a series of shrines at the fifth and sixth milestones on some of the major roads leading out of Rome.[41] These marked the edges of Rome's archaic territory, a line which was clearly obsolete by the imperial period, but continued to be celebrated through ritual. Urban boundaries, then, persisted in popular memory, legal practice and religious ritual long after their original function had been superseded, signalling a deep-seated Roman interest in the demarcation and differentiation of space.

The *continentia aedificia* and the *suburbium*

If the Servian wall still marked the edge of the *urbs* even in the imperial period, then it was beyond it that the urban periphery, strictly speaking, began. As we have seen, this periphery consisted of two major concentric zones – the extra-mural parts of the *continentia aedificia* and the *suburbium* beyond – and these will be treated separately here. Those parts of the *continentia aedificia* outside the Servian wall never became truly urban, because they lacked the special status of the walled *urbs*. However, their inclusion in Augustus' fourteen *regiones* must have made them seem very close. Just how different in character, then, were the intra-mural and extra-mural parts of Rome's built agglomeration, and how can we account for any differences between them?

Both sectors were certainly used for domestic occupation by the imperial period. A fragment of the Severan *Forma Urbis* from the Janiculum, on the right bank of the Tiber, shows a mixture of elite *domus* and *insula* blocks, interspersed with commercial buildings.[42] A similar range was found within the Servian wall, from *insula* blocks like the one built into the Capitoline hill to aristocratic residences on the Aventine, Caelian and Esquiline.[43] With the exception of the imperial palaces, however, the city's really lavish residences generally fell just outside the Servian wall, in the form of the *horti*.[44] These appeared during the first century BC, and consisted of rich mansions set into carefully landscaped gardens. They constituted extravagant displays of wealth, since only the very rich could afford to devote so much land on the fringes of the city to pleasure, rather than profit.[45] There was no legal or religious reason why *horti* could not be located within the Servian wall, and some probably were.[46] However, the density of the intra-mural occupation by the time they became popular meant that it was only really feasible to acquire enough land for them outside the walled circuit. The *horti* must also have helped to create a sense of continuity between the *continentia aedificia* and the *suburbium*. Their emphasis on luxury, display and natural idyll gave them much in common with the suburban villa, although they derived special status from being on the very perimeter of the city.[47]

The extra-mural *continentia aedificia* was also the setting for many commercial installations. Quays lined both banks of the Tiber, and large warehouses were concentrated in Transtiberim and the Emporium area south of the Servian wall.[48] Their locations were determined mainly by a need for access to the Tiber, which was probably not available from within the wall.[49] Patterson has also suggested that the imperial customs boundary affected the locations of some commercial concerns: thus, wine warehouses were located just outside it, where they might avoid taxation.[50] The Macellum (market-building) of the Republican period had lain close to the Forum Romanum, but it was displaced in the first century AD, and the markets of the imperial era occupied more peripheral locations. The Macellum Liviae was located outside the porta Esquilina, while the Macellum Magnum fell either just within or just outside the Servian wall on the Caelian hill.[51] Coarelli suggests that this reflected the flourishing agricultural activity south-east of the city, which supplied them. Patterson adds that it may also result from an imperial interest in distancing commercial activity from the new monumental *fora* in the heart of Rome.[52]

Industrial activity also seems to have gathered in Transtiberim. References in Juvenal and Martial suggest that hides were tanned in this area, while a series of water-mills powered by the Aqua Traiana functioned here in the third century AD.[53] There is no positive evidence that this was the result of any legal prohibition against workshops on the left bank of the Tiber, however. The use of the right bank for industry may have had more to do with the availability of cheap land and a water supply than an ideological or practical desire to separate industrial and domestic occupation (see further chapter 4).

The buildings of the Forum Romanum and Capitoline hill undoubtedly gave a monumental focus to the walled *urbs* from an early period, reinforced by later constructions such as the imperial *fora*, the Colosseum and some imperial baths. Yet the extra-mural *continentia aedificia* was also well endowed with public buildings, with certain regions developing particularly monumental characters. This was especially true of the Campus Martius, where, from the first century BC, competitive or self-promotional building projects were sponsored by Republican dynasts and emperors. The concentration of public monuments in this quarter may be explained by several factors. At the start of the first century BC, the Campus Martius was mainly undeveloped, and space was available for large-scale constructions.[54] The proximity of the Tiber may also have lent a special scenic attraction, enhancing the aesthetic impact of the monuments. Clodia's *horti ad Tiberim* was certainly viewed by Cicero as an attractive setting for the memorial shrine which he planned for Tullia.[55] In addition, the area was highly visible to travellers approaching Rome along the Tiber or via Flaminia.[56] Finally, figures such as Augustus may have built in the Campus Martius in conscious emulation of the *proasteia* of Greek cities like Athens and Corinth, famous for their groves, temples, monumental tombs and philosophical schools.[57]

Some monuments may also have been affected by the ideological connotations of the urban centre, and especially the course of the *pomerium*. Pliny comments that temples of Aesculapius were built first '*extra urbem*' and later on Tiber island because of Roman mistrust of physicians, while Augustus twice instigated measures to expel Egyptian cults, first from the *pomerium* and then for a further mile beyond it.[58] Yet some foreign cults were welcomed into the *urbs*, at least in certain periods. Hercules had several temples and sanctuaries within the Servian wall, while Cybele (Magna Mater) was brought from Asia Minor to be installed on the Palatine hill. Cassius Dio also reports sacrifices performed to Isis on the Capitol in 48 BC, although in the context of a subsequent order from the soothsayers to destroy all sanctuaries belonging to her or Serapis.[59] Thus, although it is clear that some temples were considered best kept outside the *pomerium*, decisions appear to have been made on an individual basis – as Vitruvius' discussion of temple locations implies – and must be interpreted as such.[60] Meanwhile, the first permanent amphitheatre at Rome, built by Statilius Taurus in 29 BC, was erected in the Campus Martius, as were several theatres. However, the earlier tradition of holding gladiatorial games in the Forum Romanum and the later construction of the Colosseum within the walls suggest that this pattern resulted from availability of space in the Campus Martius, rather than ideological objections to intra-mural games.[61]

Tombs later than the third century BC are not generally found within the Servian wall, although intra-pomerial burial could always be granted as an exceptional honour.[62] In most parts of the extra-mural *continentia aedificia*, however, they were a highly visible feature. Rome had a large population, characterised by complex social relationships and an interest in acquiring and displaying status, and all of this found vivid expression in its burial practices.[63] Lavish tomb-building became a medium for elite competition during the Republican period, especially along the via Appia,[64] while emperors such as Augustus and Hadrian advertised their importance and dynastic aspirations through grandiose mausolea. But more modest individuals also aspired to tomb-ownership, often locating them in cultivated plots to off-set the cost of the land required.[65] Meanwhile, the graves of the poor had a profound effect on the character of certain extra-mural areas. Until the first century BC, an area of the Esquiline hill immediately outside the Servian wall was used to bury paupers in open pits.[66] The area was 'gentrified' in the Augustan period, when Maecenas covered over the pits. Nevertheless, it remained an important focus for burial activity, with family or *collegium*-owned *columbaria* now used for multiple cremation burials.[67] Tombs, then, instantly signalled the difference between the intra-mural and extra-mural parts of the *continentia aedificia*. Yet the regulation of funerary activity sometimes also recognised their similarities. Over time, certain extra-mural areas became subject to the same ban on burials which affected the *urbs* through outwards shifts of the *pomerium*: particularly parts of the Campus Martius.

Dio also reports an act of 38 BC prohibiting cremation within two miles of the city: presumably in recognition of the dense, urban-style occupation in this area, and its vulnerability to fire.[68]

Finally, the extra-mural *continentia aedificia* was also home to structures connected with military activity. Some temples connected with war deities were located outside the *pomerium*, such as the temple of Mars on the via Appia, and those of Bellona and Apollo in the Campus Martius: itself named after an important altar of Mars. These were used for ceremonial activities associated with warfare: the temple of Mars was an assembly point for departing troops,[69] while the senate used the temples of Bellona and Apollo to meet with generals holding *imperium* or ambassadors from hostile nations.[70] This was forbidden within the *pomerium*, whose role as a symbolic divider between the civilian and military spheres also meant that armed soldiers were traditionally barred from the city. When emperors began to require a permanent military presence for their protection, the solution was to locate barracks such as the Praetorian camp in the extra-mural *continentia aedificia*.[71] Yet the centrality of warfare to the Roman mentality meant that structures and activities connected with it were also encountered within the walled *urbs*. Sacred spears of Mars, for example, were held within the Regia in the Forum Romanum, while Augustus established temples to Mars Ultor in his own forum and on the Capitoline hill.[72] One other structure, known as the Mutatorium Caesaris, is of interest in this context. Located on the via Appia, it may have been used for emperors to switch horses on approaching or leaving Rome, and perhaps also to make the change from civilian *toga* to military *paludamentum* involved in the ceremonies of *profectio* and *adventus*.[73] If so, this structure relates to the role of Rome's urban periphery as a formal point of transition, encountered in chapter 2.

The extra-mural sectors of Rome's *continentia aedificia*, then, shared some characteristics with the walled *urbs*. Both featured residential occupation and monumental public buildings. Yet even within these broad categories, specifics differed between the two, with *horti* and spectacle buildings more common outside the Servian wall than within. Other forms of land-use made the difference more marked: tombs, military barracks and commercial installations connected with the Tiber. Thus real differences in character and function persisted well into the imperial period, despite the inclusion of both areas within Augustus' fourteen *regiones*. Both the special status of the *urbs* and the density of its occupation by the late Republic caused it to be used in a different manner from the regions beyond the walls, and it is in these differences that the distinction between urban and periurban patterns of land-use lies.

Beyond the *continentia aedificia* lay the second of Rome's two major periurban zones: the *suburbium*. The division between the two was not, of course, as precise as the line of the Servian wall. The *continentia aedificia* probably gave way to the *suburbium* gradually, as buildings became less dense and cultivated plots appeared.[74] Nevertheless, the two terms reflect a distinct difference in character between the dense urban agglomeration and the looser landscape beyond. This latter is harder to approach from a modern perspective, since individual features within it do not share the obvious connection with the city imbued by continuity with the urban agglomeration. Instead, periurban identity must be inferred from signs of a special association with the city of Rome.

Literary texts examined in chapter 2 emphasised in particular the presence of villas within this zone. Survey work and excavation around Rome confirm that the city was surrounded by a dense halo of sites, which included sanctuaries, workshops and funerary monuments, but was dominated by agricultural establishments.[75] This is in keeping with von Thünen's belief that the land immediately outside a city will, other things being equal, be particularly intensively exploited. Thus it need not mean that any individual structures within this halo should be classed as periurban. Yet a plethora of literary texts make it clear that many villa-owners in this region *did* consider their properties to have a special connection with the city. Thus it is appropriate to ask whether anything in the archaeological record allows us, even tentatively, to identify them as periurban from a modern perspective.

Several Roman writers held that the ideal location for a suburban villa fell within a comfortable day's journey of Rome.[76] For our purposes, this helps to define a suitable arena in which to begin looking for archaeological examples. Working from literary and legal references, Champlin and Laurence concur that an easy day's travel in the environs of late Republican or early imperial Rome could cover around twenty to twenty-five Roman miles (30–37 km).[77] This fits neatly with the distribution of most 'suburban' towns within a radius of 35 km from Rome, as seen in chapter 2. Figure 2.1 (p. 21) suggested that this radius may have been skewed in favour of Latin territory on the left bank of the Tiber, but Champlin has argued that properties in the equivalent parts of Etruria were also in practice viewed as suburban.[78] This region, too, then, should be included in our enquiry. Large, well-appointed villas certainly did begin to appear within this 35 km radius from around the second century BC, albeit at different periods in different areas.[79] By the imperial period, they were scattered over most of what is now known as the Roman Campagna, with the greatest concentrations along major roads and in the areas closest to Rome.[80]

Individually, many sites do bear comparison with the suburban villas of Roman literature. Some were extensive complexes, rich in the urbane comforts which Pliny privileges when describing his Laurentine villa. The villa of the Quintilii, at the fifth milestone on the via Appia, is a vivid example, featuring broad enclosed gardens, lavish marble decoration and a monumental nymphaeum.[81] But many more modest sites also included recognisably 'urban' features such as an axial atrium and peristyle: much like those described by Pliny.[82] One example is the villa at S. Basilio, which probably acquired this layout in the first half of the first century BC.[83] The choice of plan creates an architectural link between villa and city, perhaps arising from the owner's habit of dividing his time between the two. It may also tell us something about how the property was used. In an urban *domus*, the atrium and peristyle created a grandiose approach into the house, and were used for welcoming and impressing guests.[84] The presence of such rooms in the S. Basilio villa may therefore indicate that it was indeed used for the regular visits between members of the elite encountered in literature. Certainly its location, about 8 km from Rome on a side-road linking the via Nomentana and via Tiburtina, would have made it easily accessible for both owner and guests.

The owners of some suburban properties can be identified, allowing further inferences about their usage. These include imperial properties, such as those of Domitian at Alba,[85] Hadrian at Tibur,[86] or, later, Maxentius on the via Appia.[87] Hadrian's villa offers a particularly rich combination of archaeological, literary and documentary evidence, together demonstrating that the villa did function as a privileged retreat, a place for receiving guests and an extension of urban life, in the manner of a literary *suburbanum*. The architectural remains confirm and expand upon literary reports of its extravagant facilities, while an epigraphically preserved letter sent from Hadrian at the villa to the Delphic Amphictiony indicates that he used the property for state business.[88]

Other properties are known to have been owned by high-ranking senators. The villa of the Quintilii is so named because lead pipe stamps found there indicate that it belonged to the brothers Sex. Quintilius Condianus and Sex. Quintilius Valerius Maximus, joint consuls for the year AD 151. Herodes Atticus, tutor to the young Marcus Aurelius and Lucius Verus, had a property between the second and third milestones of the via Appia, acquired as part of his Roman wife's dowry probably around the same time as his consulship in 143.[89] Another example is the villa of the Volusii, about 25 km from Rome and 500m from the town of Lucus Feroniae. The owners are known from three honorific inscriptions, commemorating the careers of L. Volusius Saturninus, consul in AD 3, and two of his descendents, consuls in AD 56 and 92.[90] Such finds attest a direct link between the villas and the city, and we can readily imagine these consuls making regular journeys to Rome to fulfil their official duties, but retiring to their villas between public engagements for social and intellectual pursuits. The inscriptions of the Volusii, set up in conjunction with portrait busts, also hint at the reception of visitors from Rome, since they appear to draw on both private and public display traditions in a manner that really required an educated and urbane audience to come off to full effect.[91]

The villa of the Volusii also sheds light on two other issues connected with suburban villas: their role in agricultural production, and their relationship with the small towns of the *suburbium*. During the first century AD, two large courts were added to this villa. One, to the west of the main building complex, appears to have been designed for leisure and display, incorporating a room housing the inscriptions and busts mentioned above and a cistern, perhaps designed to supply private baths. The other, to the north, was probably used for agricultural storage and processing. Apparently, then, the Volusii were interested in elegance *and* productivity. This is perfectly in keeping with literary discussions of the suburban villa: especially Seneca's exhortation to look after a suburban estate once it is bought, and the tailored advice of the agronomists.[92] Yet the focus of our literary sources lies in the urbane sophistication of these properties, rather than their economic productivity. Villas like that of the Volusii are a useful illustration of the balance which might be achieved in practice.[93]

Striking too is the proximity of the villa to Lucus Feroniae (figure 3.1). To the modern eye, the relationship looks remarkably like that of a medieval manor house with its dependent village. However, there is no positive evidence that the Volusii *were* closely involved in the life of Lucus Feroniae: as, for example, in the role of benefactors or town patrons. Indeed, Champlin shows that the majority of suburban villa owners took little interest in nearby settlements, with ties to home towns elsewhere in Italy and to Rome itself taking precedence.[94] The productive role of the villa does mean that Lucus Feroniae would have furnished an immediate market for its surpluses, and a source for tools and seasonal labour. But this economic relationship need not have been paralleled in social interaction. Rather, the villa of the Volusii may be placed alongside literary examples of properties which are close to towns around Rome, and yet are still '*suburbana*': in other words, their primary relationship is with Rome itself.[95] This raises the question of the status of the towns themselves, discussed later.

A distinctive type of villa was common in the immediate environs of Rome, then, and corresponded closely with literary constructions of suburban villas. The villas' remains, their locations and what is known of their owners all accord with the literary model of a halo of properties, intimately connected with the life of the city through the movements of the Roman elite. Their distribution also became sparser with increasing distance from Rome.[96] Meanwhile, evidence for serious economic activity on some properties may not find widespread resonances in the literary sources, but is clearly not incompatible with their notions of *suburbanitas*. It seems appropriate, then, to identify these properties as a functioning part of Rome's urban periphery.

Yet the challenge of the archaeological record is apparent when the properties of the *suburbium* are compared with villas in other parts of Italy. If suburban villas around Rome were characterised in part by their urbane architecture, this feature can also be recognised in villas elsewhere. The villa of San Rocco at Francolise, for instance, combines a working courtyard complex with a very urban-looking residential quarter, structured around

THE ARCHAEOLOGY OF THE URBAN PERIPHERY

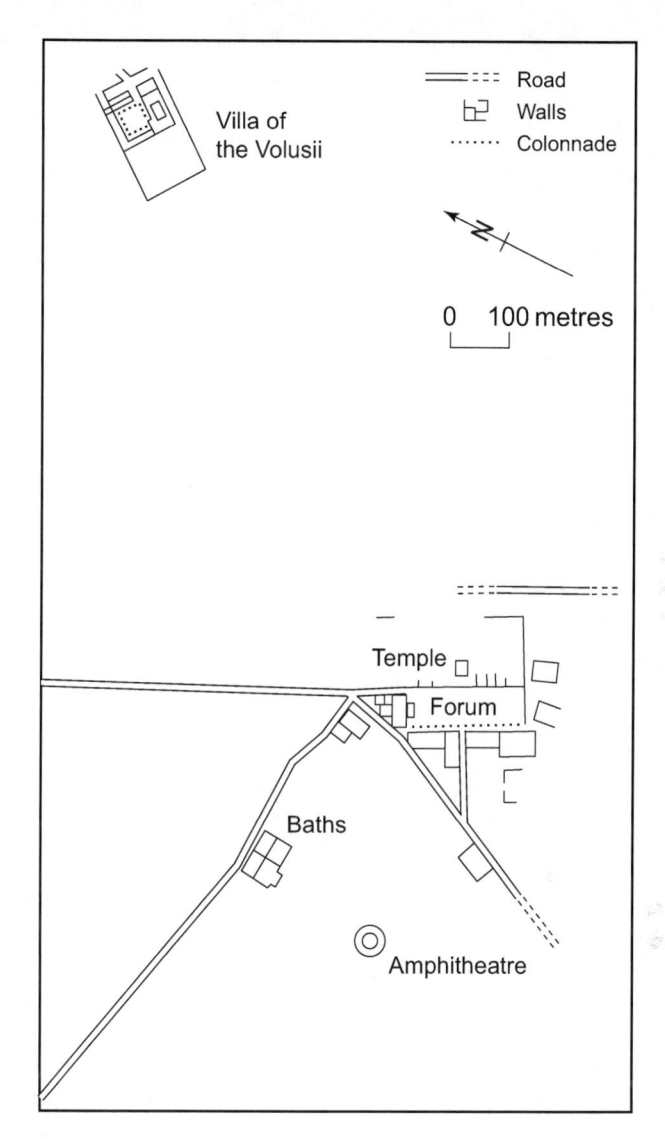

Figure 3.1 Lucus Feroniae.

an axial atrium and tablinum and including a suite of baths: all closely comparable with the villa of the Volusii.[97] It lay only 10 km each from two south Italian towns – Teanum and Cales – but the very fact that it was equidistant from both makes it hard to view it as part of the periphery of either. Rather, its location seems to maximise the benefits of proximity to *both* towns, as well as to the via Appia, via Latina, and river Savone: a setting typical for a Roman agricultural estate, and in keeping with the

53

recommendations of Cato and Columella.[98] The Bay of Naples, too, was particularly known for its ostentatious and architecturally urbane properties. Here, the villa at Oplontis also boasted an axial atrium layout and private baths, as well as extensive gardens, covered galleries, a large pool and wall-paintings which at several points mimic urban monumental architecture.[99] Again its location, 5 km from Pompeii, places it within the day's journey from that city which might allow it to be interpreted as periurban. But D'Arms has shown that such villas functioned primarily as independent leisure retreats for the elite of Rome.[100] Indeed, an inscribed amphora from the Oplontis property has led some to suggest that it belonged to the Poppaei, family of Nero's second wife Poppaea Sabina.[101]

These examples remind us that villas designed to recall the urban *domus* or decorated with scenes of urban monuments and activities should not always be interpreted as periurban. Rather, since the ownership of large villa properties and participation in urban public life were both central to Roman elite identity, it is not surprising that well-appointed private properties regularly drew upon monumental urban themes in their architecture and décor, wherever they were located.[102] It was simply one way of expressing elite status. The phenomenon may intensify around the city of Rome, but it is clear that the design and décor of an individual villa is not enough on its own to identify it as periurban.

We should also note that large, well-appointed villas were not the only agricultural establishments clustered around Rome. Survey work has identified many smaller and more modest agricultural buildings.[103] Few have been excavated in detail, especially close to the city, but two examples from the Ager Capenas survey illustrate the range of agricultural buildings concerned. At Monte Canino, around 21 km from Rome, an imperial-period property was excavated in the 1930s.[104] Much smaller than the suburban villas described above, it had a simple, compact plan. However, finds of stuccoed columns and a variety of marble types suggest that at least some parts were ornately decorated. Probably, an owner of reasonable means used it as a residence, but it is not possible to say whether this was during visits from a *domus* in the city, or whether the property was its owner's main home. Another site at Monte Forco, 35 km from Rome, was even simpler.[105] This structure also belonged to the early imperial era, and consisted of a single rectangular hall, possibly divided by wooden partitions, with several associated *dolia* (storage jars). It is more likely to have been a self-contained farm building than part of a larger complex, since it was one of several similar sites located at regular intervals along a ridge.

The presence of such sites in the *suburbium* indicates that smaller-scale agricultural production was practised alongside the large villas of literature. This may seem surprising given ancient evidence for high land prices in the area, but Morley has argued that the pattern could be explained by tenancy.[106] The land may well have been owned by the same people who built themselves ornate suburban villas, but let in small plots to dependent farmers. Economically, these small farms will have been strongly influenced by the voracious market of Rome, and we must assume that their tenants – or owners – tailored production to take best advantage of this. Whether they can be regarded as part of Rome's periphery, or simply part of the intensive cultivation which von Thünen would lead us to expect near the city, is another question. Small farmers would have had little reason to move regularly between city and farm, never mind maintain houses in Rome. Their contact with the city was probably restricted to periodic journeys to buy and sell goods: if, indeed, these transactions were not handled indirectly at the level of a smaller, local town. Thus, the social networks which tied the villas to Rome would have been all but absent for smaller farms. None the less, if Rome's suburban villas were interspersed with such properties, then they can be seen as part of the landscape of the *suburbium*. These small farms were part of the context for the more opulent suburban villas, and although seldom mentioned in the literary compositions of their owners, doubtless contributed both to their incomes and to the 'rustic' charm of their estates.

We have already noted the presence in the same landscape of centres of settlement such as Lucus Feroniae, and these require discussion in their own right. Sometimes described directly by ancient authors as 'suburban', they more often serve as points of reference for locating a suburban villa.[107] This raises the question of whether they enjoyed any independent urban identity of their own. Many had originated as autonomous Latin or Etruscan communities; for instance Bovillae, Tibur, Praeneste, Fidenae, Aricia, Gabii or Veii. Once Rome had become politically dominant over them, though, they often experienced economic and architectural decline, or at least stagnation. Some, such as Falerii Veteres, seem to have been suppressed as a punishment,[108] while others were bypassed by the network of roads converging on Rome.[109] But Morley has put forward less premeditated reasons for decline: a general shift from nucleated settlement to dispersed farms, Rome's importance as a market centre and the focus of the metropolitan elite on the city and their suburban villas.[110] Meanwhile, other settlements prospered under Roman dominance: especially those which had grown up under it. Some, like Ostia or Lucus Feroniae, were deliberate foundations, while others developed spontaneously along major roads and at junctions.[111] These roadside settlements generally appeared during the late Republic, responding to the economic opportunities of passing traffic, and flourished during the first two centuries AD.

Economically, then, the towns of the *suburbium* were profoundly affected by the presence of Rome, whether they declined in the face of its competition or profited from helping to service it. Seen from the perspective of central place theory, they are lower-order settlements, mediating between an unusually dominant city and its hinterland. Yet if they did not function as central places in their own right, this does not mean that they lacked *urbanitas* entirely. Many were either founded as or granted the status of *coloniae* or *municipia*, so had their own local councils and magistrates.[112] Some also hosted important religious sanctuaries. Meanwhile, although many older settlements suffered architectural stagnation, this was not universally true, and newer developments were a different matter. Praeneste, Tibur, Bovillae, Ostia and Lucus Feroniae were all unmistakably urban in appearance, and some roadside settlements became quite sophisticated, with fine houses, baths and temples; though almost never orthogonal road layouts.[113]

The larger settlements, then, apparently did function as urban centres. Yet in practice, their *urbanitas* was somewhat overshadowed by the 'supra-urban' identity of Rome. The focus of wealthy suburban villa owners on the metropolis to the detriment of local towns has already been mentioned, and Cicero paints a picture of suburban communities unable to find native citizens to represent them at the Latin festival.[114] Ostia's crucial importance in the defence and grain supply of Rome meant that a series of state officials were appointed to oversee activity there, and their presence can only have undermined the significance of local magistrates.[115] The architecture of Ostia was also profoundly affected by imperial building projects, and, along with Portus and the surrounding coastal area, it has been characterised as a monumental approach to the city of Rome.[116] In short, the larger settlements of the *suburbium* were at once urban centres, and yet also suburban to the metropolis that was Rome. Meanwhile, smaller settlements without urban titles, such as road-stations, are probably best understood as dependent satellite settlements: areas of development which served the needs of Rome without being physically adjacent to it.

Just as the regular journeys of villa owners tied their properties to the city, a similar relationship could apply to religious sites. Ovid describes worshippers travelling to the festival of Fors Fortuna and returning drunk from her '*suburbana . . . aede*' after nightfall.[117] Cicero, under threat from Clodius' associates, was afraid to attend the public sacrifice of the Terminalia in the *suburbium* even though he would have returned to Rome the same day.[118] Meanwhile, the inscriptions from the grove of the Arval brethren, at the temple of Dea Dia on the fifth mile of the via Campana, attest religious activity based outside the city, but fundamentally focused upon it: at least from the Augustan era. They show that the *fratres* were members of the senate and imperial household, and that their activities included rituals marking dates of importance for the emperor and his family.[119] Both privately and officially, the religious life of Rome clearly extended well into its periphery.

Many religious sites patronised by visitors from Rome were in fact based in suburban settlements; for example, the temples of Fortuna Primigenia at Praeneste,[120] Feronia at Lucus Feroniae or Hercules Victor at Tibur. As elsewhere, the contact might be pursued at a state or private level. Republican quaestors, praetors and consuls all appear in connection with either games at Praeneste, probably held in honour of Fortuna Primigenia, or the consultation of her oracle: later also patronised by emperors.[121] Possibly such state involvement was originally intended to create a formal medium for contact with previously hostile communities, and encourage settlements which had lost political independence to develop an alternative religious status. Yet the importance of these cults must also be attributed to local self-promotion. Wallace-Hadrill has argued that, during the second century BC, communities such as Tibur and Praeneste were forging and expressing their own sense of local identity through the construction of monumental religious complexes drawing on Hellenistic architectural models.[122] This sheds further light on the urban/suburban status of these settlements. In the context of Rome's extraordinary zone of influence, the very monuments which expressed their local status paradoxically also ensured their place in the religious periphery of the metropolis. Similar dualities can be observed in two other major suburban cults: Diana Nemorensis near Aricia and Jupiter Latiaris on the Mons Albanus. Both the focus of important pan-Latin festivals, Rome's participation in these cults alongside other local towns preserved some semblance of her origins as 'just another' Latin city-state. Yet the festival of Jupiter Latiaris was led by the consuls,[123] while Diana Nemorensis was strongly linked with Rome through the figure of Egeria.[124] Thus Rome at once nurtured and controlled neighbouring communities through the medium of suburban cults.

Commercial and industrial activity was absent from the literary thought-world of the *suburbium*, but clearly pursued in the suburban landscape. Again, suburban towns are important here. As indicated, we should expect them from a central place perspective to have been involved in the exchange of goods between Rome and its hinterland, and they need not be characterised as periurban on that basis. But the economic activity of some settlements made them particularly intimately associated with Rome: especially long-distance importation through Portus and Ostia, and the servicing of travellers in roadside settlements. Here, the relationship is different enough from the typical economic interaction between city and countryside for these to be regarded as periurban; even leaving aside other factors discussed above. Outside the towns, quarries, lime workshops and kilns producing bricks, tiles and pottery were also widespread.[125] Their output was not all destined for Rome, since suburban towns and villa estates also constituted important markets. But building materials flowed into the city on a grand scale.[126] Installations such as tufa quarries at Veii, travertine quarries at Tibur and brick kilns along the Tiber valley are thus best understood as features of Rome's urban periphery.

Finally, there were the funerary monuments which stretched along Rome's arterial roads, as well as the banks of the Tiber and the Anio.[127] Little different in character from those on the very fringes of the walled *urbs*, these must have created a real sense of continuity between the extra-mural *continentia aedificia* and the *suburbium*. They were a characteristic feature of the suburban landscape, visible to travellers entering Rome and accessible to its population. This, and copious epigraphic evidence linking tomb owners and occupants with the urban population, make their association with the city clear enough. They acted as a powerful indicator of Rome's presence far beyond the urban agglomeration: and, as they petered out, a sign of the transition from the urban periphery to a more truly rural landscape.

The Roman *suburbium* of literary texts was above all a landscape of elite villa properties. In practice, Rome's urban periphery was far more complex. For at least 35 km beyond the *continentia aedificia* extended villas, certainly, but also towns, sanctuaries, industries and funerary monuments, all enjoying a closer relationship with Rome than expected from normal city–country interaction. Yet the same region was also host to smaller farms and localised industries without this intensity of contact. One question which this raises is whether Rome's urban periphery is best thought of as a 'zone', within which all features were automatically periurban regardless of their specific relationship with the city, or as a collection of separate features, each individually linked to Rome. Chapter 2 concluded that periurban status was subjective, and not determined by geography alone. Yet Catullus' treatment of his Sabine/Tiburtine villa also demonstrates that geography did matter. His property is more likely to be judged suburban if it is known to fall within the territory of Tibur.[128] Thus, suburban status may have been determined *primarily* by the manner in which an owner used his property, but it was enhanced by the presence of similar villas around it. It would, after all, have been hard to have a suburban villa in isolation, when part of what that entailed was exchanging visits with other members of the metropolitan elite.

Around Rome, the density of suburban villas was such that they *can* be considered to have created a periurban 'zone' of a kind: as the use of terms such as *ager suburbanus* and *suburbium* suggests. Other structures within this zone not necessarily best understood as periurban in themselves none the less functioned within, and contributed to the character of, a suburban landscape. That landscape was also characterised by two further features not discussed above: the major roads and aqueducts which fed into the city. Built to serve the needs of Rome, yet necessarily outside it, these cannot easily be placed on an urban-suburban-rural spectrum: in some senses, their infrastructural character means that they fall outside these categories. Yet they helped to sustain not only the city on which they converged, but also the suburban landscape through which they passed. We have already met the roads in their role as essential connectors between villas and city. The aqueducts, too, helped to make suburban villa culture possible by watering suburban fields and fountains: both legally and illegally.[129]

The outer limits of the *suburbium* cannot readily be identified. Approximations such as the 35 km radius are helpful from a modern perspective, but in practice no Roman could have drawn a line indicating the precise edge of the zone, and nor should we. Rather, it must be assumed to have given way gradually to a more distinctly rural landscape, just as the *continentia aedificia* had merged into the *suburbium*. The role of roads in linking it to the city of Rome also makes plausible Arnaud's suggestion that we should conceive of the *suburbium* as radiating outwards along them, rather than as a zone of strictly equal depth.[130] It is also important to remember the unique nature of the city at the centre of this landscape. Rome's status as imperial capital made its 'zone of influence' – economic, social and political – far more powerful and extensive than can be expected for provincial cities. This is clear from suburban towns, where settlements which qualified as urban in themselves also functioned as part of the Roman *suburbium*. Perhaps the most vivid example of the phenomenon in fact relates to the 'New Rome', Constantinople: similarly an imperial capital from AD 330. The city's founder, Constantine, was described in a fourth-century biography as having died 'in an imperial villa on a suburban Constantinopolitan (estate), near Nicomedia': a major city in its own right, almost 90 km from the new capital.[131]

Urban boundaries in Italy and the provinces

Just as at Rome, boundaries of some kind marked the limits of most administrative cities in the Roman empire. This is of course in keeping with a broader Mediterranean urban tradition that had long favoured the use of urban boundaries, especially defensive walls. Cities in the Greek east, Italy and the areas of Punic colonisation were typically fortified long before they fell under Roman influence. On becoming part of the Roman world, they generally retained their fortifications, which remained desirable in the context of Roman urban ideology. Rome rarely required the demolition of the walls of her subject cities,[132] and many embellished or reinforced their fortifications under Roman rule. At Perge in Asia Minor, the embellishment by Plancia Magna of the Hellenistic main gate in the AD 120s indicated that it remained an important point of transition between the city and its exterior.[133] Even in Celtic Europe, defensive ramparts were a typical feature of the existing proto-urban *oppida*.[134] Thus the majority of cities in the Roman empire had either been fortified in the pre-Roman period, or were founded in areas whose inhabitants were likely to be receptive to the Roman interest in creating distinct urban boundaries.

We have seen the importance of the Servian wall in defining the extent of the *urbs* at Rome itself, and a passing reference in the *Digesta* confirms that walls around other Roman cities possessed similar significance. In the context of a legacy of property said to be 'at Rome', the Severan jurist Iulius Paulus ruled: 'And indeed *usually all cities are held to finish with the wall*, [but] Rome with the adjoining buildings . . .' (my emphasis).[135] Thus, for Roman cities with archaeologically traceable walls, we can expect that all occupation falling within them would have been considered urban, at least while the walls were maintained.

The role of walls as urban boundaries can be appreciated by examining the typical layout of a Roman *colonia*.[136] Aosta (Augusta Praetoria, figure 3.2), founded in north Italy in 25 BC, provides a well-documented example.[137] Its walls probably did have a defensive function: the city was built to guard the approach to the Great and Little St Bernard passes shortly after the conquest of the local tribe of the Salassi, and its security could not yet be guaranteed.[138] However, their appearance suggests that they also played an important symbolic role. The perfectly rectangular circuit, with towers at regular intervals and a squared travertine facing, would have been no more effective against a besieging army than an irregular circuit of uncut stone. But it *would* have looked more impressive and imposing within the landscape. Equally, the monumental character of the four gates would not have helped to repel attackers, but would have left travellers in no doubt that they were entering an important and sophisticated city. Elsewhere, the symbolic function of walls is made clearer still by the circumstances of their construction. An imperial donation of walls and decorative gates to the south-central Italian city of Saepinum between 2 BC and AD 4 could have had little to do with fears for security in the context of the *'pax Romana'*.[139] Rather, it is likely to have been a sign of special status and imperial favour.[140]

Roman city walls helped to express the *urbanitas* and *romanitas* of a community as monuments in their own right.[141] At the same time they would also have emphasised the same qualities in the streets and buildings within the circuit, by highlighting their identity as constituent parts of a Roman city. Walls also helped to restrict and control access to the urban centre, emphasising its status as a 'special' space. At Aosta, there were only four points of access to the city in a walled circuit 2.5 km long, and each gate was equipped with sliding gratings or portcullises, as well as flanking towers from which to observe traffic.[142] The Porta Praetoria, approached from the direction of Rome, also featured an enclosed courtyard which has led scholars to suggest that it was used to levy local taxes on goods passing through.[143] Thus it is possible that the walls also played a practical role as a customs boundary. Alternatively, the courtyard may simply have been intended to boost the impressive appearance of the gate. In the absence of more positive evidence we cannot assume that urban customs boundaries existed anywhere other than at Rome.

Coins minted by Spanish and eastern *coloniae* showing the ploughing of a *pomerium*[144] and a clause in the Urso charter forbidding burial 'within the boundaries of the town or of the colony, where [a line] shall have been drawn around by a plough,'[145] suggest that Roman *coloniae* possessed their own *pomeria*, analogous to the one at Rome. Where the *colonia* also had defensive walls, their course probably marked the line of the *pomerium*. Certainly, literary descriptions of Rome's foundation report that Romulus ploughed a

THE ARCHAEOLOGY OF THE URBAN PERIPHERY

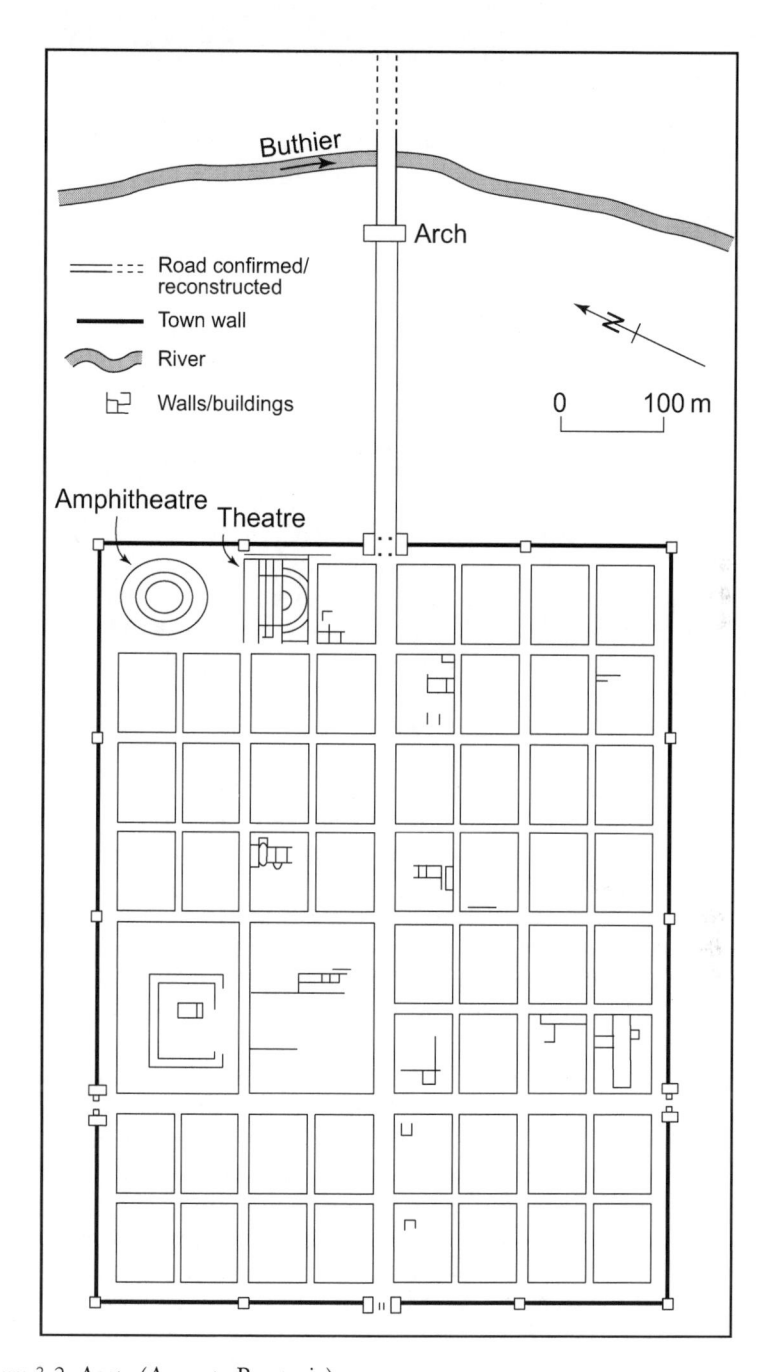

Figure 3.2 Aosta (Augusta Praetoria).

pomerium which also formed the line of the city's walls, and this probably reflects actual practice in imperial colonies.[146] For *coloniae*, then, walls had additional functions: they helped to mark out the urban centre as a religiously protected space, and defined an area within which burial was forbidden. The latter function, though, appears to have been performed by city walls even in the absence of a formal *pomerium*. The Roman law against burial within the city applied to all cities of whatever status,[147] meaning that contemporary burials are almost never found within their defensive circuits. This is in keeping with Iulius Paulus' reference to all cities being held 'to finish with the wall'.[148] City-dwellers would have understood that the intramural space was urban in status, and that burials were only appropriate in the non-urban space outside.

A pomerial circuit could apparently also exist in the absence of walls. At Capua, a *cippus* inscribed with the words 'by order of Augustus where a plough has been drawn'[149] appears to have defined a *pomerium* which must, if it needed marking out, have followed a different course from the older city walls. The presence of the *cippi* would render the *pomerium* visible to the city's occupants, allowing it to act as a meaningful boundary. From an archaeological point of view, though, the course of a *pomerium* which did not coincide with a defensive circuit is difficult to identify, and must usually be deduced from the locations of cemeteries.

City walls, then, were a characteristic feature of Roman urbanism, and served to mark the limits of that which was strictly 'urban'. None the less, a significant proportion of cities in the Roman empire were not walled, at least during the period of the high empire. This raises the question of how the 'urban' might have been defined at these cities, given the widespread interest in distinguishing between urban and non-urban space encountered so far. The issue becomes especially important in the present context, since most cities in Gaul were themselves unwalled, and the identification of urban centres here will be of great importance for the analyses in chapter 4. A close inspection of such cities reveals that, despite the absence of walls, they still had clear visual markers defining the edges of their urban centres. Examples of several may be identified at the *colonia Latina* of Bologna (Bononia, figure 3.3), founded in northern Italy in the early second century,[150] and these will be explored here to demonstrate how they could function.

One feature which helped to mark out the edges of Bologna's urban centre was the relationship between the city's orthogonally arranged street grid and the via Aemilia. As this road met the orthogonal grid on the eastern side and became Bologna's *decumanus maximus*, it turned southwards by a factor of around 14°. On the western edge of the grid, it turned northwards again by the same amount, thus performing a slight dog-leg through the city. These changes in orientation are important, since the via Aemilia was contemporary with Bologna. The relationship between them, then, was probably designed from the start as part of a co-ordinated planning project. The orientation of

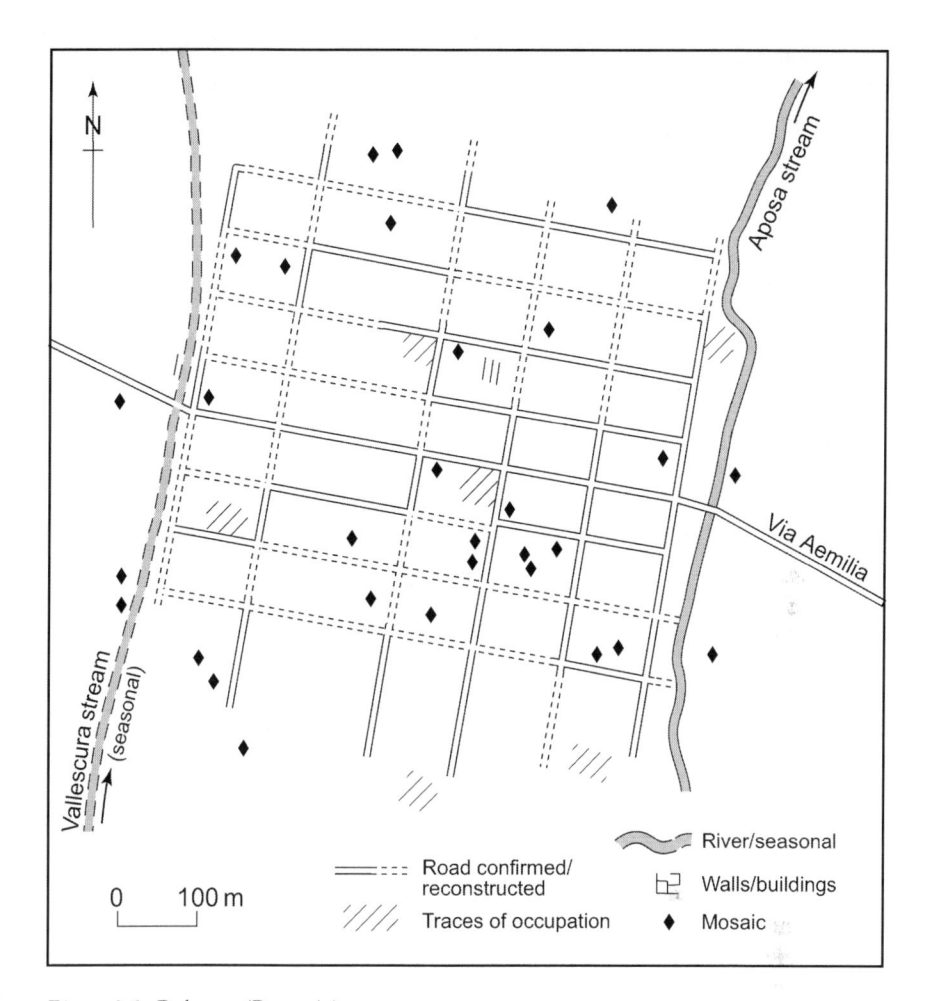

Figure 3.3 Bologna (Bononia).

roads carried great significance in the Roman empire: their famous straightness was not simply a practical exercise, but a means of demonstrating control over the landscape,[151] while urban streets were traditionally oriented towards the position of the midday sun on the day of foundation,[152] commemorating this date. For these reasons, the decision to include a change of orientation in the path of the via Aemilia as it entered Bologna must be regarded as a deliberate marking out of the point of transition between the countryside through which the road was travelling, and the city which it was entering.[153] This arrangement is regularly encountered at other Roman cities,[154] and where these were walled, like Timgad (Thamugadi) in North Africa (figure 3.5), the coincidence between the change in the direction of the road and the course of the city walls confirms that this was indeed a marker of city boundaries.

The local topography at Bologna also helped demarcate the edges of its urban centre. Along the eastern perimeter of the orthogonal grid ran the Aposa stream, bridged at a single point by the via Aemilia.[155] On the western side of the city, a seasonal stream, the Vallescura, formed a similar natural boundary, again passable only via one bridge. The northern edge of Bologna also coincided with the slope of a fluvial terrace. City planners had no control over these natural features, but *could* control the position of Bologna in relation to them, and so they can be seen as a part of the planning process. The fact that the courses of the two streams coincide with the changes in the orientation of the via Aemilia strengthens the case for both to be seen as deliberate boundary markers. Meanwhile, countless other Roman cities have one or more edges of their urban centres similarly defined by natural features, especially rivers: the Thames at London, the Guadiana at Mérida or the Adige at Verona. The phenomenon is in fact characteristic of many ancient civilisations, for obvious defensive reasons. The walls of Etruscan Veii mirrored the courses of surrounding river-cliffs for most of their circuit,[156] while the great majority of late Iron Age *oppida* in central and northern Europe were strategically located on steep-sided hill-tops or spurs.[157]

The orthogonally aligned streets of Bologna also helped to differentiate between the urban centre and the space beyond. The network of urban streets would have acted as a kind of matrix, linking buildings and *insulae* into a dense, ordered agglomeration recognisable as a city, which contrasted with the more open agricultural landscape beyond. A traveller passing out of the orthogonal grid on the via Aemilia would have been clear that he or she was leaving 'urban' space and entering something different. There is an important difference, though, between an orthogonal grid and the other methods of distinguishing an urban centre discussed above. Once city walls had been built, a change in the orientation of a road established, or a city located in relation to a particular topographical feature, these boundaries could not easily be changed. The edges of an orthogonal grid, however, could be altered to respond to urban growth through the addition of new streets. A well-known example is Leptis Magna in North Africa, where three successive areas of orthogonally arranged streets were added in phases between the early Augustan period and the mid-first century AD.[158]

We can be fairly certain that Bologna's inhabitants would have recognised that the edges of the city's orthogonal grid represented an urban boundary, not simply because the manner of land-use altered sharply at this point, but also because on at least three sides they coincided with other boundary markers. Where this was not the case, other evidence suggests that the edges of an orthogonal street network could mark the boundaries of an urban centre on their own. The edges of Amiens (Samarobriva), an unwalled *civitas*-capital in northern Gaul, were demarcated to the north by multiple branches of the river Somme, and at certain points by changes in the orientation of major roads as they met the grid. Large sections of the urban centre, however, were apparently distinguished from the space beyond only by the presence of the orthogonal grid. Yet detailed knowledge of the city's cemeteries reveals that they formed a careful ring around the edges of the orthogonal grid, and never encroached on the land within it at any time during the high empire (figure 4.10, p. 102). This confirms that the inhabitants of Amiens considered the edges of the orthogonal grid to mark a boundary between urban and non-urban land around the entire perimeter of the city. They seem to have used it as a means of distinguishing between land which was and was not suitable for burial. Once burial activity had begun, the very presence of tombs would certainly have demonstrated that the areas in which they were located were not urban. Cemeteries, then, although not intended to act as boundary markers themselves, could still help to render the edges of an urban centre visible to its inhabitants.

The boundaries of an urban centre could also be marked at certain points by monumental arches. Unlike the features discussed above, monumental arches were rarely established at the foundation of a city. But they could be added at a later date, reinforcing the lines of existing urban boundaries. As at Rome, monumental arches could be erected in a variety of settings, not all connected with urban boundaries.[159] However, De Maria has shown in his study of Italian monumental arches that they were regularly used to mark urban boundaries from the middle of the first century BC.[160] In the Augustan period in particular, he argues that city gates developed along similar stylistic lines to monumental arches. This made it easier for arches themselves to adopt the role of boundary markers, functioning almost as city gates without a wall.[161] Outside Italy, other examples confirm that monumental arches could play the same role. The arch of Caracalla at Djemila (Cuicul) marks the western entrance to both the Severan-period forum and the city itself.[162]

Six different methods for demarcating urban boundaries, then, were regularly used by Roman city planners, and it is worth summarising them here for the sake of clarity:

- City walls
- Pomerial *cippi*
- Changes in the orientation of major roads
- Natural topographical features (rivers, steep slopes, cliffs, marshes, etc.)
- The edges of an orthogonal grid
- Monumental arches

All of these served as visual cues to ancient city-dwellers, helping them to distinguish between urban and non-urban space. Cemeteries could play the same role, but were really a symptom of urban boundaries, rather than a deliberate means of marking them. Most of the features can also be used by modern scholars to reconstruct the course of an urban boundary. Meanwhile, they constituted an important part of the urban fabric in their own right, and could affect both its development and patterns of movement within the city. A particularly important distinction must be drawn between boundary markers which were visible, but did not restrict movement, and boundary markers which allowed passage only in a limited number of places. The first category might include the edges of an orthogonal grid, pomerial *cippi*, cemeteries, some topographical features such as gentle slopes, monumental arches and changes in the orientations of major roads. Defensive walls and other, less penetrable, topographical features such as rivers, marshes or steep cliffs belong in the second group. These boundary markers could usually be crossed only where roads traversed them: on bridges, over causeways or through gates.

Where a city was defined only by features belonging to the first category, the relationship between the urban centre and any periurban development beyond is likely to have been closer than where it was defined by markers from the second category. Buildings on either side of a monumental arch, for instance, might in fact be closely adjacent to and intervisible with one another. By contrast, those lying beyond a city wall or a river were physically divided from the urban centre, sometimes by quite a distance. From a modern perspective, divisions of this kind can mean that the urban periphery is easier to identify.[163] It is also likely that they created a heightened awareness of the difference between centre and periphery in their own time. A defensive wall would block visibility between the two zones, emphasising the discontinuity. Average travelling times between centre and periphery will also have been greater where urban boundaries were marked by walls or rivers that could be crossed only at specific places. Watercourses may even have presented the added inconvenience of needing to be crossed via ford or ferry. Such boundary markers, then, probably discouraged movement and contact between urban centre and periphery more than those which allowed multiple points of passage.

It is important to remember that the features discussed may have been used to mark more than one boundary within the same city. While most Roman cities appear to have had only one main urban boundary at any given time, its course could clearly be shifted, and new markers employed to define it. When this was done, earlier boundary markers were usually retained, much as at Rome. A series of such changes occurred over several centuries at the *municipium* of Verulamium (St Albans) in Britain (figure 3.4).[164] During the Claudian period, Verulamium was demarcated by a bank and ditch on at least three sides, and the river Ver to the north.[165] By the second quarter of the second century, however, the ditch had been filled in, and the city's orthogonal grid was beginning to extend over it.[166] At this point, it is difficult to be certain whether the urban centre would still have been held to end at the line of the filled-in Claudian ditch, or whether its boundaries had already shifted outwards. But by the later second century, a formal shift clearly *had* occurred. A new boundary marker, the 'Fosse earthwork', was

THE ARCHAEOLOGY OF THE URBAN PERIPHERY

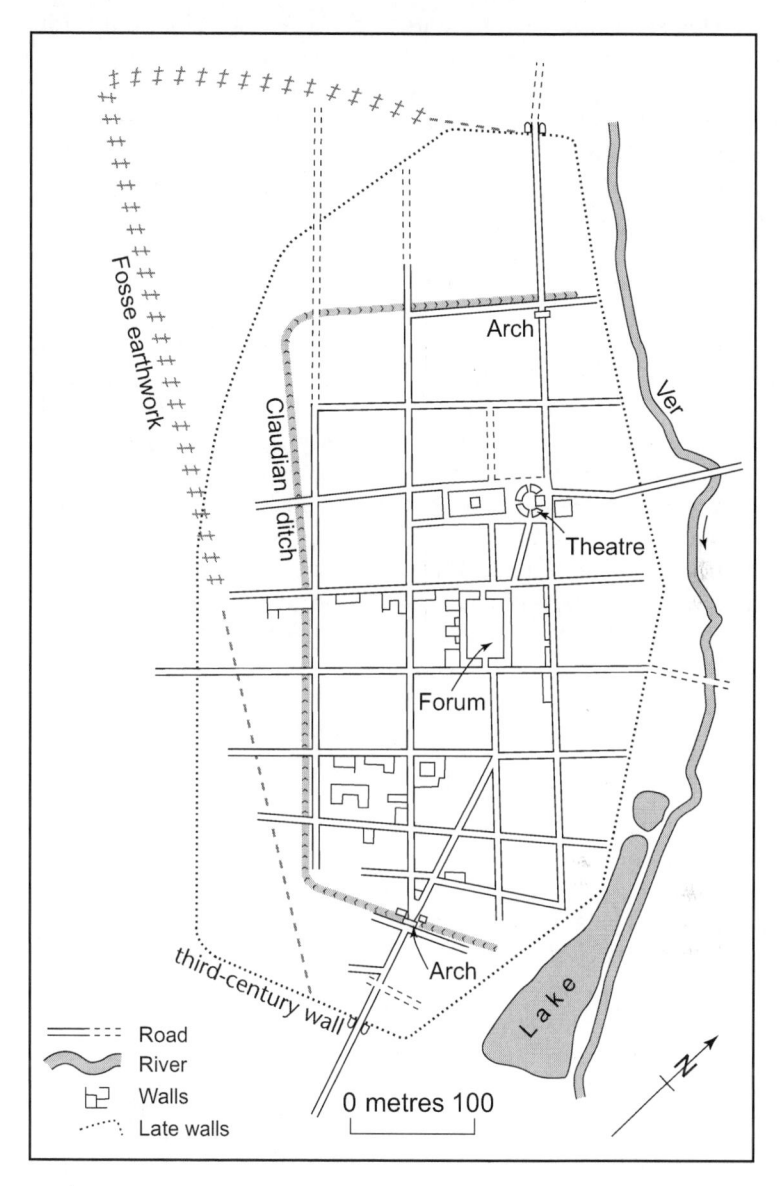

Figure 3.4 Verulamium (St Albans).

begun, although this was abandoned before completion.[167] The project was completed in slightly altered form in the third century, when a masonry-fronted bank and ditch, incorporating stone gates erected in connection with the earthwork, was built. The effort and expense of constructing this new circuit indicates a strong interest in defining a new boundary, suggesting that by this time, space falling outside the Claudian ditch but within the new wall should be considered to have acquired urban status. One issue highlighted by this change is the need for reliable chronological information when identifying periurban occupation, since it demonstrates that 'urban' and 'periurban' status could change when boundaries shifted. It is also important to remember that new urban boundaries could be established *within* older ones, rather than outside them. This was particularly common in late antiquity, and may conversely imply that areas of land left outside the new defensive walls were considered to have lost their urban status (see chapter 6).

It is also notable that the original urban boundary at Verulamium was not forgotten. Two monumental arches were constructed around the start of the third century close to the line of the old defensive ditch,[168] despite its having been filled in at least fifty years before. They appear to have been erected partly to commemorate its course: perhaps as part of a single programme of boundary commemoration and change also involving the commencement of the earthwork.[169] A similar situation applied at the *colonia* of Lincoln (Lindum) in northern Britain, where boundary shifts took place between the late first and early third centuries.[170] An original defensive circuit formed from modified military defences[171] was extended by the mid-third century through the addition of a new, larger annex to the south.[172] The now-obsolete south wall of the earlier circuit, however, was never demolished. Again, the boundary which it had marked apparently remained significant, despite the fact that the areas on either side of it were both now intra-mural. It may be suggested that in such cases, all space contained within the new boundaries was seen as 'urban', but that the area which also fell within the original boundaries retained an extra degree of prestige: 'urban plus'. Meanwhile, the commemoration of old boundaries and the creation of new ones in these cities indicates a genuine local interest in the Roman ideology of the clearly defined urban centre, since there is no evidence that these activities were prompted by direct intervention from Rome.

Periurban development in Italy and the provinces

At any Italian or provincial city, inhabitants and visitors could expect to encounter visible markers defining a special, urban centre. This was the equivalent of the *urbs* at Rome, and is referred to in municipal charters as the *oppidum*.[173] Beyond its boundaries, non-urban occupation began. Where this was physically continuous with the urban centre, it may be viewed as equivalent to the *continentia aedificia* at Rome: a concept readily applied to provincial cities in municipal charters and literature.[174] Hence, the archaeological remains of such occupation can be identified as periurban with little controversy. Beyond the continuous urban agglomeration, however, isolated features such as public monuments, villas or distinct areas of nucleated settlement might also be encountered. The challenge is to decide whether these may be interpreted as periurban by examining their archaeological remains for signs of something more than the expected city–country relationship with the nearby urban centre. The discussion here will ask what characteristics might attest a closer connection: always, of course, with the *caveat* of subjectivity in mind. It will also outline the general character of Italian and provincial periurban development, raising issues which can then be pursued in greater detail through the examination of Gallo-Roman cities in chapter 4.

Occupation falling immediately outside the urban centre, but continuous with it, was often very similar in character to that within. At Ostia, numerous structures lay beyond the late Republican walled circuit,[175] and especially outside the Porta Marina. This region featured shops, houses, a temple, a public fountain, a porticoed square and a large set of baths: all plentiful within the walled centre.[176] The African *coloniae* of Djemila and Timgad, both founded at the end of the first century AD, also saw extensive urban-style development beyond their walls during the second century. This included shops, houses, workshops and baths much like those encountered within the walled centres. More unusually, extra-mural occupation at these two cities included distinctly urban monuments *not* matched within their walls: a theatre at Djemila[177] and a Capitolium at Timgad.[178] Yet at all three cities, the extra-mural development had characteristics which marked it out as different from that of the urban centre. The Porta Marina quarter at Ostia included two large funerary monuments, standing between houses, workshops and temples in a juxtaposition that would never be encountered within the walls.[179] Meanwhile, the extra-mural development at Djemila and Timgad was distinguished from the urban centre by the absence of orthogonal planning: especially striking at Timgad (figure 3.5).

The extra-mural development at these cities was differentiated from their centres, then, not only by location but also by usage: just as at Rome. Reasons for the development of extra-mural occupation at these cities are likely to have included a lack of available building space in the urban centres. They were densely inhabited, and extra-mural development offered a way to expand beyond the walled space. Some extra-mural monuments, at Timgad in particular, were also far larger than the *insulae* of its urban centre could have accommodated, demonstrating that an unplanned urban periphery could offer extra space for individual projects as well as general expansion.[180] But the need for space does not seem to have been the only factor at play. More positive factors may have influenced the decision to locate certain structures in the urban periphery. For example, the extra-mural position of the theatre at Djemila allowed it to take advantage of a natural slope, unavailable in the urban centre,[181] while shops in the Porta Marina quarter at Ostia could have attracted travellers approaching the city from the sea *before* they came across the commercial outlets of the urban centre. The role of such

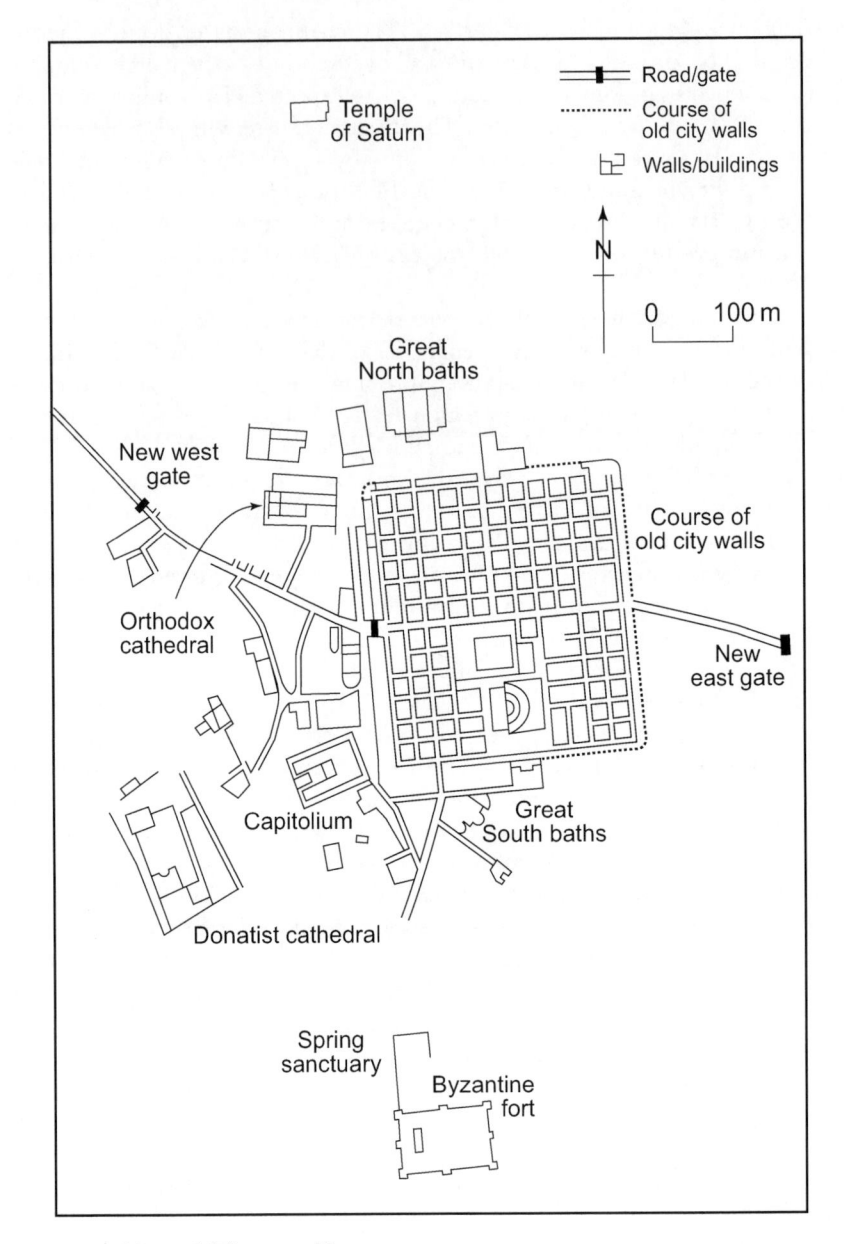

Figure 3.5 Timgad (Thamugadi).

factors in encouraging periurban development will be explored further in chapter 4.

The edges of an Italian or provincial *continentia aedificia*, like the edges of Rome, must have been difficult to identify precisely. This issue was encountered from a modern perspective by surveyors in the late 1970s attempting to identify the limits of an extensive area of periurban occupation lying across the Rhône from the Gallo-Roman *colonia* of Vienne (Vienna, figure 4.4, p. 90).[182] An area of forty hectares, including excavated periurban occupation in the area known as la Plaine, was explored through resistivity and surface survey. The study concluded that the densest archaeological remains lay immediately around la Plaine, and also identified a separate concentration of material to the north-west.[183] But the surveyors remained undecided as to whether the limits of the site could be said to lie 'with the external contours of the main buildings, with that of all the remains even the smallest, or with something else'.[184] An ancient inhabitant of the city, asked to identify the outer extent of its *continentia aedificia*, would probably have faced the same uncertainty. Vienne's urban centre was clearly defined by a walled circuit and the course of the Rhône, but no one sought to mark out the extent of the continuous periurban development beyond. Indeed, the ideological associations between boundedness and *urbanitas* in the Roman world are such that any periurban occupation which did become enclosed by visible markers must be assumed to have acquired a form of urban status: as at Verulamium and Lincoln. The limits of true periurban development were by their very nature blurred.

Beyond the continuous urban periphery might be encountered features that were isolated from the urban agglomeration, and yet intimately related to it. Amphitheatres in this situation are well attested in Italy and throughout the western provinces.[185] The Italian *colonia* of Luni (Luna), for instance, was founded in 177 BC, and acquired an amphitheatre probably in the Julio-Claudian period.[186] It fell approximately 200m outside the walled circuit, and appears to have been separated from the city by open land. None the less, it is clearly a periurban monument for several reasons. Despite the propensity for amphitheatres to be built outside city boundaries, they were essentially urban monuments.[187] The games they hosted were designed for large audiences, and a location close to a city ensured that the urban population would not be discouraged from attending by a long journey. In addition, many amphitheatres were built within urban boundaries.[188] Thus the amphitheatre at Luni may be regarded as a characteristically urban structure, displaced out of the walled centre probably mainly for reasons of space. This amphitheatre was also situated to emphasise its connections with the urban centre. It lay alongside and was oriented towards the main road into Luni from the south-west, rendering it highly visible to travellers moving in and out of the urban centre and linking it topographically with the forum at the heart of the city, to which the road led. This combination of functional and spatial links between amphitheatre and city is typical,[189] and makes it easy to categorise the monument as periurban, despite the open space between them.

More difficult to interpret are the villa properties encountered outside Italian or provincial cities. As in the case of suburban villas at Rome, we face the question of whether or not they should be seen as part of the urban periphery: did any of them have a sufficiently close relationship with the nearby city to differentiate them from rural villas? This time, however, we are less well endowed with literary references attesting such a relationship. Chapter 2 showed that suburban villa culture centred around Rome, but that the idea could also be applied to properties in Italy, Spain, Africa and the Greek east. Yet most such references occur in authors familiar with the special landscape of the *suburbium*, and often seem intended to evoke it for particular effect. Did Pliny, for example, really consider his friend Rufus to possess a *suburbanum amoenissimum* at Comum, or was the term used in order to make Rufus feel included in the lifestyle of the metropolitan elite at Rome?[190] Furthermore, the surviving references focus around a limited number of cities. If Julian, Flavius Philostratus and Aulus Gellius agree that Athens had its suburban villas,[191] this does not mean that the same was thought to apply to, for instance, London. Such references reveal that Italian or provincial villas *could* be considered suburban. But textual sources alone do not provide convincing evidence that the concept of the suburban villa, and the lifestyle associated with it, was widely subscribed to beyond Rome and a few exceptional cities. We must also allow for the possibility that some provincial villas functioned as part of an urban periphery without actually being suburban in the metropolitan sense. In other words, we should draw a distinction between a periurban villa, which only needs to have enjoyed an unusually close relationship with the city, and a special type of periurban property: the suburban villa, whose owner actively pursued a Ciceronian or Plinian lifestyle of refined intellectualism.

Archaeologically speaking, it is clear that many provincial cities were surrounded by clusters of agricultural establishments.[192] Again, this is in keeping with von Thünen's beliefs concerning the exploitation of land outside a city, and need not mean that they should be characterised as periurban *per se*. Greater evidence for a close and regularly maintained villa–city relationship is needed to diagnose periurban status. As was the case around Rome and elsewhere in Italy, the design or décor of provincial villas sometimes evoked urban themes. In a provincial context, the methods of doing this might differ. The atrium-peristyle *domus* was little-known in the urban centres of the Greek east, Britain and Gaul,[193] and so could hardly have been used to express *urbanitas* in a villa. But other devices were available. For example, mosaic depictions of public spectacles in the amphitheatre or circus have been found in urban *domus* in Italy, Spain, Gaul and north Africa.[194] They also appear in villa properties, especially in Africa. Such mosaics indicated the patron's familiarity with and involvement in the life of the city, where the games were held, as well as the urban monuments associated with them. Often they commemorated particular games financed by the patron, but they could also express religious interests or more general themes of victory and good fortune.[195]

The hinterland of Leptis Magna in Tripolitania was thoroughly studded with agricultural properties. They clustered in particular around the city, along the coast, and inland on the slopes of the Gebel Tarhuna.[196] Several properties on the coastal plain were lavishly appointed, and the decorative schemes of at least five evoked urban-based spectacles. Mosaics from a villa in the wadi Lebda, only 1.6 km south-east of the late city walls, depicted an exhausted gladiator and chariot scenes.[197] Others at Silin, 15 km to the west, showed circus games,[198] and at Zliten, 29 km to the east, gladiatorial combats.[199] Two more villas in the Silin district incorporated playful replicas of spectacle monuments. One had its own 'odeon' carved into the natural rock of the coast, and another a garden or exercise area shaped like a circus.[200] The dating of these features is not always secure, but all belong to the high imperial period, and, as such, represent a particularly strong local interest in spectacle themes during this era. This should be seen in the light of Leptis Magna's theatre, built in AD 1–2, its amphitheatre, completed in AD 56, and its circus, monumentalised in 162 but probably preceded by a simpler structure.[201] The mosaics do not depict these monuments specifically, and nor do the architectural fantasias replicate them faithfully: but they were clearly commissioned in the context of a community which placed great emphasis on public games. It would appear to have become fashionable for the Lepcitanian elite to express their connection with the city – and one another – by referencing spectacles in the decorative schemes of their private villas.

The question is whether these villas can or cannot be identified as periurban, and there are arguments on both sides. They certainly possessed the kinds of facilities associated with suburban properties in literary texts. Besides their references to urban spectacles, they boasted features such as decorative coloured marbles, wall-paintings, stucco, baths, covered porticoes and, in the villa with the circus mosaic at Silin, a library. They also fall within the easy day's journey of 35 km which we used to help identify suburban villas at Rome. Perhaps more importantly, they were not the only luxury villas within this radius. Further luxury villas in both the Silin and Zliten areas are known,[202] while two properties on the very fringes of Leptis Magna rather bridge the gap between villas and elite *domus*: the villa of the Orpheus mosaic to the west, and the villa of the Nile mosaic to the east.[203] Taken together, these properties *could* be interpreted as evidence for a suburban villa culture around this city. We should also recall that a rare literary application of the term '*suburbanus*' in a provincial context occurs in Apuleius, who uses it to describe his wife's villa outside Oea.[204] Since this was the next city west along the coast from Leptis Magna, only 100 km away, it is readily plausible that the concept was current also amongst the Lepcitanian elite. A fair case, then, can be made for sufficient links with Leptis Magna to identify these villas as periurban, and perhaps even suburban.

Yet similarly lavish or urbane villas also occur in north Africa in contexts which appear to rule this out. Another famous spectacle depiction is the so-called 'Magerius mosaic' from a villa at Smirat in Tunisia,[205] which records games financed by its patron. The venue for these games is unknown, but the villa was more or less equidistant from three local towns: Leptiminus (20 km), Thapsus (26 km, but across an oasis) and Thysdrus (27 km). Like the villa of San Rocco at Francolise, it is hard to see it as periurban, since it did not have a particularly close topographical relationship with any one city. The villas around Leptis Magna do not seem to have been significantly *more* lavish and urbane than Magerius' property, and so arguably they too should be interpreted simply as luxury villa retreats: perhaps more akin to elite properties in Campania than in the *suburbium* of Rome.

The distance of some of them from Leptis may also give pause for thought in a provincial context. In central place terms, Rome enjoyed an exceptional zone of influence, with the result that villas outside neighbouring towns could none the less be considered suburban to Rome. Leptis and Oea, however, appear to have been of roughly equal social and political status, so that, to the west at least, the Lepcitanian hinterland ended where Oea's began: no more than 65 km to the west.[206] The eastern hinterland is harder to define. The *territorium* of Leptis did not even necessarily include the villas at Zliten, and we can only say that it must have extended at least 19 km from the city.[207] At such a scale, the idea that villas 15–29 km away could be considered suburban to Leptis begins to seem rather nonsensical. If the periurban is that which is neither wholly urban nor wholly rural, the distribution of these villas leaves little room for 'true' countryside: and this for a city whose territory was unusually large by Roman standards. We might reasonably question whether a provincial noble would regularly travel half way or more to the borders of his local district to reach home after conducting his business in the forum: or, if he did, how much of a connection he would have considered his property to have with the city when he got there. The villa in the wadi Lebda, though, is a different matter. Whether or not it can be dubbed 'suburban' in the fullest sense, the proximity of this property to Leptis Magna, its position in a seasonal river valley running right past the city and the urbane theme of its mosaics are together surely enough for it to be considered periurban.

Most of the Lepcitanian villas, then, are difficult to classify definitively as either periurban or rural, and this forms an important contrast with the situation at Rome. In certain respects, the evidence from each city is similar. Within a 35 km radius of both, lavish villas with noticeably urbane features can be identified, and yet similar villas in the same regions apparently had little direct relationship with any nearby city. At Rome, though, a greater body of surviving evidence mitigates in favour of identifying the properties as periurban. Above all this includes literary texts indicating that a suburban villa culture thrived amongst and was actively pursued by the city's elite. To these may be added literary confirmation that properties 35 km away were still regarded as suburban, epigraphic documents linking particular properties with prominent urban figures and an altogether richer archaeological record. If such testimonies survived also at Leptis Magna, the villas at Silin and Zliten could readily be interpreted as periurban. But they do not: and nor do they on the same scale for any provincial city. This makes it difficult to justify the interpretation of the Lepcitanian villas as periurban, while we certainly cannot assume the specific and complex activities implied by the term 'suburban villa'. None the less, the possibility remains open for some cities, and Leptis is a plausible case: not least because Apuleius' writing on Oea associates it with a little of the kind of evidence that reveals to us the suburban villa culture of Rome.

Finally, some provincial cities were associated with areas of occupation which formed nucleated agglomerations in themselves, but were not continuous with the urban centre. One such grew up to the north of Water Newton (Durobrivae) in Britain, where it was separated from the walled town by the river Nene and a distance of around half a kilometre.[208] It was densely settled, and featured an irregular street network, numerous pottery kilns and iron workshops, and some structures which may have been shrines. As for the suburban towns around Rome, the question arises of whether this agglomeration functioned as part of the periphery of Water Newton or was an independent settlement. Archaeological data from the site may shed light on this matter. For one thing, it was clustered around a major road, Ermine Street, which also ran through the centre of Water Newton. This, along with the short distance between the two, constitutes a very close infrastructural link: much closer than would normally be expected for an independent settlement. Second, the pottery workshops identified there arose only after Water Newton was well established.[209] They are part of the wider Nene Valley pottery industry, which developed in response to the good-quality clay available in the river valley. Yet their position so close to Water Newton suggests that these particular kilns were also intended to make direct use of the town as a market in itself and a point of access to other markets. The settlement, then, may in part have grown up around these kilns in order to service the needs of Water Newton. As such, it is analogous to the road stations in the Roman *suburbium*, and may be interpreted as a periurban satellite agglomeration.

Conclusion

The methods proposed here for identifying periurban remains in the archaeological record rest above all on the definition of the periurban established in chapter 1, and confirmed through the examination of ancient evidence in chapter 2: we are looking for that which was neither entirely urban nor entirely rural. On these terms, occupation within the urban boundaries can, for the most part, be ruled out, since it drew *urbanitas* from its very location.

Outside the boundaries, distinguishing between the periurban and the rural is more difficult, since geography alone is no longer a reliable indicator of status. Occupation that was physically continuous with the bounded urban centre can usually be taken as periurban, since it belongs to the *continentia aedificia*. Chapter 2 showed that such occupation was considered part of the urban agglomeration, although not 'urban' in the truest sense. It is when features are separated from the main agglomeration by open land that periurban status becomes hardest to identify. In these cases, we must search for positive evidence of links with the city that indicate something other than a purely rural character. At Rome, the wealth of surviving evidence often illuminates these links. In a provincial context, the evidence is predominantly archaeological, and frequently the limitations of this material mean that periurban status cannot be identified with certainty: especially in the case of villa properties.

Alongside these general guidelines, we must allow for ambiguities and overlaps. The distinction between the urban, the periurban and the rural should not be seen as a series of discrete steps, but rather a sliding scale, with one merging into the next and no category being completely exclusive. In chapter 2, we encountered activities such as the cultivation of city plots, or self-conscious elite displays of *rusticitas* in an urban context.[210] Even within a bounded centre, then, activities normally considered 'rural' might be pursued, and individual features could be judged 'more' or 'less' urban. Rome's multiple boundaries also created a more complex hierarchy of space than a simple urban–periurban division allows, extending from the ideologically charged walled *urbs* and through the monumentalised Campus Martius to the humbler district of Transtiberim and beyond. Similar gradations probably also applied in provincial cities which saw boundary shifts, as the commemoration or preservation of old boundaries at Verulamium and Lincoln suggests. The rural landscape, too, was not homogeneous. Von Thünen argued that land close to a city would normally be more intensively exploited than land further away, and in a Roman context this is manifested in the tendency of agricultural establishments to cluster around cities. Arguably, land exploited in this way was more intimately connected with the city than land which was not, through the medium of economic exchange. Thus the countryside, too, could be 'more' or 'less' rural: until the point where its relationship with the city was so intense that it is more helpful to view it as periurban.

This chapter also showed that the feature hardest to fit into archaeological assessments of the urban periphery was the villa, and it is worth saying a few more words here on the nature of the problem. Two related difficulties are involved: the fact that literary references to suburban villa culture focus almost exclusively on the city of Rome, and the lack of any distinct correspondence between those literary references and the archaeological record. At Rome itself, literary and epigraphic sources reveal suburban lifestyles to us, allowing us to associate them with archaeological remains. But even here it is clear that the archaeological record alone would not be able to support such an interpretation, since the physical remains of the villas look little different from luxury properties elsewhere in Italy. The distinction rests in behavioural patterns too subtle to be detected in the archaeological record. In fact, elite Romans used luxury villas outside the *suburbium* in a manner not greatly different from their suburban estates. They visited their own properties for extended periods, and the properties of others as they were moving around Italy.[211] Pliny wrote literature on his estate at Tifernum, received friends there, and enjoyed covered arcades, formal gardens, fountains, baths and fine views.[212] His description of this property actually differs little from that of his Laurentine estate, except in its greater emphasis on agricultural productivity. What made a suburban villa different was partly the frequency of the journeys between the villa and the city, and partly self-perception: what the owners thought they were doing. These temporal and cognitive factors may be attested in texts or implied through epigraphy, but they are not directly detectable through archaeology.

Arguably, suburban villa culture was not only attested in texts, but actually constructed *by* them to signal the sophistication of their authors. Yet we need not believe that the suburban villa was only a literary conceit. It is perfectly likely that *suburbanitas* also extended to real behaviour, enhancing the owners' status in the eyes of others, and their own enjoyment of their villas.[213] Having a suburban villa consisted of performing to a particular script, characterised by activities such as regular journeys to and from the city, philosophical debate, neighbourly visits, the enjoyment of 'nature', and literary composition: sometimes on this very theme. Our difficulty is that the set required for this performance was also used for elite display elsewhere. And this is not surprising, given that the script followed in other villas was not so radically different either.

In the provinces, we can see a comparable pattern. Villas with lavish or urbane architecture and décor do occur in close association with cities, but also elsewhere. Yet with archaeological evidence alone to work from, we cannot be sure that *any* of them were used in the pursuit of a metropolitan-style suburban villa culture, nor distinguish the relevant villas even if they were. Individual cases of provincial *suburbanitas* are attested, and Herodes Atticus furnishes a good example. He would have been familiar with the Roman concept of the suburban villa from his estate on the via Appia, and developed a similar property at Kephisia, 10 km outside Athens, which Aulus Gellius and Flavius Philostratus apparently considered suburban.[214] Herodes, however, was one exceptional man, and even his case serves to illuminate the problem elsewhere. He owned two further estates, at Marathon, 30 km from Athens, and at Loukou, in a rural district of Kynouria far distant from any major city. Yet what is known of their architecture and décor suggests that all four villas were much alike. In Herodes' case, literary testimonies allow us to draw some distinctions between the four properties. But for most provincial villas, this is lacking: and, as we have seen, the behaviour pursued in each may not really have been very different. Archaeological evidence may allow us to identify *peri*urban villas in the provinces, where properties enjoyed an unusually close topographical relationship with the city; for example, the wadi Lebda villa at Leptis Magna. But *suburbanitas* is destined to remain elusive outside the pages of literature.

4

GAUL IN THE HIGH EMPIRE: ADMINISTRATIVE CITIES

Introduction

The previous two chapters have discussed the urban periphery as a phenomenon of the Roman empire in general. It is now time to turn to the specific province of Gaul for a more detailed exploration of periurban development in practice. The next three chapters will examine and analyse the evidence for periurban land-use in Gaul, mainly through the medium of archaeological evidence. The special characteristics of periurban development will be identified through comparison with the urban centre and the countryside, and the factors giving rise to them explored. Regional patterns of similarity or difference across Gaul will also be sought, and their implications considered. Finally, the conclusions drawn from these chapters will be discussed in chapter 7 in relation to three wider issues: the nature of the Roman city, its relationship with the country and the relationship between the provincial and metropolitan elites.

Gaul

The choice of Gaul as a 'case study' for this analysis needs to be explained. One thing the region has to offer is a form of urbanism forged primarily out of a process of cooperation between the Roman state and the local elite.[1] Before the Roman conquest, the Gallic interior had known only proto-urban *oppida* (hill-forts),[2] and although the Mediterranean coast and Rhône valley were populated with Greek and Celto-Ligurian settlements,[3] even their pre-Roman features were generally left behind in the Roman era. With a few exceptions, such as Marseille (Massilia), pre-Roman Gaul may justly be considered 'a world of villages'.[4] Yet Rome's system of government required the establishment of a comprehensive network of cities across the province. It was probably Rome's administrators, surveyors and engineers who provided the encouragement and expertise needed to begin work on individual cities, as well as the network of roads, bridges and docks which connected them. But it was the new Gallo-Roman elite who provided most of the resources necessary for the task, and who made the cities a social and political success by filling their magistracies and priesthoods, using them as centres for social interaction and administering the communities based around them on Rome's behalf.[5] The very existence of periurban development in Gaul, then, was the result of interactions between the provincial elite and the Roman government, while its evolution over time will have been shaped by the continuing relationship between the two. Thus the extent to which the Gallo-Roman elite absorbed the thought-world of the urban periphery explored in chapter 2, and sought to apply it to their own cities, can readily be explored here.

These circumstances, however, apply equally to most provinces in the western part of the Roman empire. The four Gallic provinces offer further advantages. The region contains a substantial enough number of cities to sustain a detailed study, and allow meaningful patterns to emerge: the exact number varies depending on calculations of provincial borders or classifications of status, but eighty to ninety major administrative cities will serve as a round number.[6] The modern countries where these cities now lie also have a strong archaeological tradition, meaning that their Roman-period remains tend to be well documented. This is not to say that the evidence available is consistently spectacular. Some cities, such as Vienne (Vienna), have seen the systematic excavation of whole quarters of periurban occupation. But many more have witnessed little exploration beyond their urban boundaries. In her exhaustive treatment of Roman Béziers (Baeterrae), Clavel could cite only two periurban finds, although she believed that these hinted at further, undiscovered occupation.[7] Continuous living occupation on the sites of most Gallo-Roman cities has also meant that the archaeology of their centres and their peripheries is often restricted to chance finds and limited rescue excavations, making systematic comparisons between the two difficult. Neither problem is unique to Gaul, though. Esmonde Cleary for Britain and Quilici for Rome have both observed a historical tendency for archaeologists to concentrate on the 'spectacular' buildings of the urban centres to the detriment of the periphery.[8] Meanwhile, the problems of continuous occupation apply to all western provinces with the exception of north Africa, where modern political agendas have created their own difficulties. Thus Gaul is certainly at no more of a disadvantage that any other western province. And, as the discussion which follows will reveal, the quantity and quality of the evidence available *is* enough to sustain a detailed examination of periurban development in Roman Gaul. It is simply necessary to remember that an absence of known periurban remains at a given site may reflect only a lack of surviving evidence, rather than past activity.

The different social, political and geographical circumstances in which the cities of the Four Gauls developed mean that they also offer an interesting degree of variation, while still forming a coherent data-set. The region which came to be known as Gaul did not all come under Roman control at once.

The southern part, Gallia Transalpina (the 'Provincia', later Narbonensis) was acquired in the wake of a request for Roman help against the Ligures by Marseille in 125 BC, while Gallia Comata (later the 'Three Gauls') was conquered in 58–51 BC by Julius Caesar. A sharp distinction between these two 'halves' of Gaul persisted in geographical accounts of the region,[9] but, administratively, the reorganisations of the Augustan era eroded it.[10] Gallia Transalpina was renamed 'Narbonensis' at the same time as the three new provinces of Aquitania, Belgica and Lugdunensis were defined, suggesting that Augustus intended all four to be seen as roughly equivalent parts of the same whole. The Agrippan road system radiating outwards from the approximate centre of the four provinces also stressed the unity of the region, and the importance of communication between its component parts. The Gaul of the imperial period may thus be viewed as a unit, but one with significant regional variations.

The cities of Gaul are also more readily comparable than the different histories of Narbonensis and the 'Three Gauls' might suggest. The development of its urban network in fact took place over a relatively brief period. After the foundation of Narbonne (Narbo Martius) in 118 BC,[11] little more was done to encourage Roman-style urbanisation in the south, and major development began under Caesar during the 50s BC.[12] It was completed a generation later by Augustus, who simultaneously initiated the widespread urbanisation of Aquitania, Belgica and Lugdunensis. Most Gallo-Roman cities were thus founded within fifty years of one another, and existed at least in embryonic form by the start of the first century AD. This means that the model of Roman urbanism current when they were being planned and developed would have been much the same for cities across the region. An important difference must be acknowledged, though: the predominance of *coloniae* as administrative units in Narbonensis, and *civitates* in the Three Gauls. This would imply a significant social divide, due to the greater presence of veteran soldiers in the south. But many of the *coloniae* in Narbonensis were actually indigenous communities granted the title of *colonia Latina*,[13] while even the populations of the *coloniae Romanae* founded to settle veteran soldiers are now thought to have included locals too from an early stage.[14] Here then, as well as in the Three Gauls, the cities developed under local, as well as central Roman, influences.

A word should also be said on the geographical limits adopted for this study. The boundaries of Gaul did not remain static over the period of the high empire. In particular, some communities which had originally been part of Gaul were later allocated to the two new provinces of Germania Inferior and Germania Superior, created around AD 90.[15] Their inclusion does not seem to have altered their character markedly: in fact, the Sequani continued to send representatives to the council of the Three Gauls at Lyon.[16] It could therefore be argued that, culturally speaking, they remained Gallo-Roman, and the archaeological evidence from their urban peripheries should be considered alongside that from the other cities of Roman Gaul. However, attempting to determine exactly which of the cities in the two Germanies should be considered 'more' German or 'more' Gallic would be a complex and somewhat questionable exercise, unlikely to result in a significant improvement of our understanding of periurban development in Roman Gaul. For this reason, then, the chapters which follow will treat only those cities which remained within the Gallic provinces throughout the high empire.

Administrative cities

Our exploration of Gaul begins in this chapter with cities that acted as administrative centres during the period of the high empire; in other words, the seats of local councils from which the Gallic communities and their territories were governed. As already mentioned, the types of communities established tended to be *coloniae* in Narbonensis, and *civitates* in the Three Gauls. There were exceptions, however. In Narbonensis, a small number of *civitates* with Latin rights and *civitates foederatae* were established alongside the *coloniae Romanae* and *coloniae Latinae*.[17] *Civitas* status in this region was normally used as a means of rewarding loyal communities with a degree of autonomy: examples include Rome's old ally, Marseille, and the Vocontii, perhaps for supporting Rome during a revolt by the Allobroges in 62 BC.[18] Conversely, a small number of *coloniae* were established in the Three Gauls during the mid-to-late 40s BC: Lyon (Lugdunum) in Lugdunensis, and Nyon (Noviodunum) and Augst (Augusta Raurica) in territory later allocated to Germania Superior. The distribution of these *coloniae* along a potential German invasion route towards Narbonensis and Italy suggested to Drinkwater that their foundation had more to do with the security of the frontiers than the urbanisation of Gaul.[19] Lyon, however, did go on to play a pivotal role within the Gallo-Roman urban network. Some *civitates* also attained the rank of *colonia* later on as a sign of imperial favour; for example, Trier (Augusta Treverorum), which probably received the honour from Claudius.

Meanwhile, besides governing *coloniae* or *civitates*, a small group of cities also served as provincial capitals. These include Narbonne, Lyon and Reims (Durocortorum), identified as the capitals of Narbonensis, Lugdunensis and Belgica. The capital of Aquitania is less certain, and may have shifted from Saintes (Mediolanum) to Poitiers (Limonum) and finally Bordeaux (Burdigala).[20] These cities acted as seats for provincial governors, and would thus have enjoyed closer links with the central government at Rome than the ordinary *coloniae* and *civitas*-capitals, as well as a higher status. Narbonne and Lyon also had the added privilege of acting as religious centres for Narbonensis and the Three Gauls respectively. They hosted official sanctuaries of the imperial cult, which acted as a focus for province-wide worship of the imperial household, and were also associated with provincial councils (*concilia*) made up of representatives from all the communities of the two regions.[21] Thus the communities of Gaul, and the cities which administered them, were arranged into a hierarchical structure: from *civitates* and *coloniae* – which came to be seen as the more prestigious of the two – to the provincial capitals, and especially Lyon and Narbonne, at the top.

The archaeological material from the cities which administered these communities has here been divided up thematically. Periurban remains are grouped according to the different types of activity connected with them; for example, houses, baths or cemeteries. This grouping allows activities which were pursued separately, and affected by different social, economic or political concerns, to be explored in their own right. Workshops, after all, will have been located in the urban periphery for different reasons than temples. Examined in isolation, each periurban activity can readily be compared with similar examples in other parts of Gaul, as well as with equivalent activity in the urban centre or countryside. Yet chapter 3 has already shown that periurban development often featured several different types of land-use going on simultaneously in the same district: shops, houses, temples, baths and tombs outside the Porta Marina at Ostia, for instance. Workshops and temples, then, did not really exist in isolation, but affected one another, and could potentially develop a symbiotic – or competitive – relationship. For this reason, I shall also discuss the overall organisation of periurban space, before going on to examine its individual components separately.

The Gallo-Roman urban fabric

We begin by outlining the general characteristics of the Gallo-Roman administrative cities, as context for the specific examination of their peripheries (figure 4.1, p. 84). Most were little affected by either buildings or street plans which had existed in the pre-Roman period. In Narbonensis, the *coloniae Romanae* were usually founded on virgin sites, meaning that their urban form could be determined entirely by the new colonists. The *coloniae Latinae* and other cities in this area usually had their locations at least determined by pre-Roman settlements, and sometimes retained features from them. The walls of Nîmes (Nemausus), though Augustan in themselves, carefully incorporated an Iron Age tower into an octagonal structure now known as the Tour Magne, and Marseille retained a Hellenistic defensive wall throughout the Roman period.[22] But even in these cases, the rest of the city was completely remodelled in the Roman era.

In the Three Gauls, the *civitates* often established capitals which related closely to an existing tribal *oppidum*.[23] Sometimes, they were founded on the same site, but more usually they were established nearby, on a flat plain below the older settlement. Such locations were more accessible and easier to develop than hill-tops, and as such were in keeping with the general preferences of Mediterranean urbanism by this period. Meanwhile, other

HIGH EMPIRE: ADMINISTRATIVE CITIES

Figure 4.1 Major Roman cities in Gaul.

civitas-capitals abandoned the *oppidum* altogether, in favour of better access to communications and transport networks. Where new sites were used, the city could be laid out entirely *ex nihilo*, without being affected by the positions of existing structures. But even on occupied sites, existing structures were usually demolished at the foundation of the city or soon afterwards, meaning that an effectively virgin site was created.[24]

The general principles of foundation and construction used at cities of all kinds in Gaul were very much in keeping with those current elsewhere in the empire, and documented in Roman literature. All administrative cities appear to have been laid out on an orthogonal grid plan: certainly, none are known not to have been.[25] A forum was usually located somewhere at the centre of that grid, and the rest of the city embellished with public buildings drawn from the Italo-Roman tradition.[26] The amphitheatres at Arles (Arelate) and Nîmes, for instance, bear close comparison with that of Verona in north Italy, as well as the Colosseum in Rome,[27] the Barbarathermen at Trier fit into the tradition of imperial bath-buildings exemplified by the Baths of Titus, Trajan or Caracalla in Rome,[28] and the gates of Autun (Augustodunum) resemble those of Aosta, Turin or Verona.[29] Apparently, then, the Gallo-Roman elite were keen to adopt the basic model of urbanism to which they were exposed on becoming part of the Roman empire. Their awareness of this model will have come largely from contact with the Roman administration, and especially provincial governors, surveyors and architects. But literary sources and coin images will also have contributed, while some Gauls must have had experience of urbanism in other parts of the empire: particularly Rome and north Italy.[30] The *coloniae Romanae* of Narbonensis, and those at Lyon, Nyon and Augst in the Three Gauls, could also have provided inspiration for other communities.

Literary texts in particular would also have acquainted the Gallo-Roman elite with the thought-world of Roman urbanism.[31] We know that both Latin and Greek were taught in Gaul from an early period. A school was active in Autun by the Tiberian period, and a mosaic from the same city showing at least five Greek poets holding extracts from their work suggests that its lessons were taken to heart.[32] Caligula held games at Lyon which included a competition in Greek and Latin oratory, and a letter from Pliny reveals that his books were on sale in the same city.[33] Such influences would of course have reached only a small proportion of Gauls, but the best-educated were probably also the most wealthy, and the most likely to influence the development of cities. We can expect these people, then, to have been familiar with most of the *topoi* encountered in chapter 2, including the city–country antithesis and the notion of an urban periphery, and to have been influenced by them when making decisions about how to build and use their cities.

Yet despite the obvious place of Gallo-Roman cities within the Roman urban tradition, they also had distinct local characteristics. One of the most obvious is that very few of them were walled.[34] Here, a difference may be detected between the cities of the Three Gauls and those of Narbonensis, resulting from the different circumstances of their foundation. Narbonensis had seen both internal revolts and external attacks between its foundation and the period of Caesarian colonisation,[35] and until the success of Caesar's campaigns to the north were assured, the security of the region remained under question. By the Augustan era, however, the Rhine frontier was heavily patrolled and expected to be pushed still further forward, and the empire was ruled by a man with an immense vested interest in promoting the idea of the *pax Romana*.[36] Thus, on current knowledge, nine cities in Narbonensis were given defensive circuits during the late Republic or early empire, but only three in the Three Gauls were fortified at any time during the high empire.[37] This demonstrated that the cities of the Augustan world did not *need* walls: besides having the practical advantage of meaning that they could not be used as strongpoints by rebellious factions. The situation may be viewed as a development in the model of Roman provincial urbanism, later also applied in Britain.[38] Where walls were built, including those in Narbonensis, they were frequently irregular, unlike the square or rectangular circuits preferred at north Italian cities such as Aosta or Turin. They might incorporate surrounding hill-tops into their circuits, rendering them visible from a distance, and were rarely more than 2.5 m thick, making it likely that their purpose was as much ornamental as military.[39]

The absence of defensive walls around many Gallo-Roman cities did not, however, mean that they departed from the usual Roman practice of marking out a distinct urban centre. As for Bologna in Italy, this could readily be achieved without walls. We have already seen that it was normal practice for administrative cities in Gaul to be laid out on an orthogonal grid, creating a visible distinction between the urban centre and the surrounding countryside. Major roads entering the city generally changed orientation as they entered this grid,[40] and the city's cemeteries were usually located just beyond it.[41] Rivers, too, might skirt the gridded centre on one or more sides. Metz (Divodurum), for instance, was surrounded on three sides by the Moselle and the Seille, while Meaux (Iatinum) was entirely enclosed by a branch of the Marne (figure 4.2). The centre of Reims was also marked out by four monumental arches from the late second or early third century.[42] Evidently, the figures involved in planning and maintaining these cities were keen to make the limits of the urban centres clear, with or without walls. The placement of the cemeteries shows that their boundaries were widely recognised and respected.

The amount of space contained within these boundary markers often differed greatly from the actual extent of later occupation.[43] At Arles and Fréjus, parts of the walled circuits were demolished to make room for other monuments as the cities expanded,[44] while orthogonal grids at Trier and Amiens seem quickly to have been extended.[45] Conversely, areas covered by orthogonal grids at Limoges, Angers and Carhaix, and enclosed by a wall at Toulouse, seem never to have been entirely filled.[46] Mismatches between planning and development are of course central to the issue of periurban development, since it offered one means of handling a failure to provide enough space within the urban centre. They are by no means unique to Gaul, however, and are in fact a common phenomenon of Roman urbanism. The examples seen in chapter 3 of cities whose boundaries were shifted outwards will stand as cases of under-provision. Meanwhile, urban centres which remained partially vacant include Avenches in Germania Superior[47] or the Hadrianic extension of Itálica in Hispania Baetica.[48]

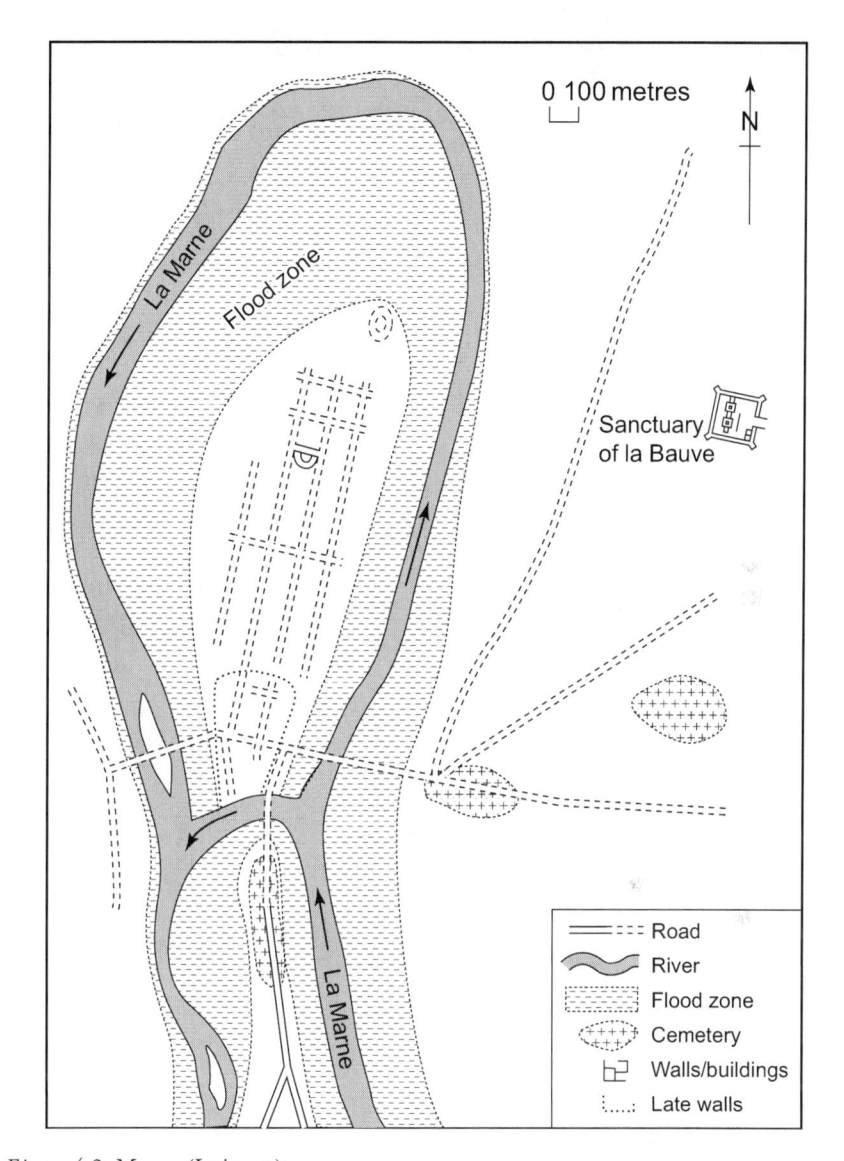

Figure 4.2 Meaux (Iatinum).

While the Gallic elite followed Roman precedents in erecting monumental public buildings in their cities, those buildings did not always correspond with the established Italo-Roman architectural tradition. In particular, local versions of temples, theatres and amphitheatres developed, which differed markedly from their classical equivalents (figure 4.3). Their distribution across the province again reveals a difference between Narbonensis and

HIGH EMPIRE: ADMINISTRATIVE CITIES

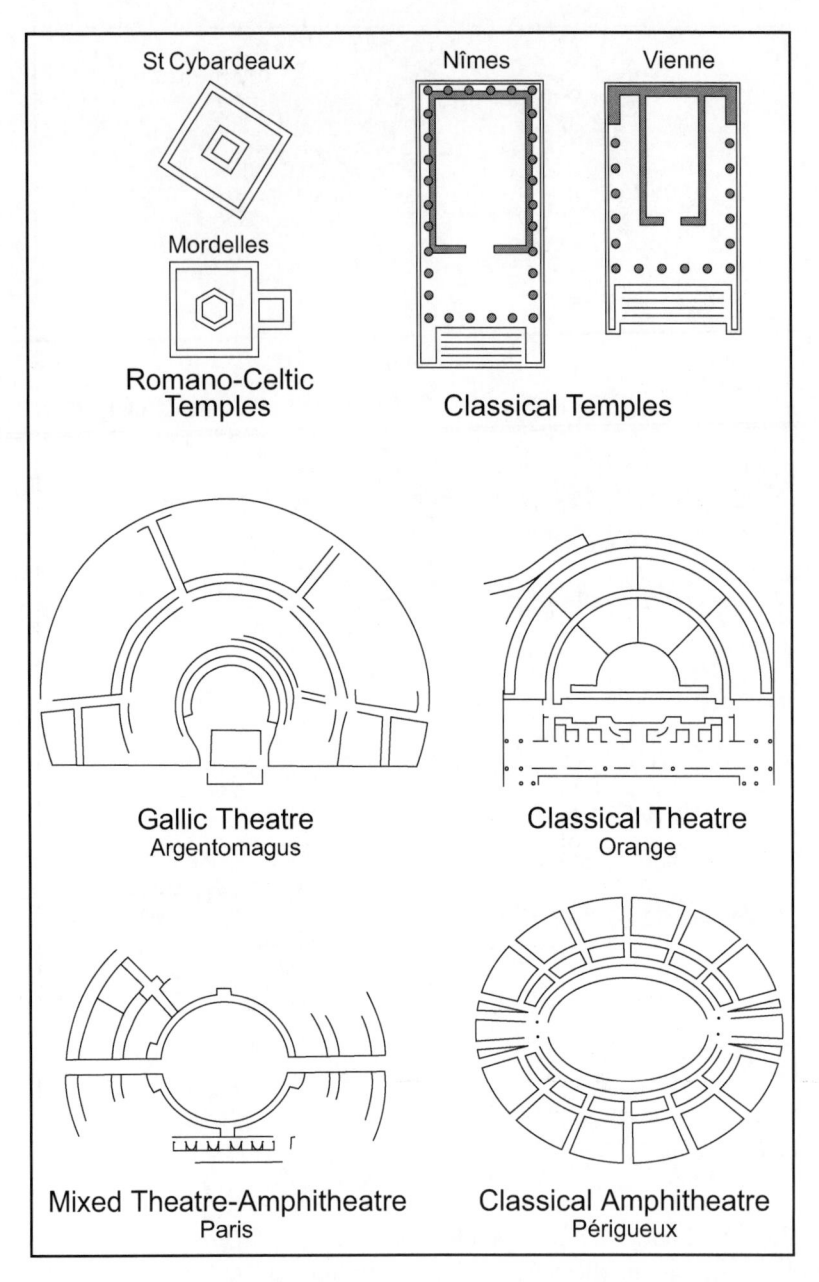

Figure 4.3 Gallo-Roman variants on classical-type monumental public buildings.

the Three Gauls. Although monuments of classical and local type are encountered in both regions, classical buildings were usually preferred in Narbonensis, while the local variants were predominantly a feature of the Three Gauls. Hence, monumental arches are relatively common in Narbonensis, but few examples are known in the Three Gauls.[49] Conversely, the local type of Romano-Celtic temple is rarely encountered in Narbonensis, but predominates in northern Gaul.[50] Wherever they occur, strong differences may also be observed in the typical locations of each type of building. The details will be explored as they are discussed individually later in the chapter, but, in general, buildings of classical type were found almost exclusively at administrative cities, while the local variants usually occurred in the countryside or at secondary settlements. This will be important when considering the factors which might have led either to be erected in the urban periphery, or the roles that they played once there.

Periurban quarters

Periurban development in Gaul could take many forms. At some cities, the only known periurban features are cemeteries or isolated monuments such as temples or amphitheatres. In these cases, only one type of activity is involved, so the factors affecting their character, position or orientation are best discussed alongside other examples of the same kind. But there are also many examples of periurban 'quarters', where a range of different types of land-use developed alongside each other to form a cluster of occupation. The individual structures within these areas will of course have responded to their own specific influences. But it is also important to ask what factors may have affected the topography, infrastructure and development of periurban quarters as a whole, and helped to link them to the nearby urban centres.

It is important first to outline the chronological relationship between periurban development and the associated urban centre. Often, periurban development seems to have grown up primarily because the urban centre had been outgrown. This occurred very quickly at Vienne (figure 4.4). The walled circuit here, probably Augustan, was over 6 km long and enclosed the summits of four hills.[51] This seems, however, to have been done to render the circuit visible from afar rather than to provide building space. In fact, much of the land enclosed was very steep, and unattractive to building. As a result, the slopes and summits of the hills remained largely unused. Meanwhile, occupation had spread across the Rhône on to the flat plain opposite by the end of the first century BC,[52] and to the south of the walls by the early first century AD.[53] This suggests that the intra-mural space had quickly become inadequate for the building needs of the population.

Not all periurban occupation, however, grew up for this reason. The chronological relationship between urban centre and periphery can sometimes indicate that other explanations need to be sought. At Lyon, for

HIGH EMPIRE: ADMINISTRATIVE CITIES

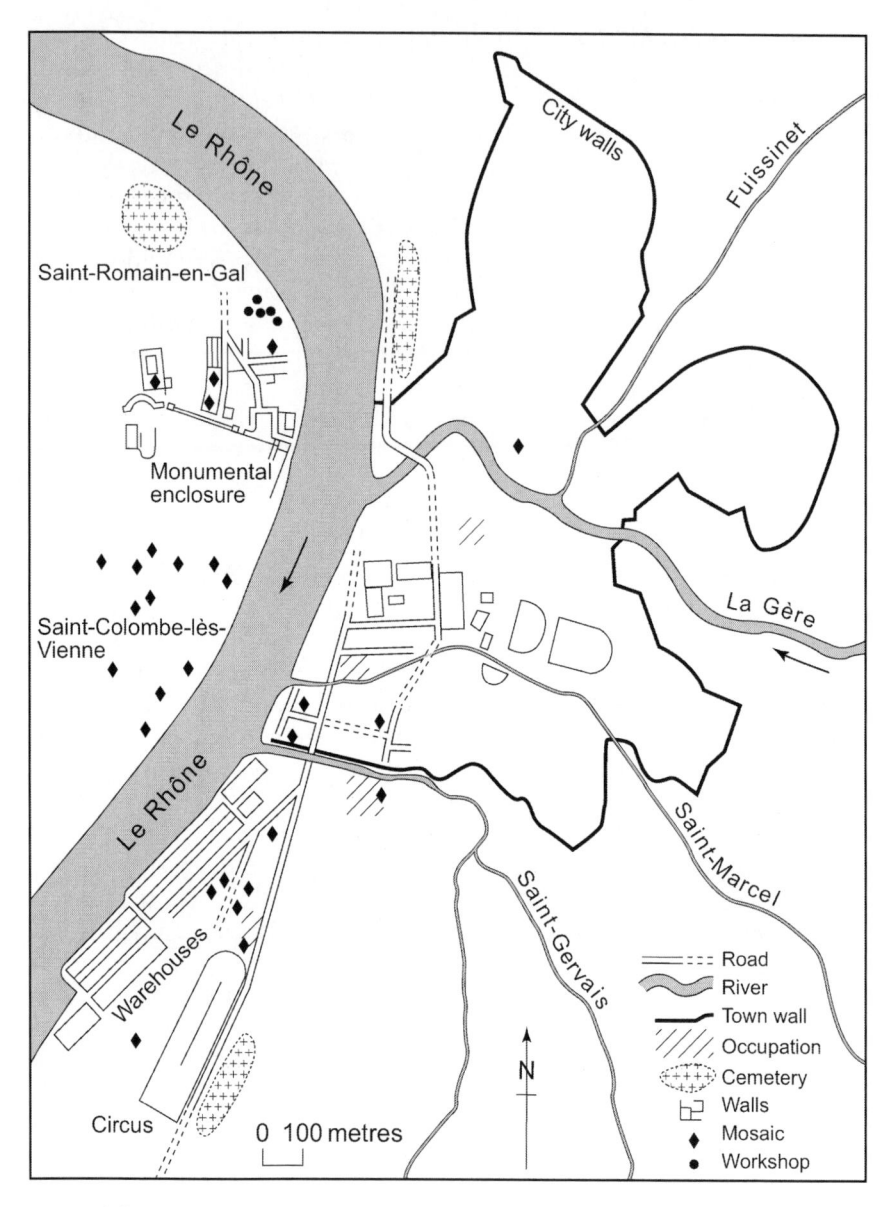

Figure 4.4 Vienne (Vienna).

example, the earliest known occupation was not on the Fourvière plateau, where the Roman *colonia* was established in 43 BC (figure 4.15, p. 120). Instead, it was on the plain of Vaise to the north-west, where occupation had begun by the Bronze Age.[54] Vaise went on to become an important sector of the Roman city, hosting warehouses, cemeteries, workshops, and some elite houses. Yet the occupation here did not develop purely in response to the establishment of the urban centre at Fourvière. Rather, it can be seen as an existing feature which was incorporated into Lyon's periphery, and continued to develop in that context. Such examples highlight the importance of chronological data for our understanding of periurban development, and warn against the assumption that periurban development was always prompted by a need for space.

Even where periurban occupation did post-date the urban centre, explanations for its development other than a need for space must be considered, lest a simple equation between periurban development and urban growth should obscure other, more interesting, factors. Two other periurban quarters at Lyon – the Presqu'île area between the Rhône and the Saône (known in the Roman period as the *Canabae*), and the Saint-Jean quarter at the foot of the colline de Fourvière – were rendered habitable in different periods through land-altering projects designed to drain and fill secondary river channels which ran through them.[55] The result on the Presqu'île was that warehouses and *domus* grew up from the middle of the first century AD.[56] Meanwhile, in the Saint-Jean quarter, domestic and commercial buildings appeared from the third quarter of the second century,[57] and a road was built running close to the foot of the colline de Fourvière.[58] Both of these projects could be interpreted as evidence for pressure on space within the urban centre, prompting the exploitation of difficult nearby terrain. For the Presqu'île development, this is plausible, since it occurred around the middle of the first century AD, just when the Fourvière plateau seems to have become filled with occupation.[59] Yet the commercial nature of the development which occurred may also mean that occupation was drawn to the Presqu'île simply because of the easy access which it offered to the rivers, regardless of issues of space.

Meanwhile, the Saint-Jean site does not seem to have been habitable before the later second century, and occupation there did not become dense until the third.[60] Had the development here occurred purely due to pressures on space in the urban centre, the process of making the area habitable would surely have been completed more quickly. A more satisfying explanation may be reached by looking at the changes which occurred on the Fourvière plateau during the third century. In this period, the urban centre was slowly abandoned, and the focus of occupation at Lyon appears to have shifted to the low ground on the banks of the two rivers.[61] The reasons for this move are not fully understood. Audin suggested that the population of Fourvière was forced down from the plateau after the city's aqueducts were cut by invaders,[62] but Villedieu has pointed towards the economic and political difficulties of the third century in a more general sense, provoking changes in the nature of the city.[63] Whatever the reasons, the occupation at the Saint-Jean quarter in the third century should be interpreted not as an extension to flourishing occupation within the urban centre, but as a direct alternative to it.

When periurban land was developed, a key factor at work in shaping its development will have been the status and interests of those in control of it. The precise identities of these people are not usually known. However, the way in which an area was developed may reveal what the concerns of those who controlled it were, and this in turn may help to indicate what sort of people may have been involved. Two major scenarios may be envisaged. First, periurban land might be owned directly by the local community. If so, its development would be at the discretion of the civic council: whether they chose to build on it themselves, or to grant permission for private individuals to do so.[64] Land controlled by the civic council is more likely than privately owned land to have been subject to large-scale projects like the land improvements seen at Lyon, or the installation of infrastructural networks (roads, sewers, etc.), since the council could command the authority and the resources necessary to put such work into action. Such projects are certainly well attested in urban centres, where work such as the diversion or stabilisation of streams or rivers[65] and the creation of terracing[66] was regularly carried out at the foundation of a city, usually to aid the establishment of an orthogonal grid.[67] In the urban periphery, work of this kind would allow or encourage the occupation of the land by private individuals, and might occur if there was pressure on space within the urban centre, and a need for expansion was perceived.

Second, periurban land might be owned by private individuals or groups of individuals. In these cases, its development would be largely at their discretion. The local council, though, could still exercise authority if it wished, since the work would be taking place within their sphere of jurisdiction. They might, for example, act to protect publicly owned structures such as roads or aqueducts from private encroachment.[68] Where individuals owned large areas of land, they could potentially choose to undertake large-scale planning projects of their own, in order to improve the value of whole areas of land for private use, sale or rent. It is more likely, however, that private individuals would choose to develop small areas of land at a time. For instance, a property owner whose holdings lay alongside a major route into a city might decide that land immediately adjoining the road would be more profitable if sold off or rented to artisans or merchants than if used for agriculture. Such small-scale developments would be unlikely to follow a unified topographical scheme, responding instead to individual, *ad hoc* decisions.

Whether initiated by civic authorities or private land-owners, periurban development was usually affected by existing landscape features: both natural and man-made. Natural features such as hills, cliffs, rivers and marshes all determined whether or not particular areas of land could readily be developed, as well as influencing the orientation of buildings which were constructed. As already noted in the context of Lyon, though, the imperatives towards periurban development were sometimes strong enough to prompt land-altering projects designed to overcome natural difficulties. Before periurban development occurred, the landscape around a city had generally also been altered by human agents through the construction of major roads, bridges, harbours and ports: to say nothing of the city itself. In Gaul, such installations were usually established at the same time as the cities,[69] but they could also be developed later on. By analogy with Spain and Italy, senior magistrates were probably permitted to carry out new road-building anywhere within their jurisdiction, so long as it did not damage the interests of private individuals.[70] Man-made features were, of course, also influenced by the local geography. Thus, the harbour at Fréjus (Forum Iulii, figure 4.13, p. 110) made use of marshes between the limestone hill occupied by the city and the coast, while the roads approaching Lyon generally followed the courses of valleys or tacked diagonally up hill-sides in order to reach the urban centre on the Fourvière plateau (figure 4.15, p. 120).

Periurban development responded in particular to the courses of major roads, frequently growing up along them, and especially immediately beyond the points where they left the urban centre. At Orange (Arausio), for example, an amphitheatre and a probable *domus* lay just outside the north-west gate.[71] Similarly, at Paris (Lutetia), the original urban centre lay on the left bank of the Seine, but a cluster of occupation is attested on the right bank, just where the city's *cardo maximus* crossed the river and headed north (figure 4.5).[72] Such locations would have held many attractions as a focus for occupation. Individuals establishing shops, houses or workshops there had easy access to travellers passing in and out of the urban centre, as well as a ready-made communications link with both city and country. Similarly, public monuments or tombs would be visible to travellers and accessible to both city- and country-dwellers. From a modern perspective, it is also easy to classify such development as periurban, since its location immediately beyond the urban boundaries made it part of the *continentia aedificia*.

Yet development which occurred at some distance from an urban centre could also be closely associated with it. An example is Saint-Michel-du-Touch, a nucleated settlement 4 km north of Toulouse (Tolosa, figure 4.6), and separated from it by open country.[73] This site featured a natural spring and stood at the confluence between the Garonne and its tributary, the Touch. It had already been occupied in the pre-Roman period,[74] but in the Roman era saw the construction of a temple, a monumental fountain, three sets of baths, a classical amphitheatre and various domestic and artisanal installations. Baccrabère, the excavator of the settlement, believed that it grew up primarily in response to religious beliefs associated with the spring and confluence.[75] Yet, despite its distance from Toulouse, several factors suggest that it should be seen as periurban. Its location on the Garonne gave it one link, since this river also flowed past Toulouse. One of the main roads north-west from Toulouse also led to the settlement, meaning that it could be reached from the urban centre in an hour's walk.[76] Meanwhile, since the classical amphitheatre at Saint-Michel is the only one in the area, it almost

HIGH EMPIRE: ADMINISTRATIVE CITIES

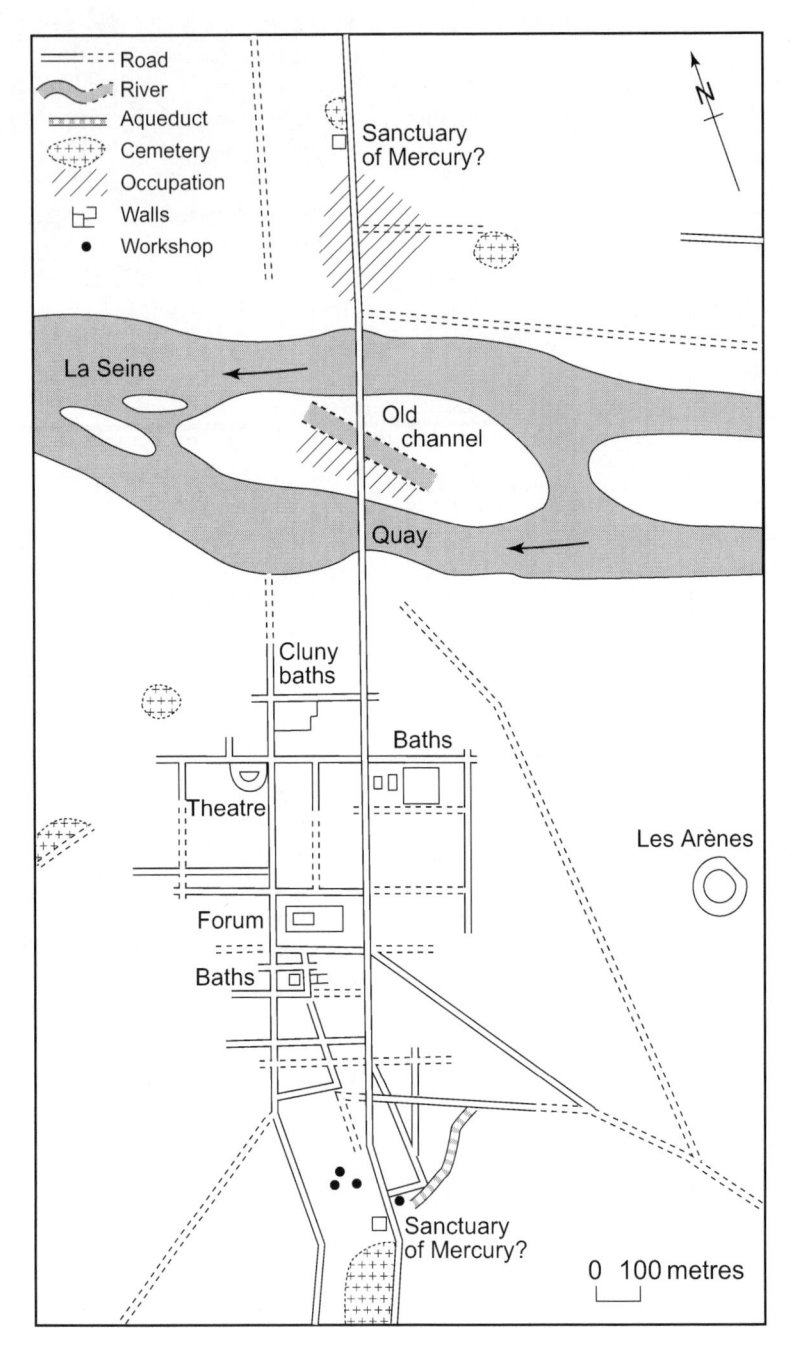

Figure 4.5 Paris (Lutetia).

HIGH EMPIRE: ADMINISTRATIVE CITIES

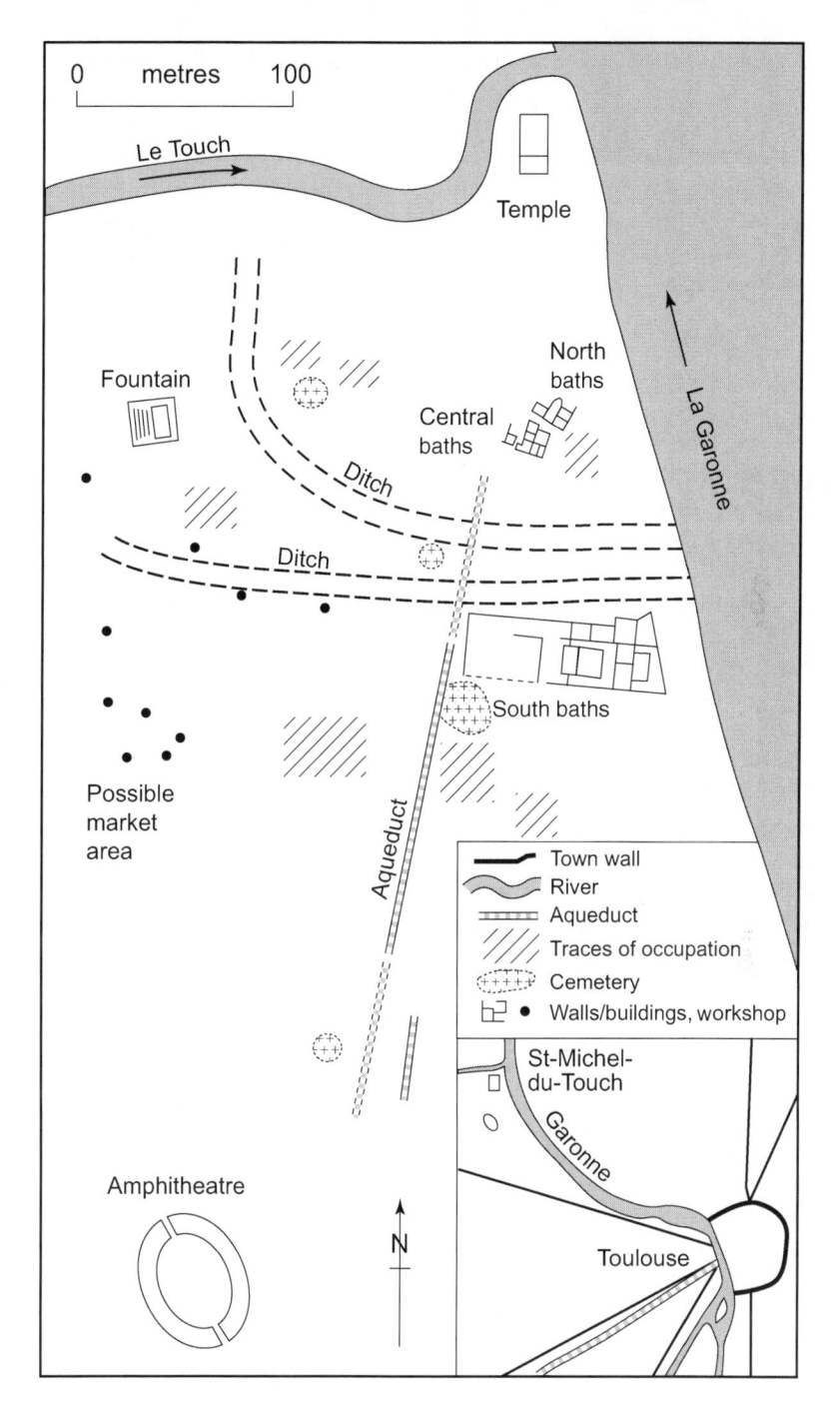

Figure 4.6 The satellite agglomeration of Saint-Michel-du-Touch, with inset showing relationship with Toulouse (Tolosa).

certainly functioned as Toulouse's main spectacle building:[77] especially given its classical form, which never occurs except in association with major administrative cities in Gaul.[78] Inhabitants of the urban centre would thus probably have journeyed to Saint-Michel-du-Touch to attend games, and also for religious reasons associated with its temple and spring, thus creating regular and intensive contact between the two. Finally, the presence of several contemporary burials on the site also strongly suggest that it should be seen as a periurban satellite, rather than an independent settlement which would surely have separate cemeteries.[79]

It has already been stated that the centres of Gallo-Roman administrative cities were normally laid out in an orthogonal grid. The streets themselves could be surfaced with stone paving, as was done in the urban centre at Lyon during the Claudian period.[80] However, this was generally an improvement carried out during periods of urban monumentalisation, and not at the establishment of a city. More often, even at large and important cities such as Saintes, streets were surfaced with gravel over a base of larger stones.[81] The urban periphery of course did not generally share the orthogonal layout of the centre, since this was one of the very features which distinguished urban from periurban. Instead, the roads encountered in periurban quarters were often simply the major roads running into the urban centre. This is the case at la Genetoye, just across the river Arroux from Autun, where an important area of periurban development grew up from the Augustan period (figure 4.7). Two main roads ran north and west through this area from Autun, while another feature which may have been a road headed from a bridge across the Arroux towards a periurban theatre.[82] Between these routes, secondary roads may have existed,[83] but the quarter does not appear to have developed an extensive road network of its own.

Where denser periurban road networks did grow up, they usually appear to have done so without the influence of an overall planning project. This was certainly the case at Vienne, where excavations at Saint-Romain-en-Gal and Sainte-Colombe, across the Rhône from the main urban centre, have revealed parts of a major periurban quarter (figure 4.4, p. 90).[84] At Saint-Romain-en-Gal, a large continuous area has been excavated, and it is clear that occupation here grew up around two early axes: one perpendicular to the river, and one curving roughly north-west along its course.[85] As dense, urban-style occupation developed between these axes, further roads were added to serve it. However, there is no sign of any attempt to create an orthogonal plan in this quarter. This makes it likely that most of the roads in the area were built through private initiative, to serve a series of small-scale developments. A similar process seems to have determined the development of the road network to the south of the walled circuit on the opposite bank of the Rhône, although the chronology here is less secure.[86] Here, too, occupation grew up around the axes of two major inter-city routes, to which further roads were added as required.

HIGH EMPIRE: ADMINISTRATIVE CITIES

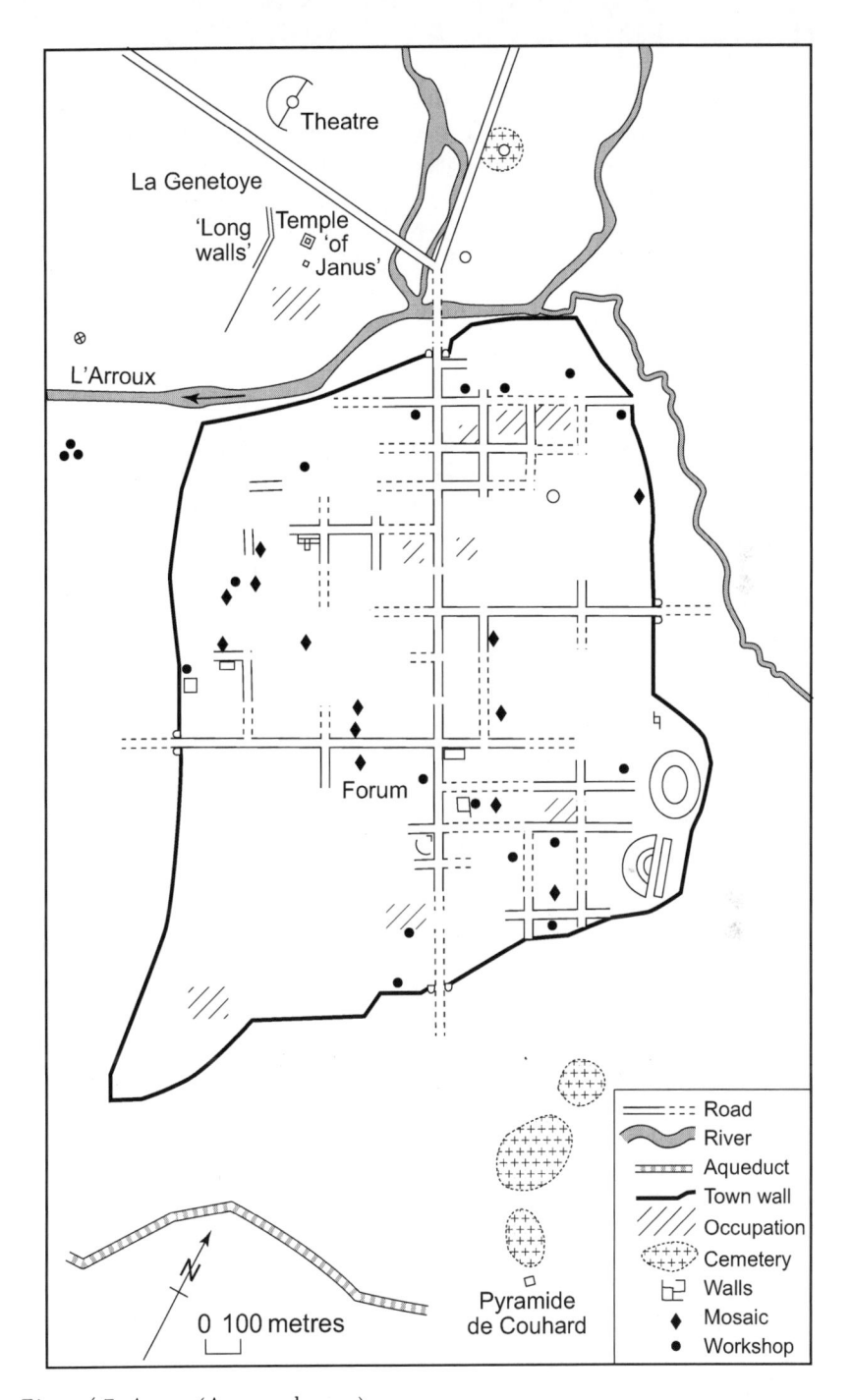

Figure 4.7 Autun (Augustodunum).

At a small number of cities, limited orthogonal layouts *do* occur in the urban periphery.[87] These may attest deliberate planning. However, an example from the 'site Michelet' to the north-east of Lisieux (Noviomagus) shows how they could evolve without it. This site was separated from the main urban centre at Lisieux by the stream of the Rouges Fontaines (figure 4.8).[88] Here, a north-south road 6.5 m wide was constructed at the end of the first century AD. At this time, only one small building existed on the site, but during the second century around ten more grew up, aligned roughly with the road. A pair of secondary roads, 4.5 and 3 m wide, were also added at right angles to the first. These roads do not appear to have been planned as part of an orthogonal network, since they do not face each other directly across the main road, and nor are they perfectly perpendicular to it. Instead their orientation seems to have been determined by a need for access to the new buildings. The limits of the excavation at the Michelet site mean that we cannot know whether further roads, parallel to the first, were constructed beyond the area observed. However, it would be quite possible for a development of this type to give rise to an extended area of more-or-less orthogonal roads and buildings, without the need for any large-scale planning.

Local civic councils, then, do not generally seem to have been particularly concerned to impose unifying planning principles on periurban development, but preferred to let it grow up 'organically'. The Rhône valley cities of Arles (Arelate) and Vienne, however, do provide suggestive evidence for high-level interest in the development of their urban peripheries. At Arles, a porticoed square bordered by at least two roads has been identified in the periurban quarter of Trinquetaille (figure 4.9).[89] Vienne, meanwhile, saw the installation of a similar colonnaded area at Saint-Romain-en-Gal in the AD 60s (see plate 4.1, p. 101 and figure 4.4, p. 90).[90] The square at Arles is poorly documented, but we know that existing structures were demolished to make way for its counterpart at Saint-Romain-en-Gal.[91] This certainly suggests the involvement of a body with considerable authority and spending power: either the civic council or a wealthy individual in consultation with it.

The complexes at Arles and Vienne have both cautiously been interpreted as secondary *fora*, built in addition to the Augusto-Tiberian *fora* in the adjacent urban centres.[92] But whether or not this was actually the case, their topographical function was equivalent. They created monumental foci for the areas, and would have been unmistakable expressions of *urbanitas*. At both cities, then, the local councils seem to have been actively concerned with enhancing the character of these transfluvial quarters through major construction projects. This may have been a response to the elite housing which had already developed there. But for Gauls who had visited Rome or read Strabo's description of it, the squares may also have recalled the colonnades, baths and temples of the Campus Martius, especially given the position of both close to the Rhône. In both cities, then, we may be seeing a deliberate

HIGH EMPIRE: ADMINISTRATIVE CITIES

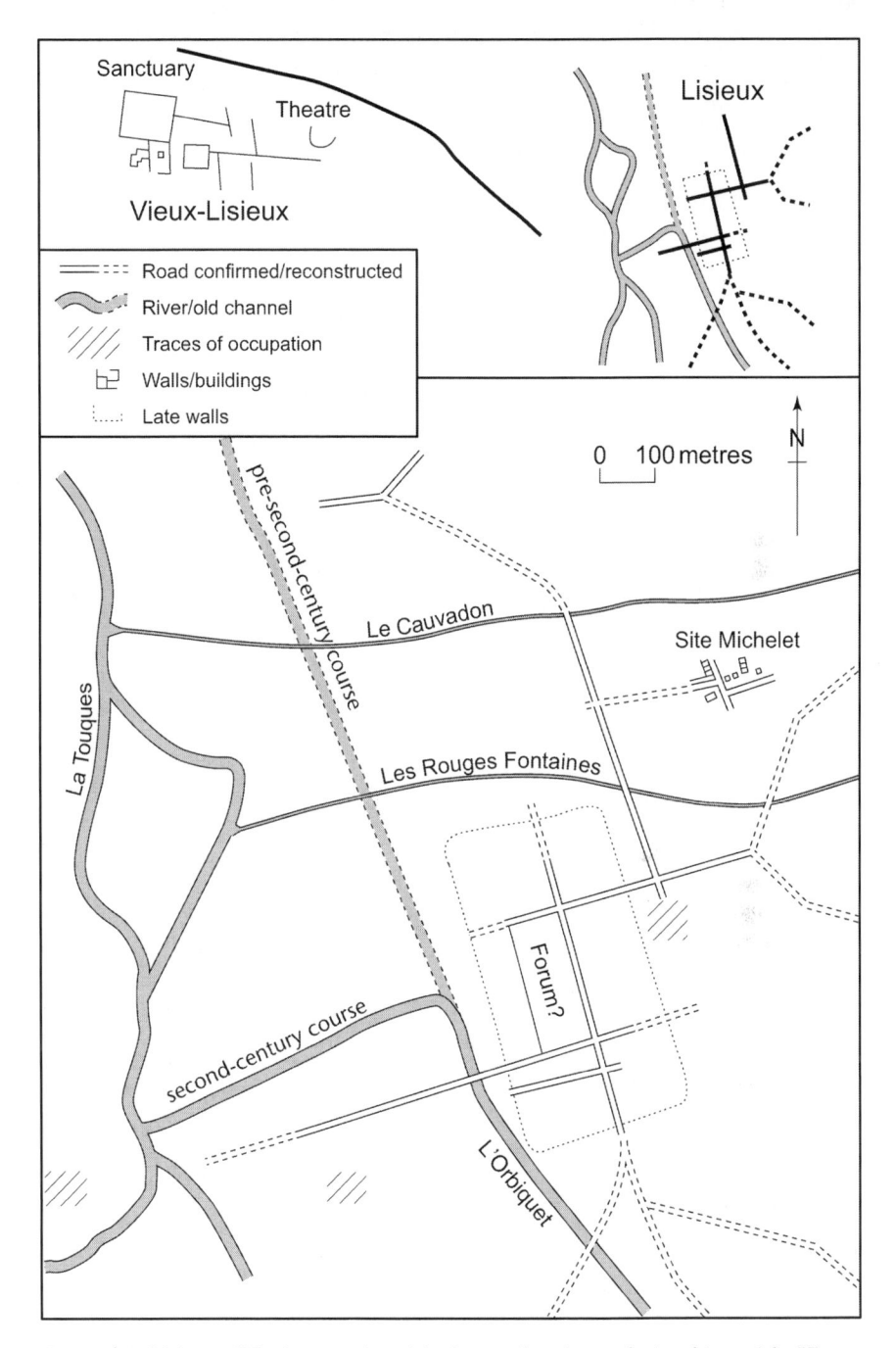

Figure 4.8 Lisieux (Noviomagus), with inset showing relationship with Vieux-Lisieux.

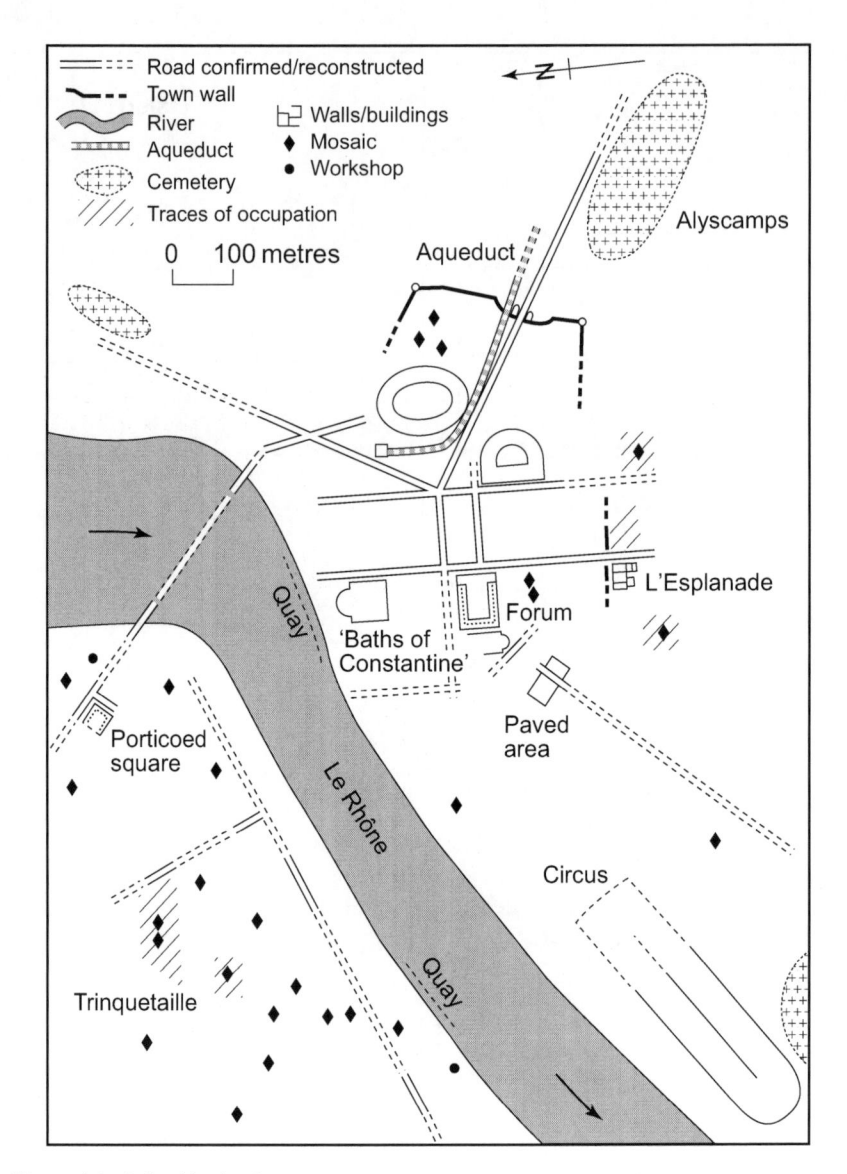

Figure 4.9 Arles (Arelate).

attempt to emulate this very formal style of periurban development – and thus Rome itself.

Most Gallo-Roman urban centres were provided at some point with running water by means of an aqueduct, although rivers, wells and springs always continued to contribute. Sewers and drains were also commonly laid out at the foundation of the city, to run beneath its streets.[93] The provision of

HIGH EMPIRE: ADMINISTRATIVE CITIES

Plate 4.1 East–west road and northern wall of the colonnaded enclosure at Saint-Romain-en-Gal, Vienne.

such facilities, though, rarely extended to the urban periphery. A typical example is Amiens (Samarobriva), where water-pipe finds attest a running supply in the urban centre, and a system of collection sewers has been identified.[94] Here, a periurban quarter developed north of the Somme in the area known as Saint-Maurice (figure 4.10).[95] It consisted mainly of houses made of perishable materials, with cellars cut into the natural chalk. A total of nine wells are known from the area, of which five have been fully or partially excavated.[96] These extended down through the chalk plateau to the water-table of the Somme valley, 20m below, and seem to have been the main source of local water.[97] This contrasts strongly with the provisions for the urban centre, and suggests that the civic authorities were not interested in providing the Saint-Maurice development with the same amenities. Instead, the water supply here seems to have been left to private individuals.

In some cases, however, sophisticated infrastructural systems *were* set up in periurban quarters. Saint-Romain-en-Gal, opposite Vienne, again provides an example. At the end of the first century BC, the water here came largely from cisterns and wells, but in some areas these were superseded by wooden and then lead water-pipes, apparently supplying localised needs.[98] Between the middle and end of the first century AD, these too were replaced by a comprehensive water-supply and sewer network, suggesting the intervention of the civic council.[99] After this, the provision at Saint-Romain compared

101

HIGH EMPIRE: ADMINISTRATIVE CITIES

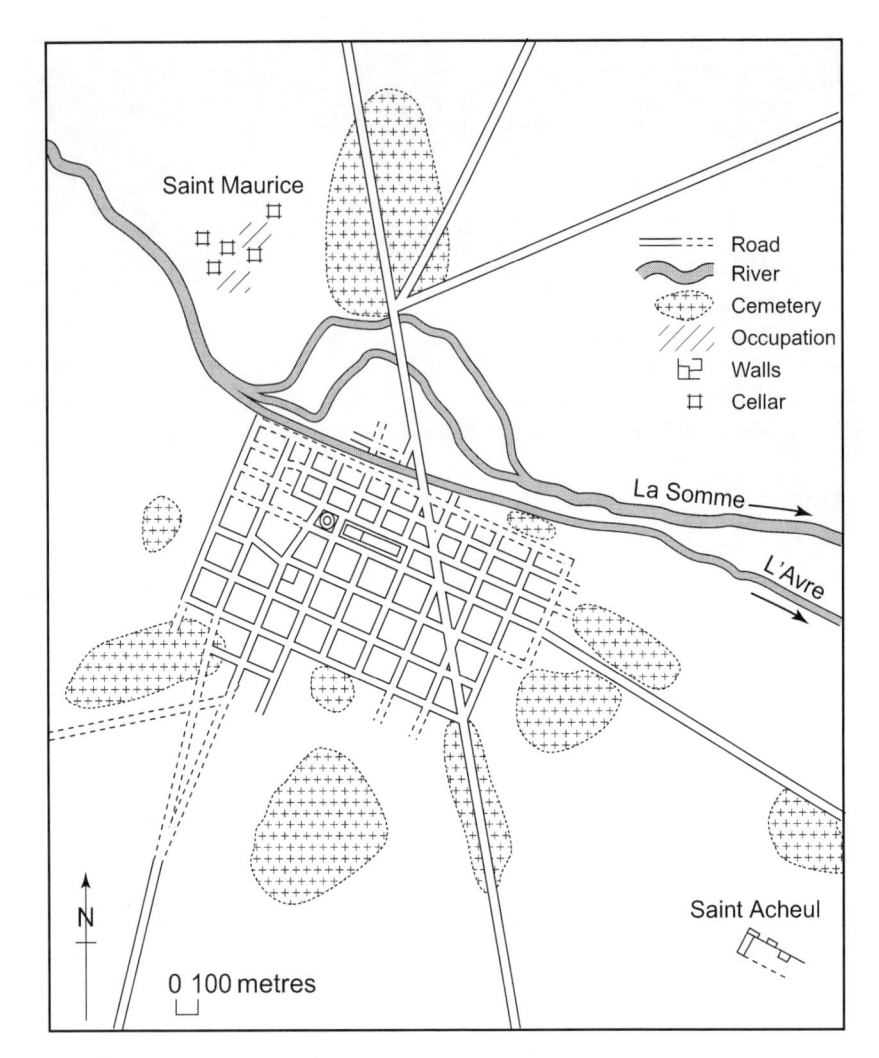

Figure 4.10 Amiens (Samarobriva).

extremely favourably with the urban centre, which was supplied by several aqueducts and had its own sewers.[100] Similarly, the roads at Saint-Romain-en-Gal were at an early stage surfaced with densely packed gravel and pebbles.[101] During the second century AD, however, most of them were paved with stone, again bringing them up to the same standard as the urban centre.[102] This attention to the local infrastructure suggests that, by the second century, the occupation at Saint-Romain was considered by the local council to be little different in status from the main urban centre. At Arles, similar projects also affected Trinquetaille, although here they are less well dated.

Lead water-pipes found on the bed of the Rhône and in north-east Trinquetaille suggest that an inverted siphon was installed to carry water to the area from the two aqueducts supplying the urban centre.[103] Again, this points towards an unusual level of interest in the development of the periurban quarter, possibly connected with the elite housing which grew up there.

Another important element in the topography of a Gallo-Roman urban periphery was the spatial distribution of different types of buildings and activities. Within Gallo-Roman urban centres, a degree of distribution by function can be observed. For instance, temples might be concentrated in the area around the forum, while tombs were always located outside the city's boundaries.[104] But in general, distinct 'zoning' was not practised. Instead, large and small houses, shops and public buildings were juxtaposed in all areas of the city: as was normal in Roman urbanism generally.[105] In the urban periphery, a similar situation can be seen. Outside the south-west corner of the walls of Fréjus, for example, houses and funerary monuments occurred in close association.[106] To be sure, some areas of occupation were dominated by one form of land-use. We have already encountered la Genetoye, across the Arroux from Autun. Here, at least seven Romano-Celtic sanctuaries and a theatre, probably with a religious function, are found together.[107] A similar site is the Altbachtal sanctuary at Trier, where numerous temples, shrines, altars and another theatre cluster just beyond the edges of the city's orthogonal grid (figure 4.14, p. 116).[108] At Sens (Agedincum), an area of two to three hectares across the river Yonne from the urban centre appears to have been occupied almost exclusively by ceramics workshops (figure 4.11),[109] while the site Michelet at Lisieux yielded evidence for some fifteen forges and metal-working debris.[110]

In several of these cases, however, the dominant form of land-use was not the *only* one practised in the area. At Autun, the public buildings of la Genetoye were close to the remains of other buildings, possibly houses, as well as two large funerary monuments and an associated burial area.[111] At Sens, the potters' quarter has also yielded domestic finds, suggesting that the potters lived alongside their kilns.[112] Meanwhile, two perpendicular walls in the north-west corner of the Michelet site at Lisieux may belong to a large private property, and a row of short foundation walls built up against them probably supported wooden shops lining the main road.[113] The Altbachtal sanctuary complex at Trier does appear to be a genuine example of 'zoned' land-use, as are some extensive cemetery areas; for example, at Trion, to the south-west of the urban centre at Lyon.[114] However, the most typical situation in a Gallo-Roman urban periphery appears to have been for different buildings and activities to exist side by side. The greatest difference from the urban centre will have been the potential for cemeteries and funerary monuments to appear as part of the mix. But we should note that even this did not apply in all periurban quarters. The most densely occupied sectors of Trinquetaille at Arles and Saint-Romain-en-Gal at Vienne, for instance, were

HIGH EMPIRE: ADMINISTRATIVE CITIES

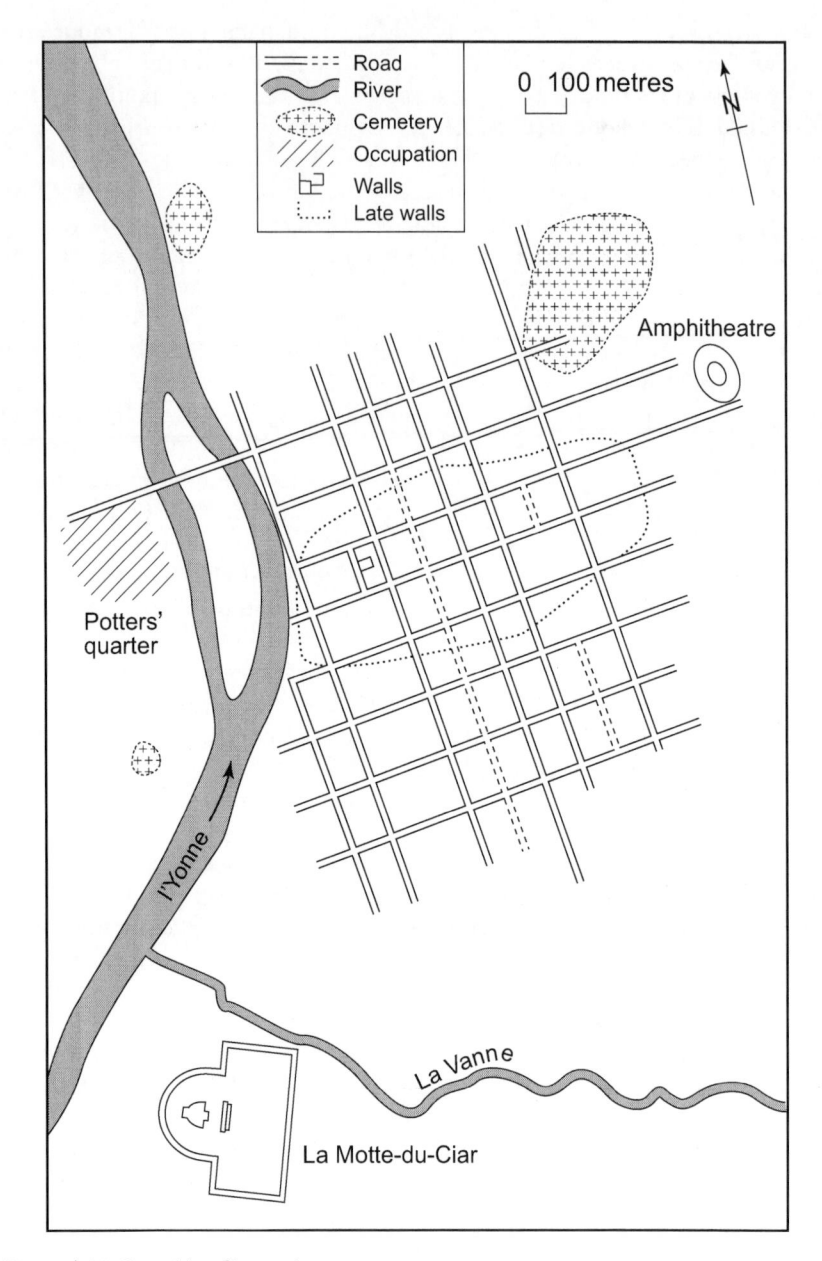

Figure 4.11 Sens (Agedincum).

devoid of burials, at least during the high empire. This is another indication of the 'special' nature of these quarters, again suggesting that they were perceived as little different from the nearby urban centres on the opposite bank of the Rhône.

Industry

The word 'industry' is used here to refer to secondary production on whatever scale: the manufacture of goods, from domestic weaving to extensive kiln complexes. Assessing this type of activity in a Roman context poses some archaeological challenges. Manufacture that did not require purpose-built workshops can be difficult to spot archaeologically, especially if the goods produced were made of perishable materials; for instance, spinning or basket-weaving. Meanwhile, even if units of production are successfully identified, the small scale of much ancient industry can make it difficult to be certain whether a single excavated workshop was an isolated concern, or one of many similar units.[115] Such factors render comparisons between the urban centre and the urban periphery difficult. Yet there is no reason to believe that they did not apply equally to both. Thus, although conditions may not be ideal in either case, comparisons can still be drawn.

The distribution of Gallo-Roman industrial activity clearly responded above all to economic factors, such as the availability of raw materials and land or ease of access to markets and transport networks. Frequently, this meant locations away from administrative cities. Workshops often occur alongside roads or in association with villas,[116] as well as in secondary agglomerations.[117] For the most part, the goods produced were sold locally, but wider markets were also accessible.[118] The classic example is the terra sigillata (Samian ware) industry.[119] Gaul was the main producer of high-quality terra sigillata in the first and second centuries AD, and its pottery was sold all over the empire. The location of sigillata-producing kilns near cities, from where their goods could easily be sold on, might therefore be expected. Yet with the exception of workshops at Lyon and Trier, most Gallic sigillata was produced at small artisanal settlements. This can be explained to some extent by the presence of suitable clay deposits, but these were not sufficiently rare to be the only factor. Peacock suggests that another important aspect was the distinct separation between production and sale in the sigillata industry. Because the market for sigillata was empire-wide, the pottery was usually transported over long distances to reach its consumers anyway, so that proximity to one urban market was not a significant advantage. Meanwhile, most sigillata-producing settlements *were* close to major watercourses or their tributaries, giving them access to long-distance trading networks.

For other industries, though, an urban location could be attractive. If raw materials and building space were available, a city could offer a concentrated market, supplies of labour and equipment, and access to transport networks. The immediate market was probably of particular importance, since – exceptions such as the sigillata industry apart – Roman manufacturers generally sold goods directly from their place of production as well as sending them for sale elsewhere. Artisans will therefore have responded to commercial, as well as productive, concerns when deciding where to locate their workshops. In early Roman Gaul, locations in the urban centre were not unusual. Workshops were scattered across the centres of both Saintes and Autun in the early first century AD, side by side with domestic occupation. Over time, though, they tended to move outwards.[120] At Saintes, the local potters established themselves on the opposite bank of the river Charente (figure 4.12),[121] while at Autun, artisans shifted towards the very edges of the urban centre, although remaining just within its walls.[122] Similar patterns have also been noted at Chartres (Autricum) and Tours (Caesarodunum).[123]

By the end of the first century AD, then, kilns and purpose-built workshops tended to be concentrated in the peripheries of Gallo-Roman cities, rather than their centres. This is often explained in terms of a deliberate policy of excluding industry from the urban centre due to practical factors, such as fire and pollution,[124] or ideological factors connected with the sophisticated appearance of the city.[125] Such explanations, also given for other parts of the empire, are often made with reference to chapter 76 of the Urso charter.[126] This begins with a clause forbidding anyone to have a tile-works with a capacity of more than three hundred tiles or tile-like objects within the *oppidum* from which the *colonia* was administered.[127] Reference may also be made to literary evidence from Rome indicating that tanning was concentrated in Transtiberim, and especially Juvenal's reference to goods 'for banishing beyond the Tiber'.[128] These sources would indeed seem, at face value, to point to an interest in keeping dangerous or unpleasant industries outside Roman urban centres.

However, a closer examination of the Urso charter calls this picture into question. After the restrictions on tile-works are outlined, the same chapter continues with a description of the action to be taken if they are disregarded:

> Whoever will have had [a tile-works], that building and the place shall be the public property of the colonia Iulia, and whoever will preside over jurisdiction in the colonia Genetiva Iulia shall pay into the public funds that money [derived] from the building, without fraud or wrongdoing.[129]

Here we see that, when the original injunction is disobeyed, the concern of the civic authorities is not to remove the offending kiln, as we might expect if the intention was to 'protect' the urban centre from industry, either practically or ideologically. Instead, the authorities want to make the kiln and its revenue public property. We should also note that the law concerns only tile-kilns, even though pottery kilns, glass workshops and forges would surely

HIGH EMPIRE: ADMINISTRATIVE CITIES

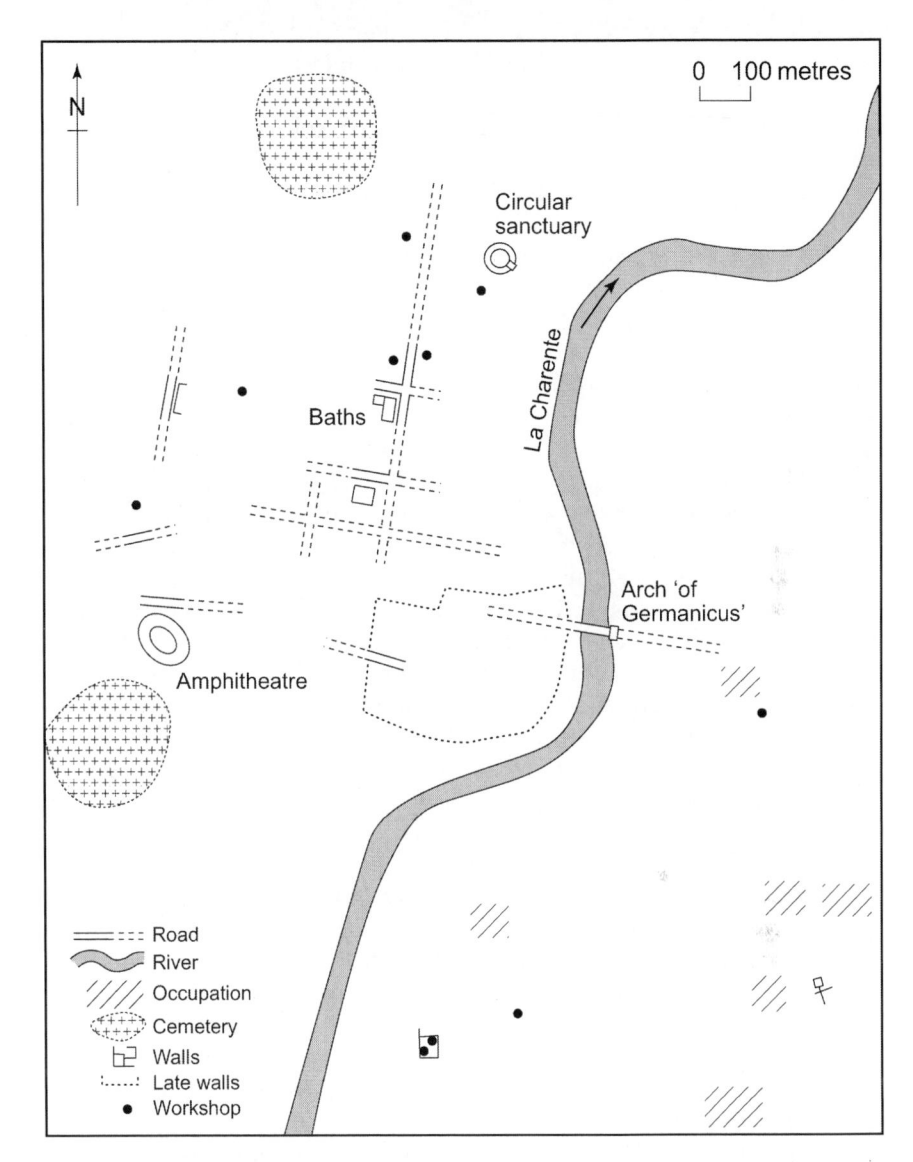

Figure 4.12 Saintes (Mediolanum).

have posed just as great a fire risk. Even the tile kilns are only problematic when over a certain size: Crawford comments that the purpose of the law 'is clearly to limit production of tiles to a number suitable for private house building'.[130] Thus the Urso charter cannot be used as straightforward evidence for a widespread interest in keeping *all* industries out of Roman urban centres. Possibly it was instead intended to protect the production of tiles for public building-works from private competition. Furthermore, archaeological evidence from many Roman cities shows that industry often *was* located in the urban centre,[131] while rulings in the *Digesta* seem to assume that domestic and industrial occupation were normally found side by side in an urban setting.[132] There is no reason, then, to assume that Gallo-Roman civic councils were actively concerned with excluding workshops from their urban centres.

Other reasons for the migration of industries into the urban periphery must therefore be sought, and one may have been the price of land in the urban centre. It is difficult to prove that land in the urban centre was more expensive than land in the periphery, since no specific information on the subject survives.[133] But it is clear from the archaeological record that urban land *was* coveted. The focus of occupation was always the urban centre, and a general preference for progressively denser development here, rather than a spread into the periphery, is obvious: and in accordance with our knowledge of the elite interest in closely defined cities. Central land should therefore have fetched a higher price than periurban land, for sale or for rent, from the earliest history of a city. The extent of the difference probably also increased over time, as the supply of available land in the centre was used up. From the point of view of an artisan, then, establishing a workshop in the centre of a city would have been more expensive than establishing one in the periphery: and increasingly so, as competition for central land became more intense. Unless there were particularly pressing reasons for favouring a central location, then, a periurban situation is likely to have been more profitable. It could offer much the same opportunities in terms of access to the city and its benefits, but for a lower price.

The workshops at Autun strongly support the idea that industry congregated in the urban periphery for economic reasons, rather than as a result of any deliberate civic policy. These workshops did shift outwards over time, but remained just within the urban centre, as defined by Autun's defensive circuit. This circuit, though, was unusually extensive, enclosing around 200 ha (see plate 4.2).[134] Although most of the space within it eventually became built up, there was probably never a great deal of pressure on it. The locations of the workshops, then, suggest that the relationship between centre and periphery at Autun was rather different when viewed from an economic perspective than when viewed from an ideological one. Elite ideas about *urbanitas* demanded a sharp distinction between urban and non-urban space. Thus, if Autun's civic council had pronounced any kind of ban on industrial activity in the city, the workshops would surely have had to move outside the walled circuit. Since they actually remained within it, we are alerted to the possibility of a smoother economic transition from centre to periphery, with no such distinct division, but a gradual decrease in land prices from the heart of the city to the edges of the urban agglomeration. At other cities, where the defined urban centre was smaller, the point at which rents became low enough to attract artisans may well have been beyond the urban boundaries:

HIGH EMPIRE: ADMINISTRATIVE CITIES

Plate 4.2 Part of the walled circuit at Autun.

but this does not mean that the boundaries themselves were the decisive factor.

Other economic factors may also have made a periurban location positively attractive, even without the effects of land price differentials. Some are illustrated by a group of at least fifteen potters' kilns to the north-east of Fréjus (figure 4.13).[135] Here, a large seam of very plastic clay was available near the ground surface, and potters clearly located their kilns in order to be close to it. As a result, most fell in the urban periphery, where most of the seam was located. However, two were located in the urban centre, where the seam penetrated just within the walls. Another attraction in the area must have been the road leading north-east from Fréjus. This would have aided the transport of both raw materials and finished goods to and from the kilns, and offered the added possibility of selling products to passers-by travelling along the road. Similar circumstances apply to the group of potters' kilns on the left bank of the Yonne opposite Sens (figure 4.11).[136] Here, the kilns had access to water, fuel from woods above the valley, and large deposits of silty white clay.[137] Their relationship to the river Yonne, as well as the city of Sens and the roads passing through it, also gave them access to the urban market, transport networks and passing trade. Again, at Saintes, the kilns and other workshops located across the Charente from the urban centre enjoyed access to sandy clay, a road running east towards Lyon, the river and of course the city itself.[138] In each case, the positive attractions of the urban periphery are

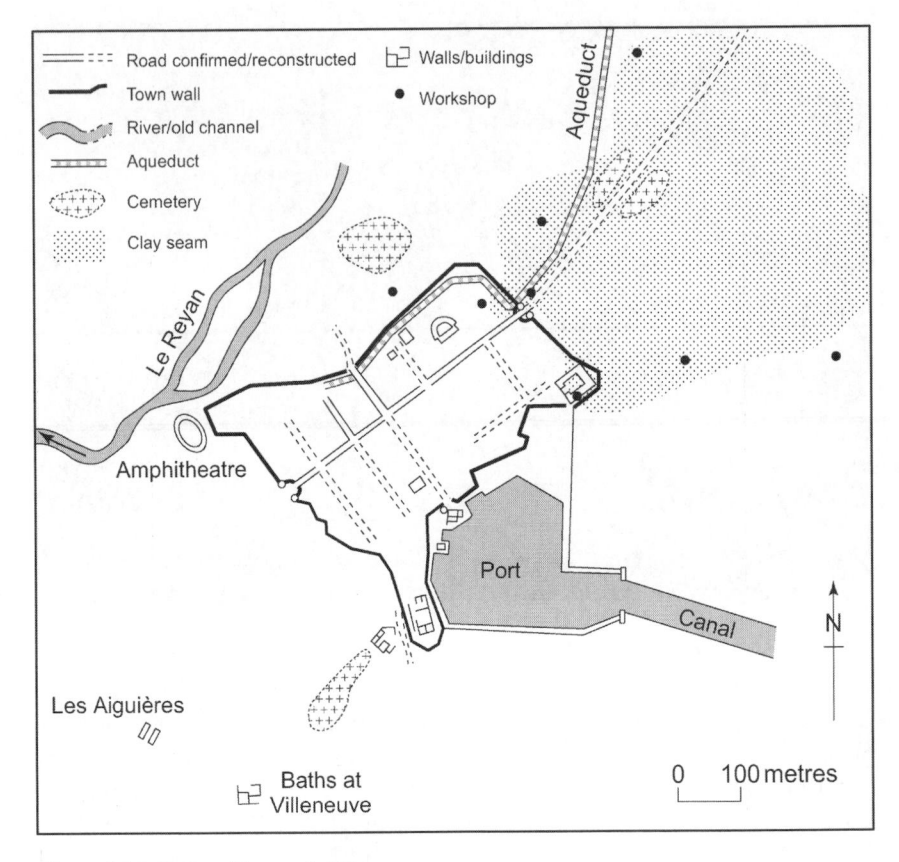

Figure 4.13 Fréjus (Forum Iulii).

quite enough to explain both the presence of industry here in the first place, and the clustering of several workshops in the same locations.

We should also consider the attractions which a periurban location had to offer over a location away from the city altogether. Studies of the products of periurban kilns have shown that their output was generally more varied and sophisticated than that of their rural counterparts. At the Senonian potters' quarter, goods produced which were not supplied by rural kilns in the area include amphorae, fineware and utilitarian objects such as lamps and loom-weights.[139] Apparently, then, the potters were actively seeking to meet a wide range of consumer demand. The market available to them from the periphery of Sens was clearly extensive, since their goods have been found not only within the nearby urban centre, but also throughout its territory, and in other neighbouring cities such as Paris, Troyes and Melun.[140] Similarly, potters at Reims during the early imperial period produced a range of stamped Gallo-Belgic fineware in the Saint-Rémi district, to the south of the urban centre and close to the river Vesle and a major south-running road.[141] Their goods have been found all over Gallia Belgica and Germany, as well as in Britain, showing that the potters took full advantage of the trading routes accessible to them from this position. As the example of terra sigillata showed, long-distance trade of this kind clearly *could* be accomplished from a non-urban location. But proximity to a city does appear to have opened up fruitful opportunities for some artisans.

The workshops discussed so far were all located in the immediate periphery of the city. Here, industry regularly occurred alongside other types of occupation, as several examples from Lyon demonstrate (figure 4.15, p. 120). On the slopes below the amphitheatre of the Three Gauls at Condate, a kiln was built next to residential rooms within a *domus* during the second century, and a glass-workshop was active from the end of the second to the middle of the third century in a house only metres from the amphitheatre.[142] Meanwhile, on the plain at Vaise, a large, well-appointed house known as the 'Maison aux Xenia' had a workshop producing bronze or copper right outside it, and another artisanal installation used for dyeing, fulling or tanning about 30m to the north-east.[143] Apparently, then, there was little interest in attempting to separate industrial activity from other types of occupation in the urban periphery, including elite houses.

However, nucleated groups of workshops could also form in the periurban *continentia aedificia*. We have already encountered the fifteen metal-working forges on the site Michelet at Lisieux and the potters' quarter across the river Yonne from the urban centre at Sens. Multiple groups of kilns also produced fineware from the Augustan period onwards on the left bank of the Saône at Lyon,[144] while a complex of nine kilns was concentrated into two buildings in the north part of Saint-Romain-en-Gal at Vienne.[145] This was evidently a communal workshop, staffed by several potters. Nucleated groups such as these might offer several advantages to their workers. For example, craftsmen could arrange to buy in raw materials or send products to nearby markets together, sharing the cost of transport. A group of kilns may also have allowed potters to specialise, increasing their efficiency. At least one kiln could be in use at all times, allowing some workers to concentrate on throwing pots while others tended the kilns. Such specialisation may have made it easier for artisans to produce the range and quality of goods required by the urban market, boosting their ability to take full economic advantage of their periurban situation.

Finally, some industries from beyond the *continentia aedificia* are also best interpreted as periurban. One such is quarrying: an industry particularly closely associated with urban markets thanks to the construction of monumental public buildings. Stone was expensive to transport over long distances, making a location close to the point of use particularly attractive. Yet quarries could hardly be opened in the urban centre, especially since the favoured method was open-cast quarrying, which involved opening up large tracts of land for access to the stone. They therefore tended to develop in the urban periphery, where their precise location was of course determined by geology.[146] At least five were situated within a 1.5 km radius of Nîmes, and three more lay 3, 9 and 20 km away to the north-west, where the best stone was available.[147] All are known to have supplied Nîmes directly, although the most distant quarry, at Bois de Lens, also supplied other southern cities. Arles, meanwhile, provides an interesting example of industrial activity making direct use of a city's system of infrastructural support. Seven kilometres east of Arles, a flour mill at Barbegal was powered during the second and third centuries by an offshoot from its aqueduct, and probably also sold most of its produce in the city.[148] As for the quarries, then, production apparently developed here in response to specific opportunities stemming from proximity to Arles, but in a position where raw materials – in this case, grain – were readily available.

Commerce

Commerce can be defined as any activity concerned with the movement and exchange of goods for profit, including retail, trade, storage and transport. It begins at the point where goods are produced, through agriculture or industry, and ends with their acquisition by consumers. Not all goods in the ancient world passed through commercial networks. A high proportion of agricultural output was produced and consumed within the same household in the context of subsistence farming,[149] and the same could apply to manufactured goods. Goods were also exchanged through mechanisms other than the free market; for instance, gifts passed amongst the elite or taxation in kind by the Roman government.[150] In these cases, though, the produce underwent much the same process as free market goods in its journey from producers to consumers; for example, during transit or storage. Non-free market exchange, then, can be viewed as part of the world of Roman commerce, and left its own traces in the archaeological record.

Goods exchanged on the free market were often retailed directly to consumers from the point of production. This saved on transport costs, and must have been an attractive method of sale. But it was not sufficient to ensure the efficient exchange of goods between producers and consumers on its own. Goods were also sold through a sophisticated system of markets, either by their producers or by professional traders, and usually within a relatively short distance of their point of production.[151] In cities, some retail took place in permanent shops. These were usually used for high-value goods such as terra sigillata, glass or lamps,[152] when the protection against theft or damage which a shop could offer was clearly considered worth the extra expense involved. But shops were not the only retail outlets, even in cities, and markets, itinerant peddlers and direct sales from warehouses also played a major role in commercial exchange. Finally, goods bought up from producers or at local markets might also be traded over longer distances. The significance of such trade in the Roman empire has long been debated, but it clearly did occur, and involved numerous 'middle-men' along the way: small-scale traders, merchants or corporations of merchants, river boatmen, marine shippers, dockers, warehouse owners, and even bankers, money-lenders and insurance brokers.[153]

A great deal of commercial activity clearly went on in the centres of Gallo-Roman cities. Forums were often equipped with permanent shops,[154] and would generally have been used for regular markets. Shops were also built into the façades of houses fronting onto major thoroughfares.[155] The 'Maison du Laraire' in Lyon, for example, faced on to a *decumanus* leading towards the nearby municipal sanctuary of the imperial cult, and had two pairs of shops on either side of its entrance-way.[156] Small storehouses are also attested,[157] and, less commonly, purpose-built *macella*. One such is attested by an inscription at Béziers[158] and another has been excavated at Saint-Bertrand-de-Comminges (Lugdunum Convenarum),[159] but they do not seem to have been as widespread in Gaul as they were in Italy and North Africa. Meanwhile, large cryptoporticoes in the centres of Arles, Bavay (Bagacum), Narbonne and Reims have sometimes been interpreted by French archaeologists as *horrea*, or large store-houses.[160] Rickman, though, has argued that the plans and décor of these monuments, the difficulty of access to them and the damp conditions within all make this unlikely. Instead, he suggests that they were simply intended to support weighty superstructures such as forum porticoes and create level terraces where necessary.

In the countryside, the main mechanism for exchange was regular markets. These are not easily visible through archaeology, since they generally did not take place in permanent buildings. But literary and epigraphic evidence from Gaul and elsewhere makes it clear that regular markets were held on agricultural estates[161] at rural sanctuaries[162] and in small towns.[163] Meanwhile, in both city and country, games or religious festivals were usually accompanied by commercial activity.[164] This could mean the sale of small-scale consumables to the attendant crowds (de Ligt's 'accessory festal markets'), or larger, official markets (de Ligt's '(genuine) fairs'). The venues for such events, of course, were determined primarily by the spectacle buildings or temples around which they focused, but they also deserve consideration here from a commercial perspective.

Commercial activity in the urban periphery was often associated with industry. The metal-working forges of the site Michelet at Lisieux faced what appears to have been a row of shops built into the perimeter of a private property.[165] If these structures were shops, then they may be considered analogous to those built into houses in the urban centre. In either context, the owner could maximise his income by renting out units built into his property, or using them to sell the produce of his own country estates. The position of the shops facing on to a major road leading north from the city,

HIGH EMPIRE: ADMINISTRATIVE CITIES

also suggests that they were intended to attract passing trade, like the shops lining urban streets. Whether they were used to sell the products of the adjacent forges is uncertain, but this would certainly seem sensible from the point of view of the smiths working in the area, even if it was not their main market.

At Saint-Romain-en-Gal, across the Rhône from Vienne, commercial and industrial activity again appear together, and in close association with elite *domus* and public buildings. Several first-century *domus* here had shops built into their façades,[166] suggesting that the area was already sufficiently affluent and well populated for them to be considered a worthwhile investment. In the centre of the excavated area, a triangular *insula* housed a group of nine shops and workshops at its northernmost end, a large fulling establishment in the centre (see plate 4.3), and what seems to have been a covered market to the south: all built around the turn of the second century.[167] The market itself incorporated shops, a set of latrines, two hearths, staircases which probably led to living quarters, and a metal-workshop. Further south, a rectangular plot occupied by storehouses or shops and another fullers' or dyers' workshop has also been excavated.[168] This complex, developed during the second half of the first century, was directly adjacent to two elite *domus*: the Maison des Dieux Océans (and its earlier predecessors) to the west, and the Maison aux Cinq Mosaïques to the north. Occupation at Saint-Romain was highly mixed, then, just as was usually the case in an urban centre. Meanwhile, the frequent juxtaposition of shops, storehouses and workshops again

Plate 4.3 Vats in the large fullery, Saint-Romain-en-Gal, Vienne.

draws attention to the close links between commerce and industry in the Roman world. All three will have interacted, with the shops being used to sell goods produced in the workshops and/or stored in the warehouses. They are also likely to have grown up in the area in the first place for much the same reasons, including the transport opportunities offered by the Rhône, as well as the consumers based in Saint-Romain-en-Gal itself and the other quarters of Vienne across the river.

A large rectangular building constructed at Saint-Romain-en-Gal in the second half of the first century AD has also been identified as a *horreum* (large warehouse), on the basis of its plan and a damp course made of rows of inverted amphorae set into its floor.[169] This must have been used to store goods on a large scale, probably in connection with traffic along the Rhône. Unlike the other structures discussed above, such a *horreum* would not normally be found in a Gallo-Roman urban centre, and its presence suggests an unusually high degree of commercial activity at Saint-Romain-en-Gal. However, it was clearly not a deterrent to the construction of urban-style *domus* or monumental public buildings in the area. It lay only just north of the Maisons des Dieux Océans, which continued to undergo major embellishments long after the warehouse had been erected,[170] and is roughly contemporary with the construction of the large monumental square nearby. We have already seen that Saint-Romain enjoyed unusually elevated status for a quarter of periurban occupation in the eyes of the local council, receiving an infrastructural system comparable to the urban centre and a monumental public square. Apparently, the commercial activities of the quarter were no impediment to this kind of treatment; indeed it is possible that they generated part of the wealth behind it.

The warehouse at Saint-Romain-en-Gal also draws attention to the importance of fluvial – and marine – trade in shaping the character of periurban commercial activity in Gaul. Rivers were clearly an important factor in the Gallic economy, facilitating both local and longer-distance trade. Their impact on transport and communications is eulogised by Strabo,[171] and confirmed by pottery distribution maps, which normally show a close relationship between the spread of pottery from its point of production and the river network.[172] Most Gallo-Roman cities were situated on or near navigable rivers, and equipped with port installations such as harbours, quays and warehouses. This shows that they were used as stopping-points for river-boats, allowing goods to be taken from the city to other markets, or transferred from the river for sale in the city itself or transportation along the road network. Meanwhile, few cities were located directly on the sea,[173] but many were close to river-mouths, allowing sea-going craft to conduct the same kinds of exchanges.[174]

The spatial relationship between Gallo-Roman cities and these watercourses had a marked effect on the urban periphery. The capacity for rivers to act as urban boundaries has already been discussed, and numerous Gallo-Roman

HIGH EMPIRE: ADMINISTRATIVE CITIES

examples illustrate the principle clearly. At Vienne, the occupation on the left bank of the Rhône is clearly identifiable as the urban centre, despite the sophisticated character of the occupation at Saint-Romain-en-Gal, because it is the location of the city's forum, and is surrounded by walls. The walls do not continue on to the right bank of the river, indicating that the western boundary of the urban centre was marked by the Rhône itself. At Autun and Trier (figure 4.14), similar configurations apply, except that in these cases the arrangement is made even clearer by walls which mirror the courses of the rivers Arroux and Mosel. Even without walls to reinforce the point, urban centres throughout Gaul were consistently located on only one side of a river.

Commercial installations associated with the rivers thus naturally fell either on the very perimeter of the urban centre, or completely outside it. A typical example is Rouen (Rotomagus), where excavations have revealed first- and second-century quays and a warehouse on the bank of the Seine at the southern edge of the urban centre.[175] The role of the Seine as an urban

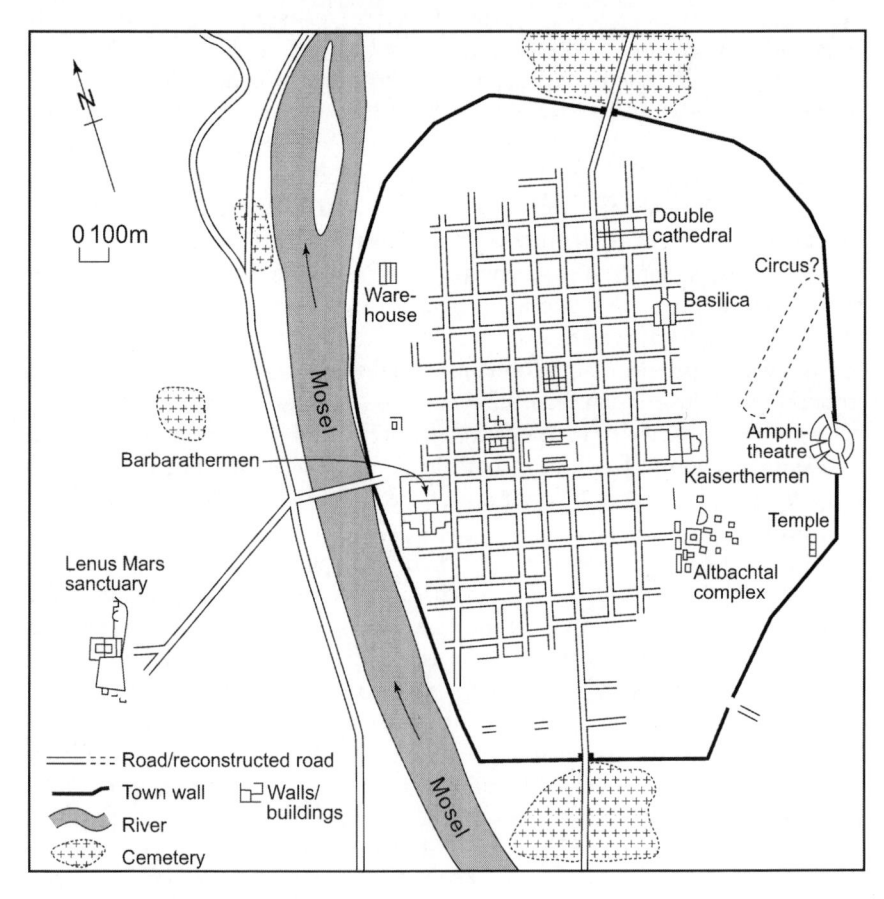

Figure 4.14 Trier (Augusta Treverorum).

boundary placed these features on the very edge of the urban centre: neither fully integrated into it nor fully relegated to the periphery. Elsewhere, similar structures fell more explicitly in the urban periphery. The *horreum* at Saint-Romain-en-Gal is one such example. Several larger *horrea* also lined the left bank of the Rhône to the south of Vienne's walled circuit,[176] where their construction had been made possible by major terracing and stabilisation works between AD 15 and 40,[177] and a series of first- to third-century warehouses have been identified upstream of Lyon at Vaise.[178]

Some of these periurban warehouses were extremely substantial. At Vienne, the Saint-Romain-en-Gal *horreum* covered 2600m^2, while that at the Nympheas II site on the left bank of the Rhône covered at least 6000m^2. This may help to explain their explicitly periurban location. Vienne's urban centre abutted directly on to the Rhône for a stretch of only around 900m, yet the warehouses to the south of its walls extended for at least 750m along the bank. The riverside parts of the urban centre, then, would have been completely dominated by these structures if they had been built within the city walls. Such a location may also have been unattractive if the bulk of the goods stored in the warehouses were not destined for consumption in Vienne, but were instead merely passing between different converging elements in Gaul's transport infrastructure. Rickman has argued that there was a high degree of state involvement in the building and running of provincial *horrea*, especially those connected with the public grain supply.[179] Certainly, the size of these warehouses, the fact that major land-alterations were undertaken in order to build them and their location on a river used to convey goods towards Germany all raise the possibility that these warehouses were involved in supplying the armies on the Rhine frontier. In this case, a location even on the perimeter of the urban centre may simply have made access to the warehouses more difficult, without bringing any compensatory advantages.

All of these practical factors, then, help to explain the concentration of river trade installations in the urban periphery. In the specific case of Vienne, meanwhile, we may also add some more ideological considerations. We have already seen how, at this city, the monumentalising treatment of Saint-Romain-en-Gal could potentially have recalled the character of the Campus Martius in Rome. The warehouses, too, may be seen in a similar light. Although Vienne was a great deal further up the Rhône than Rome was up the Tiber, the two cities were alike in having a walled urban centre incorporating several hills on the left bank of a major river, and a warehouse district just to the south of those walls.[180] Possibly, then, experience of Rome itself had suggested to the elite of Vienne that this was simply the most appropriate location for warehouses in a Roman city. Meanwhile, the depiction of periurban storehouses on Trajan's column, though post-dating Vienne's examples by a century, further suggests that the urban periphery was widely considered the proper setting for such structures in Roman thought.

Finally, the satellite agglomeration of Saint-Michel-du-Touch near Toulouse, with its amphitheatre, temple and group of baths, also appears to have been the focus of a seasonal periurban market.[181] First- and second-century domestic structures with related wells were discovered here, as well as twenty-seven gravelled surfaces: most of them circular or quadrilateral in shape and some associated with amphora sherds (figure 4.6, p. 95).[182] Baccrabère has suggested that a cluster of these surfaces just north of the amphitheatre constituted a kind of temporary marketplace, and that both the gravelled areas and the domestic structures were used mainly on a seasonal basis as a commercial encampment.[183] Given the association between fairs and public festivals, this is certainly plausible for a site featuring religious and entertainment buildings. Traders could converge on Saint-Michel either for short periods, or perhaps during a more extended festival 'season'. In doing so, they would be taking advantage of custom drawn into the urban periphery for reasons other than commerce: a topic for further discussion later in this chapter, in connection with the public monuments involved. Meanwhile, ten first-century potters' kilns interspersed with the other occupation at Saint-Michel again confirm the tendency for periurban occupation to be mixed in character, and especially for commercial and industrial activity to occur together.[184]

Domestic occupation

The urban periphery was of course home to many Gallo-Roman city-dwellers. Not all of them lived in purely residential buildings. We have already encountered cases of close associations between industrial, commercial and domestic occupation, and some residents in the urban periphery will have lived in their shops and workshops.[185] But others lived in a range of purpose-built domestic structures, from the simple to the lavish. Assessing the range of housing in the urban periphery and comparing it with the urban centre allows us to ask whether any kind of social divide existed between the two. Did the equivalents of affluent suburbs and inner-city slums exist in Roman Gaul? Or, indeed, city-centre penthouses and run-down housing estates? We might certainly expect that the ideologies connected with the urban centre made it an attractive place for the elite to live. But did the urban periphery have its own appeal?

Some archaeological difficulties must be addressed here. First, houses in Gaul did not develop in the same manner as houses in Italy, so we cannot expect even the wealthiest residences of Roman Gaul to look like those of Pompeii or Herculaneum. A few houses, mainly in Narbonensis, did use the axial atrium-peristyle plan,[186] but it was never widespread, even amongst the elite. In the Three Gauls, meanwhile, the houses of the wealthy would have been hard to distinguish from those of the poor until the second half of the first century AD, when masonry houses began to be built.[187] Before this, urban houses had differed little in size, and were usually built of perishable materials such as wood, sun-baked bricks or cob (a mixture of clay and straw).[188] Even after this, houses were built to a wide variety of plans, although some kind of courtyard was a common feature in all contexts.[189] Wealth, then, must be judged not from layout, but from other features such as décor, overall size, quality of construction and associated artefacts.

It is also often difficult to understand Gallo-Roman houses in context, due to the limited scope of most urban excavations. A house excavated in isolation may not be sufficient evidence for the overall character of occupation in a particular area, particularly because we know from other parts of the empire that housing in Roman cities was not usually arranged into social 'zones'. For many administrative cities, then, it is difficult to draw meaningful comparisons between domestic occupation in the urban centre and in the periphery. Lyon, however, offers an unusual wealth of data from both areas (figure 4.15). Its housing may not, it is true, be typical of other administrative cities in Gaul, given its status as a provincial and religious capital, but it can provide a model for testing against other cities, in order to see whether the same patterns may plausibly apply elsewhere.

Domestic occupation in the centre of Lyon is known from two major excavated sites: the Rue des Farges[190] to the south of the theatre and odeon, and the Clos du Verbe Incarné,[191] alongside the municipal sanctuary of the imperial cult. Both reveal very mixed occupation. By the mid-first century AD, the Rue des Farges site had developed a set of monumental baths, a number of small storehouses and several shops, as well as a variety of houses. The largest house was the 'Maison aux Masques'. Built by around AD 40, this extended over 700–1000m^2, and consisted of about fifteen rooms, grouped around a peristyled garden containing a pool fed by running water.[192] Opposite this, and contemporary with it, were two houses known collectively as the 'Maison au Char'.[193] Each was around 120m^2, with one house consisting of three independent rooms facing on to a portico, and the other of a group of six rooms. By the same period, the sanctuary of the imperial cult had been constructed at the Clos du Verbe Incarné, and was surrounded by largely residential *insulae* lined with shops. South of the sanctuary were at least two large houses, parts of which were excavated and planned in the early twentieth century. To the east of the sanctuary, however, were a number of smaller houses occupying plots from 100m^2 to 500m^2, many with simple courtyards. In both of these areas, then, the quality of occupation varied considerably. Clearly, people of very different means were living in close proximity to one another: as well as alongside public buildings and commercial outlets, some of which probably served as dwelling-places in themselves.

Lyon's urban periphery has yielded extensive evidence for domestic occupation. Antiquarian finds of mosaics, hypocausts or other remains have been recorded in all of the occupied areas outside the urban centre.[194] More recently, excavations have revealed fuller house plans. At les Hauts Saint-Just, near the

HIGH EMPIRE: ADMINISTRATIVE CITIES

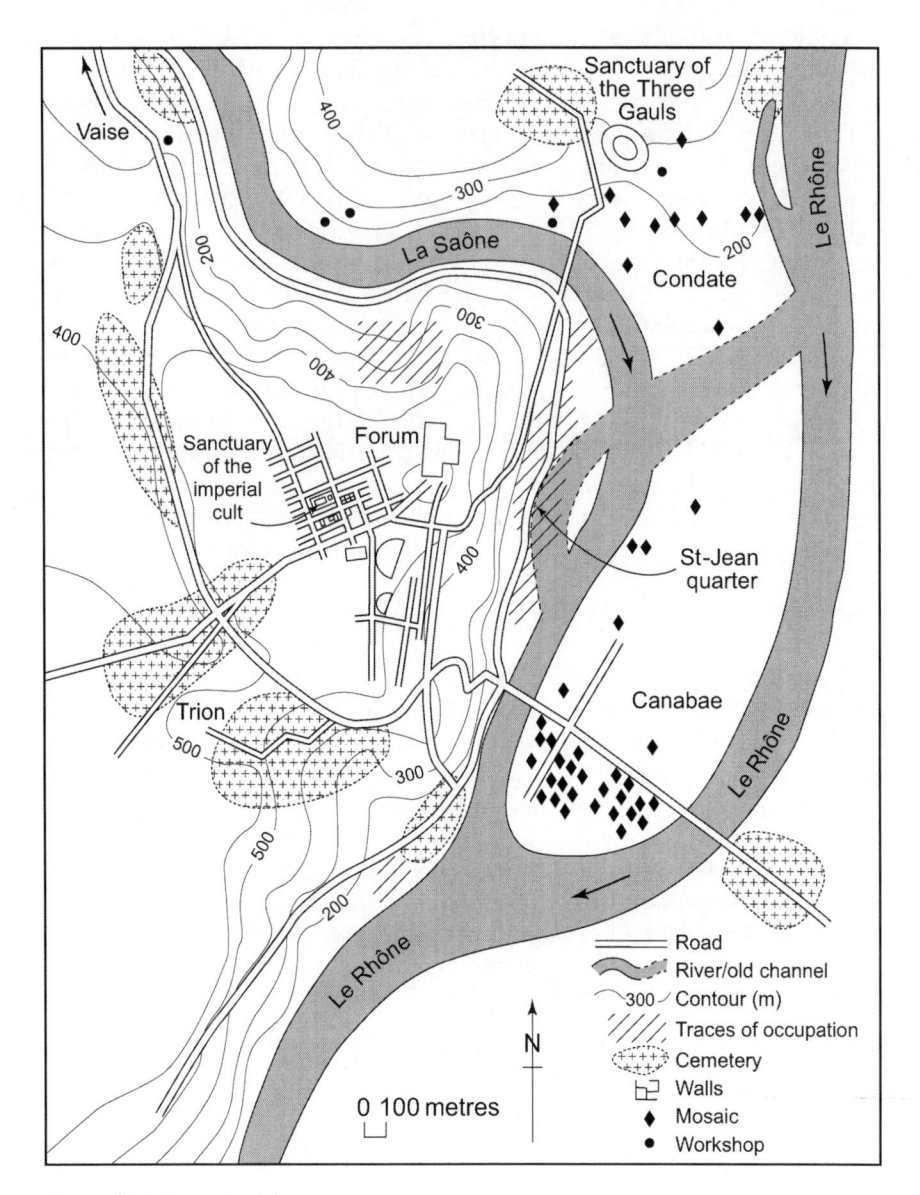

Figure 4.15 Lyon (Lugdunum).

cemetery area at Trion, residential occupation began in the Augustan period, making it contemporary with the earliest houses observed at the Rue des Farges and Clos du Verbe Incarné.[195] The earliest domestic structure observed here had its own small bath-suite and a probable atrium. By the mid-first century, another house had been built a little to the west, at the other end of a portico. It consisted of rooms grouped around two sides of a court, with no evidence for baths or an atrium. Yet it was comparable in size to the eastern house, and, at 550m^2, larger than many of the Clos du Verbe Incarné houses. Both houses, then, must have belonged to people of fair means, but they were nevertheless built in the urban periphery at a time when the urban centre at Lyon was still being developed. We must assume that space was still available for their owners to have lived in the urban centre, but that they chose not to do so. Meanwhile, the portico between the two houses was converted in the Flavian period into a series of small rooms, some with hearths. This new building was clearly residential, and has been interpreted as an inn.[196] Along with the two houses, it then remained in use until the end of the second century, constituting another example of well-appointed houses existing alongside humbler residential/commercial land-use.

On the right bank of the Rhône just where it was joined by the Saône, parts of at least four houses were uncovered at the Clos de la Solitude site in the 1960s.[197] The best known was a masonry structure with rich wall-paintings and a large monumental nymphaeum comparable with those of Pompeii.[198] Apparently, then, its owner was interested in adopting symbols of status from Roman culture, and was wealthy enough to afford them. Meanwhile, at Vaise, a single house known as the Maison aux Xenia was built in the Tiberian period,[199] so is again roughly contemporary with those on the Rue des Farges and Clos du Verbe Incarné sites. Unlike the other housing discussed so far, the Maison aux Xenia appears to have been relatively isolated. It does not seem to have been adjoined by other houses or set into an *insula*, but was reached by a single road which ran directly to its front entrance. Both its layout and an absence of evidence for agricultural activity, however, suggest that it should be interpreted as an urban *domus*, not a villa.

In fact, the layout of the Maison aux Xenia – ten rooms arranged around two sides of a peristyled courtyard – was markedly similar to that of the Maison aux Masques in the urban centre. The similarity extended also to décor and construction techniques: both featured wall-paintings, concrete and beaten-earth floors, and wood and sun-dried brick walls on masonry foundations.[200] Furthermore, the courtyard of the Maison aux Xenia contained a garden, which by the Claudian period had been equipped with a fountain fed by running water, probably drawn from nearby springs.[201] Only one of Lyon's four aqueducts entered the urban centre at a point high enough to supply all areas of the Fourvière plateau: the aqueduct of Gier, now thought to have been built in the Claudian period itself.[202] Thus, the Maison aux Xenia may have had its own water supply before many of the central houses at Lyon: though not before the Maison aux Masques itself. Certainly, the houses at the Clos du Verbe Incarné are not known to have had private supplies by this time.[203] This need not mean that the owner of the Maison aux Xenia was *more* wealthy than the inhabitants of the Clos du Verbe Incarné. But it does point towards different opportunities available to home-owners in the urban centre and urban periphery at Lyon. The possibility of installing a private water supply may have been an extra attraction of the Maison aux Xenia site.

Clearly, then, wealthy individuals were living in the urban periphery at Lyon. In some cases, specific factors like the availability of water may have influenced their decisions to do so. But we should also look for more universal issues. An absence of space in the centre of the city is not sufficient explanation, since houses appeared in Lyon's periphery when parts of its centre were still only just becoming built up. Competition for space, though, probably *was* an issue. Land price differentials, raised earlier in the context of workshop distribution, almost certainly meant that a house-builder could acquire more periurban than central land for his money. At 630m^2, the Maison aux Xenia was larger than many houses on the Rue des Farges or Clos du Verbe Incarné sites, perhaps because its owner could afford to build a larger house in this setting. Meanwhile, although living outside the urban centre, he was still close enough to participate fully in city living. We should remember here that the authors of Urso charter were happy to allow the city's decurions, augurs and pontiffs to live outside the urban centre, so long as they remained within a thousand paces of it.[204]

The modern mind, accustomed to the idea of the 'leafy suburb', might also imagine that living outside the urban centre offered an escape from the noise and smell of its other inhabitants. The evidence of Lyon, though, does not support this interpretation. The Maison aux Xenia does seem to have been relatively isolated, but the establishment of artisanal constructions to the south of the house around AD 25, and of a bronze or copper-making workshop against its south-west corner in the Claudian period do not suggest that the owner was making any particular effort to keep such activities away from his house.[205] In fact, the metal workshop was probably built in connection with a new room added to the same corner of the house at this time,[206] so the house owner may well have initiated its construction. Similarly, the occupants of the two houses at les Hauts Saint-Just do not seem to have been troubled by the establishment of an inn between their properties.

Well-appointed houses from the peripheries of other Gallo-Roman cities suggest that similar factors did apply elsewhere. Large periurban *domus* are known at Apt (Apta),[207] Arles,[208] Bordeaux,[209] Orange,[210] Saintes,[211] and Vienne.[212] In each case, they seem to have existed alongside other types of occupation, just as in an urban centre. Certainly, the elite houses of Trinquetaille at Arles and Saint-Romain-en-Gal at Vienne existed side by side with public, commercial and industrial buildings.[213] It is less easy to say from the available evidence whether humbler individuals also lived in the same quarters, but it is unlikely that the dock-workers, potters, shop-keepers or warehouse staff who worked in Trinquetaille or Saint-Romain-en-Gal would have lived far away.

At other Gallo-Roman cities, more extensive evidence for non-elite housing in the urban periphery is known. Often, small or poor-quality houses are found in conjunction with evidence for commercial or industrial activity. This applies to the potters' quarter at Sens, and the domestic structures found at Saint-Michel-du-Touch outside Toulouse. Here, the housing can be regarded as an accessory to industry or commerce, meaning that the factors influencing these activities are enough to explain its location in the urban periphery. Two concentrations of poor-quality periurban housing at Amiens and Metz, however, are not so easily explained. In the areas of Saint-Maurice across the Somme from Amiens,[214] and Pontiffroy across the Moselle from Metz,[215] distinct periurban agglomerations developed during the first century AD (figure 4.16). At Saint-Maurice, the remains consist of cellars cut into the natural chalk, together with wells and rubbish-pits. The elevations of the houses do not survive, and were probably of perishable materials. At Pontiffroy, most of the observed features were again subterranean masonry cellars. Here, however, at least one house was built with a stone elevation at the turn of the second century, and boasted features such as wall-paintings and a hypocaust by the third,[216] while there is also some evidence for a public building in the area.[217]

Caution must be exercised in interpreting these sites, since both were revealed through a combination of chance discoveries and rescue excavations. But, at least in the early period of their development, they do appear to have consisted almost exclusively of simple domestic occupation, without related commercial or industrial activity.[218] We may thus ask why people of such apparently small means were choosing to live in the periphery of a Gallo-Roman city. Price differentials can readily explain their location outside the urban centre. But they do not tell us what positive attractions the urban periphery may have held for them, particularly in terms of employment. One possibility is that they were cultivating land in the urban periphery: an activity which Garnsey argues must have been common outside urban centres in Italy.[219] But nothing from either site confirms this, and the hypothesis does not adequately explain the locations of both areas close to bridges carrying major roads into the urban centre. If the inhabitants of these houses were principally engaged in agriculture, it seems strange that they should have been so interested in access into the urban centre.

Another possibility is that these quarters housed free unskilled workers who were attracted to the city by the availability of manual labour. Both Brunt and Treggiari have argued that, despite the prominence of slave labour in Rome, free labourers were employed there in large numbers on construction sites, on docks and in warehouses, shops and small businesses.[220] Amiens and Metz may not have been able to match the imperial capital for the scale or frequency of building projects, or the volume of trade. But both were on major rivers, so employment probably was available in loading and unloading cargoes and staffing warehouses and shops. They were also equipped with public bath-houses, roads, sewers and aqueducts, all of which

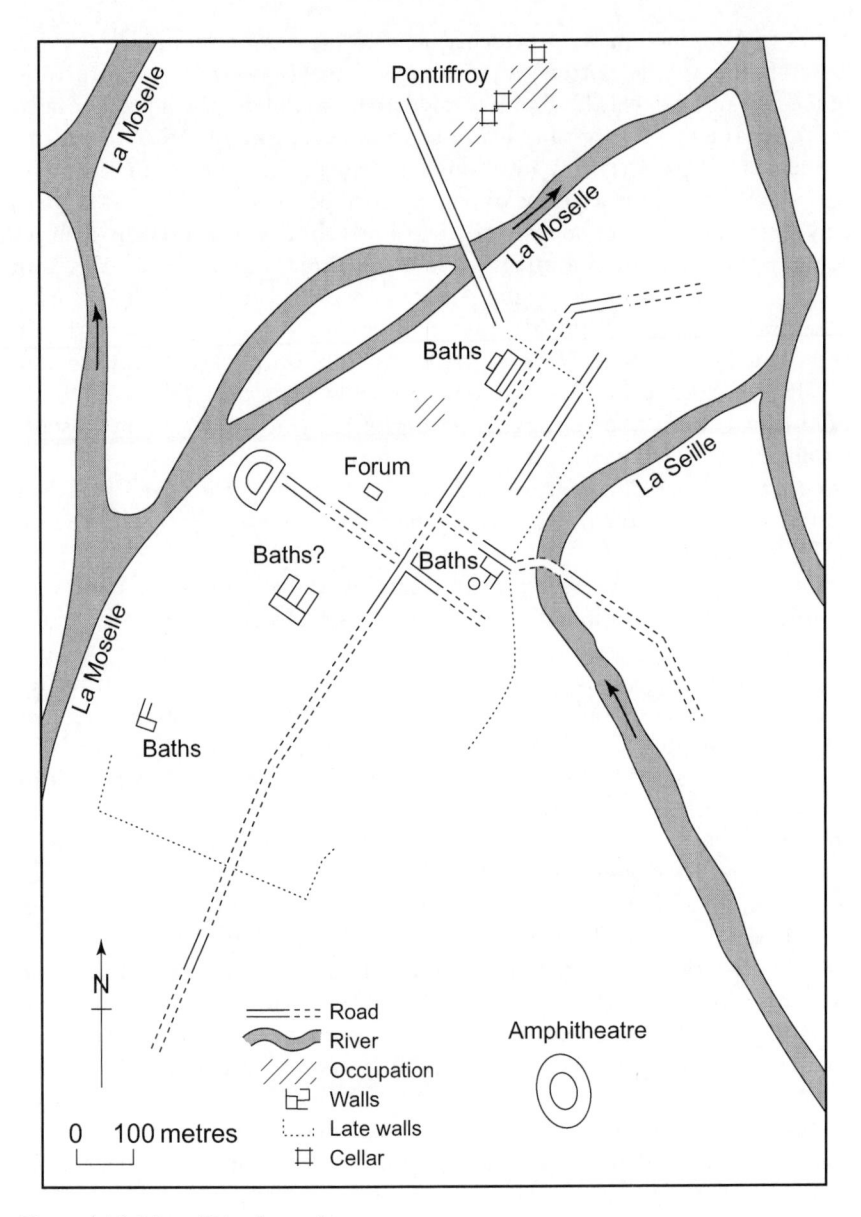

Figure 4.16 Metz (Divodurum).

needed building in the first place, and then staffing and maintaining. Meanwhile, Whittaker has argued that, in the Gallo-Roman countryside at least, slave labour was not very widespread, and the majority of the workforce was made up of dependent peasants.[221] This may not have applied to the same extent in cities, but if slave ownership was in general less widespread in Gaul than in Rome, then greater opportunities for manual labour may in fact have existed in Gallo-Roman administrative cities. Furthermore, dating evidence from Pontiffroy indicates that the occupation here was more than usually sensitive to interruption. No less than three periods of temporary abandonment are attested on the site during the Roman period: during the late first century AD, the late second to early third century and again in the late third.[222] Though interpreted by Schlemaire with reference to political disturbances, these could equally well represent periods of local economic decline, when a reduction in casual employment in the urban centre caused the unskilled labourers at Pontiffroy to seek opportunities elsewhere.

Baths

Bathing establishments were common features in Gallo-Roman cities, and could be found at any point within the urban centre. They also occur at smaller agglomerations, or in association with rural sanctuaries.[223] This association sometimes arose from a healing role played by the baths, but it could also reflect their use in cleansing before religious activities.[224] Baths at rural sanctuaries were architecturally similar to urban baths, but could have special features, such as a water supply drawn directly from natural springs. In Gaul, periurban baths are known at eight different cities (see table 4.4, p. 165). This certainly shows that baths could be located in the urban periphery, but the urban centre does seem to have been preferred. We need to look for positive reasons for going against this preference when they occur in the periphery.

The process may be aided by dividing up the baths according to their size and the apparent lavishness of their construction. Two broad architectural 'registers' can be identified by doing this: simple, functional buildings, and larger monumental buildings. Baths at opposite extremes of these two groups looked very different from one another, and were probably built for different reasons. The monumental buildings are more likely to have been public benefactions, intended to enhance the status of their donors and express the sophisticated nature of the community. The smaller, simpler buildings are more likely to have been privately owned business ventures.[225] The constructors of each type of establishment will have weighed up different considerations when deciding where to build them. It should thus be easier to understand why the urban periphery was chosen by considering the two groups separately.

Baths from the simple, functional end of the scale are known at four periurban sites in Gaul: the rue des Frères-Bonie at Bordeaux,[226] the Saint-Jean quarter at Lyon,[227] L'Esplanade at Arles[228] and the North baths at Saint-Romain-en-Gal opposite Vienne.[229] All covered areas of 1500m^2 or less, and were laid out asymmetrically. But the details of their plans and construction strongly suggest that they were open to the paying public. Except for those at Lyon, all are known to have had a full set of *tepidarium, caldarium* and *frigidarium*. The North baths at Saint-Romain had a set of latrines and an entrance opening directly on to a main road, while the Frères-Bonie baths at Bordeaux had a *piscina* and probably also latrines. They could offer all the facilities required for bathing in the traditional Roman style, then, on a scale somewhat surpassing that usually found in a private house. Only the third-century baths at Lyon are debatable, since their remains were badly disturbed by later constructions. But a larger bath complex built on the same site after a fire in the early fourth century was almost certainly public. Probably, then, the earlier establishment was too.

These sets of baths were all built in areas which already featured some residential occupation, and in some cases were expanding rapidly. The Frères-Bonie baths were part of a wave of expansion to the south of Bordeaux's urban centre in the early imperial period, and were surrounded by houses which both pre- and post-date them.[230] Similarly, occupation had already appeared in Lyon's Saint-Jean quarter at least a generation before the baths.[231] The Esplanade baths at Arles followed relatively later, appearing around AD 190 in an area which had been occupied since the start of the first century AD (figure 4.9, p. 100). Here, the neighbourhood had recently suffered a serious fire, and the new baths were part of its redevelopment.[232] Finally, the North baths at Vienne, built around AD 160, were fitted into a plot of land within the already-thriving quarter of Saint-Romain-en-Gal, probably replacing earlier structures.

The residential context is unlikely to have been a coincidence. It has already been suggested that these baths were profit-making establishments. They were really commercial buildings, then, and the main reasons for their construction in the urban periphery will have been economic. Almost certainly, the intention was to make money by providing baths which were more directly accessible to local residents than those of the urban centre. At Bordeaux and Lyon, entrepreneurs seem to have gambled – apparently successfully – on continued expansion in areas which were only just beginning to be occupied. Meanwhile, the constructors of the baths at Arles and Vienne took the safer course of opening up their businesses when plots of land became available in established residential areas.

More lavish periurban baths from Gaul include three, or perhaps four, sets from the plain opposite Vienne,[233] three at Saint-Michel-du-Touch near Toulouse,[234] one at Chamiers near Périgueux (Vesunna),[235] the Villeneuve baths at Fréjus[236] and baths associated with the sanctuary of the imperial cult at Narbonne.[237] The baths at Narbonne will be passed over for the moment, and discussed along with the provincial sanctuary in the context of religious buildings. Meanwhile, the baths at Périgueux and Fréjus are known only through antiquarian observations, coupled with partial excavation in the 1920s at Fréjus. Details of their structure, dating and local context are therefore scanty. The discussion here, then, will focus on the baths at Vienne and Toulouse. With the exception of the baths of the Palais du Miroir, excavated and planned in the early twentieth century, these have all been the subject of recent excavations.

These baths differ markedly from those discussed above in size, layout, décor and facilities. With the exception of the Central and North baths at Saint-Michel, included here because of their obvious relationship with the larger South baths, all extended over 3000m^2 or more. At Vienne, the Thermes des Lutteurs also had a more or less symmetrical layout, at least in so far as the irregular plot which they occupied would allow. Other monumentalising features in these baths include two symmetrical *caldaria* with curved apses in the Villeneuve baths at Fréjus and a semi-circular portico in the Palais du Miroir at Vienne. The latrines of the Thermes des Lutteurs displayed high-quality wall-paintings of boxers fighting, while the South baths at Saint-Michel-du-Touch, the Place de l'Égalité baths at Vienne and the baths at Chamiers had mosaic floors. All of the baths at Saint-Michel-du-Touch and in Vienne's Saint-Romain-en-Gal quarter are also known to have been supplied by aqueducts.[238] Of the simpler baths described above, only the North baths at Saint-Romain are known to have had this advantage: and then only because an established supply of water was already serving the area.

At Vienne, the Thermes des Lutteurs and the baths of the Palais du Miroir were set into the monumental enclosure built at Saint-Romain-en-Gal in the mid-first century AD.[239] The Thermes des Lutteurs, built around AD 65, faced into the centre of the complex through a monumental hemicycle on its edge.[240] The baths of the Palais du Miroir sat within the enclosure, and, although less well dated, almost certainly post-date its construction.[241] We have already seen that the enclosure itself was probably built to enhance the appearance of Saint-Romain-en-Gal, perhaps in direct emulation of Rome's Campus Martius. The construction of the baths could only have added to its impact, as well as providing attractive and sophisticated bathing facilities for the wealthy residents of nearby *domus*. They may even have drawn visitors into the quarter from the urban centre across the river.

Meanwhile, the three sets of baths at Saint-Michel-du-Touch seem to have been built largely for religious reasons. They were established on a site which apparently had a strong sacred identity, probably connected with the nearby confluence of the Touch and Garonne. Certainly, it included a temple at the confluence, and a monumental fountain built around a natural spring (figure 4.6, p. 95).[242] Thus, the earliest baths on the site – the South baths, built in the mid-first century AD – were probably erected to serve the needs of pilgrims to the site.[243] The smaller Central and North baths, built a generation later, were then doubtless added to extend capacity. Objects found in the Central baths suggest that these were used mainly by women, pointing towards greater specialisation.[244] The baths at Chamiers, outside Périgueux, may have served a similar purpose. Long thought to belong to a private villa, they have now been reinterpreted as part of a periurban satellite settlement much like Saint-Michel-du-Touch.[245] It, too, featured a probable sanctuary, and was linked to the urban centre 2 km away physically by a bridge over the Isle, and topographically by the use of a very similar orientation. Finally, a set of baths at the Place de l'Égalité, opposite Vienne, were equipped with a series of small pairs of hot and cold rooms, which Bouet has suggested may point towards curative use.[246]

Two major reasons for building larger sets of baths have emerged, then. Those set into the monumental enclosure at Saint-Romain-en-Gal were probably the product of the same factors which applied in an urban centre: a desire to express and enhance the status of the area, and to increase the standing of the benefactor. But the nearby more functional North baths demonstrate that this did not need to apply to all of the baths in one quarter. Meanwhile, the baths at Saint-Michel-du-Touch, Chamiers and perhaps also the Place de l'Égalité, Vienne, are better viewed in a religious light. The position of the first two in periurban satellite agglomerations also illustrates a very different principle of location. All of the other baths discussed here were located within the *continentia aedificia* where many people would see or pass by them, and this is entirely in keeping with their profit or display function. The baths at Saint-Michel-du-Touch and Chamiers, though, were clearly located in response to the nearby sanctuaries. They were part of what visitors to these sanctuaries travelled for, and did not need to attract 'passing trade'.

Temples

Temples occur in the peripheries of over twenty Gallo-Roman cities, in all four of the Gallic provinces (see table 4.4, p. 165). The buildings concerned fall into two main types: classical temples in the Mediterranean architectural tradition, and Romano-Celtic temples, a local variant.[247] The principal difference between the two lay in the shape of the central space, or cella (figure 4.3, p. 88). The classical temple usually had a rectangular cella, while that of a Romano-Celtic temple could vary. It was often square, but could also be circular or octagonal. In place of the *pronaos* ('porch') which normally fronted a classical temple, a Romano-Celtic temple was also usually surrounded by a low porticoed gallery, and often enclosed within a walled precinct, which could again vary in shape but was usually square or rectangular.[248] These features echo the indigenous sanctuaries of the pre-Roman period, of which the Romano-Celtic temple seems essentially to have been a translation into stone.[249] An examination of the usual context for each type of temple shows that the vast majority of classical temples were built at administrative cities (here taken to include both centre and periphery). By contrast, almost all of the 650 known Romano-Celtic temples were erected in the countryside or in smaller settlements.[250] A small number of examples of each are known outside of these typical contexts,[251] but in general terms the division between classical temples in the cities and Romano-Celtic temples beyond is clear: except, of course, in Narbonensis where the Romano-Celtic type was not used. When each type appears in the urban periphery, then, it is likely to be for different reasons, since variation from a different norm is involved. For this reason they will be treated separately here.

Classical temples in the urban centre most often stood in or close to the forum.[252] Yet the conventions were clearly flexible. At Toulouse, for example, the 'Temple de St-Etienne' was located on the *decumanus maximus* close to a major city gate, probably in order to ensure the maximum impact on travellers passing through it.[253] We might expect to find that this flexibility extended to the construction of classical temples in the urban periphery, just as it did for baths, but only three or four examples of periurban classical temples are known. Clearly there was a very strong preference in this case for building such temples within the urban centre, and special circumstances must have applied when it was disregarded.

The exploration of those circumstances is hampered by the state of the evidence. Judging from their plans, temples in the peripheries of Toulouse, at Saint-Michel-du-Touch, and Trier, at Herrenbrünnchen, were almost certainly of classical type. But we lack reliable evidence for the dates of their construction or the deities worshipped in them.[254] It is not even possible to say whether the Herrenbrünnchen temple predates the construction of the walls at Trier, since both are dated simply to the second century. If it did, it should certainly be considered periurban, since it stood at some distance from the city's orthogonal grid, on a different alignment. But the ambiguity means that it is of little help here. The temple at Saint-Michel-du-Touch is more fruitful, since the agglomeration here is fairly well documented (figure 4.6, p. 95). We can therefore understand it in context, and perhaps the most important aspect of that context was the nearby classical amphitheatre. Although such amphitheatres were regularly built in the urban periphery, this one is unusually far from an urban centre. The occurrence of the two classical-type buildings together indicates a site with a unique character: probably generated by a water-cult associated with the nearby confluence and spring. Thus, this temple *can* be seen as an exceptional monument.

The provincial sanctuaries of the imperial cult at Lyon and Narbonne provide much richer grounds for comment.[255] These were extensive complexes, which acted as a focus for religious rites performed on behalf of all the Gallic communities, and belonged to a series of similar sanctuaries established in most western provinces during the early imperial period.[256] At each one, a provincial *concilium* (council), made up of representatives sent by the individual communities of the province, gathered annually. At Lyon, this included all the communities of the Three Gauls, while at Narbonne it meant the communities of Narbonensis. The councils were primarily religious bodies, charged with the celebration of rites at the provincial sanctuaries. But they also had an administrative and political function, which included electing officials, liaising with imperial representatives and sending embassies to Rome. In the Three Gauls at least, the post of high priest of the council appears to have been viewed as the peak of a political career.[257] The religious observances of the councils demonstrated collective loyalty to Rome and the imperial house, while their membership could provide the imperial administration with a useful insight into provincial interests and opinions. Fishwick has also suggested that they may have helped to create a sense of shared identity between the various communities of a province.[258]

At Lyon, the provincial sanctuary site centred round an altar, described by Strabo and depicted on coins, and probably established by Drusus in 12 BC.[259] An amphitheatre, of classical type, was added by a citizen of Saintes in the Tiberian period (see plate 4.4),[260] while a temple may have been built during the reign of Hadrian.[261] The amphitheatre is the only element in the complex to have been identified and excavated,[262] but the altar must have lain nearby. The connection between amphitheatre and sanctuary is clear from seat inscriptions marking places for cult officials and council representatives,[263] while its location at Condate accords with Strabo's description of the sanctuary as being 'in front of the city at the junction of the rivers' (figure 4.15, p. 120). Audin suggested that the sanctuary itself was located on a wide esplanade, built into the hill-side to the east of the amphitheatre.[264] Here,

Plate 4.4 Amphitheatre associated with the sanctuary of the Three Gauls, Condate, Lyon.

then, we do not have actual archaeological remains of a classical temple. But the complex as a whole was all about demonstrating connections with imperial Rome. If a temple *was* added in the Hadrianic era, no other form would have been appropriate.

At Narbonne, the location of the sanctuary is attested above all by the discovery of a bronze inscription in the *piscina* of some monumental baths on the eastern perimeter of the city in 1887.[265] This inscription, the *lex de flamonio provinciae Narbonensis*, refers to a provincial temple of the imperial cult based at Narbonne, and sets out the rights and duties of its high priest.[266] Another inscription attesting the restoration of some baths by Antoninus Pius after a fire has been associated with the same site.[267] Both have led the baths to be interpreted as part of the provincial sanctuary of the imperial cult. Meanwhile, earlier excavations in the same area in 1838 had uncovered a large portico, believed to have surrounded a temple, and part of an amphitheatre.[268] In the light of the inscriptions, these, too, are considered to have been part of the provincial sanctuary. Again, actual temple remains are lacking, but this time we know that one existed, and it must have been of classical type. The precise spatial relationship between the complex and the urban centre is difficult to gauge, since the boundaries of Narbonne, and especially the extent of its orthogonal grid, are not well known. However, during the early first century, a number of rich houses were built around the perimeter of the city, and represent the greatest known extent of its growth.[269] The sanctuary, established in the Vespasianic period,[270] lies beyond them, suggesting that it was built on the very edge of the city (figure 4.17).

Both sanctuaries, then, can be regarded as periurban, and we should view this situation in the light of their special role in the celebration of the imperial cult at a province-wide level: not least because it is typical for sanctuaries of the same type in other western provinces.[271] At Lyon, it is virtually certain that the cult altar was established by Augustus' step-son, Drusus, and therefore likely that he or his representatives influenced the choice of site. No such evidence is available for Narbonne, but if the baths restored by Antoninus Pius were indeed connected with this sanctuary, then there does seem to have been a degree of imperial involvement. In both cases, then, it is valid to consider the locations of the sanctuaries from the perspective of the imperial administration, and to assume that they were guided by a concern to maximise their effectiveness in fostering loyalty towards Rome and cultural cohesion within Gaul.

One factor which may have helped to achieve these goals was the relationship between the sanctuaries and the nearby urban centres. At Lyon, the sanctuary of the Three Gauls was intervisible with the city's forum, which lay in approximately the same position as the modern Basilique Notre Dame, visible on the Fourvière plateau in plate 4.5. At Narbonne, the provincial sanctuary lay on one of the major roads into the city, which ran directly to its

HIGH EMPIRE: ADMINISTRATIVE CITIES

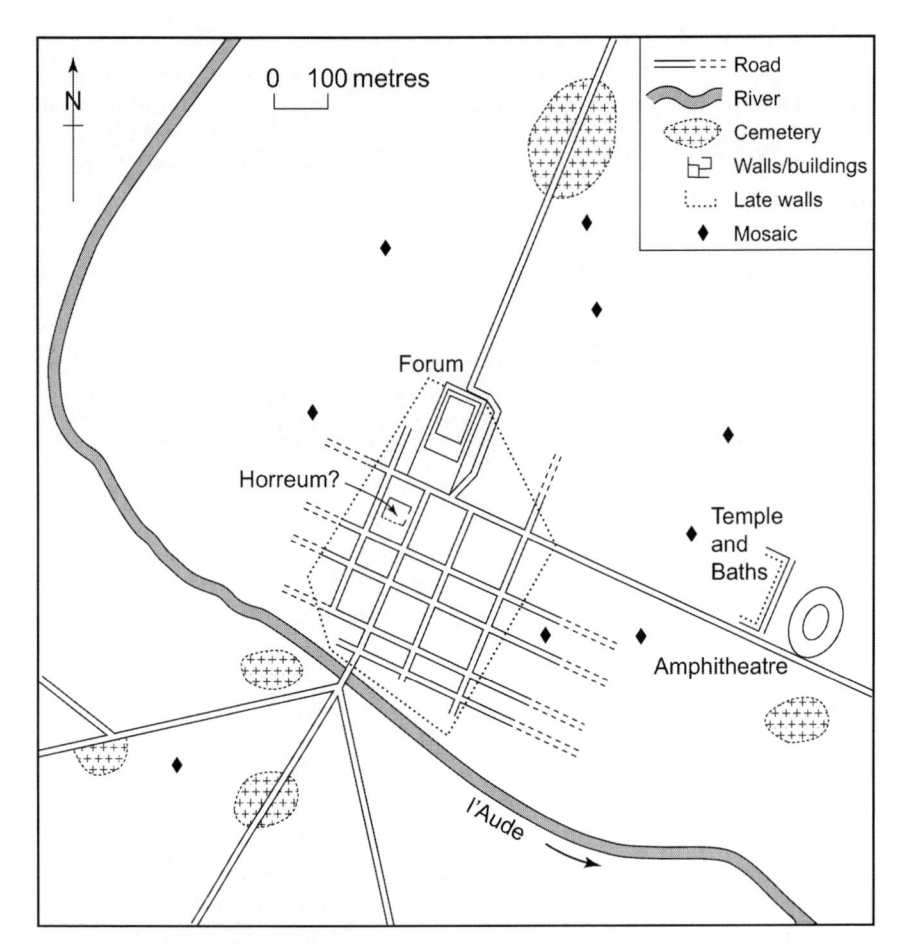

Figure 4.17 Narbonne (Narbo Martius).

forum. These positions certainly suit the role of both sanctuaries in province-wide worship, since they were linked with the administrative hearts of the relevant provincial capitals. Yet, if this had been of primary importance, we might expect them to have been located within the actual centres of these cities. Instead, they were not. Perhaps this was partly for reasons of space. The sanctuaries certainly developed into large complexes, and if they were conceived of as such from the start, then their planners will have wanted to be sure that they had room to expand. At Narbonne, this is very plausible, since the sanctuary here was established at a time when the urban centre was already densely occupied. But its equivalent at Lyon was founded in the Augustan era, when the city was only three decades old. The urban centre was far from full at this time, and room could surely have been set aside for such an important monument if this had been considered desirable.

Plate 4.5 View from the amphitheatre at the sanctuary of the Three Gauls towards the urban centre on the Fourvière plateau, Lyon.

Another factor behind the choice of a periurban location may have been a concern to differentiate between the worship of the emperor on a province-wide scale, and worship mounted by the communities of Lyon and Narbonne on their own account. Both communities clearly did celebrate the imperial cult on a local level, and, importantly, they did so in the urban centre. The people of Narbonne established an altar to the *numen* of Augustus in their forum in AD 12,[272] while Lyon developed a municipal sanctuary of the imperial cult at the Clos du Verbe Incarné site early in the reign of Tiberius.[273] Notably, this *was* a large structure, supporting the theory that a central site could indeed have been found for the provincial sanctuary a few decades earlier. By contrast, the periurban locations of the two provincial sanctuaries may have been intended to demonstrate that they operated in a wider world, and belonged not to Lyon or Narbonne themselves, but to the people of Gaul as a whole. Financially their affairs do appear to have been kept strictly separate, with the Lugdunese council certainly and the Narbonese one probably administering their own treasuries, distinct from those of the nearby *coloniae*.[274] Spatially, the urban periphery could offer a compromise between an appropriate connection with the provincial capitals, and a dissociation from the communities of Lyon and Narbonne themselves.

At least seventeen single Romano-Celtic temples or groups of these temples are known from the peripheries of administrative cities in the Three

Gauls. This type of temple, then, was more common in a periurban context than a classical one, at least outside Narbonensis. But it was still most often found in the countryside. The locations of Romano-Celtic temples have been studied in detail by Fauduet,[275] and a summary of her findings will help to indicate whether Romano-Celtic temples in the urban periphery were influenced by similar factors to those elsewhere. Fauduet found that Romano-Celtic temples could be located anywhere within a community's rural territory, including in association with a settlement or group of buildings, in complete isolation, or close to the boundary with a neighbouring *civitas*. They were rarely built near major roads, but were often located on slopes, hill-tops or raised ground, and near rivers, lakes, or springs. At least eighty examples are also known to be situated directly over pre-Roman cult sites.

In the urban periphery, similar principles seem to have applied. The sanctuaries of the Altbachtal complex at Trier[276] and le Haut-Bécherel at Corseul (Fanum Martis)[277] were located close to rivers or streams, while those of Icovellauna at Metz[278] and Vieux-Lisieux opposite Lisieux[279] both featured springs. The group of temples at la Genetoye opposite Autun[280] and the sanctuary of the 'Motte-du-Ciar' at Sens[281] were located at confluences: also key features in the Gallo-Roman sacred landscape. Others were located on hill-sides or hill-tops; for example, the temple of Lenus Mars at Trier,[282] the sanctuary at the north end of Jublains (Noviodunum),[283] the temple of la Bauve at Meaux,[284] and, again, those at Corseul and Vieux-Lisieux (figure 4.8, p. 99). Finally, the temples at Jublains and Meaux, as well as examples on the northern edge of Saintes,[285] the western edge of Poitiers[286] and a hill overlooking Bayeux (Augustodurum),[287] all appear to have been built over pre-Roman cult sites.

At a micro level, then, Romano-Celtic temples appear to have been attracted to the same sorts of sites whether they were built in the urban periphery or the countryside. The question is, why were they built in the urban periphery at all? Central to answering this will be understanding why they were so rarely built in the urban centre. The relationship between these temples and their pre-Roman forerunners tempts the suggestion that they represent the persistence of 'indigenous' religious beliefs,[288] and that these were deliberately excluded from the urban centre. But this view is difficult to sustain. For one thing, although Romano-Celtic temples may have looked much like their pre-Roman equivalents, they were clearly used in a different way. Practices such as the display of human heads, mixtures of human and animal sacrifices and offerings of weapons were left behind in the pre-Roman era.[289] More modern interpretations stress instead the creation of a new, Gallo-Roman religion, visible to us in very self-aware syncretisms of names and iconography.[290] Nor should the tendency for these temples to be located near water or on hill-tops be interpreted as a sign of 'un-Roman' religious beliefs. Such situations attracted sanctuaries in Italy, too.[291]

There is no reason, then, to believe that Romano-Celtic temples were kept out of the urban centre because the practices associated with them were not

'Roman'. Another possibility is that the deities who inhabited these temples were considered best worshipped in the urban periphery, and that this, rather than the form of the temple itself, was the primary issue at stake. Such principles certainly applied at Rome, and are prominent in Vitruvius' advice about how to situate public buildings.[292] But two issues make it difficult to pursue this question. First, the localised nature of Gallo-Roman deities means that we rarely have a very developed understanding of what they represented to their worshippers. Was the Treveran god, Lenus Mars,[293] for instance, similar enough to the Roman Mars to mean that his temple was situated in Trier's urban periphery (figure 4.14, p. 116) out of a Vitruvian concern for keeping dissension out of the urban centre, or because of other beliefs about him which escape us? Second, and more fundamentally, the identities of the deities concerned are too infrequently attested to allow any systematic comparison between urban, periurban and rural cults. We can only acknowledge the likelihood that such factors were at work, and concentrate instead on what we *can* see: the architectural form of the temples.

A helpful approach might be to see the micro-locational principles which governed the positions of temples in the urban centre, the urban periphery and the countryside as part of a unified set of conventions, rather than assuming that one set of rules applied to temples of classical type, and another to those of Romano-Celtic type. In other words, we could say that *any* temple built in the urban centre was likely to be located near the forum or on main roads, while any temple built outside its boundaries was likely to be on a hill-top, near water, etc. It is simply that the temples in the urban centre were normally built in a classical form, and the ones outside it in Romano-Celtic form. Indeed, the few examples that we have of classical temples outside urban centres, or Romano-Celtic temples within them, support the principle. The periurban classical temples at Trier, Toulouse and Lyon, discussed above, *were* all situated on hill-sides, at confluences, or both,[294] while Romano-Celtic temples at Limoges (Augustoritum), Périgueux and Tours were located in the very centres of the cities: definitely next to the forum at Limoges and Périgueux, and almost certainly so at Tours.[295] This observation frees us from the need to believe that Romano-Celtic temples were part of a separate religious landscape from classical temples, which began at the edges of the urban centre. Instead, the issue becomes one of appropriate architectural language. The apparent division between classical temples in the urban centre and Romano-Celtic ones outside it may in fact have arisen primarily because, when the decision was taken to build a temple, a classical form was felt to be most appropriate in the monumental context of the urban centre, and a Romano-Celtic one elsewhere.

Another noticeable factor is the scale and decorative style of several of the periurban Romano-Celtic temples. Some, it is true, differed little from their rural counterparts. But a significant number were either unusually large, decorated in a classicising style, or both. In the first category belong examples such as the sanctuaries of Lenus Mars at Trier, of la Bauve at Meaux, of the Motte-du-Ciar at Sens (figure 4.11, p. 104), of le Haut-Bécherel at Corseul, on the north perimeter of Jublains and probably also at Chamiers near Périgueux.[296] Groups of temples, such as those at la Genetoye opposite Autun or the Altbachtal sanctuary at Trier, arguably need to be seen in the same light for their cumulative effect, especially since both include large 'dominant' temples, as well as theatres. Meanwhile, temples which were Romano-Celtic in plan, but decorated with pilasters, columns, capitals and cornices drawn from the classical orders include Lenus Mars at Trier, la Bauve at Meaux, the north sanctuary at Jublains and the temple building of Vieux-Lisieux near Lisieux.[297] Interestingly, much the same applied when such temples were built in the urban centre. The circular 'Tour de Vésone' at Périgueux was 21m in diameter, and occupied a sacred enclosure measuring approximately 120m by 140m. A similar temple at Tours had a diameter of 34.5m and a *pronaos* 18m wide on its east façade, in an arrangement not unlike Rome's later Pantheon.[298] We are dealing with temples of Romano-Celtic plan in both urban centre *and* urban periphery which achieved a monumentalised appearance through size, classical ornamentation, or both.

Perhaps, then, the most significant architectural division was not between classical and Romano-Celtic temples after all, but between self-consciously 'monumentalising' temples and their humbler counterparts.[299] Viewed from this perspective, both classical temples and monumentalised Romano-Celtic temples could be seen as part of a single architectural phenomenon: one which occurred in urban centres, urban peripheries, and also in secondary agglomerations such as Sanxay or Ribemont-sur-Ancre. If this is accurate, then the monumentalising Romano-Celtic temples of the urban periphery may be seen as part of the same imperative to embellish the city with splendid public monuments as the classical temples of the urban centre: just like the larger bath buildings discussed earlier in this chapter, or the amphitheatres and circuses to be encountered shortly. The precise reasons for their construction in the periphery *instead* of the centre still remain obscure, but factors such as the availability of space or religious reasons connected with the deities being worshipped are plausible enough in this context. Meanwhile, beyond the urban agglomeration, a monumentalising style – whether that meant 'pure' classicism or an aggrandisement of the Romano-Celtic temple – may simply have been considered unnecessary.

Temples of any kind may also have been built in the urban periphery as a means of linking the city and its population with a wider religious world. It has already been suggested that the provincial sanctuaries of the imperial cult at Lyon and Narbonne were situated in the urban periphery partly in order to signal their role in the religious life of whole provinces, rather than just individual communities. The positions of some Romano-Celtic temples in isolated spots a short distance from the urban centre may have helped them to achieve a similar effect. Examples include the temples of le Haut-Bécherel at Corseul, la Bauve at Meaux (figure 4.2, p. 87), and Saint-Vigor-le-Grand at Bayeux,[300] all approximately 1.5 km from their respective urban centres. That these temples should be seen as periurban, rather than rural, is made clear by a number of factors. The first two temples were close to at least one major road running into the urban centre: a situation which Fauduet noted was unusual for Romano-Celtic temples, and suggests a special concern for enabling travel between them. That at le Haut-Bécherel also lay on the same watercourse as Corseul. Finally, each temple stood on raised land, making it visible from the urban centre. All of these factors connected the temples with the cities. But their isolated positions will also have recalled other Romano-Celtic temples in more explicitly rural locations. Thus, they could be viewed, literally and metaphorically, as constituting an interface between the religious worlds of the city and of its territory.

Finally, where temples were built directly over pre-Roman religious sites, slightly different factors come into play. In these cases, the original choice of site was not made in the context of a thought-world which included periurban space, although the decision to perpetuate a cult there will have been. The case of the north sanctuary at Jublains illustrates the issues involved. Originating in the Iron Age, this sanctuary was rebuilt in Romano-Celtic form in the Neronian era, making it one of the first monumental public buildings constructed in the city.[301] Naveau has suggested that the pre-Roman sanctuary, already accompanied by occupation, was politically, as well as religiously, important.[302] Despite this, it was not included in the new Gallo-Roman urban centre (figure 4.18). Rather, the entire city of Jublains seems to have been planned to ensure that the sanctuary would fall in its northern periphery. Although very close to the orthogonal grid, the temple is marked out as periurban by several factors, including a 6° difference in orientation, changes in direction by the two roads which passed it, and burials along its western and southern perimeters.[303]

This planning strategy is likely to have been implemented by the leading citizens of the Aulerci Diablintes, whose *civitas*-capital Jublains was, under guidance from Roman surveyors. It is natural that this local elite should wish to associate their new city with a sanctuary which already held religious and political importance. Indeed, Bedon has suggested that such concerns may explain the locations of more Gallo-Roman *civitas*-capitals than is currently realised.[304] But they may also have wished to indicate that they recognised the greater sophistication and importance of a fully developed city over a single sanctuary site. If so, setting the temple in their new urban periphery represented the perfect compromise. It created an intimate link between the sanctuary and the new city, allowing each to enhance the status and importance of the other. Yet the sanctuary was not the focal point of Jublains. This role had been taken over by the forum, symbolising membership of a wider and more complex world.

HIGH EMPIRE: ADMINISTRATIVE CITIES

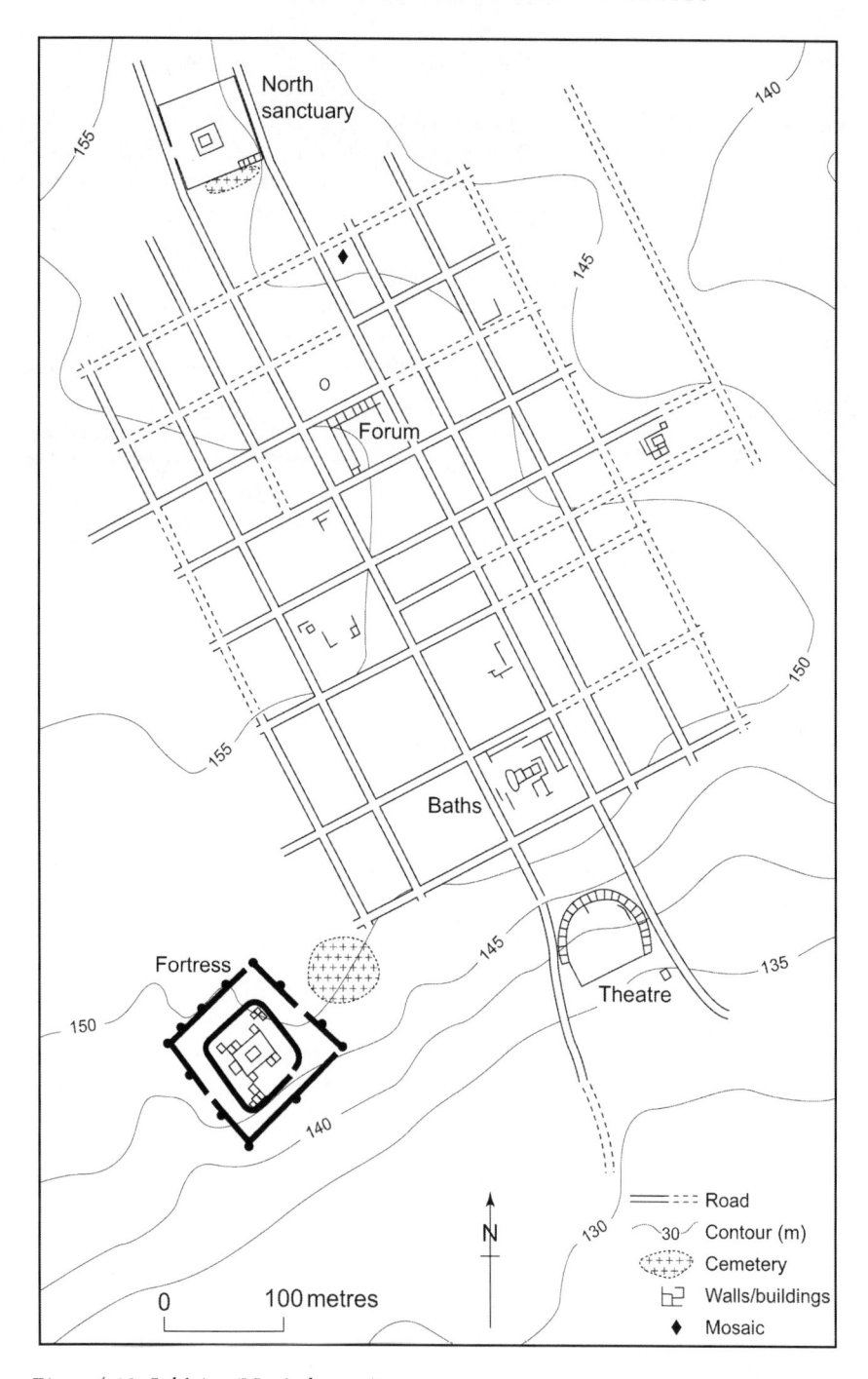

Figure 4.18 Jublains (Noviodunum).

Spectacle buildings

Theatres

As for temples, two types of theatre existed in Roman Gaul: the classical theatre, and the theatre of Gallic type.[305] Gallic theatres differed from classical theatres in having a *cavea* (seating area) which extended beyond the line of a true semi-circle, and a stage-building which projected into the *orchestra* (figure 4.3, p. 88). The Gallic theatre, though, was not a masonry version of a pre-Roman building type. Instead, it developed after the conquest, and must be viewed as the product of interaction between Gallic and Roman culture. Once again, a clear division can be observed in the locations of these buildings. Of twenty-one positively identified classical theatres, all were built at cities of administrative status.[306] Most Gallic theatres, however, were located at secondary agglomerations or in the countryside: often in association with a sanctuary.[307]

Comprehensive studies of Gallo-Roman theatres allow the known urban examples to be divided up by architectural type (i.e. classical or Gallic) and by location (i.e. central or periurban). The results are presented in table 4.1. This reveals a very strong preference for locating classical theatres within the urban centre. By contrast, when theatres of Gallic type *were* built at administrative cities, this was always done in the urban periphery. At a micro level, both kinds of theatre could also be affected by the availability of sloping land to support their *caveae*. Theatres of Gallic type were always built into slopes, and so were many classical theatres.[308] This practice reduced construction costs, and in an urban centre was also an excellent way to make use of a steep slope. Most other monuments were difficult to build into a hill-side, but a theatre could turn it into a positive asset.

Where a slope was not available within the urban centre, the constructors of classical theatres usually preferred to erect a free-standing monument, like those at Paris, Meaux or Fréjus, rather than go into the urban periphery in search of sloping land. As a result, only three rather ambiguous cases of periurban classical theatres are known in Gaul. One, at Béziers, is too poorly documented for analysis.[309] The other two, at Saint-Bertrand-de-Comminges (figure 6.4, p. 226) and Soissons (Augusta Suessionum), were both built into hills on the edges of their cities' orthogonal grids.[310] The availability of a slope on the very perimeter of the city appears to have overturned the normal preference for building classical theatres in the urban centre on these rare occasions. But measures were still taken to link them as closely as possible with the city. Both faced directly into the urban centre, while that at Saint-Bertrand was embellished with a porticoed square, itself integrated into the orthogonal grid. These appear to be deliberate devices designed to minimise the impact of the periurban location.

Table 4.1 Types and locations of urban theatres in Gaul

City	Classical theatre	Theatre of Gallic type
Aquitania		
Agen	C	
Cahors	C	
Clermont-Ferrand	C	
Limoges	C	
Saint-Bertrand-de-Comminges	P	
Belgica		
Bavay	C?	
Soissons	P	
Trier		P, P
Lugdunensis		
Autun	C	P
Évreux		P
Jublains		P
Lillebonne		P
Lisieux		P
Lyon	C	
Meaux	C	
Orléans		P?
Paris	C	
Narbonensis		
Alba	C	
Apt	C	
Arles	C	
Béziers	P?	
Fréjus	C	
Marseille	C	
Nîmes	C	
Orange	C	
Toulouse	C	
Vaison-la-Romaine	C	
Valence	C	
Vienne	C	

Sources: Grenier 1958; Bedon *et al.* 1988; Rivet 1988; Landes 1989; Dumasy and Fincker 1992; Bedon 2001

Note: C = urban centre, P = urban periphery

Of the eight theatres of Gallic type built in the urban periphery, five were closely related to Romano-Celtic temples.[311] At Trier, one small theatre stood in the middle of the Altbachtal sanctuary and one formed part of the Lenus Mars sanctuary across the Mosel.[312] Another theatre was associated with the sanctuary agglomeration of Vieux-Lisieux near Lisieux,[313] and a fourth lay near the temples of la Genetoye outside Autun.[314] A more unusual piece of urban planning linked the Romano-Celtic sanctuary at the northern edge of Jublains with a theatre of Gallic type 800m away (figure 4.18).[315] This theatre was set into a slope on the southern edge of the orthogonal grid. But the slope extended east–west for some distance, meaning that the theatre could have been built anywhere along it. Clearly, a deliberate decision was made to locate it between two major north–south streets leaving the orthogonal grid. These streets in fact framed most of Jublains' public monuments: the forum, a bath complex *and* the temple at the northern end of the city.[316] Thus they gave the theatre a strong infrastructural link with the sanctuary, and created a sense of symmetry between the two monuments, despite their positions at opposite ends of the city. Dating evidence also suggests that this was planned as a single project. The monumentalisation of the sanctuary began late in the reign of Nero, while the theatre was dedicated in AD 81–3.[317] Thus, the two monuments could easily have been under construction simultaneously.

Associations between theatre and temple were in fact extremely common in Gaul, and by no means limited to the urban periphery. Gallic theatres and Romano-Celtic temples frequently occurred together away from administrative cities,[318] while classical theatres and temples often did the same in the urban centre.[319] This type of association was part of the Roman architectural tradition, and had precedents going back to and beyond the first permanent theatre erected in Rome: the theatre of Pompey.[320] In Gaul, though, theatre-temple complexes seem to have been adopted with a special enthusiasm. Van Andringa has pointed out that the frequency of their appearance outside administrative cities in the Three Gauls is almost unique to this region.[321] In her study of theatres in Belgica and the two Germanies, Bouley has also argued that the phenomenon often gave rise to alterations in the architecture of classical theatres, and explained some of the peculiarities of the Gallic theatre.[322] For example, the *scena* (stage-building) of a classical theatre might be reduced in height, to allow spectators to see a temple beyond. Theatres of both types, then, were probably used in a slightly different way from classical theatres in Italy.[323]

The locations of theatres in Gaul, then, were often determined by their association with a temple. And this brings us back to the same question which we faced in the previous section: why the consistent division between a classical architectural form in the urban centre, and a local one in the urban periphery? Again, the most plausible reason for this seems to be one of appropriate architectural language. Wealthy Gallo-Roman benefactors may simply have considered that theatres within the urban centre were best built in classical style to suit and enhance the sophisticated *romanitas* of the surrounding urban fabric. Meanwhile, in the urban periphery, a more localised style became acceptable: especially if the theatre was associated with a temple which also deviated from the classical tradition.

Amphitheatres

Once again, the amphitheatre of classical type is matched in Gaul by a local variant: the mixed spectacle edifice, which could serve as either amphitheatre or theatre.[324] This type of building appeared in Gaul only after the Roman conquest. It differed from a classical amphitheatre in that its *cavea* did not always form a complete oval, and that it had a small stage set into one side of the building (figure 4.3, p. 88). Yet, unlike a Gallic theatre, it did have an enclosed arena, suitable for gladiatorial fights or beast-hunts. Twenty-nine classical amphitheatres have been positively identified in Gaul, all located at administrative cities.[325] However, of the sixteen clear examples of mixed edifices, only five were built at administrative cities.[326] The usual context for this building, then, was away from the city: often at a secondary agglomeration.

As was done for theatres, amphitheatres located at administrative cities in Gaul can be divided into monuments of classical and local type, as well as those in a central or periurban location (see table 4.2). This reveals that only three amphitheatres across all of Gaul were explicitly located in the centres of administrative cities: all of classical type. Another twenty-six classical amphitheatres were built in the urban periphery, or sometimes on the very edge of the urban centre. This is very different from the obvious preference for locating classical temples and classical theatres within the urban centre. Meanwhile, five, or possibly six, examples of mixed edifices were found in periurban locations, but never within an urban centre. The distribution pattern for these buildings, then, is similar to that seen for Romano-Celtic temples and Gallic theatres.

The availability of space was clearly a major influence governing the location of a classical amphitheatre.[327] These were large buildings, which normally exceeded the size of an urban *insula*, and in any case did not accord well with its quadrangular shape. When they were built in urban centres, this was usually only possible because space had been set aside for the purpose at an early stage: as was clearly the case at Aosta in Italy.[328] In Gaul, classical amphitheatres generally did not appear until at least the Flavian period: a century or more after most cities had been established.[329] Unless their construction had been foreseen early on, sufficient space was unlikely to have remained available for their construction.

Notably, two of the three central examples from Gaul, at Autun and Nîmes, were only just within the urban boundaries. This was probably because of the unusually large areas enclosed by the walls of these cities: 200 ha and 220 ha respectively. When the amphitheatres came to be built,

Table 4.2 Types and locations of urban amphitheatres in Gaul

City	Classical amphitheatre	Mixed edifice
Aquitania		
Agen	P	
Bordeaux	P	
Bourges		P
Limoges	P	
Périgueux	P	
Poitiers	P	
Rodez	P	
Saint-Bertrand-de-Comminges	P	
Saintes	P	
Belgica		
Amiens	C	
Beauvais	P?	
Metz	P	
Reims	P	
Senlis		P
Trier	P	
Lugdunensis		
Angers		P
Autun	C	
Carhaix		P
Chartres	E?	
Le Mans	P	
Lyon	P	
Meaux	E?	
Paris		P
Rouen	P	
Sens	P	
Tours	P	
Vieux		P
Narbonensis		
Aix-en-Provence	P	
Antibes	P	
Apt	P?	
Arles	E	
Béziers	P	
Die	P?	
Fréjus	P	
Narbonne	P	
Nîmes	C	
Orange	P	
Toulouse	P	

Sources: Grenier 1958; Bedon *et al.* 1988; Rivet 1988; Futrell 1997; Golvin 1988; Bedon 2001.

Note: C = urban centre, P = urban periphery, E = on very edge of urban centre.

in the Flavian period at Nîmes and around the same era at Autun,[330] the edges of the urban centres were probably still relatively undeveloped. At Autun, it is also possible that space had been deliberately set aside for the amphitheatre. It stood immediately adjacent to a theatre and in a strong axial relationship with the probable site of the forum, perhaps indicating that an 'entertainment quarter' had been planned here early on (figure 4.7, p. 97).[331] A related case is Arles, where the amphitheatre again stood next to the city's theatre, and must be viewed as straddling the very boundaries of the urban centre, since a part of the Augustan walled circuit was demolished to make room for it.[332] The classical amphitheatre at Amiens is in a more unusual position, immediately adjacent to the city's forum (figure 4.10, p. 102).[333] Various theories have been advanced to explain this location, although the question remains unresolved. Suggestions include the possibility that it also functioned as a theatre, or that it had superseded an early wooden structure engulfed by subsequent expansion of the street-grid. Its near-circular shape has also led some to suggest that it was inserted into an existing plot after this expansion.[334] This would mean that its unusual location was simply the chance result of space becoming available in the urban centre at the right time.

A more typical relationship between a classical amphitheatre and an urban centre can be seen at Bordeaux (figure 6.3, p. 218). The amphitheatre here lay just on the edge of the city's orthogonal grid, close to a major road leaving the city. It also had a monumental entrance in its south-east façade, oriented towards the urban centre.[335] Thus, it was closely associated with the urban centre, but did fall just beyond it. This type of arrangement is matched in most of the cities with classical amphitheatres in Gaul, not to mention throughout the western provinces.[336] Clearly, the issues of space outlined above will have been a major factor in creating this pattern. But other practical factors may have contributed. At Saintes, the construction of an amphitheatre in a natural valley on the edge of the urban centre began in the Tiberian era (see plate 4.6).[337] At this time, space *would* have been available for a free-standing amphitheatre in the urban centre,[338] but the availability of the slope appears to have made the urban periphery preferable. As we have seen, though, the same issue did not prevent most classical theatres from being built in urban centres, and so it must be counted as a fairly minor factor overall.

Another issue may have been accessibility. Although clearly built close to the city so that they could be reached easily by a concentrated population mass, amphitheatres would also have been patronised by visitors travelling in from the rest of a community's territory.[339] A location just outside the urban centre would have made it easy for these people to find the amphitheatre, and kept large crowds out of the city streets. A periurban location may also have been considered most appropriate for a building which was only used on a periodic basis, but took up a large area of land. Yet we should allow for the

Plate 4.6 The amphitheatre at Saintes.

possibility that provincial amphitheatres *were* used between shows, for instance as marketplaces, like the Circus Maximus at Rome.[340] The same issue of accessibility for rural, as well as urban, visitors would certainly have favoured such use. Specific issues relating to the functions of individual amphitheatres could also apply. At Lyon and Narbonne, the close connection between the amphitheatres and the provincial sanctuaries is enough to explain their construction in the urban periphery. It is also tempting to suggest that the amphitheatre at Saint-Michel-du-Touch outside Toulouse was built here because of an unattested religious association with the nearby water sanctuary.[341]

Clearly, multiple practical factors weighed in favour of locating amphitheatres in the urban periphery. But the willingness of the Gallo-Roman elite to locate classical theatres in the urban centre despite many of the same issues shows that these could have been overcome with sufficient determination. Further explanation is necessary, and various ideological factors have been put forward in this context. One issue is the association between gladiatorial games and death, which has led some to argue that, like cemeteries, amphitheatres had to be built outside the city for religious reasons.[342] The association was certainly very real. The Romans believed that the first ever gladiatorial games had been held at a funeral in 264 BC,[343] and similar occasions remained the basis for shows until the late Republic.[344] Under the empire, the connection dropped away, but some games continued in a funeral context.[345] The amphitheatre was of course also a place of violent death: for Futrell even a ritualised form of human sacrifice.[346] Whether this is accurate or not, corpses certainly resulted, and were often stored temporarily in chambers below the arena.[347] Apparently associated with this was a belief in the amphitheatre's potential for liminal magic. Lead *defixiones* (inscribed magical tablets) have been found in subterranean chambers in the amphitheatres of Carthage and Trier: possibly those used for storing their victims.[348] Yet citing this connection as a straightforward reason for the periurban locations of amphitheatres runs into serious difficulties when confronted with two facts. First, gladiatorial games were regularly held in the forum in the very heart of Rome in the Republican era,[349] and second, many amphitheatres *were* built within urban centres, including the earliest known permanent arena at Pompeii, and the much-emulated Colosseum at Rome. Religious scruples as strong as those connected with cemeteries could not have tolerated this.

Another factor used to explain the locations of classical amphitheatres is the agonistic nature of the games. In the amphitheatre, established Roman society came into ritualised confrontation with its enemies, including criminals, barbarians and wild animals. These representatives of a dangerous external world were symbolically 'conquered' before the watching spectators.[350] Wiedemann has suggested that the most appropriate place for this controlled confrontation was on the margins of that most potent Roman symbol of civilisation: the urban centre.[351] Yet amphitheatres also celebrated the social order. Although funerary in origin, by the imperial period gladiatorial games had also become offerings to the gods. Many amphitheatres incorporated shrines,[352] and chapters 70 to 71 of the Urso charter required that spectacles should be held in honour of Jupiter, Juno and Minerva.[353] Games could also be connected with the imperial cult, as at Lyon, or given in honour of living emperors.[354] Finally, the very structure of the amphitheatre itself also consolidated the established social order. Spectators were organised hierarchically around the *cavea* according to class, while the nature of the spectacles which they witnessed helped to confirm the legitimacy and supremacy of Roman civilisation.[355] Thus amphitheatres were places where existing social and political structures were reverenced and upheld. Arguably, this was as good a reason to build amphitheatres within the civilised space of the urban centre as it was to build them at the point where that space confronted the external world.

The ideology of the classical amphitheatre was thus complex and rather ambiguous. With no explicit ancient commentary on the issue of their location, it is difficult to build a completely convincing case for the exclusion of amphitheatres on ideological grounds reconstructed by us. We return, then, to practical factors as the most plausible reasons so far for the phenomenon. These clearly did mitigate in favour of a periurban location, but, as indicated, they could have been overcome with sufficient will to build in the urban centre. One more issue, then, may have tipped the balance in favour of the urban periphery. Free-standing amphitheatres had large and often decorative façades, which must have made a striking impression on the viewer. Within a built-up urban centre the façade might be partially obscured, detracting from its impact. But in the urban periphery, these splendid monuments – compared by Golvin to the great medieval cathedrals – could be properly appreciated.[356] For both benefactor and community, then, the urban periphery may simply have offered the best opportunities for showing off their monument. Certainly, the positioning of most of Gaul's periurban classical amphitheatres on major roads and/or raised ground suggests an interest in maximising their visibility and potential to impress.[357]

Turning to the five or six examples of mixed spectacle edifices built in the urban periphery, it is notable that only one was built at a city known to have possessed any other spectacle buildings: Paris (figure 4.5, p. 94).[358] In fact, most of the cities which constructed these mixed edifices could be characterised as belonging to the smaller and less monumental end of the urban spectrum. Apart from Paris, they include Angers, Bourges, Carhaix, Senlis and Vieux: all *civitas*-capitals, but yielding little evidence for the kind of sophisticated and competitive monumentalism known at cities like Trier, Lyon, Vienne or Arles. Their decision to build mixed edifices may be explained to some extent through reference to the function which these buildings fulfilled when built in a non-urban context. Mixed spectacle edifices are most common in Aquitania and in the Parisian basin, where *civitas* territories were generally larger than those in other parts of Gaul.[359] It has been suggested that they were built in order to bring shows and games to those living far away from the nearest city, and that the construction of a building which could host two types of spectacle in this context was primarily a choice of economy.[360] These arguments find support in the relatively small seating capacity of most mixed edifices (averaging around 7,000), and the fact that they were almost always built into natural slopes.[361]

Since most of the mixed edifices built in the urban periphery seem to have been built as an alternative to a separate theatre and amphitheatre, economic considerations do seem a plausible factor in this context. Yet other aspects of mixed edifices have suggested that economy may not have been the only concern in their construction. Drinkwater has argued that the careful construction of these buildings, and especially their stages, indicates that they were designed to host spectacles which differed from classical performances, but were of special importance in Gaul.[362] Meanwhile, Futrell has pointed out that if economy had been the highest priority, these buildings could have been constructed out of wood and earth banks, rather than employing stone.[363] In this case, another reason for the construction of mixed spectacle edifices at some cities may simply have been a demand for the localised spectacle performances postulated by Drinkwater. Certainly, some explanation beyond simple economy is needed for Paris, where the mixed edifice known locally as 'Les Arènes', was probably built *after* the construction of a classical theatre in the city's urban centre.[364] Meanwhile, any of the factors which applied to either classical amphitheatres or Gallic theatres could also have encouraged the construction of these buildings in the urban periphery. Les Arènes at Paris, at least, was positioned in order to make use of the slope of the colline Sainte-Geneviève.

Circuses

There is no known local equivalent of the classical circus in Gaul, and indeed circuses of any kind appear to have been rare here. Four examples are attested, but those at Lyon and Trier are known only through epigraphy and late literary accounts respectively.[365] The only securely *located* circuses are at Arles and Vienne,[366] where they occupy remarkably similar positions. Each was built on the left bank of the Rhône, just south of the urban centre on the same side of the river. Vienne's circus was established at the end of the first century on land reclaimed through terracing (figure 4.4, p. 90).[367] By this period, the available land in the urban centre had been filled, and there was no question of accommodating a circus. Its position was thus determined by factors of space, and its orientation governed by the river and the hills to the east. The circus was flanked by two main roads, linking it with the urban centre.

The circus at Arles was also built at the end of the first century.[368] It was located well to the south-west of the urban centre, and close to a cemetery, in a position probably determined largely by local marshes (figure 4.9, p. 100). Even where it was built, oak piles had to be sunk to stabilise the ground, and the land raised to avoid flooding.[369] The building's orientation relates directly to the course of the Rhône, but may also have been influenced by a major road leading towards the coast. In fact, excavations in the urban centre have revealed a monumental paved area at the start of this road, embellished during the Flavian period.[370] Possibly, it was enhanced with the imminent construction of the circus in mind, to establish a monumental interface between the new building and the urban centre.

For both circuses, it is clear that size ruled out a central location. Of more interest is the position of each monument within the periphery. Either could have been built on the right bank of the Rhône, where extensive areas of flat land at Trinquetaille and Saint-Romain-en-Gal were already being put to use. Yet they were located on the left bank instead, despite this necessitating land reclamation and stabilisation. This indicates a profoundly felt interest in this side of the Rhône as a location for the circuses, surely stemming from the positions of the urban centres on the same bank. Perhaps a monument as large and expensive as a circus was considered too important to allow it to be separated from the ideologically significant urban centre by a boundary as divisive as a river.

The riverside locations also carry resonances of Rome's Campus Martius. This would certainly have been an appropriate evocation, since chariot races were held on the Campus Martius during the *Ludi Taurenses* and *Ludi Saeculares*.[371] Finally, the positions of Arles and Vienne along the same river and within the same province of Narbonensis also raise the possibility of local rivalry, especially since the circuses were near contemporaneous. Either city, becoming aware of the construction plans of the other, may have decided to assert their own sophisticated urban status by building a similar monument in a similar location.

Festivals and shows

Temples, theatres, amphitheatres and circuses were not simply empty edifices, of course, but the focal points of religious festivals and shows. These have been touched upon in earlier parts of this chapter. We saw that commercial activity might be drawn into the urban periphery by crowds attending such events, and encountered possible evidence for seasonal fairs connected with the water-sanctuary, amphitheatre or both at Saint-Michel-du-Touch. We have also seen that accessibility for large crowds might have been one practical reason for situating amphitheatres in the urban periphery. Now that each of the building types involved has been examined separately, it is worth returning to the issue to consider the overall impact of such events.

Festivals and shows were community occasions, and it is clear that people travelled to attend them, sometimes over long distances. We have already met people going out from Rome for suburban religious festivals in chapter 3, while games held in 46 BC to celebrate Julius Caesar's victories in the Civil Wars attracted such crowds that people were camping in tents along the city streets.[372] Evidence from Gaul is scantier, but Eusebius does describe attendees at the festival of the Three Gauls at Lyon in AD 177, when relating martyrdoms enacted in the amphitheatre that year. The crowds were large, and made up of 'many people from all *ethne*'.[373] Of course, this was one of Gaul's biggest festivals, and such throngs are unlikely to have attended most local shows or festivals. But we can certainly assume that the larger events attracted visitors from all over a community's territory, and possibly beyond.

Not all festivals and shows took place in the urban periphery. Arguably, though, those which did must have attracted some of the largest crowds. Certainly, amphitheatres and circuses, which were regularly located in the urban periphery, had larger seating capacities than theatres, which were not. No such direct equation can be drawn between temple size and crowd size, but the extent of some periurban sanctuaries certainly suggests that they played an important role in local religious life. Scheid has pointed out that benches and altars dedicated by *pagi* at Trier's sanctuary of Lenus Mars indicate official participation in the cult,[374] meaning that representatives from communities throughout Treveran territory can be expected to have attended its festivals. Public shows and festivals, then, will regularly have brought large numbers of city- and country-dwellers together in activities focused on the urban periphery.

The effect must have been to draw attention to the potential for this zone to act as a successful venue for celebrations of local status and community identity. The ideology of *urbanitas* and the concern for marking out a formal urban centre implied that the proper show-place for the sophistication of a community was within its boundaries. But the presence of temples and spectacle buildings, and the festivals and shows associated with them, in the urban periphery must have demonstrated very visibly that it, too, was an integral and important part of the city which could play the same role, and not just an incidental adjunct to the urban centre.

Cemeteries and tombs

The burial of the dead is the first activity discussed so far that never occurred in a Gallo-Roman urban centre. It is also an activity which we can take for granted as occurring in the periphery of every administrative city in Gaul. Burial beyond the urban boundaries was standard practice throughout the Roman world, and Gaul did not go against the trend. In fact, the custom may already have been established amongst some Gallic communities before the conquest. In Narbonensis, pre-Roman burials seem to have been grouped into cemeteries outside the *oppida* of Ambrussum and Ugernum,[375] while in Celtic Europe, a cemetery containing eighty inhumation burials lay a short distance north of the pre-Roman settlement on the Gasfabrik site at Basel, Switzerland.[376] Yet burials have been found in houses within the fortifications of Mont Beuvray (Bibracte): a major *oppidum* of the Aedui which Woolf has described as demonstrating 'how Gauls could build a Roman city without a grid'.[377] The final consolidation of the practice, then, took the direct involvement of Rome.

The reasons for extra-urban burial in the Roman world – and indeed most ancient Mediterranean cultures – must have been partly practical. Corpses posed a threat to health, whilst cremation constituted a fire risk: certainly considered by Cicero to have been the reason for the ban at Rome.[378] It was also a concern for the compilers of the Urso charter, who followed their clause banning burial within the *pomerium* with another banning the construction of new funeral pyres closer than 500 paces to the town.[379] Taboos associated with death and the dead, and a desire to maintain a distinct separation between the dead and the living were also clearly important, however.[380] As Lindsay has argued, practical and spiritual concerns may have reinforced one another.[381]

The spatial relationship between burials and the urban centre was much the same across Gaul. A typical example is Amiens, where known burials were all located either just beyond the orthogonal grid, or across the river

Somme (figure 4.10, p. 102). They were beyond the boundaries, but very close to the urban centre, and also clustered around the major roads leaving the city. As elsewhere in the Roman world, this attests an interest in a close association between cemetery areas and the living population of the city, despite the desire to keep them out of the actual urban centre. It meant that the tombs of the dead were regularly and clearly visible to large numbers of people, helping to perpetuate their memory. It also meant that they were easily accessible for living relatives to visit and make offerings; for instance on the anniversary of the person's death, or during festivals such as the Parentalia.[382] The distribution of cemeteries around Gallo-Roman urban centres, then, reflects the universal paradox of the dead: 'the corpse evokes both fear and solicitude'.[383]

The size and layout of individual cemetery areas will have been affected by patterns of land-ownership in the urban periphery. At some cities, large areas of land appear to have been dedicated specifically for burials. One such is Trion, on the south-west edges of the urban centre at Lyon. Here, cemeteries established in the early first century AD along the roads to Aquitania and Narbonensis, had joined to form a vast continuous necropolis by the start of the second century, and continued to be used until the end of the third.[384] Such a development points towards publicly owned land, since sufficient authority was obviously being exercised to stop other kinds of development in the area. This could have been set aside by planners at the foundation of the city or donated soon after as a benefaction.[385]

Elsewhere, tombs and cemeteries occurred alongside other forms of land-use. To the north of Narbonne, a large, densely packed cemetery developed from the beginning of the first century AD along the via Domitia.[386] In the middle of it, however, lay an artisanal and commercial area, where metal-workers, potters and probably also oyster-traders worked during the late first century BC and first century AD.[387] By the mid-first century AD, then, the area must have had a very mixed character. We might speculate that private land-owners in the area were simply making whatever use of their land seemed to promise the highest income, on an *ad hoc* basis.[388] The result was a juxtaposition of burials and living occupation which would never have occurred within the urban boundaries. In Gaul as elsewhere, then, the desire to separate the living and the dead did not extend beyond the special space of the urban centre.

The character of individual tombs could vary dramatically. Cemeteries to the north and north-east of Fréjus feature cremations and inhumations, as well as a range of simple burials, burial enclosures and large individual monuments.[389] Evidently, wealth, social status and individual identity were being expressed through burial practices: a custom already established in pre-Roman Gaul, and firmly entrenched at Rome.[390] The burial concerns of the Gallo-Roman elite are well illustrated by a group of five mausolea from Trion.[391] All were large, decorated with sculptural mouldings, and, in their original state, equipped with inscriptions identifying their occupants. They stood on the very edge of Lyon's urban centre along the road leading southeast towards Aquitania, immediately outside the conjectural position of a city gate in the course most usually reconstructed for a walled circuit. The monuments were aligned along the road, ensuring that passers-by would see them, and perhaps read their inscriptions.

The monument of a *sevir* named Q. Calvius Turpio appears to have been one of the earliest, built closest to the city in the second half of the first century AD.[392] It was followed from the end of that century by a row of similar monuments on the slope below, belonging to other *seviri* and decurions. The location, then, seems to have become increasingly attractive to the local elite over time. This may be explained partly by the factors which initially attracted Turpio: chief amongst them its proximity to a major entrance or exit to the city. But a 'snowball effect' seems also to have been at work. Once a few spectacular elite tombs had been established here, they drew attention to the site and inspired competitive attempts to outdo them. In this respect, the tombs at Trion resemble those lining the via Appia outside Rome or the Via dei Sepolcri outside the Herculaneum gate at Pompeii.[393] It seems unsurprising that this phenomenon should be encountered in such a developed form outside Lyon, the political and religious centre of the Three Gauls. But the Trion monuments were not unique. Examples of similar clusters of lavish tombs occur north of Orange and across the Arroux from Autun.[394]

Tombs such as these helped to monumentalise the urban periphery. But despite this, and the apparent lack of interest in separating them from living occupation, tombs must also have lent it something of a sinister aspect. The ghostly and magical associations of cemetery areas are clear from the Roman literary tradition; for instance, Petronius' story about a werewolf or Horace's account of witches in the former Esquiline burial grounds.[395] They seem also to have applied in Gaul. A monument known as the 'Pyramide de Couhard' stood on a hill-top approximately 1 km from the south gate of Autun, strikingly visible from within the walls and across the surrounding landscape (plate 4.7).[396] It may be a cenotaph, since no burial, or burial-chamber, has been found within it, but its funerary purpose is clear from its shape and location in an established cemetery area.[397] At its foot, excavations in the 1980s uncovered a *defixio*: an inscribed tablet used for invoking gods and demons to fulfil wishes or enact curses. It contained a list of Latin *cognomina*, presumably naming those to be cursed, along with two symbols and several magical and nonsense words in Greek script.[398] Such tablets could be transmitted to the spiritual world via a well, spring or river, but they were often targeted at the spirits of the dead: especially those who had suffered violent or premature deaths, and those denied proper burial.[399] If the Pyramide de Couhard was indeed a cenotaph, any or all of these criteria could well have applied to the person for whom it was built. It was therefore doubtless

Plate 4.7 The 'Pyramide de Couhard' funerary monument, Autun.

a particularly appropriate target for necromantic magic, but the fact that any funerary monument was used in this way confirms the connotations of cemetery areas in Gaul. They gave the urban periphery a distinct character, not shared by the urban centre, which included an aspect of danger and threat.

Villas and farms

Chapter 3 established that true 'suburban' villas, of the kind described in Roman literature, would be next to impossible to identify in the provinces. Provincial villas equipped with urbane features and located within a day's journey of an urban centre may well have been considered suburban by their owners. But, archaeologically speaking, they look much the same as other elite villas which had little connection with any city. This is of no great surprise, since the behaviour associated with suburban villas in literary texts is not actually enormously different from that linked with elite villas in any setting. The distinction only becomes apparent through literary or epigraphic evidence able to attest the rhythms of villa use or the mind-set of villa owners: and this is all but absent in the provinces. The suburban villa, though, is arguably only a special kind of periurban villa; that is, a villa which, like the other forms of land-use discussed in this chapter, was distinguished from the majority of its rural equivalents by an unusually close link with the city. Characteristics which have identified other isolated features as periurban, such as intervisibility with a city, a position on a major road running into it, or simply a location very close to its boundaries, can be seen in villas too. We may then ask what prompted some villas to develop in such positions, and whether it is indeed helpful to interpret them as part of the urban periphery.

Gaul was home to a range of agricultural properties. Studies have shown that they varied from small, simple buildings to large complexes covering several hectares, and that their plans and distribution within the landscape vary from region to region.[400] There has been a long history of seeking to divide them up into two broad categories: 'farms' and 'villas'. But such a distinction is unlikely to have been applied in the Roman era, and the modern heading 'villa' generally covers a wide range of buildings of very different sizes and degrees of complexity.[401] Indeed, Garmy and Leveau remind us that even the opposition between villa and village may not have been so stark as modern scholars often assume.[402]

Our knowledge of these properties is not always ideal. Many, of course, have not survived in the archaeological record at all, making it difficult to reconstruct ancient patterns of distribution across the landscape. Meanwhile, most of those which have are known only through aerial photography, chance finds, surface survey, restricted sondages or antiquarian reports.[403] This means that dating, layout, décor and the details of the villa's context in the landscape may all be poorly documented. Of particular importance in the present context is the impact of modern urbanism. Continuous occupation on the sites of Gallo-Roman cities has meant that villas close to the urban centre are most likely to have been disturbed or destroyed by subsequent building work. Walker's observations around Lyon typify the problem.[404] As a major political and economic centre with extensive development in its immediate periphery, we could well expect the landscape around Lyon to have been studded with villas. Indeed, as a provincial capital which clearly enjoyed close links with Rome, we might even expect its elite to have subscribed to the idea of a suburban villa culture. Yet the environs of the city have yielded only a very small number of ambiguous or poorly documented villa remains, none of which have been properly excavated. The main reason for this is the rapid and extensive growth of the modern city, but Walker argued that a relative lack of interest in the history of the countryside around Lyon had also played its part.

Some distortion in the archaeological record is inevitable, then. None the less, some lavish villa properties *are* known close to administrative cities in Gaul, and it is clear that they were very similar to other examples a great distance away. The situation is well illustrated in north-eastern Gaul. At Saint-Acheul, approximately 1.5 km from the south-east corner of Amiens, a large villa was found during the creation of a housing estate (figure 4.10, p. 102).[405] It had already been destroyed to foundation level or below, allowing little to be said about its décor, although a Doric capital and two column drums suggest the presence of a portico. But enough is known of the plan to recognise an arrangement favoured at the top end of the villa spectrum in this part of Gaul. A group of residential buildings at the north-western end of the site looked out over what was probably a medium-sized court followed by a larger court, with various buildings around its perimeter. The type is referred to by Agache as a '*grande maison à longues ailes latérales*', and likened by him to the 'courtyard villas' known in Britain.[406] Very similar examples are known at Estrées-sur-Noye, about 10 km south of Amiens, at Warfusée-Abancourt, about 20 km to the east of Amiens, and at Anthée, around 60–70 km each from the Bavay and Tongres.[407] These are clearly the villas of the region's elite, but nothing about the Saint-Acheul villa marks it out as notably different from the others. It looks like any other wealthy villa, which simply happens to be located very close to Amiens.

These north-eastern villas do not reveal any great interest in the specific evocation of *urbanitas* noted in the properties discussed in chapter 3. Elsewhere in Gaul, though, this is documented. An example from the immediate environs of a city is Montmain, 3 km south of Autun.[408] This villa was partially excavated and planned in 1834, meaning that our information is limited in quantity and quality. But much can still be said. Its plan shows two main groups of rooms, each covering around 1000m^2: a bath-complex to the north and what Rebourg interprets as '*salles de réception*' to the west.[409] They appear to face on to a central court containing a large pool and a fountain. Finds include a millstone and iron tools, as well as pieces of marble, an *opus signinum* floor and fragments of inscriptions. The overall impression, then, is of a villa which had a productive function, but was also equipped with the sophisticated décor and facilities its owner might expect to enjoy in the city.[410]

Again, though, equally urbane features appear far distant from any city. An eighteen-hectare complex at Chiragan, for example, famous for its collection of second-century sculpture and equipped also with mosaic-floored reception rooms and extensive baths, lay 45 km from Saint-Bertrand-de-Comminges and 60 km from Toulouse.[411] Montmaurin in the same region boasted porticoed courts, a strong axial layout and fine reception rooms even in its mid-first century phase, yet lay 35 km north of Saint-Bertrand-de-Comminges.[412] Meanwhile, spectacle mosaics of the kind noted in north Africa occur also in Gaul. Some decorated *domus* in the very centres of cities or the extra-urban *continentia aedificia*.[413] But chariot-racing scenes found in a property at Sennecey-le-Grand were a full 90 km away from the nearest administrative city at Autun, and even 30 km and 60 km respectively from the largest secondary agglomerations in the region: Châlon-sur-Saône and Mâcon.[414] Similar examples can be cited all over Gaul.[415]

If the character of villa properties did not change markedly in the vicinity of a city, though, their density did. Studies have shown that agricultural properties in Gaul, from the lavish examples discussed above to much simpler farms, tended to cluster more densely around settlements, including administrative cities but also secondary agglomerations.[416] This is unsurprising, since it is in keeping with patterns in other western provinces, and with the ideas of von Thünen (see chapter 3). Market factors of the type which he envisaged will have been prominent in encouraging these patterns of distribution. Both cities and the roads converging on them were central to the sale and transportation of surplus produce. But cities may have offered other spurs to the development of nearby agricultural properties. Woolf has argued that skilled craftsmen and good-quality building materials were more easily available close to the city, encouraging the development of grander villas in particular.[417] Meanwhile, recent work has drawn attention to the possible contribution of aqueducts. Although installed primarily to feed administrative cities, these also affected rural settlement patterns. They probably encouraged agricultural activity along their courses by offering a source of irrigation (both officially and unofficially), while for wealthier villa owners they also created an opportunity for the supply of private baths.[418]

All of this of course demonstrates the impact of the city on the surrounding landscape, and it is undeniable that cities and their surrounding agricultural properties were engaged in a social and economic relationship with one another. But if we interpret properties as periurban on this basis, then we would have to do the same for everything throughout the territory governed by any city. All the people in that territory, and the property which they owned, were after all governed from its urban centre, and thus affected by it. Throughout this book, periurban development has been defined as something which fell between the fully urban and the fully rural: not merely something exhibiting any kind of relationship with the city. Patterns of villa and farm distribution may well indicate that the impact of the city was felt more strongly in the areas nearest to it, and from one perspective this *is* a weaker example of the same phenomenon as periurban development. But to interpret it explicitly as periurban in itself would be to obscure more interesting examples of development which bridged the urban–rural divide. Furthermore, the impact of cities and secondary settlements on patterns of agricultural exploitation may anyway be viewed as only one amongst many elements which could affect villa and farm distribution within the landscape. A similar example might be clustering on fertile plains, which Agache argued were especially attractive to villas in Picardy.[419]

The archaeology of villas in Gaul, then, reveals much the same patterns observed in other parts of the western empire. Just as in Italy and north Africa, agricultural properties of all kinds clustered around cities, and lavish elite villas occurred not only within a day's journey of the cities, but also well beyond that range. From the archaeological record alone, nothing warrants drawing any special distinction between elite villa properties closest to the cities, and those furthest away. Yet we must remember that it is not archaeology but literature and epigraphy that reveal to us that lavish villas around Rome were bound to the city through regular journeys and the mind-set of the metropolitan elite. To be sure, no Gallo-Roman city has yielded anything approaching the same density of villa remains around it as Rome, and the difference in character between even the richest of the provincial cities and the metropolis makes this unsurprising. But if the archaeological evidence from Gaul does not offer positive evidence for any special links between villas and cities, the case of Rome shows that it also does not allow us to rule it out in the absence of literary and epigraphic evidence.

In fact, as chapter 6 will show, literary texts testify that the idea of the suburban villa was indeed current amongst at least some parts of the Gallo-Roman elite during the late antique era. It is quite plausible, then, that it had also been absorbed earlier on: especially since we know that the writings of Pliny were readily available in Lyon.[420] Some Gallo-Roman villa owners, then, perhaps *did* think of their properties as suburban. Certainly, some villas were situated in places that would have allowed their owners to travel regularly between them and the city and use them as a leisured retreat from urban duties, if they had wished to do so. The villa at Saint-Acheul lay a few hundred metres from one of the main roads into Amiens, while Montmain had easy access to Autun via its own well-built service road.[421] These sorts of links would clearly have allowed a close relationship with the city, whether or not that was enacted in the context of an explicit suburban villa culture. And it is perfectly logical to imagine that wealthy Gallo-Roman villa owners whose properties happened to lie near to cities would have worked out for themselves that they could be used as an extension to their urban lifestyles, without needing Pliny or Cicero to teach them to construct this as '*suburbanitas*'. Perhaps, then, we can justify calling such villas periurban, in the sense of properties which were clearly owned by an urban-based elite and, at least physically, more than usually closely connected with the city. But we do not have any direct evidence that proximity to the city was conceived of as anything more than a pleasant bonus in high imperial Gaul. Views of such properties as essential badges of elite status, or as fundamentally different from 'rural' villas, are simply not attested.

Conclusion

Perhaps the most important point to emphasise at the end of this chapter is the sheer number of sites upon which the discussion has been able to draw. In

Table 4.3 Overall occurrence of periurban development at Gallo-Roman administrative cities

Region	Number of cities	Number with periurban features	Percentage with periurban features
Aquitania	20	11	55.0%
Belgica	13	7	53.8%
Lugdunensis	25	19	76.0%
Three Gauls	58	37	63.7%
Narbonensis	26	12	46.4%
All Gaul	84	49	58.3%

fact, at least forty-nine out of the eighty-four administrative cities in Gaul have yielded positive evidence for some kind of periurban development (see table 4.3). Even if in many cases this meant only a single amphitheatre or sanctuary, these were still important features in the urban landscape. Meanwhile, the totals shown in table 4.3 reflect the hazards of the archaeological record, and almost certainly underestimate the true extent of periurban development in Gaul by a significant margin. This is a type of occupation that has been consistently under-explored by comparison with central equivalents, and the table does not take account of periurban finds so fragmentary or ambiguous that they cannot readily be attributed to any specific form of occupation. As future discoveries are made and our knowledge of Gallo-Roman urbanism improves, the numbers of cities known to have generated an urban periphery can only go up.

The character of the Gallo-Roman urban periphery

Periurban development of course varied from city to city, and this issue is treated later. But it is helpful first to outline some of the general characteristics of the occupation discussed in this chapter. Most often, it was situated just beyond the urban boundaries, and particularly around the city's entrances or exits. In common with the urban centre, it was rarely 'zoned'. But nor was any interest usually shown in shaping or enhancing the urban periphery through planning projects or infrastructural provisions. This suggests that civic councils were generally less concerned with the appearance of or quality of life in the urban periphery than the urban centre, and this is fully in keeping with the elite ideologies of the city encountered in chapter 2. But it was not always the case, as the examples of Saint-Romain-en-Gal at Vienne and Trinquetaille at Arles indicate.

The Gallo-Roman urban periphery was certainly *not* a lower-class artisano-commercial zone. Industry, commerce and simple housing could all be found there. But they were also common in the urban centre, and, even in the periphery, they were by no means the defining form of occupation. Wealthy *domus* and splendid public monuments found their place there, too, and there is little sign of any efforts to keep them apart. Arguably, the very idea that the periphery of a Roman city might have been an unsavoury exclusion zone is inspired by assumptions based on medieval and early modern urbanism (see chapter 1). Certainly, there is an unjustified over-emphasis on archaeological evidence for periurban industry, and on the idea that it was prompted by the deliberate 'expulsion' of such activity from the urban centre. Ziegert, for example, is ready to reconstruct a vast 'factory zone' around Leptis Magna on the basis of one glass workshop, one potter's kiln and literary references to production and trade:[422] an extrapolation which would never be accepted for an urban centre. Meanwhile, scholar after scholar has seen a widespread policy of exclusion in one very specific ruling from the Urso charter and Martial and Juvenal's jibes at a particular area of Rome. Civic councils certainly did expel some activity from the urban centre: notably burials. But the evidence of Gaul suggests that industry and commerce gathered in the urban periphery mainly for independent economic reasons.

Periurban structures might stand in isolation, and this seems to have been particularly common for public monuments. If they did, devices such as orientation, a relationship with a major road or intervisibility were usually employed to emphasise the building's relationship with the urban centre. Frequently, though, continuous areas of periurban occupation grew up. They might begin just outside the urban boundaries, forming part of the urban *continentia aedificia*. But they could also form distinct areas of nucleated occupation in their own right. Such nuclei have been encountered in this chapter at Amiens and Metz, where they consisted mainly of low-quality housing, at Vaise outside Lyon, where housing, warehouses, workshops and cemeteries were mixed, and at Lisieux, Périgueux and Toulouse, where they seem to have centred around sanctuaries. A number of further examples are considered by Bouet and Carponsin-Martin in the context of their discussion of the Chamiers site at Périgueux, including Thenac (7 km from Saintes), Allones (5 km from Le Mans), Vieil-Évreux (7 km from Évreux) and Vaugrenier (4 km from Antibes).[423] I am not entirely convinced that there is enough evidence for a close relationship with the nearby cities in these cases to justify calling them periurban satellites, rather than independent sanctuary agglomerations located near to administrative cities. None the less, the phenomenon of the periurban satellite settlement was clearly real in Roman Gaul, and perhaps quite widespread. Its significance will be further explored in chapter 5, in the light of patterns of spatial organisation observed in secondary agglomerations.

Reasons for periurban development

Periurban occupation developed for many reasons, and these varied greatly according to the type of building or land-use, and the local circumstances of the city concerned. Pressure on space was certainly a major factor. It could apply in cases where there simply was no room for a particular feature within the urban centre, such as the circuses at Vienne and Arles. But it also gave rise to competition for the space that was available, and this often seems to have prompted a location in the urban periphery as a cheaper alternative. This is likely to have been an issue for artisans and people with little money to spend, but it probably also applied to the owners of some wealthy *domus*.

An over-emphasis on space as a factor, though, can obscure other reasons for periurban development. The potters of Sens and Fréjus may well have been able to pursue their profession more cheaply in the urban periphery, but they also had easier access to the resources they needed: particularly suitable clay, but also water and timber. Similarly, amphitheatres and circuses were difficult to accommodate in an urban centre. But a periurban location could also enhance their impact as display monuments, by allowing a fuller view of their impressive façades.

Ideological concerns about the character of the urban centre have also been shown to be less significant than is often assumed. They certainly *were* at work in the siting of cemeteries and tombs. But there is no real evidence that they applied to industry and commerce, while arguments for their significance in the case of amphitheatres are not wholly convincing. It is also unlikely that Romano-Celtic temples appear in the urban periphery because of any sense that the practices associated with them were 'un-Roman', and therefore unsuitable for integration into the urban centre. The possibility that these monuments – and local spectacle buildings – were considered *architecturally* unsuitable for construction in the urban centre, though, will be returned to in chapter 7 in the context of the relationship between the provincial and metropolitan elites. Meanwhile, in some circumstances, the urban periphery appears to have been able to make a positive contribution to the ideological impact of a building. Thus the intended role of the sanctuaries of the imperial cult at Narbonne and Lyon as province-wide, rather than local, monuments was almost certainly enhanced by their periurban location.

Regional and provincial patterns

The issue of whether periurban development in Gaul showed any patterns of regional variation can be addressed by returning to table 4.3. The province by province figures on this table show that, in our current state of knowledge, periurban land-use of any kind was most common at cities in Lugdunensis (76 per cent), and least common in Narbonensis (46.4 per cent). The difference is quite marked, but given the hazards of the archaeological record, it should not in itself be overemphasised. It does, though, raise the question of how such a difference might be explained.

Closer investigation of tables 4.1 and 4.2, showing the positions of theatres and amphitheatres at Gallo-Roman cities, helps to illuminate the issue. These tables reveal significant differences in the placement of spectacle buildings, not only between Lugdunensis and Narbonensis, but also between Lugdunensis and the other two northern Gallic provinces. In Narbonensis, Aquitania and Belgica, the great majority of spectacle buildings erected at administrative cities were of classical type, with theatres usually situated in the urban centre, and amphitheatres in the periphery. For Narbonensis, this is the whole story. For Aquitania and Belgica, Gallic theatres and mixed spectacle edifices also need to be taken into account. But in these provinces, the local variants were almost always erected away from administrative cities, which remained the preserve of classical spectacle buildings.[424] In Lugdunensis, the usual pattern of central theatres and periurban amphitheatres, both of classical type, is present. Here, though, around ten cities also set up local types of spectacle building in their urban peripheries. This is a significant departure from the practices observed in the other provinces, and it has the effect of causing four Lugdunese cities – Angers, Évreux, Orléans and Vieux – to appear on table 4.3 where they would not otherwise have done so. If these four cities are subtracted from the totals in the table and the figures recalculated, the percentage of cities in Lugdunensis known to have generated some form of periurban development comes down to 60 per cent: much more in line with the figures for the other three provinces.

The pattern in Lugdunensis could be portrayed as a deviation from the standard model of Roman urbanism. The communities of Narbonensis echoed Italian practice in building classical theatres in the centres of their administrative cities, and classical amphitheatres outside them. The communities of Aquitania and Belgica followed the same pattern where classical buildings were concerned, but were clearly also interested in Gallic theatres and mixed spectacle edifices. These buildings were not part of the Roman architectural tradition, however, and, perhaps for this reason, were generally kept away from the places where the communities were working hardest to fit in with that tradition: their cities. Only in Lugdunensis was the Roman model altered by the construction of local types of spectacle building in the urban periphery.

From another perspective, though, the Lugdunese practice of situating local spectacle buildings in the urban periphery could illustrate the extent to which the Roman urban model had been understood in this region, and the success with which it had been adapted to local interests. The communities of Lugdunensis may well have recognised that theatres of Gallic type and mixed spectacle edifices were not part of the standard equipment of a Roman city. But they also seem to have realised that Roman urbanism offered a way to make these building types available to urban populations without compromising the sophisticated *romanitas* of the urban centre. In using the urban periphery as a location for these buildings, it could be said that the local communities were actually recognising and capitalising on the flexibility of the Roman urban model. Arguably, they had absorbed its principles more fully and achieved greater success in making it suit their needs than the people of Aquitania or Belgica. In Narbonensis, meanwhile, the issue did not arise, since the communities here did not develop building types which fell outside the standard Roman urban model.

It should also be noted that, although this phenomenon was concentrated in Lugdunensis, it was not rigidly defined by the province's boundaries. Only three cities outside of Lugdunensis are known to have built local types of spectacle buildings in their urban peripheries: Bourges in Aquitania and Senlis and Trier in Belgica (see tables 4.1 and 4.2). But, of these, Bourges (Avaricum) and Senlis (Augustomagus) were both close to the borders of Lugdunensis, and, perhaps more importantly, fell within the extended basins of the Seine and the Loire. Most of the Lugdunese cities which followed the same practice were also concentrated around these river basins, raising the possibility that we should view it as characteristic of this geographical region, rather than the politically defined province of Lugdunensis, which had simply made intelligent use of the natural landscape. The river basins are more likely to have encouraged contact between these communities than the political boundaries, perhaps causing the idea of constructing local spectacle buildings in the urban periphery to catch on and spread amongst them through local emulation.

Variations in periurban development

As noted above, the character and apparent extent of periurban occupation also varied from city to city all across Gaul. We have seen that a wide range of specific factors, including particular local circumstances, could encourage periurban development. But, on a province-wide scale, it is also possible to identify some recurring characteristics which seem to have made the development of an urban periphery inherently more likely. We will start by considering those cities which appear to have made very limited use of the urban periphery, and those which made reasonable, but not extensive, use of it: leaving aside for the moment particularly spectacular examples such as Arles, Lyon and Vienne. Many of the sites listed in table 4.4 (p. 165) actually appear thanks to a single form of periurban land-use: perhaps an amphitheatre, a sanctuary or some limited occupation. Examples include Antibes, Béziers, Corseul, Évreux, Limoges, Meaux, Rodez, Senlis and Soissons. In some cases, this may reflect a lack of archaeological exploration, but many cities must simply have generated very little periurban development. The middle ground is occupied by cities which have yielded periurban remains of a varied character on several sites. Examples include Apt, Autun, Fréjus,

Lisieux, Metz, Orange, Reims, Saintes and Sens. In general the differences between these two groups lie in size, status and apparent prosperity. With the exception of legal status, these are difficult factors to quantify. But a comparison between Fréjus in Narbonensis and Corseul in north-western Lugdunensis will serve to illustrate the sorts of factors which appear to have been relevant.

Fréjus, founded by Julius Caesar in the 40s BC, was made a Roman *colonia* by Augustus in the early 20s and used as a base for part of the Roman fleet during the first century of the principate.[425] Situated around 1.5 km inland from the Mediterranean, it had a port linked to the sea by a canal, and was also on the main land route along the south coast of Gaul between Italy and Spain. It was walled in the Augustan period, and had its street layout defined in the late first century BC.[426] Corseul was established as a *civitas*-capital during the last decade of the first century BC, but does not appear to have had its streets laid out formally until the Claudian period.[427] It was located on a minor watercourse, around 15 km from the coast, and could not have participated directly in marine trade. It was also not on the routes between any major settlements. Fréjus, then, was in a much better position to take advantage of trading opportunities than Corseul, had better links with other cities along the south coast, and for a while enjoyed political importance as a naval base.

The differences between the two settlements are reflected in the development of their urban centres. Fréjus became host to a theatre and several lavish *domus*, and was supplied by an aqueduct. Corseul, meanwhile, has yielded little in the way of monumental buildings, besides a small temple on the southern perimeter and some fourth-century baths. Even its finest houses were modest by comparison with those of Fréjus, and supplied by wells. But perhaps the most eloquent testimony to the differences between them is their periurban development. At Corseul, the only known feature is the sanctuary of le Haut-Bécherel. The periphery of Fréjus, by contrast, featured housing, lavish baths, a large classical amphitheatre, what was probably part of the naval base at Les Aiguières,[428] and kilns producing amphorae which travelled as far afield as Ostia and Ventimiglia.[429] Making due allowance for specific circumstances, then, we might say that periurban development tended to be more extensive at well-connected cities with flourishing economies and/or political significance.

At the top end of the scale, Vienne and Arles in Narbonensis and Lyon in Lugdunensis developed particularly extensive or spectacular urban peripheries. One characteristic which all certainly shared was the restrictive nature of their urban centres. Lyon's, on the colline de Fourvière was extremely inaccessible, requiring ascents up steep slopes to reach it on virtually every side. This was an unusual position by comparison with other Gallo-Roman cities,[430] and probably chosen because Lyon was one of the first cities established beyond Narbonensis, at a time when the region was barely pacified. It would have aided defence, but made access to the Rhône and Saône below difficult. Arles and Vienne, by contrast, were founded at river level. But Arles had a relatively small walled circuit: in part perhaps because marshy ground to the south-east left little room for an extensive urban centre. Its inadequacy for the needs of the population is demonstrated by their willingness to demolish it within a century of Arles' foundation, in order to make room for their amphitheatre.[431] Vienne, meanwhile, boasted a walled circuit 6 km long. But the inclusion of several hills in the circuit meant that much of the land it enclosed was in fact unsuitable for urban development, leaving only around 40 ha of good building ground available.

Vienne and Arles, then, clearly faced problems of space, while Lyon's urban centre was poorly suited to the climate of the *pax Romana*. In all three cases, periurban development offered a solution to these problems. But the difficulties presented by the urban centres are not enough in themselves to explain the extent and character of their peripheries. We are also dealing with unusually successful urban foundations. The position of all three on the lower and middle reaches of the Rhône cannot be a coincidence. It created opportunities for trade, and the very nature of the periurban development at all three cities demonstrates the importance of this. Vienne and Arles both undertook terracing and stabilisation work which allowed them to make fuller use of periurban land along the banks of the Rhône. Lyon, meanwhile, seems to have seen an outright shift in its urban centre over the course of the third century from the Fourvière site in favour of the lower land around the Rhône-Saône confluence.[432]

Finally, the locations of the three cities along the same river may also have led to direct emulation between them, encouraged by the regular contact it allowed. The possibility of competition between Arles and Vienne has already been raised in the context of their circuses, and could equally have applied to the public squares built in the transfluvial quarters at each. No such direct similarities can be drawn with periurban development at Lyon, but the amphitheatre associated with the sanctuary of the Three Gauls at Condate could well have been in the minds of the local elites at Arles and Vienne when they built circuses in their urban peripheries. Certainly, the presence of very similar theatre, sanctuary and odeon complexes in the centres of Lyon and Vienne makes competitive interaction between the two of them very likely. The possibility that all three communities were also looking beyond Gaul for models of periurban development will be returned to in chapter 7.

Appendix: table of major periurban remains

This table presents the major known periurban features from the administrative cities of Roman Gaul during the high empire, in an easily accessible form. It draws on information from numerous works listed in the bibliography, but the first and most helpful point of reference for further reading

HIGH EMPIRE: ADMINISTRATIVE CITIES

on any of the features indicated will be Bedon 2001. It includes only soundly documented features, omitting trace remains which cannot be confidently linked with any specific type of activity. It also omits funerary remains and villas or farms, since these were found outside all Roman cities, and can be taken as read for any given site.

Table 4.4 Major periurban remains at Gallo-Roman administrative cities

City	Industrial activity	Commercial activity	Domestic occupation	Baths	Temples	Spectacle buildings
Aquitania						
Agen						✓
Bordeaux	✓	✓	✓	✓	✓	✓
Bourges						✓
Cahors					✓	
Clermont-Ferrand			?		✓	
Limoges						✓
Périgueux				✓	?	✓
Poitiers	✓				✓	✓
Rodez						✓
Saint-Bertrand-de-Comminges						✓
Saintes	✓		✓		✓	✓
Belgica						
Amiens	✓		✓	?	✓	
Beauvais					✓	?
Metz		✓			✓	✓
Reims	✓	✓				✓
Senlis						✓
Soissons						✓
Trier			?		✓	✓
Lugdunensis						
Angers						✓
Autun		?	?		✓	✓
Bayeux					✓	
Carhaix						✓
Chartres	✓					
Corseul					✓	
Évreux						✓
Jublains					✓	✓
Le Mans						✓
Lillebonne					✓	✓
Lisieux	✓	✓	✓			✓
Lyon	✓	✓	✓	✓	✓	✓
Meaux					✓	

Continued overleaf

Table 4.4 Continued

City	Industrial activity	Commercial activity	Domestic occupation	Baths	Temples	Spectacle buildings
Orléans						✓
Paris		✓	✓			✓
Rouen						✓
Sens	✓		✓		✓	✓
Tours	✓					✓
Vieux						✓
Narbonensis						
Aix-en-Provence						✓
Antibes						✓
Apt			✓		✓	?
Arles		✓	✓	✓		✓
Béziers						✓
Die						?
Fréjus	✓	✓	✓	✓		✓
Narbonne	✓			✓	✓	✓
Nîmes	✓					
Orange			✓			✓
Toulouse	✓	✓	✓	✓	✓	✓
Vienne	✓	✓	✓	✓	✓	✓

5

GAUL IN THE HIGH EMPIRE: SECONDARY AGGLOMERATIONS

Introduction

Within the territory of an administrative city, substantial numbers of smaller settlements, or 'secondary agglomerations'[1] were usually to be found (figure 4.1, p. 84). This chapter addresses the question of whether development analogous to that discussed in the previous chapter can also be identified at the secondary agglomerations of Gaul.

Secondary settlements are usually viewed as a coherent group on the grounds that they, and their inhabitants, were all administered on a day-to-day basis by the council of decurions based in the local administrative city. They were therefore subordinate in status to this city, and could not act independently of it. Beyond this common factor, however, the size, appearance, status and function of Gallo-Roman secondary agglomerations in fact varied widely: much like the towns, villages, hamlets and other settlements administered from a modern British county town. We shall begin by establishing the extent of this variation, and some of its manifestations.

Something of the physical variations between secondary agglomerations may be illustrated by comparing Mandeure (Epomanduorum, figure 5.1), a small town in the territory of the Sequani,[2] and Taden (figure 5.2), a port settlement in north-western Lugdunensis.[3] These two settlements differed markedly from one another in almost every aspect of their physical appearance. While Mandeure was organised around a more or less regular street-grid, Taden consisted of a scatter of buildings following various alignments: most apparently determined by features such as the nearby river Rance and a winding road passing through the centre of the site. The occupation at Mandeure also covered a total of over 120 ha, in contrast with an occupied area of around 50 ha at Taden. In addition, Mandeure has yielded evidence for several monumental buildings in the form of a temple, a theatre, two sets of baths and a portico. Taden, meanwhile, is only known to have possessed two small Romano-Celtic temples.

Taken together, Mandeure and Taden may be characterised as representing different points along a spectrum of aspirations towards *urbanitas*. The

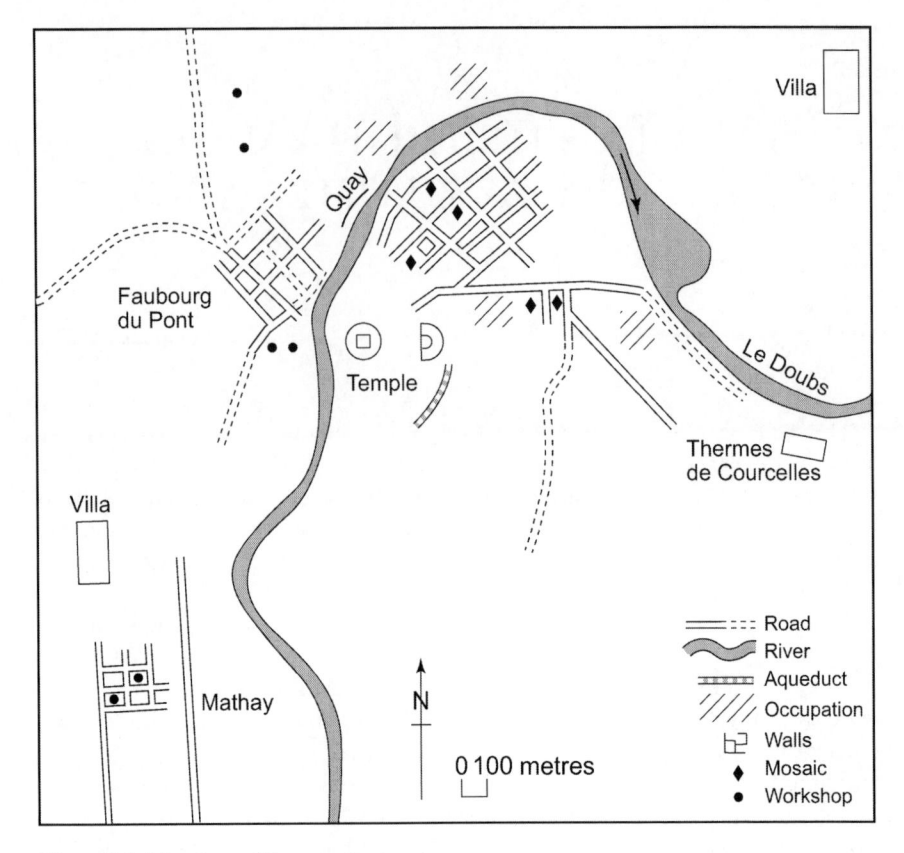

Figure 5.1 Mandeure (Epomanduorum).

orthogonal street layout and monumental buildings of Mandeure are features which would be expected in any of the administrative cities of Gaul. Meanwhile, other indications from the site also point towards customs and practices typical of cities with administrative status. For example, Mandeure has yielded thirty-four inscriptions of different types – more than some actual *civitas*-capitals[4] – while none are known from Taden. We might comment that although Mandeure lacked the administrative role necessary to qualify as 'urban' in the strictest sense, certain individuals involved with the settlement apparently hoped to acquire a less strictly technical form of urban status for it by equipping it with the monumental façade which Pausanias, at least, considered of almost equal importance in identifying a Greek settlement as a full *polis*.[5] At Taden, such individuals were clearly lacking.

Individuals with the capacity to affect the appearance of a secondary agglomeration such as Mandeure must by definition have been members of the local elite, since they were clearly people who possessed the wealth, the

HIGH EMPIRE: SECONDARY AGGLOMERATIONS

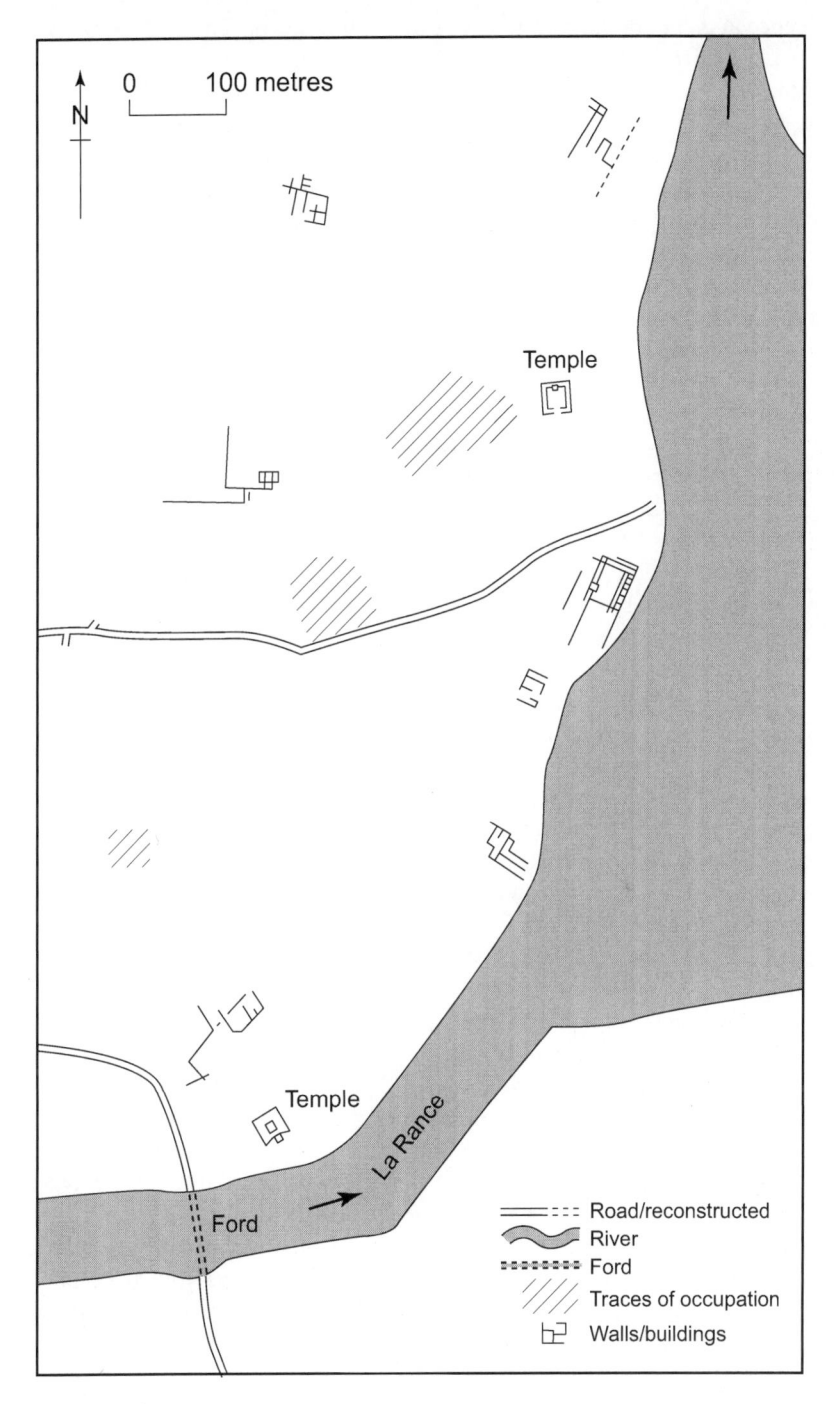

Figure 5.2 Taden.

influence and the inclination to instigate such projects. The establishment of an orthogonal grid in particular indicates a significant outlay of both effort and money, since these were expensive to establish, especially on sites which were already occupied.[6] Although local elites in Gaul, as elsewhere in the Roman empire, are traditionally considered to have focused most of their activities on administrative cities, there is also significant evidence for elite involvement with secondary agglomerations, of a kind which may have led to such monumentalisation.

In part, elite involvement may have been encouraged by the Roman system of administration. Some of the larger secondary agglomerations, for example, probably acted as centres for the administration of *pagi* (subsidiary districts within the territory of an administrative city). As such, they may have had their own local assemblies, or have been used as bases by junior magistrates.[7] If so, this system probably encouraged the magistrates or assembly members to make benefactions of monumental public architecture in the secondary agglomerations, as a means of boosting their own local status and ensuring progress up the political ladder. In addition, Mangin and Tassaux have argued that the councils of decurions who oversaw the affairs of the *civitas* as a whole may also, on occasion, have ordered the construction of monumental buildings in secondary agglomerations,[8] perhaps indicating that the appearance of these settlements, like the appearance of the main administrative city, could contribute to displays of the whole community's status and identity. Other evidence from secondary agglomerations may suggest that some elite individuals felt a more personal concern for their development. For example, lavish funerary monuments found close to these settlements[9] may indicate a desire to establish or display a long-running interest in the settlement on the part of certain local families. Indeed, Woolf has argued that some aspects of elite involvement with secondary agglomerations may reflect the persistence of loyalties to pre-Roman settlements which remained occupied in the Roman period, but were not made into *civitas*-capitals.[10]

Of course, the pre-Roman origins of some secondary agglomerations could have a significant influence on their physical appearance. Not all secondary agglomerations of the Gallo-Roman period had their origins in pre-Roman settlements, but where such a history did apply, it could have a far greater effect on the topographical development of the site than was usually the case for an administrative city with similar origins. When a pre-Roman settlement was marked out for transformation into a new, Gallo-Roman *civitas*-capital, the local elite was generally quick to set about turning it into a city in the Roman style, and existing pre-Roman structures were often demolished.[11] However, less emphasis was placed on transforming secondary centres in the same manner. In some secondary agglomerations, particularly in southern Gaul, pre-Roman structures remained in place, and continued to affect the local topography well into the Roman period.[12] Most strikingly, numerous secondary agglomerations can be identified today as having had pre-Roman origins precisely because of the continued presence of a pre-Roman earthen rampart around the site. In fact, it is clear that in some cases, pre-Roman ramparts were deliberately maintained at such settlements, rather than simply never demolished. For example, the pre-Roman fortifications of the settlement at Mont Afrique, near Dijon in Germania Superior, were repaired at least twice during the Roman period.[13]

Various technical terms for describing the status of secondary settlements are known; for example, '*vicus*' or '*conciliabulum*'.[14] But it is rare to be able to attribute them securely to any specific settlement. Some Gallo-Roman secondary agglomerations can be identified as *vici* from local epigraphy, the Peutinger Table or land itineraries. However, many are not mentioned in these sources. Scholars are thus left to invent criteria by which to identify their legal status from their archaeological remains:[15] a problematic exercise, given that we cannot be certain that a particular status was always linked with specific physical features. Furthermore, the precise technical meaning of either '*vicus*' or '*conciliabulum*' in a Gallo-Roman context is in any case still only partially understood. Leveau reminds us that we still do not know whether a *vicus* was always found in association with a *pagus*, or whether the *vicus* was always dominant over the *pagus* rather than vice versa.[16] Meanwhile, the application of the term '*conciliabulum*' to certain settlements in the centre-west of Gaul, championed by Picard in the 1970s,[17] is now generally rejected, partly because there is no evidence that it was ever used in Gaul as a technical term at all.[18] The very existence of isolated monumental centres at these sites, a feature considered characteristic of a '*conciliabulum*' by Picard, is also increasingly coming into doubt, as aerial photography and further excavations reveal substantial areas of associated housing which were hitherto unknown.[19]

Of greater importance than the quest to identify the status of specific secondary agglomerations is the fact that the division in status between these settlements and administrative cities was in any case not entirely static.[20] Sources such as Strabo, Pliny, road itineraries and local epigraphy, which can be used to identify the status of particular settlements during a given period, also reveal that this status could change over time. Thus, Carcassonne and Château-Roussillon were both *coloniae* in the early imperial period, but had been demoted to the status of *castella* by the time the Bordeaux-Jerusalem itinerary was written in AD 333.[21] Conversely, certain particularly successful secondary agglomerations were promoted in the late imperial period to become the administrative centres of their own territories: examples include Boulogne, Geneva, Grenoble and Tournai. The importance of such documented changes is that urban status in Roman Gaul *was* negotiable. Settlements such as Mandeure did stand a genuine chance of attaining full administrative status if a sufficient display of local importance was made: something which benefactions of orthogonal street layouts or monumental public buildings could only aid.

Whilst it is difficult to identify the legal status of a secondary agglomeration with certainty, variations in the roles which they played within wider settlement networks are proving a fruitful focus of current scholarship. Archaeological evidence makes it clear that secondary settlements were capable of performing a wide range of different social, administrative and economic functions.[22] Certain secondary agglomerations also developed a specialised function, and may thus have been visited by people from the surrounding region who required a specific service. Some settlements, for example, developed a specialised religious function, attested by the remains of temple complexes or baths fed by thermal springs.[23] Others had a strong industrial or commercial element,[24] or acted primarily as road-stations meeting the needs of travellers.[25] Such specialisation was not universal, and many secondary agglomerations performed a combination of functions. However, it does point towards the development of local settlement hierarchies in Gaul during the Roman period, consisting of groups of interdependent secondary agglomerations headed by the administrative cities.[26]

Finally, secondary agglomerations also varied in terms of their distribution across the landscape. Location studies have shown that certain geographical factors were particularly conducive to the successful development of Gallo-Roman secondary agglomerations. They are often found, for example, at sites with good communications links. Waterways had already been attractive to settlement in the pre-Roman period, but the development of the Gallo-Roman road system played a still greater role in influencing the distribution of secondary agglomerations.[27] Sites where one or more transport routes intersected, such as cross-roads, river-crossings or estuary mouths were especially favoured. Secondary agglomerations could also be located at points of special significance within the political or physical landscape, such as near the boundaries of *civitates*, close to *civitas*-capitals, at valley entrances or on hill-tops.[28] Many Gallo-Roman secondary agglomerations had of course already had their locations determined in the pre-Roman period. However, sites with pre-Roman origins could only have survived and flourished if their locations also gave them a relevance and function within the new Gallo-Roman settlement networks. It is also clear that secondary agglomerations were not evenly distributed across all of Gaul in the Roman period, and nor were they consistent in character from one region to another.[29] For instance, studies in Aquitania have revealed a striking contrast between those *civitates* north of the Garonne, which generally had dense networks of secondary agglomerations, and those to the south, which contained very few such settlements.[30] In part, this reflects geographical factors which made some regions more hospitable to secondary centres than others, as well as differences in settlement patterns in the pre-Roman period.[31] However, Woolf has argued that variations in the density of secondary agglomerations may also have resulted from the different levels of interest shown by local elites in fostering their development.[32]

In terms of appearance, status, function, distribution and extent of elite involvement, then, the secondary agglomerations in Roman Gaul, were a highly diverse group: arguably much more diverse than the administrative cities from which they are usually distinguished. As a result, research into these settlements has frequently sought to approach them by grouping them into different typological categories. In France, a typology created in 1990 by Mangin and Tassaux for the secondary agglomerations of Aquitania[33] had a significant impact on modern research, and has since been applied to other parts of Gaul.[34] Mangin and Tassaux defined five types of secondary agglomeration, which may be translated as follows:

1   Cities, including 'true' cities and semi-urban agglomerations.
2   Small market towns (specialised or diversified economic centres).
3   Agglomerations with a predominantly religious function.
4   Relay stations.
5   Rural agglomerations or villages.

These categories have not been without their critics, who have argued that there is not yet sufficient evidence available to group secondary agglomerations in this way, or, who suggested that the categories do not do justice to the full range of secondary settlement types in Gaul.[35] However, Tassaux defended the typology in 1994, arguing that it is more useful to attempt to examine the different functions of secondary agglomerations than simply to list them without distinction, even if this can currently be done only as a preliminary exercise.[36] In Britain, Burnham and Wacher devised a similar typology for their book, *The Small Towns of Roman Britain*.[37] Burnham and Wacher, however, split Mangin and Tassaux's first category into three different levels of cities and towns, and introduced 'minor defended settlements' and 'undefended settlements' in the place of their last two categories. These changes in part reflect differences in the development of Britain and Gaul during the Roman period, since most British settlements were defended by the end of the second century, while their Gallo-Roman equivalents remained open.

Here, a typological approach will also be adopted, in order to discover whether there are consistent patterns in the development or non-development of any peripheral features around different types of secondary agglomerations. However, the categories defined by both Mangin and Tassaux and Burnham and Wacher have limitations which make them inappropriate in the present context. The criteria used by both sets of researchers to define their categories are somewhat mixed, grouping the settlements by a combination of their physical appearance (e.g. size, monumentality, presence of defences) and their apparent socio-economic function. In my view, this undermines the usefulness of the typologies, since it creates the potential for a settlement to belong equally to two different categories depending on whether its physical appearance or local function is privileged. In this chapter, I propose instead to group the secondary agglomerations of Gaul into two broad categories on the basis of a single criterion:

1   Those, such as Mandeure, which show significant evidence for aspirations towards *urbanitas*.
2   All other settlements.

In practice, the line between these two categories is of course hard to define, and classifications are bound to remain somewhat subjective. However, in the context of an enquiry into the periurban, it is worth at least attempting to make this division, for two main reasons. First, examining the 'more urbanised' secondary agglomerations as a separate group allows valuable comparisons to be drawn between these settlements and the primary administrative centres of Gaul. As the example of Mandeure shows, the most urban secondary agglomerations had much in common with administrative cities in terms of size, appearance and culture. If, then, they are also found to display patterns of periurban development similar to those associated with administrative cities, this may indicate that the two types of settlement had more in common on a socio-economic level than the legal differences between them might suggest. Second, an examination of the 'less urbanised' secondary agglomerations as a separate group will allow the assumption, made thus far, that periurban occupation requires a distinctly urban centre against which to be defined to be put to the test. Since these settlements were not markedly urban in nature, we might assume that they could not have possessed an urban periphery. The second part of this chapter will determine whether they could, none the less, be organised according to some form of centre–periphery divide and, if they could not, what alternative forms of topographical organisation they *did* display. While the discussion of both types of secondary agglomeration is underway, the terms 'periurban' and 'urban periphery' will be avoided until and unless it becomes possible to determine whether they can justifiably be applied to the occupation encountered at these settlements. 'Centre' and 'periphery' will be preferred, since they avoid assumptions about the *urbanitas* of the settlements under discussion.

As a final point, it must be acknowledged that any study of Gallo-Roman secondary agglomerations is made difficult by the limited nature of the archaeological evidence available: especially dating evidence.[38] Even where systematic excavations are carried out, they are often too limited in scope to provide detailed chronological information,[39] while many features are known only through aerial photography. Modern research into secondary agglomerations has also been uneven, meaning that settlements in some areas of Gaul have been studied in great detail, while those in other areas remain poorly known. Comprehensive regional syntheses of secondary settlements in Aquitania,[40] Belgica and the Germanies[41] and the modern regions of

Franche-Comté and Bourgogne[42] and Languedoc-Roussillon[43] have all been published, but other parts of Lugdunensis and Narbonensis remain to be covered. This makes it difficult to compare secondary agglomerations in different parts of Gaul. Likewise, few of the sites are known in enough detail to draw firm conclusions about the nature, or even the existence, of any development around their peripheries. Therefore, in this chapter the study area has been expanded slightly in order to increase the available data-set, with a small number of sites from areas allocated to the Germanies in the AD 90s included in the discussion.

Settlements with distinct aspirations towards *urbanitas*

Introduction

Few Gallo-Roman secondary agglomerations have yielded clear evidence for significant aspirations towards urban status. Mangin and Tassaux, when creating their typologies of secondary agglomerations in Aquitania, were able to identify only ten ' "true" cities' and a further twenty 'semi-urban agglomerations' amongst a data-set of 180 secondary settlements known in the region.[44] Naturally, still less of those secondary agglomerations which *do* show signs of urban aspirations have been investigated thoroughly enough to reveal evidence for any peripheral development. A recent discussion of eight of the largest and best-known secondary agglomerations in Aquitania includes the comment, '*Notons à cette occasion que l'environnement immédiat des agglomérations n'est pour ainsi dire pas connu: aucun faubourg, aucun nécropole n'ont été repérés.*'[45] As a result, it has been possible to draw on evidence from only eleven settlements for the present discussion: Naintré,[46] Antigny,[47] Sanxay, Saint-Germain-d'Esteuil[48] and Argentomagus[49] in Aquitania, Dalheim, Château-Porcien and Beaumont-sur-Oise in Belgica,[50] Ambrussum and Glanum[51] in Narbonensis and Mandeure in Germania Superior.

The small size of this group need not be taken to indicate that occupation on the periphery of urbanised secondary agglomerations was especially unusual *per se*, given the current state of research. It does, however, mean that it is difficult to be certain how widely the patterns of occupation observed may actually have applied in the past. Within the group, a preponderance of settlements in Aquitania and Belgica must be acknowledged; however, this is more likely to reflect the concentrations of modern scholarship than ancient patterns. It should also be noted that three of the settlements – Naintré, Antigny and Sanxay – were all located in the territory of the Pictones, where they formed an arc of highly urbanised secondary agglomerations between 18 and 30 km from the *civitas*-capital, Poitiers.[52] Thus, any patterns of occupation observed at these particular towns may in fact have resulted from local circumstances (including direct emulation of one another), rather than from factors which applied all over Gaul.[53]

The main features which mark out the settlements in this group as having had strong aspirations towards *urbanitas* are the presence of an orthogonal street layout or monumental public buildings. Naintré, Antigny, Dalheim, Château-Porcien, Beaumont-sur-Oise and Mandeure all have well-documented orthogonal layouts, and Sanxay clearly had a strongly axial plan, although only fragments of an actual street-grid have been identified. Not all of these layouts are entirely regular across the site. For example, at Mandeure, the orientations of some roads were clearly influenced by the curving course of the nearby river Doubs. Yet a degree of irregularity can also be identified in the street plans of some administrative cities; for example, Amiens, Arles, Lyon, Paris, Rouen, Saintes or Toulouse. Meanwhile, with the exception of the poorly explored Château-Porcien, each one of these settlements is known to have possessed a theatre and at least one temple. Mandeure also boasted a set of baths and Antigny and Sanxay both possessed complexes of related monuments, unified through architectural devices such as a common orientation or an enclosure wall. Saint-Germain-d'Esteuil, Argentomagus, Ambrussum and Glanum did not have orthogonal layouts, but all were well-equipped with urban-style public monuments or houses.[54] Ambrussum also appears to have minted its own coins during the closing years of the Republic,[55] while Glanum has yielded an inscription of the second century AD describing it as a '*res publica*' with its own treasury.[56] Both, then, may in fact have enjoyed full urban status for a time, although it is not thought to have been long-lasting in either case.

Boundaries

If the secondary agglomerations under consideration here shared with full administrative cities characteristics such as orthogonal street layouts or the presence of monumental public buildings, it should not come as a surprise to find that they also shared the distinctly urban trait of using visible boundary markers to define the core of the settlement. The orthogonal grids already discussed of course contributed to this, by creating a visual distinction between the area covered by and aligned with the grid, and the area beyond it. Furthermore, those parts of the settlements which possessed orthogonal grids, or, in the absence of a grid, featured the heaviest concentration of monumental buildings, were also often demarcated by natural features such as watercourses or steep slopes, suggesting that they were deliberately placed to make use of these as boundary markers. Watercourses appear to have acted as boundary markers at Antigny, Beaumont, Mandeure, Naintré and Sanxay, while steep slopes also performed the same function at Antigny, Argentomagus, Château-Porcien, Dalheim, Naintré and Saint-Germain-d'Esteuil. Finally, Ambrussum, Glanum (figure 5.3) and Argentomagus (figure 5.4, p. 182) also retained into the Roman period defensive circuits which had been established before the Roman occupation.

HIGH EMPIRE: SECONDARY AGGLOMERATIONS

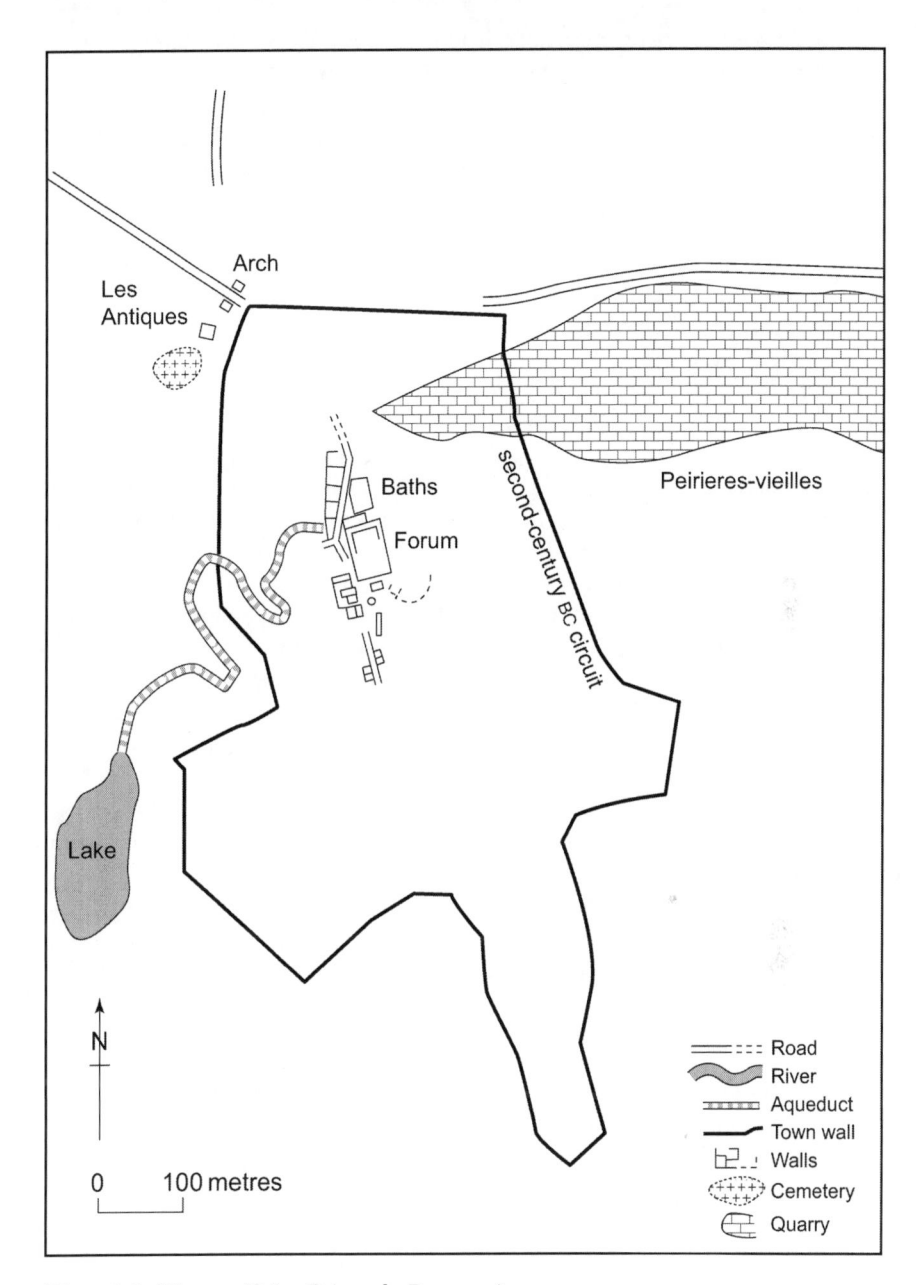

Figure 5.3 Glanum (Saint-Rémy-de-Provence).

Glanum had had two successive defensive circuits by the time it was incorporated into the Roman empire: initially one of earth and dry stone built around the sixth century BC, and then a rebuilding of this circuit in *grand appareil* and its extension northwards in the second century BC.[57] Ambrussum, too, had known two successive sets of masonry ramparts by the second half of the third century BC, both furnished with towers.[58] Meanwhile, part of Argentomagus was located on a steep-sided plateau, known today as 'les Mersans', with an earthwork consisting of a bank and ditch restricting access to the plateau from its one readily approachable side.[59]

That all of these boundary markers performed the same sorts of functions as the boundary markers found in administrative cities is already strongly suggested by their location around parts of the settlements which were embellished with orthogonal grids or monumental public buildings. It may in some cases be further strengthened by an examination of the position of the settlements' cemeteries: features which, as established in chapter 3, can help modern observers to identify the probable courses of urban boundaries, even if they did not constitute boundary markers in themselves. We find that cemeteries have been identified at Dalheim at the northern and southern ends of the orthogonal grid, as well as to the east, in the valley below the edge of the plateau where the settlement was situated.[60] Beaumont-sur-Oise also had a cemetery immediately to the south of its orthogonal grid.[61] At Argentomagus, imperial-period cemeteries were located outside the pre-Roman earthwork,[62] strengthening the idea that it helped to define a special area of occupation on the plateau itself. At Glanum, a cemetery was in use by the first century BC about 600m north of the probable line of the second century BC circuit,[63] while no tombs of this period have been found within the circuit. The best-known tomb from the imperial period here is a mausoleum at 'les Antiques', built just outside the north-west corner of the defensive circuit, but inhumation burials and a funerary inscription have also been found close by,[64] all suggesting that the pre-Roman circuit continued to be used as a form of pomerial boundary. Perhaps more significantly, around 20 BC a monumental arch was built in the same area of 'les Antiques' on the approach into the town.[65] Thus, a typically Roman-style boundary marker supplemented the nearby line of the existing ramparts, marking a point of transition here between countryside and settlement. Similarly, the south gate at Ambrussum was rebuilt in the late first century BC, again reinforcing in a Roman context the significance of the existing pre-Roman circuit.

If it is by now clear that boundaries similar to those found in administrative cities were used to define distinct 'centres' in the most urbanised secondary agglomerations, we should nevertheless note that in several cases, the state of the evidence makes it difficult to identify the line of the boundaries precisely. For instance, it may not be clear how far an orthogonal grid extended. It is also arguable that the concern to mark settlement boundaries clearly, and to maintain them over time, was less strong in these secondary agglomerations than was usually the case in the administrative cities of Gaul. The irregularities in some of their street plans, for instance, may reflect a lower level of commitment to the idea of creating a precisely ordered urban centre than was felt at some administrative centres. Some orthogonal layouts also appear to have developed over a longer period of time than the grids laid out in administrative cities, or have been established at a later date.[66] Occupation at Dalheim, for example, began in the Augustan period, but an orthogonal grid was only added on to the existing ribbon development at the site in the AD 70s.[67] At Château-Porcien, on the other hand, excavations on the plateau de Nandin make it reasonably certain that the occupation here was both established for the first time and organised into an orthogonal grid during the Augustan period.[68] In addition, the use of features such as rivers or steep slopes to define the edges of these settlements should not be interpreted purely as a sign of interest in conforming to the Roman ideal of urbanism. Natural features such as these were often employed as boundaries for indigenous settlements, prior to the beginnings of Roman influence in Gaul.[69]

Chronology

Some of the settlements in this group are known to have been occupied in the pre-Roman period. This is certainly the case for Argentomagus, Ambrussum and Glanum, as evidenced by their pre-Roman defences, and extensive Hellenistic-period remains in the case of Glanum.[70] The establishment of Roman rule did not always have an immediate effect on the topography of such settlements. In Narbonensis, Ambrussum and Glanum begin to show unequivocal evidence for change only in the latter half of the first century BC, while the earliest recognisably Roman constructions at Argentomagus were not built until the first half of the first century AD. Even once the settlement had become recognisably Gallo-Roman, existing pre-Roman features could continue to have a marked effect on topographical development. The pre-Roman buildings at Glanum in the mouth of the valley of Notre-Dame determined the organisation and later development of the town's monumental centre, while the defensive circuits at all three settlements seem to have continued to define their 'central' cores throughout the Roman period.

Whilst such dramatic legacies of pre-Roman occupation are absent from the other secondary agglomerations being considered here, pre-Roman origins can be detected in several other cases. A la Tène house has been identified at Dalheim,[71] while Iron Age coins and fibulae were discovered beneath the sanctuary at Mandeure.[72] Saint-Germain-d'Esteuil has yielded evidence for at least sporadic occupation since the mid-third century BC, and Naintré appears to have resulted from a shift in the early Roman period from a hilltop *oppidum* into the river-plain below, which itself may already have been partially occupied.[73] Meanwhile, the site of Château-Porcien on a closely defined plateau has led some commentators to suggest that it may have been the location of a pre-Roman settlement.[74] In most cases, however, the earliest significant signs of nucleated settlement appeared during the reign of Augustus, with noticeable flourishing beginning in the Claudian period.[75]

Occupation beyond the visible boundary markers at these settlements is rarely well enough documented to allow detailed commentary on its chronological relationship with the demarcated centres. However, at none of these sites is any peripheral feature known to have *pre*-dated the establishment of the defined settlement centre. Argentomagus does offer an example of the appearance of a peripheral monument almost concurrently with the beginnings of monumentalisation on the defended plateau. Here, a wooden theatre of Gallo-Roman type was built at le Virou in the second quarter of the first century AD, around 100m west of the plateau (see plate 5.1).[76] Perhaps more typical, however, is the situation seen at Mandeure. Here, an area of peripheral development at Mathay probably grew up for the first time during the first century AD.[77] If this is correct, Mathay became occupied well after the establishment of Mandeure's central nucleus in the Augustan period.

General topography

A number of the settlements in this group have yielded evidence for individual public buildings such as theatres, temples or baths, which seem to

Plate 5.1 Theatre of le Virou, Argentomagus.

have stood beyond their demarcated centres and in isolation from other structures. The level of archaeological information available in most cases means that the possibility of as-yet-unidentified structures around these buildings, or between them and the settlement centre, cannot be discounted. However, on the basis of the current evidence, examples of apparently isolated peripheral buildings include a theatre at Dalheim,[78] another at Saint-Germain-d'Esteuil,[79] a further theatre, temple and enclosed spring basin at Sanxay,[80] a theatre and small temple at Argentomagus[81] and one more theatre and temple as well as a set of baths at Mandeure.[82] All were set apart from the centres of their respective settlements, and yet linked to them through devices such as roads or physical orientation (see discussion below). The placement of such public buildings in the settlement periphery, with no immediately adjacent occupation, is something which has already been encountered at administrative cities, and hence may point towards similar principles of topographical organisation being used. It is also worth noting that, again just as at administrative cities, isolated public buildings could either be the only peripheral features at a secondary agglomeration (e.g. at Dalheim, Sanxay and Saint-Germain-d'Esteuil), or occur together with clusters of occupation elsewhere in the settlement periphery (e.g. at Mandeure and Argentomagus).

At certain secondary agglomerations, occupation has been identified which is continuous with the centre of the settlement but distinguished from it by the boundary markers discussed above. This is particularly clear at Argentomagus, where most of the peripheral occupation was clustered immediately around the defended plateau of les Mersans, just beyond the pre-Roman rampart (figure 5.4). To the north of the rampart lay an amphitheatre, which was probably built in the second century AD.[83] This quickly became surrounded by an area of loose residential and artisanal occupation on the plateau of les Courates, which grew up from around the same period and is known through antiquarian reports, aerial photography and surface survey.[84] Meanwhile, between the southern foot of les Mersans and the bank of the river Creuse lay a set of public baths, probably also built in the second century, and again almost certainly surrounded by further occupation.[85] Both les Courates and the river valley, then, appear to have been used as expansion zones during the second century, providing extra space for the construction of both public monuments and residential occupation. Again, this is a pattern which can be seen in the peripheries of administrative cities in Gaul such as Lyon or Vienne. Indeed, the relatively small size of the defended plateau at Argentomagus may indicate that continuous areas of occupation grew up on its periphery for similar reasons to the equivalent developments at Lyon and Vienne: the presence of an original defined 'centre' which was closely constricted by natural topography and/or man-made defences.

Rather different settlement patterns are seen at Mandeure, Antigny, Château-Porcien and Ambrussum. These four settlements all featured separate

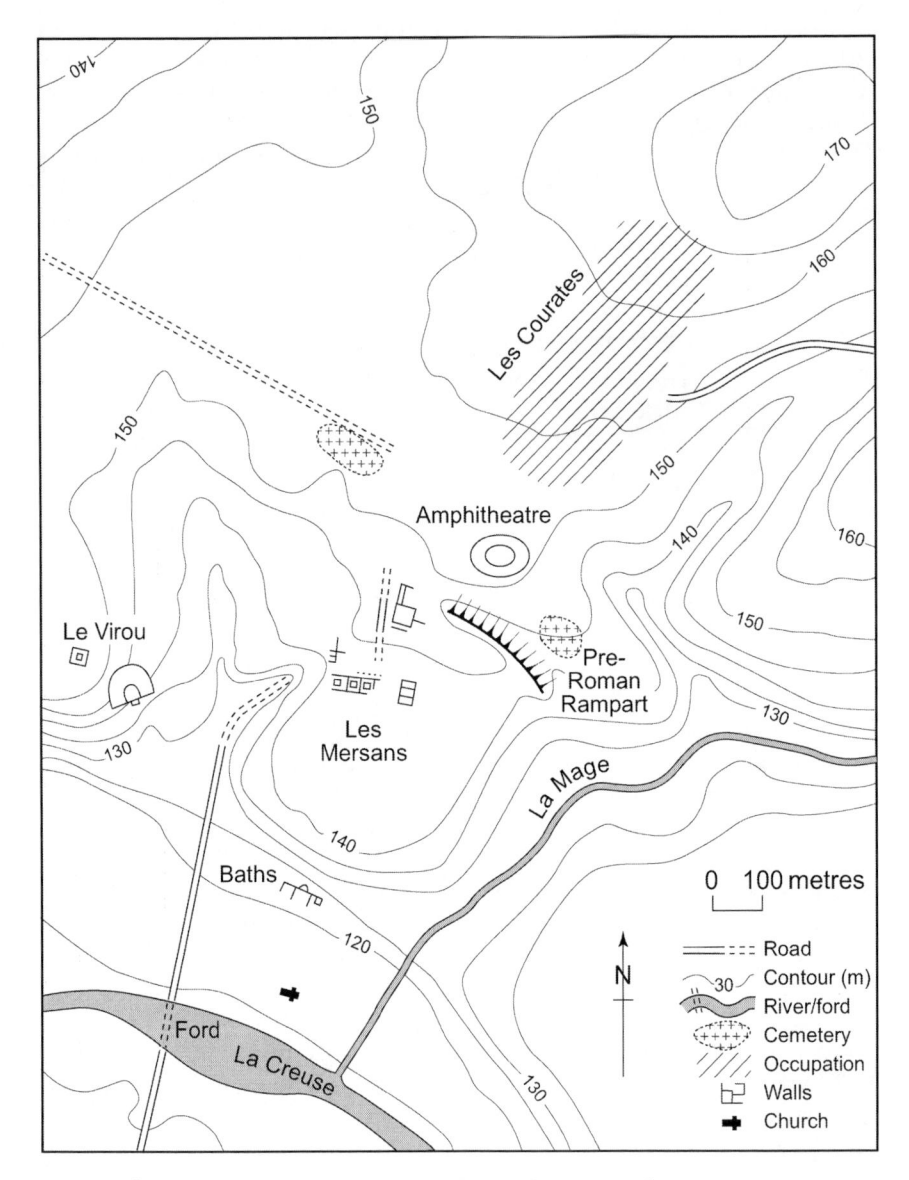

Figure 5.4 Argentomagus (Argenton-sur-Creuse/Saint-Marcel).

nuclei of occupation which were not directly continuous with their demarcated centres, but nevertheless appears to have been closely related to them. At Mandeure, two such nuclei, covering around 100 ha between them, existed in addition to the 60 ha of the settlement centre.[86] The first of these, the 'Faubourg du Pont', lay across the river Doubs, where two major roads converged in order to cross it by bridge.[87] This can arguably be interpreted as a directly continuous development, which was separated only by the river from the main core of Mandeure. However, the second nucleus, Mathay, lay approximately 1.5 km from the demarcated centre, separated from it by both the river Doubs and an extent of apparently open space. Nevertheless, several factors suggest that it should be interpreted as a satellite settlement rather than an independent agglomeration. Mathay was linked to the settlement centre at Mandeure by its position on the main road leading out of Mandeure towards Besançon and by a ford across the Doubs. It also appears to have performed a specialised commercial and industrial function, believed to have been linked with trading activities based in the larger centre.[88] At Antigny, a similar area of occupation lay across the Gartempe and around 250m from the main settlement, but was connected to it by a ford across the river. Here, 4000m^2 of built-up occupation has been recognised through aerial photography, including the ground-plans of buildings which appear to be houses.[89] At Ambrussum, a separate nucleus of occupation grew up around 30 BC at Sablas, which lay on the Via Domitia 250m from the fortified centre, and close to the river Vidourle.[90] Finally, at Château-Porcien, another nucleus of occupation, at la Briqueterie and les Coutures, lay approximately 1.5 km east of the main settlement centre and was connected to it by the road towards Köln.[91]

These distinct satellite nuclei may again be compared with similar developments already observed at certain administrative cities: in particular, Amiens, Metz, Lisieux, Périgueux and Toulouse. It is also of interest to note that the satellite nuclei at both Mandeure and Antigny have yielded evidence for the presence of orthogonal street layouts. The Faubourg du Pont at Mandeure was not only laid out with orthogonal streets itself, but also shared an identical alignment with the main centre: perhaps supporting the earlier suggestion that it should really be seen as a continuous peripheral development rather than a separate satellite. Mathay, however, also had an extensive and very regular orthogonal grid, which has been thoroughly explored through modern excavations, although here it was aligned with the main road towards Besançon rather than with the streets of Mandeure. Meanwhile, the nucleus across the Gartempe at Antigny featured at least two roads which were perpendicular to the main route leading through it towards Bourges.[92] This suggests that this quarter was also organised around an orthogonal grid, although it is not certain in this case whether the grid was deliberately planned or developed spontaneously, like the example seen at Lisieux. Orthogonal planning of this kind was extremely rare in the urban peripheries of the major administrative cities in Gaul, and its appearance outside Mandeure, and possibly Antigny, is rather surprising. It could perhaps be characterised as the result of a local enthusiasm for adopting indicators of urban status, such as the orthogonal grid, which was less constrained by the usual focus upon the urban centre than it might have been in a primary city.

However, given that these two cases are the only examples known, they need not be viewed as evidence for a widespread practice.

Uses of peripheral space

The secondary agglomerations which are grouped together in this chapter because of their apparent aspirations towards *urbanitas* are separated in other contexts because of the different activities which went on within them. Such functional distinctions should generally not be drawn too sharply, since the evidence is rarely strong enough to be certain that any given activity was *not* practised within a particular secondary agglomeration in the past. It is also clear that many settlements performed a range of functions. Researchers at Sanxay, for instance, usually categorised as a religious settlement, have suggested that it was also the setting for fairs during religious festivals, thus combining an economic with a sacred function.[93] However, it is noticeable that, among the settlements under discussion here, Antigny, Sanxay and Glanum have produced evidence for particularly large or extensive sanctuary complexes, but little or no industrial activity. By contrast, the other settlements being examined have yielded plentiful evidence for economic activity, although all of them also had at least one temple. At Beaumont-sur-Oise, Mandeure, Dalheim, Naintré and Argentomagus, industries such as ceramic production, metal-working, meat-processing, stone-working and textile production are well attested within the centres of the settlements.[94] This is perfectly in keeping with the evidence from administrative cities in Gaul, where there also seems to have been no deliberate policy of excluding industrial production from the urban centre.

Beyond the centres of these secondary agglomerations, industrial activity is also attested, but often appears to have taken on a more specialised character. At Naintré, several potters' kilns, and possibly some metal-working forges, were clustered together immediately east of the town's orthogonal grid.[95] Aerial photographs of the site suggest that some of these kilns were grouped within a rectangular enclosure, while excavations in 1985 uncovered an organised potters' workshop.[96] This area, then, was clearly dominated by industrial activity, and was probably used by groups of potters working together. Excavations at Mathay near Mandeure have also revealed evidence of specialised activity. Here, the dominant industry appears to have been the manufacture of pitchers, which, along with other ceramic goods, were produced in at least seven workshops, some featuring more than one kiln or specialised rooms for different stages in the production process.[97] With several shops and storage silos also identified on the site, Mathay appears to have functioned primarily as a centre of production and exchange, with links to the main centre at Mandeure, and perhaps also other markets along the course of the Doubs or along the road to Besançon.[98] At Sablas, just outside Ambrussum, a building with a courtyard has been excavated in detail.[99] This building was host to a range of economic activities, including milling, smithing and ceramic production, while the prints of numerous horse-shoes in the floor suggested that horses regularly passed through the court, and a series of rooms along its north wall may have been used as bedrooms. The site as a whole has been interpreted as a relay-station servicing travellers on the Via Domitia,[100] which may be seen in itself as a specialised function. Finally, at Glanum, major quarrying work went on during the early imperial period to the north-east of the settlement, where large deposits of shelly limestone were available (labelled 'Peirieres-vieilles' on figure 5.3, p. 177).[101] These quarries must have been a major source of wealth for Glanum, since their stone was used not only for many of the buildings within the town, but also for construction works at Lyon and Vienne.[102]

It would thus appear to have been possible for industrial activity to develop almost anywhere within an urbanised secondary agglomeration, but for it to gather in the settlement periphery in certain circumstances, often as a specialised cluster of related activity. At Glanum, the location of the quarrying industry was obviously determined by the limestone deposits. The activity here may be compared with that at Nîmes, or the clusters of potters attracted to clay seams in the peripheries of Fréjus, Saintes and Sens. The relay station outside Ambrussum evidently developed in response to the course of the Via Domitia, and perhaps also the nearby river Vidourle. The clusters at Mathay and to the east of Naintré are currently less easily explicable, but it would be of no great surprise to find that they, too, were influenced by superior ease of access to economic attractors such as raw materials, space for building workshops and markets for their goods.

The periphery of an urban secondary agglomeration could also be used for domestic occupation, again as was the case at an administrative city. Such occupation is known from the area of les Courates at Argentomagus, and also in the satellite nuclei at Mandeure, Antigny and Château-Porcien. At Antigny, no houses have been directly excavated, but aerial photographs indicate that the houses across the Gartempe were similar to those in the settlement centre, consisting of rectilinear walls aligned with the nearby roads.[103] At Mandeure, systematic excavations have revealed some differences between centre and periphery in terms of domestic occupation, and especially between the main nucleus in the curve of the Doubs and the development at Mathay. In both the demarcated centre and the Faubourg du Pont, masonry houses with features such as painted plaster and large rooms have been excavated, while mosaics have also been discovered in the central part of the settlement. In both cases, there was also evidence for metal-working being pursued on some of the same sites, revealing a close link between domestic and economic activity.[104] By contrast, most of the domestic structures excavated at Mathay took the form of annexes behind shops and workshops which lined the streets,[105] rather than large, independent houses. Given the specialist economic function which Mathay seems to have fulfilled, though, this may reflect the difference between a primarily artisanal and a primarily residential area as much as it does the differences between a settlement centre and its periphery.

All of the settlements under discussion here except for Château-Porcien and Glanum are known to have possessed a theatre of some kind.[106] Most of these appear to have been of Gallic type, although those at Naintré and Saint-Germain-d'Esteuil were apparently classical in style. With the exception of those at Beaumont-sur-Oise and Saint-Germain-d'Esteuil, they were also all built using sloping ground to support their seating. At Beaumont, the free-standing design of the theatre meant that it could be fitted into one of the *insulae* of the orthogonal grid, making it an unusual example of a Gallic theatre built within the centre of an urbanised settlement.[107] The locations of most of the other theatres, however, appear to have been determined largely by the availability of sloping ground. This had the effect of placing them either on the very perimeter of a settlement (as at Antigny, Dalheim, Naintré and Mandeure) or in areas which were more clearly beyond the limits of the urbanised centre (as at Argentomagus, Saint-Germain-d'Esteuil and Sanxay). Here, then, the periphery was being used as a zone in which to construct public monuments at relatively low expense, but within easy reach of the settlement centre.

The relationship between these peripheral theatres and the nearby centres, however, was still made clear. The theatres at Naintré, Sanxay and Saint-Germain-d'Esteuil were all oriented so that their seating faced towards the centre of the agglomeration, much as was the case for the periurban classical theatre at Saint-Bertrand-de-Comminges. At Dalheim, the slope into which the theatre was set caused it to face away from the settlement centre, but here, a road appears to have provided a link between the two, as was also the case for the theatre at Naintré. The situation at Dalheim is again comparable to the theatre at the administrative city of Jublains, which also faced away from the urban centre but was linked to it by a pair of roads. Meanwhile, at Argentomagus, the theatre at le Virou faced out across the river Creuse and towards the main route towards the settlement from the south. This theatre appears to have been situated in order to render it highly visible to visitors approaching the settlement: probably also the case for the theatre at Saint-Germain-d'Esteuil, on the end of a low ridge. The theatre at Mandeure faced towards a nearby sanctuary set into a round enclosure, rather than the main settlement centre. However, both theatre and sanctuary lay within 200m of the gridded centre, and would have been highly visible to anyone approaching the settlement across the Doubs from Besançon. They can therefore also be interpreted as closely related to the central nucleus.

Generally, then, theatres at urbanised secondary agglomerations were of Gallic type, and fell in the settlement periphery but were closely related to the centre. In these respects, they much resemble theatres at administrative cities, although the Gallic theatre located within the settlement centre at

Beaumont-sur-Oise is not currently known to have been matched at any administrative city. The links between settlement centres and theatres suggest that these buildings were perceived as important features of the agglomerations where they were found, with people travelling regularly from the centre to attend spectacles held in them, and indeed often looking back over that centre as they watched the shows. It is also important to note that the use of orientation to associate several of these theatres with their settlements is very characteristic of Roman urban planning, and again reflects their urban aspirations.

The relationship between the theatre and round sanctuary at Mandeure has already been noted, and a similar temple–theatre relationship appears to have applied at Argentomagus, where a small Romano-Celtic temple has been identified close to the theatre at le Virou through aerial photography.[108] Elsewhere, small temples which do not appear to have had a direct relationship with a theatre are known in the peripheries of Antigny, Sanxay and Château-Porcien. These temples were all of Romano-Celtic type, and their appearance in the settlement periphery is thus in keeping with patterns seen at administrative cities. However, most of the urbanised secondary agglomerations under investigation here also featured at least one, and often several, Romano-Celtic temples *within* their demarcated centres. This is a significant departure from the model of administrative cities in Gaul, where this was extremely rare, and it must be treated as a sign of the difference in character between administrative cities and even the most urbanised secondary agglomerations. The only exception to the rule is Glanum, where a pair of Corinthian temples in honour of Roma and the imperial family were built in the monumental centre of the settlement during the Augustan period.[109] Glanum's position in Narbonensis, where temples of Romano-Celtic type are virtually unknown, is enough to explain this, however. The central area of Antigny also featured a temple of classical type, probably dedicated to Minerva,[110] but this seems to have been an isolated example amongst a further eight or more Romano-Celtic temples also located within the settlement centre.

Returning to the temples which were located in the peripheries of urbanised secondary agglomerations, we find that those which did not have a close physical or axial relationship with a nearby theatre were generally linked instead, using similar devices, with the centre of the settlement. At Sanxay, a small temple on the far bank of the Vonne lay on the same axis as the main octagonal sanctuary in the centre of the agglomeration. At Antigny, another sanctuary was located on a plateau with an excellent view over the whole settlement, and probably faced towards its centre.[111] Both of these temples, in fact, were on raised ground overlooking the settlements, perhaps indicating that they had some kind of tutelary function. A slightly different case is encountered in the nucleus of la Briqueterie/les Courcelles at Château-Porcien, where a building set into a large enclosure has also been interpreted as a temple.[112] If this is correct, it constitutes an example of a temple which was not isolated, but associated with residential occupation. However, with no detailed dating evidence from either the temple or the surrounding occupation, it is not possible to say whether it was built to serve an existing population nucleus, or whether the occupation grew up around the temple.

The theatres and temples discussed above represent the great majority of the public buildings encountered in the peripheries of urbanised secondary agglomerations. However, two further types of public building remain to be discussed. At both Mandeure and Argentomagus, public baths have been encountered outside the defined centres of these settlements. Mandeure in fact possessed at least two sets of baths: one within the orthogonal grid of the settlement centre, known as the Thermes de Muraille-Bourg, and a second about 1 km to the south-east of this centre, known as the Thermes de Courcelles. The central baths, excavated during the late eighteenth century, were equipped with marble-panelled walls and mosaic floors, as well as lead pipes suggesting a running water-supply.[113] Meanwhile, the peripheral Thermes de Courcelles featured multiple rooms and pools decorated with several different colours of marble panelling, slate, polished yellow stone and stucco.[114] There thus appears to have been little discernable difference in quality between the two complexes. Mangin and collaborators suggest that the Thermes de Courcelles may have been built outside the centre of Mandeure because they were linked with an unknown sanctuary.[115] Equally, the probable Flavian date of these baths may mean that space did not exist within the settlement centre for a monument as ambitious as this by the time it was built.

At Argentomagus, the probable second-century date of the baths situated between the plateau of les Mersans and the river Creuse similarly suggests that they were built when there was already little space left within the fortified centre.[116] At neither Argentomagus nor Mandeure does ease of access to a water supply from the nearby river seem to have been an overriding factor in influencing the location of their peripheral baths. Running water was clearly available in the centre of Argentomagus, since it was supplied to a monumental public basin there through a conduit.[117] Finally, Argentomagus also possessed an amphitheatre, again of probable second century date, situated a little to the north of its earthen rampart. The presence of such a monument is very unusual in a secondary agglomeration, and especially one which already featured a theatre. However, the amphitheatre has been very little explored, and is known only through limited investigations in the late nineteenth century.[118] Information about its exact date of construction, or even whether it was a mixed edifice or of classical type is therefore lacking. What can be said is that the presence of such a monument in the settlement periphery is once again entirely in keeping with patterns observed at administrative cities, as is the absence of amphitheatres from the centres of these secondary agglomerations.

Another prominent feature which can be observed around secondary agglomerations of urban type is the villa. One or more villas are known close to six of the eleven settlements discussed here, at distances varying from 1 to 4 km.[119] The best documented are probably two situated along a road running past the eastern end of Naintré, observed through aerial photography,[120] and the villa of les Murgelots at Mandeure, which has been the subject of restricted excavations. The villas at Naintré both cover a large surface area, and the one further from the town has revealed traces of a semi-circular entrance-way facing on to the road.[121] The villa of les Murgelots, which was actually closer to Mandeure than the occupation at Mathay, had heated rooms which may have constituted a bath suite, and has yielded fragments of black marble streaked with white from quarries in the Haute-Saône region, about 20 km away.[122] Some of these villas, then, were richly furnished, and they were certainly physically close to the nearby agglomerations. Probably, this reflects the importance of small-scale trade in agricultural produce within the Gallo-Roman economy. Nearby villas could use the town as a source of labour and a market for their produce, which might also be gathered and stored within the town before being transported for sale elsewhere. The relationship, then, may well have been similar to that seen at administrative cities, and some villas may even have been owned by elite families with a special interest in particular secondary agglomerations. But, once again, the relationship does not seem to have been significantly more intense than that between a settlement centre and any agricultural property, and there is certainly no sign of anything approaching Ciceronian *suburbanitas*.

Conclusion

In general terms, the character and organisation of the peripheral development discussed above would appear to have a great deal in common with periurban development encountered at *coloniae* or *civitas*-capitals in Gaul. Just as the centres of these secondary settlements resemble the centres of administrative cities in their use of monumental architecture and orthogonal street layouts, their peripheries were also home to a number of features familiar from primary cities: industrial installations, domestic occupation, public buildings, cemeteries and villas. The spatial principles by which these features were organised are likewise comparable, including isolated buildings, areas of continuous occupation and distinct nuclei. In addition, similar structural links served to connect peripheries and centres in each case. Roads, bridges and the orientations of buildings provided physical or visual connectors, while religious, social and economic activity must have ensured regular movement between the two zones.

Such similarities cast a valuable light on the factors which encouraged the development of this type of occupation, at either administrative cities or the most urbanised secondary agglomerations. Since the two types of settlement held a different legal status, and yet developed similar patterns of occupation outside their centres, we can conclude that the character of this occupation was not significantly affected by the administrative status of the settlement around which it grew up. Instead, its development must have been influenced by some or all of the other characteristics which these types of settlements both shared; for example, a closely defined urban centre, a relatively large population and a role as a significant socio-economic centre within the local landscape. Meanwhile, the very case for describing the agglomerations discussed in this section as 'urban' would seem to be strengthened by the discovery that not only their centres, but their settlement peripheries too, were closely akin to the equivalent areas of administrative cities. Both the urban nature of these secondary agglomerations, and the similarities between their peripheries and those of administrative cities, would now seem sufficient grounds for describing development beyond their centres as 'periurban'.

Nevertheless, differences can also be observed between the periurban development seen at these centres and that encountered at full administrative cities. In particular, even at the most urban secondary agglomerations, it was clearly considered perfectly appropriate to build Romano-Celtic temples in either the urban centre or the urban periphery. By contrast, Romano-Celtic temples built at administrative cities tended to be kept to the urban periphery, while a classical form was almost always favoured instead when temples were built within the urban centre. This difference may relate to the chronological development of the secondary agglomerations. Often, the temples located within the centres of these settlements have their origins early on within the history of the towns, and potentially in a period before serious ambitions towards urban status had been conceived.[123] As we have seen, some of the monumentalising features which developed at these settlements were not established until well into the Roman period: the orthogonal grid of the AD 70s at Dalheim, for example. Thus, Romano-Celtic temples could be founded in the centre of a secondary agglomeration early on in its history, at a time when the idea of building a classical temple instead might not have been considered. The effort and expense of then converting them into a classical form when the local elite became more interested in emulating the forms of Roman urbanism may simply have been too great for such an operation to be undertaken. This model is supported by the chronology of the classical temple which, unusually, was built in the centre of Antigny, since this was apparently built on an empty site around the start of the second century.[124] It could thus readily belong to an era in which the local elite had developed greater ambitions for Antigny than were current when the earlier Romano-Celtic temples nearby were built.

Amphitheatres, a common periurban feature at administrative cities, are also almost entirely missing from the peripheries of the secondary agglomerations discussed here. This is relatively unsurprising, however, since only eleven examples of amphitheatres of any type are known to have been built anywhere away from administrative cities in Gaul, as compared to thirty four built at administrative cities.[125] The amphitheatre is therefore not a common feature of secondary agglomerations at all, although the one example encountered at Argentomagus did fall within the urban periphery. Another potential difference between these secondary agglomerations and the administrative cities discussed in chapter 4 is the number of villas found close to them. There is no more evidence that the villas located outside urbanised secondary agglomerations functioned as part of a developed suburban villa culture than there is for villas located outside the *coloniae* and *civitas*-capitals of Gaul. However, there do seem to be more known examples of villas located immediately outside these settlements than was the case for administrative cities. This may simply be because the modern cities which have succeeded so many of Gaul's *coloniae* and *civitas*-capitals have destroyed a greater proportion of villa remains outside them. Other possible explanations will be discussed in the general conclusion, after the full range of different types of secondary agglomerations has been examined.

Finally, the existence of periurban nuclei at some distance from the centres of Mandeure, Antigny, Château-Porcien and Ambrussum is also worthy of special note. Although this has been treated so far as a feature shared with certain administrative cities, the following sections of this chapter will reveal that such nuclei were also common at secondary agglomerations where aspirations towards *urbanitas* appear to have been lacking. They may therefore transpire to be a feature which is not exclusively associated with urban-style occupation, despite the fact that they did occur outside the most urbanised secondary agglomerations and at some administrative cities.

Settlements with little sign of urban aspirations

Introduction

The great majority of known Gallo-Roman secondary agglomerations do not seem to have possessed the concentrations of public buildings or orthogonal street layouts seen in the settlements discussed so far, and thus probably lacked the significant aspirations towards *urbanitas* which these features would imply. Instead, like Taden, they often consisted simply of clusters of buildings grouped into a settlement nucleus, often along a road, around a junction or at a river-crossing. However, the less urbanised secondary agglomerations of Gaul were not all the same. They, too, fulfilled a range of religious, social and economic functions, and also varied in size, setting and topography. These different agglomerations are treated here as a group simply in order to test the proposition that periurban occupation can only exist outside a settlement centre which is distinctively 'urban'.

A settlement periphery?

We have seen that a distinctive characteristic of Roman urbanism was an interest in marking out a well-defined urban centre, using devices such as orthogonal street layouts, defensive walls, natural features such as rivers or steep slopes, monumental arches and changes in the orientation of major roads. In the settlements under discussion here, however, explicit markers of this sort are generally absent. This can mean that it is actually difficult to be certain what might have been considered the central 'core' of a non-urbanised secondary agglomeration, if indeed anything was. As a result, it is equally difficult to be certain whether any features might have been considered 'peripheral' to the rest of the settlement. The main guiding principle available is the clustering of the structures within the settlement, and sometimes their setting within a naturally defined space such as a plateau. On these grounds, it is sometimes possible to identify non-urbanised secondary agglomerations which did feature a distinct nucleated cluster of buildings, but also had either a single, isolated building or another similar cluster of buildings located a small distance away. For such settlements, then, we may ask whether the relationship between the clustered nucleus and the isolated building, or between one clustered nucleus and another, can helpfully be understood in terms of 'centre' and 'periphery'.

Clustered settlements with a single outlying feature are not common, but one example is Évaux (Evaunum) in Aquitania.[126] Here, a large thermal bath-complex lay 600m north of the main settlement, in a narrow valley where hot springs rose. The presence of these hot springs is in fact likely to be the main reason for the development of a settlement here, and it has been suggested that the town was built 600m to the south simply because the valley itself was unsuitable for the construction of a settlement.[127] Certainly, very close links were maintained between the town and its baths. An aqueduct which fed the town with cold water probably had a branch carrying extra water to the baths,[128] while a long, covered gallery allowed bathers to pass between town and baths without being exposed to the elements.[129] The fact that the gallery arrived in Évaux at the point where the modern church stands, and where traces of Gallo-Roman masonry have also been found, has even led Lintz to suggest that it may had provided a direct route between the baths and a related temple beneath the church.[130] In any case, it is fairly clear that the separation between the baths and the rest of the agglomeration at Évaux was made necessary only by the natural geography of the area, and that every effort was made to link the baths with the main area of occupation. The baths, then, were less a peripheral monument of Évaux than an essential feature of the settlement, and were displaced only because of an awkward physical site.

The settlement of Kérilien, in Armorica (north-western Lugdunensis), was first occupied in the late la Tène period, and until the early second century

AD consisted mainly of a clustered nucleus of unordered artisanal and domestic occupation.[131] In the early second century, however, a theatre was built into a slope 300m south-west of this nucleus. This theatre, too, could potentially be interpreted as a monument which was peripheral to the main 'central' nucleus of Kérilien. However, it needs to be seen in the context of an apparent effort to raise the status of the whole settlement in this period, by equipping it with other characteristically urban features. At the same time as the theatre was being built, there are also signs of an attempt to impose north–south and east–west orientations on to the main occupied nucleus. Thus, Kérilien did acquire a typically periurban building, but only at a time when it seems to have been transforming itself wholesale into an urbanised settlement. Its theatre therefore needs to be understood alongside the similar examples at more urbanised secondary agglomerations already discussed above. In this context, it is fairly typical in apparently having been built in the settlement periphery in order to take advantage of a natural slope, not available on the plateau where the main nucleus lay.

Rather more common than these examples of non-urban secondary agglomerations with single outlying features were settlements of the same type which were made up of several nuclei of occupation. These sites consist of a number of distinct clusters of buildings, which are close enough to one another to be considered part of the same group, but are separated by unoccupied areas, and may have had different functions from one another. Some secondary agglomerations of this type seem to have developed a nucleated structure already prior to the Roman period. For example, at Quimper, also in Armorica, a group of adjacent hillocks are known to have harboured small clusters of occupation during the la Tène period.[132] The scattered nature of the pre-Roman settlement persisted after the conquest, and during the Roman period the town consisted of at least three major occupied nuclei and several other smaller areas, most still located on raised land. The topographical organisation of the settlement at Quimper had thus already been determined during the pre-Roman period, and does not seem to have changed markedly after the conquest. Other secondary agglomerations with a similar structure, however, appear to have developed after Gaul's incorporation into the Roman empire. Examples include Charleville-Mezières in Belgica, where isolated traces of pre-Roman occupation are known but dense, nucleated settlement developed only in the Augustan period,[133] or Aoste (Augusta/um) in Narbonensis and Roanne (Rodumna) in Lugdunensis, neither of which are known to have any pre-Roman origins.[134]

The organisation of small settlements into multiple occupied nuclei, then, was an established feature of pre-Roman occupation in Gaul, and also a characteristic of Gallo-Roman secondary agglomerations. It must have continued to be seen as an attractive form of settlement layout after the establishment of Roman influence in Gaul. In order to discover whether any one of the nuclei in such a settlement functioned as a dominant 'centre' with an associated 'periphery', it is necessary to ask whether any of them were marked out as distinct by features such as their size, location, historical origins or function. Certainly, at Quimper, Charleville-Mezières, Aoste, Roanne and Blicquy one area of occupation appears to have been noticeably larger than the other nuclei around it. In some cases, the larger nucleus has also yielded the earliest traces of occupation. This applies at Charleville-Mezières, where pre-Roman remains have been discovered beneath the largest nucleus, on the plateau of Berthaucourt in the bend of the Meuse,[135] and also at Blicquy, likewise in Belgica, where traces of la Tène occupation have been found beneath the largest nucleus at Ville d'Anderlecht.[136] In cases such as these, it seems likely that the largest nucleus of the settlement was the earliest focus of occupation, and remained the major population centre as it developed. This does not mean that the earlier origins of the nucleus were known to the people living there by the mid-Gallo-Roman period. However, the size of the nucleus alone may have meant that it retained some sense of an identity that was distinct from the other nuclei which grew up around it.

At some non-urban secondary agglomerations, the largest and earliest settlement nucleus was also distinguished by either natural features or man-made earthworks which had defended the site in the pre-Roman period. This applies, for example, to the largest nucleus at Charleville-Mezières, situated as it was on a plateau with a watercourse looping around three of its sides. Another example, this time with a man-made circuit, is Vermand (Viromandis), again in Belgica.[137] Here, one of three associated nuclei was surrounded by an earthen rampart. This particular nucleus was not, however the oldest of the three, since an earlier religious site already existed at le Champ des Noyers on the opposite side of a marshy river valley by the middle la Tène period. In a province where distinct boundary markers were regularly used at administrative cities as a sign of *urbanitas*, the existence of natural or man-made boundaries around one nucleus of occupation at these secondary agglomerations must have marked those nuclei out as being of special status. They should not, however, be regarded as direct equivalents to the urban boundaries encountered at *coloniae* and *civitas*-capitals, since there are no other signs from these settlements to suggest that they were significantly urban in character. Rather, they constitute a remnant of a proto-urban form of occupation from the pre-Roman period, which did not go on to develop into something that Roman eyes would recognise as truly urban.

At settlements composed of a cluster of nuclei, then, it was possible for one nucleus to be marked out from the others by its size, location, historical origins or a combination of the three. This is not enough in itself, however, to mean that such nuclei were necessarily seen as having the same kind of 'special' identity as the urban centre at an administrative city. To be certain that an identity of this kind was attached to one out of a cluster of nuclei, we would need to see evidence that this part of the settlement was used in a different way from the other nuclei: a way which suggested that a special ideological significance was attributed to the nucleus and the buildings within it. In the cases of Aoste, Blicquy and Quimper, enough is known about the occupation at both the largest/oldest nuclei and some of the surrounding nuclei to go some way towards allowing this kind of comparison. At Aoste, we find that the larger of the two main nuclei on the site featured domestic occupation, a sanctuary and some kilns.[138] A smaller nucleus to the west, meanwhile, consisted of a cluster of kilns with some domestic structures. At Blicquy, the largest nucleus at Ville d'Anderlecht has revealed a mix of features, including a building with a hypocaust, a Romano-Celtic temple and a bronze workshop.[139] One smaller nucleus at Aubechies featured public baths which were probably used in religious activities, while another at Camp Romain has yielded mainly artisanal and domestic occupation. Finally, at Quimper, the largest nucleus at Locmaria was home to a great variety of structures, including houses, workshops, kilns, storehouses and at least two sanctuaries.[140] Meanwhile, surrounding nuclei have revealed primarily domestic structures, with baths also located on the Roz-Avel prominence.

The excavated evidence from these settlements is patchy enough to require caution. None the less, a broad pattern of fairly mixed occupation in the largest nuclei, often including a sanctuary of some kind, and more specialised occupation in the smaller nuclei would appear to emerge. The picture is supported by evidence from a few other secondary agglomerations where the centre is poorly known due to modern settlement, but surrounding nuclei have been explored. Thus at Vermand, although the defended nucleus is little known, one nearby nucleus at le Champ des Noyers featured at least four Romano-Celtic temples and numerous other smaller shrines, as well as some domestic occupation, while another at le Calvaire has yielded several potters' kilns and a probable glass workshop.[141] All of this does point to differences in function between the nuclei in settlements of this sort, with some being identifiable as the 'main' focus of occupation, and others as specialised satellites. Such a situation is comparable with that seen at either administrative cities or highly urbanised secondary agglomerations with similar satellite nuclei. However, at these less urbanised secondary agglomerations, the extent of the difference between the 'main' and other nuclei would appear to have been less marked, and it is perhaps over-stating the case to label one as 'central' and the others as 'peripheral'. More helpful might be the approach taken by Pape, the excavator of Quimper, who described the occupation there as *'polynucléaire'*.[142] This term is able to express the idea that all the occupied areas at such settlements functioned as broadly equal components of a single agglomeration, with none of them unequivocally dominant over the others.

Finally, there is also the matter of the numerous villas which were located close to non-urban secondary agglomerations: both those which had only one main nucleus, and those which were polynuclear. A villa featuring ten rooms arranged symmetrically around a court is known 2.5 km from Évaux on the road between Néris and Ahun,[143] while Quimper featured a complex of agricultural buildings at the Parc-ar-groas site just east of the main nucleus, and a large villa at Kervéguen, 3 km to the north-east.[144] However, perhaps the most interesting example of a villa associated with a non-urban secondary agglomeration is provided by Bliesbruck-Reinheim (figure 5.5). Here, a complex consisting of a residential area (80m by 70m) and a large court (300m by 150m) was built at the north-west corner of the settlement towards the end of the first century AD.[145] Excavations in the centre of the agglomeration have revealed rectangular strip-houses arranged along its main road: some made of masonry, but most using perishable materials with stone foundations, and many yielding evidence for artisanal activity. By comparison with these houses, the villa was extremely luxurious, certainly by the time it had reached its heyday in the third century. Not only was it large,

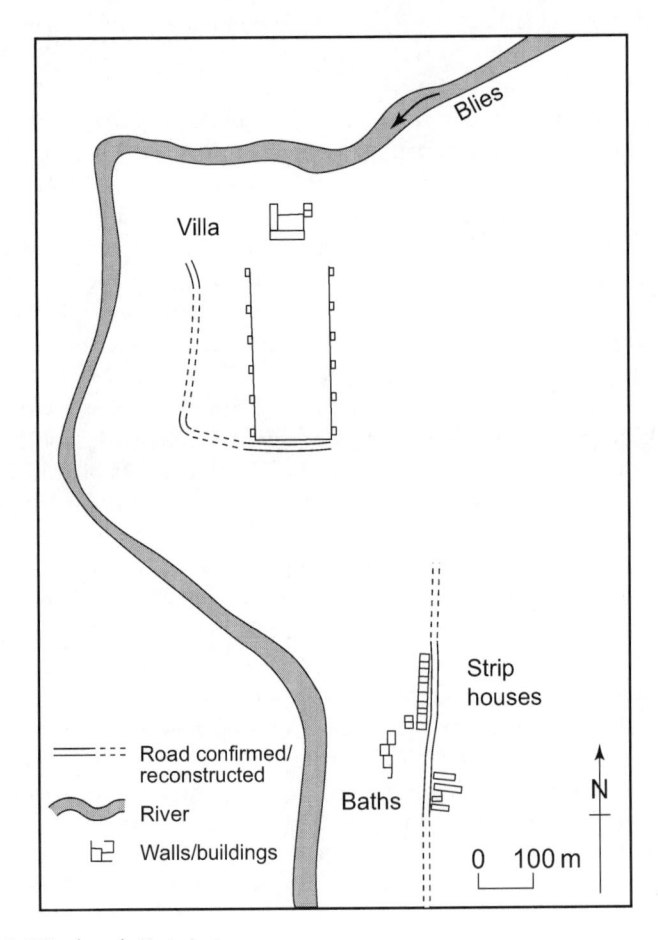

Figure 5.5 Bliesbruck-Reinheim.

but it was also embellished with stone and bronze statuary, sandstone columns, painted wall-plaster and a bath-suite.[146]

This villa, then, was clearly the residence of a wealthy family, and it seems, topographically at least, to have been dominant over the nearby settlement. The known buildings extend over approximately one hectare, while the settlement itself was not much larger: perhaps around 4–5 ha for the nucleated core. Thus the villa was a very significant addition to the town, and it does not need to have had particularly extensive estates for the total land-holdings of its owner to have exceeded the size of the settlement. It was also located only about 250m from the settlement, very much recalling the relationship between the villa of the Volusii and Lucus Feroniae near Rome. This time, though, there is no obvious large city in the area with which the villa might have enjoyed a more significant relationship than it did with Bliesbruck-Reinheim, and to which it could be interpreted as suburban. In fact, it lies over 110 km from each of the two nearest cities, Metz and Trier.

Perhaps in this case, then, a relationship of social dependence between the settlement and the villa can more safely be postulated. Certainly, Bliesbruck-Reinheim could readily have acted as a place of exchange for the villa's produce and as a source of labour. It is also tempting to interpret the construction of public baths within the town at around the time of the villa's appearance as a benefaction to the community by its owners. If these speculations are correct, then something rather different from the relationship between a suburban villa and a major city was at work. The suburban villas of literature clearly arose in response to the social and political importance of cities such as Rome. The city was the dominant partner in the relationship, with the villas situated to allow access to it, but also an escape from it. At Bliesbruck-Reinheim, although the villa post-dates the settlement, it seems likely that, once established, it became the dominant entity. Far from needing a place to escape from the burdens of urban life, we can imagine its owners enjoying the position of their property close to the settlement, where they could easily control its inhabitants. The fact that only one villa is known this near to Bliesbruck-Reinheim, in contrast with the halo of properties surrounding a city such as Rome, strengthens this impression, implying as it does a monopoly of local influence.

Conclusion

The patterns of spatial organisation seen at these less urbanised secondary agglomerations are comparable to a degree with the organisation of Gallo-Roman cities into urban centre and urban periphery. In the polynuclear settlements, a 'main' nucleus can often be identified, which was distinguished from the other nuclei by being larger, less specialised and often older than them. However, the degree of difference between the 'main' nucleus and its satellites generally appears much less marked than that seen between a true urban centre and its periphery. While the highly urbanised secondary agglomerations examined in the previous section could fairly be said to have much in common with administrative cities in terms of the presence of an identifiable centre and periphery, the same point becomes sorely stretched in the case of the settlements discussed here. It is perhaps more helpful to recognise that the non-urban nature of these secondary agglomerations precluded the division into a distinct centre and periphery commonly observed at urban settlements. Non-urbanised secondary agglomerations either consisted of one undifferentiated nucleus, like Taden, or developed a polynuclear structure: a system of spatial organisation which was already established in Gaul before the region came under Roman control.

Conclusion

The settlements discussed in this chapter are distinguished from those of chapter 4 by their legal status. In terms of the overall social and political organisation of Gaul, however, administrative cities and secondary agglomerations of all kinds may be viewed as elements in a continuous settlement hierarchy: a hierarchy which incorporated the largest provincial capitals as well as the smallest villages. In this context, the legal division between primary and secondary settlements is only one of many factors which distinguish settlements at different levels within the hierarchy. Administrative cities and secondary agglomerations have been considered separately thus far because the division between them presented a convenient means of breaking up the available evidence. But new observations about patterns of topographical organisation in Gaul can be made if they are brought back together here.

First, it is striking that the greatest differences in spatial organisation amongst Gallo-Roman settlements do not occur at the dividing line between administrative cities and secondary agglomerations, but further down the scale from the most to the least urbanised settlements. The most urbanised secondary agglomerations possessed an identifiable urban centre, and often an urban periphery beyond it, just as the majority of administrative cities did. Despite their lesser legal status, then, it is arguable that in terms of their actual appearance and character, these more urbanised agglomerations really had more in common with administrative cities than with most other secondary settlements.

Second, over the range of settlements known in Gaul, it is possible to identify two broad approaches to spatial organisation which are comparable, but not the same. At administrative cities and the most urbanised secondary agglomerations, the dominant mode of organisation was the clearly defined urban centre, generally accompanied by an urban periphery which was closely related to, but distinct from, that centre. This method of spatial organisation is inherent in the Roman urban tradition, and was used at Rome itself. At many of the less urbanised secondary agglomerations, however, we instead encounter a polynuclear settlement structure. This could involve some degree of differentiation between a 'main' and subsidiary nuclei, but it was generally nothing like as sharp as the centre–periphery divide at an urban settlement. Thus, these agglomerations cannot really be said to have possessed anything characterisable as an 'urban periphery'. Polynuclear settlements of this kind were a feature of pre-Roman Gaul, but also developed and flourished in a Gallo-Roman context.

A degree of common ground can be observed between the two patterns of organisation, however. Some of the more urbanised settlements in Gaul, besides having a closely defined core, also had distinct satellite nuclei which were separate from the main urban centre, but clearly related to it. This phenomenon may be observed at highly urbanised secondary agglomerations such as Mandeure, Antigny, Château-Porcien and Ambrussum. It also applied at a number of administrative cities, such as Amiens, Metz, Lyon, Lisieux, Périgueux and Toulouse (see chapter 4). These sites are not directly equivalent to polynuclear secondary agglomerations like Charleville-Mezières, Aoste, Roanne or Blicquy, since at the more urbanised settlements, the distinction between a centre of special status and its subsidiary satellites is much more marked. The combination of a defined urban centre and peripheral satellite(s) is also not unique to Gaul: again, the same arrangement may be observed at Rome and other western provincial cities (see chapter 3). Nevertheless, the Gallo-Roman urban settlements can be characterised as drawing upon and combining two traditions of spatial organisation: the localised tradition of non-urbanised polynuclear settlements *and* the Roman urban tradition, which itself allowed for more than one related nucleus so long as one of the nuclei was clearly marked out as an urban centre.

Finally, an important phenomenon observed in this chapter is the close relationship between secondary agglomerations and villas. Both highly urbanised and non-urbanised secondary agglomerations commonly had at least one villa situated only a short distance away from the main settlement. In fact, in eastern Gaul systematic research has shown that out of seventy secondary agglomerations in Bourgogne, Franche-Comté and Lorraine, forty-three had villas less than 5 km away, and eighteen of those had villas within only 1 km.[147] The relationship between these villas and the nearby settlements, however, may have been very different from the relationship between a suburban villa and Rome, as the example of Bliesbruck-Reinheim demonstrates. The close association between Gallo-Roman secondary settlements and villas may in fact reflect local social hierarchies rather than an interest in emulating the Roman conceit of the suburban villa. This would certainly accord well with the idea that certain elite families in Gaul took a close interest in secondary agglomerations.[148] Such villas could have functioned as their local residences, where they maintained their links with the community and expressed their status within it through the richness of the villas themselves. If so, they were hardly suburban to the local settlement, but rather dominant over it.

6

GAUL IN LATE ANTIQUITY

Introduction

The period of the high empire saw its own changes in the nature of western provincial urbanism. The significance of juridical titles such as *'colonia'* or *'municipium'* evolved, the prominence of the imperial cult and imperial images increased, and some cities developed new monumental complexes rivalling their forums.[1] However, major political, social and economic changes in the west from around the middle of the third century AD altered the character and topography of the Roman provincial city to such a degree that it becomes unhelpful to discuss urban development in this period alongside that of the high empire. This chapter examines the effects of these changes on Gallo-Roman urban peripheries as a separate issue, set within the specific context of late antiquity.

The intention here is not to attempt to treat the late period in the same level of detail as the high empire, but to raise and highlight some of the major issues involved in the study of late antique urban peripheries, and compare them with those prominent in the discussion so far. Identifying changes in the use of periurban land, and particularly distinguishing between those functions which persist into late antiquity and those which do not, should reveal much about the strength and significance of the patterns so far encountered. A survey of these changes thus forms an appropriate closure to the study of the Gallo-Roman urban periphery in the high empire.

Modern scholarship on the late antique city is striking in that it generally attributes far greater importance to the urban periphery than equivalent work on the high empire.[2] A glance through any volume of the *Topographie Chrétienne des Cités de la Gaule* quickly reveals that there are plentiful references in late antique and early medieval literature to churches described as *'extra muros'* or indeed *'in suburbio'*: a term which lost its special connections with Rome in the late antique era. These descriptions immediately demonstrate that the centre–periphery divide remained significant, and the churches themselves have of course drawn scholarly interest towards the periphery. In the context of the *Topographie Chrétienne*, churches are listed for each city according to whether they formed part of the episcopal complex, were intramural, extra-mural or are as yet unlocated: an arrangement unmatched in comparable topographical works on cities of the high empire. Another aim of this chapter is to ask whether this difference in scholarly approach is justified by the nature of the periurban land use in each period. In other words, *did* late antique urban peripheries really make a more important contribution to urban life than their earlier predecessors?

The chronological scope of the discussion will deliberately be left imprecisely defined, for two reasons. First, Roman cities were always dynamic entities, making it impossible to identify a single moment when the usual rate of change within them increased sufficiently to indicate the 'onset' of late antiquity. Second, even if the beginnings of major urban change are located within a wider time bracket, such as a quarter- or half-century, this is still unlikely to have been identical across all of Gaul. The material discussed in this chapter, then, has been selected on the grounds that it represents major urban change of a type normally associated with late antiquity, rather than according to exact dating criteria. Such change might include the appearance of new types of buildings like churches and cathedrals, the erection of walled circuits, the demolition, destruction and abandonment of some existing buildings and changes in the functions of others. These developments, and their impact on the city, form the subject-matter of this chapter.

Late antique Gaul

First, however, it will be helpful to set these changes into the context of general social and political change in Gaul during this period. Like most of the empire, Gaul appears to have experienced economic regression during the third century, manifested by a reduction in long-distance trade and the decline of some villas.[3] But this should not be exaggerated, and its apparent symptoms may simply have resulted from changes in taste and trading patterns. From the mid-fourth century, more serious economic decline is observable, although its effects vary from city to city. Meanwhile, the province was also affected by political and military unrest. Serious incursions and uprisings on the Rhine and Danube frontiers began during the reign of Marcus Aurelius, while the Gallic interior also suffered the effects of internal power-struggles. The civil war between Septimius Severus and Clodius Albinus, for instance, ended in battle at Lyon in AD 197, and the city was penalised for supporting Albinus.[4]

By AD 260, internal rivalries and external invasions had created an atmosphere of disruption serious enough to prompt the emergence of the breakaway 'Gallic empire': a succession of usurpers based at Trier who exercised power at their height over the four Gallic provinces, Britain and Spain, but did not attempt to seize power in Rome.[5] The success of this rival administration probably rested largely on the perceived inadequacy of the imperial government in dealing with invasions across the Rhine and Danube. In 274, however, the Gallic empire was suppressed by Aurelian, and further invasions quickly followed. The military reforms of Diocletian, followed by the attention paid by the Constantinian dynasty to the north-eastern frontiers, did much to improve the situation in Gaul, and resulted in a period of peace and relative economic recovery. However, from the mid-fourth century onwards, the pattern of usurpations and invasions resumed, aggravated by the appearance of local brigands taking advantage of the turbulent circumstances.[6] By 407, the Rhine frontier was effectively abandoned. Franks and Burgundians began to establish kingdoms in north-eastern Gaul, and Visigoths in Aquitania. The imperial administration tolerated and liaised with these new powers for several decades,[7] but Rome's influence gradually decreased, and the last holdings in southern Gaul were ceded on the deposition of Romulus Augustulus in 476. For Gaul itself, this was not the end of unrest. Battles between rival invaders, civil wars between Frankish kings and further invasions by Germanic Lombards perpetuated a climate of military and economic instability.[8]

As Gaul evolved from a stable and wealthy province to a region troubled by conflict and hardship, major political and administrative changes also occurred. In the late third century, Diocletian initiated reforms leading to the division of the empire into east and west and the establishment of the Tetrarchy. Three large administrative regions known as praetorian prefectures were created, one of which, the 'Gauls' (including Britain and Spain), had its capital at Trier. These prefectures were subdivided into dioceses, of which two – Galliae and Viennensis – incorporated the former provinces of Gaul. The dioceses were themselves subdivided into fifteen (later seventeen) smaller provinces. For some cities, particularly the new diocesan or provincial capitals, these administrative changes brought increased status. Others, however, lost influence. Lyon went from being religious centre of the Three Gauls and political capital for the twenty-four communities of Lugdunensis, to being capital only of the three communities which made up Lugdunensis Prima.[9] Changes at a local level also affected the fortunes of individual cities. The tendency in late antique Gaul was for the territories of larger cities to be divided up, and for large secondary agglomerations to become new *civitas*-capitals. But the opposite could also occur. Jublains, for instance, ceased to be capital of the Aulerci Diablintes and was absorbed into the *civitas* of the Aulerci Cenomanni, administered from Le Mans (Vindinum).[10]

Urban administration also changed. The *curia* retained some importance, continuing to collect taxes and witness legal procedures into the fifth century.[11] But magistrates' roles and titles altered. *Duumviri* and *quattuorviri* vanish in the fourth century, while a new office, the *defensor civitatis*, arose under Valentinian I and Valens. The actual power of both *curia* and magistrates probably also decreased as new players appeared. These included bishops and the clergy, the *duces* who commanded the frontier forces, and the *comites*: representatives of the imperial court created by Constantine, and later powerful agents of the barbarian kings.[12] In the fifth century, the administrative system altered again as the Frankish, Burgundian and Visigothic kingdoms were established. Under the new rule, individual cities could still prosper. Paris was chosen by the Frankish king Clovis as his capital in the early sixth century,[13] and saw several churches built at royal initiative. Other cities became the seats of royal mints in the sixth century.[14] But the true centres of administrative power in the early barbarian kingdoms were the royal palaces, and these were not always located at cities.

Meanwhile, the growing influence of the Christian church, and especially its bishops, played a crucial role in ensuring the continuing social and administrative significance of the cities into the early medieval period. In Gaul, as elsewhere, Christianity flourished in an urban environment.[15] The earliest attested Christian communities in Gaul were based in Lyon and Vienne, known through Eusebius' record of their letter reporting martyrdoms at Lyon in AD 177 to churches in Asia and Phrygia.[16] In 314, all but one of the Gallic bishops present at the council of Arles described themselves as having come from a city.[17] The religion seems to have spread from southern Gaul through the cities of the Rhône valley towards the Rhine, reflecting the importance of this axis as a trading route, and the function of cities as nodes along it.[18] Episcopal seats were usually established in existing *civitas*-capitals, but sometimes also important secondary centres.[19] Networks of rural churches were then fostered by the bishops after their position in the urban centre was secured.[20] By the fifth century, bishops had taken on many of the roles previously played by civic magistrates – urban builders, administrators, financial managers and negotiators[21] – and their presence in a city had become synonymous with urban status.[22] Although it brought important changes in urban topography, then, the rise of Christianity also ensured that the city remained a focus of religious, social and administrative activity.

Urban defences

Perhaps the most striking change to affect cities in late antique Gaul was the widespread construction of new defensive walls. This was a significant modification for most Gallo-Roman cities, which until then had remained unwalled: though not, as we have seen, undefined. Until the late antique era, the majority of cities in Gaul had maintained the urban boundaries established at their foundation, although many had expanded through periurban development, and a few such as Trier had established new, more capacious, boundaries.[23] The new walls, however, generally followed an entirely different course from the existing boundaries, often surrounding only a small portion of the area previously marked out as the urban centre. Thus, they represent a rupture in the erstwhile stability of Gallo-Roman urban boundaries, as well as a reversal of the general trend towards expansion for the first time since the establishment of urbanism in Gaul.

The appearance of new defensive circuits was usually accompanied by other transformations in the urban fabric. For example, streets might be blocked by their construction. That walls were allowed to have such an impact suggests profound changes in attitudes towards the urban fabric. Clearly, unimpeded circulation or sight-lines within the city were no longer considered as important as a defensive wall. Similarly, public buildings and funerary monuments outside the walls were often demolished to provide materials for them. At Saintes, the course of the defensive wall built in the last quarter of the third century excluded the high imperial forum and its surrounding monumental buildings (figure 4.12, p. 107). Excavations of the wall have revealed that many of them were demolished and used to provide stone for its foundations and its façades.[24] This could be seen as an effect of the construction of the walls. But it also indicates broader changes in priorities, which had eroded the significance of the forum monuments and simultaneously lent greater urgency to defence.

In the present context, the most important issue surrounding the construction of new walled circuits concerns their effect on areas which had previously been part of the urban centre, but now lay outside them. Had these newly excluded areas exchanged an urban identity for a periurban one, and if so, how was that change manifested? Intuitively, we might assume that the identity of the regions left outside the walls had indeed changed. The apparent willingness to leave these areas vulnerable to attack certainly suggests that they were now seen as different in status from the defended centre. This assumption can be tested by examining and comparing land-use in different areas of the late antique city. For instance, the presence or absence of burials in the defended centres, the areas newly excluded by the walls and the old urban periphery can help to indicate the status of each, as can the uses made of existing buildings and the construction of new buildings. This chapter will gather and examine such evidence in order to decide which, if any, parts of late Gallo-Roman cities may be characterised as periurban.

First, however, the walls themselves need to be discussed, since the details of their dates and circumstances of construction, lengths and courses can reveal much about changing urban priorities in this period. Their appearance in Gaul is often considered to be a phenomenon of the last quarter of the third century, prompted by invasions of Franks and Alamanni in the 270s.[25] However, precise dating evidence is rarely available, and they are often dated only on the basis of a *terminus post quem* provided by coins or reused inscriptions built into the wall.[26] The evidence that is available also suggests that the peak period of late antique wall-building occurred at different times in different areas. Thus, many cities in the north and east of Gaul did indeed build defensive circuits during the late third century, yet several in the south-western region of Novempopulania did not do so until well into the fourth.[27] Meanwhile the cities of Narbonensis, little affected by external attacks until the fifth century, often did not receive new walls until the medieval period.[28] This is partly because many of them still had viable early imperial defences. Yet even at Arles, where the Augustan wall had been partially demolished during the Flavian period, new defences cannot be dated to earlier than the mid-sixth century and may be as late as the ninth.[29] Meanwhile, at Aix-en-Provence (Aquae Sextiae), excavations along the south-west part of the original city wall have suggested that it was actually demolished over the course of the fourth century, and new walls are not attested before the eleventh.[30]

As already mentioned, most late antique defences enclosed significantly smaller areas than the urban centres of the high empire. A typical example is Sens, where the original orthogonal grid covered around 225 ha, yet the late third-century rampart enclosed only about 40 ha at the centre of that grid (figure 4.11, p. 104).[31] Some cities, however, were able to construct circuits enclosing most of their former urban centres. The walls built at Metz in the late third century enclosed approximately 70 ha, encompassing most of the existing centre (figure 4.16, p. 124).[32] Similarly, the mid-fourth-century walls at Dax (Aquae Tarbellicae) enclosed around 13 ha as compared to the 20 ha or less covered by the earlier orthogonal grid.[33] Of these two cities, Metz fits into a general pattern of north-eastern cities with larger defended centres than those of central and western Gaul.[34] The circuit at Dax, however, is unusual for Novempopulania, where reduced circuits were typically built around raised ground above the existing cities.[35]

Examples of cities retaining older walled circuits in the late antique period include Trier, where the second-century walls were never replaced by a shorter circuit, and Toulouse, where the early imperial circuit was retained,[36] but closed off by an addition along the previously undefended bank of the Garonne.[37] At some of these cities, though, the area of actual occupation seems to have shrunk dramatically, leaving large abandoned areas within the circuit; for example, Autun.[38] Here, the entirety of the area within the walls can no longer be referred to meaningfully as an 'urban centre', since some parts of it had clearly ceased to function as part of the city. Yet in the absence of any smaller circuit, it is also difficult to speak of a new urban centre. At Fréjus, by contrast, the full extent of the urban centre defined by the Augustan walled circuit seems to have remained in use until at least the mid-fourth century.[39] Here, there was apparently little change in the identity and function of this area.

Where cities did erect reduced defensive circuits, a number of persuasive factors may have lain behind this decision. One is likely to have been the availability of financial resources. During the high imperial period in Gaul, walls had been associated almost exclusively with *coloniae*.[40] Many were probably built as part of the foundation process, and, if not, were still likely to have been imperial benefactions; for example, the 'walls and gates' presented to Nîmes by Augustus.[41] By late antiquity, though, the financial demands of military campaigning and the increased need for defensive circuits must have made it difficult for the emperors to be so generous.[42] Local resources, too, were often stretched, especially in view of the increasing reluctance of local elites to participate in the traditional system of private euergetism.[43] In such circumstances, a reduced circuit could provide acceptable defence at a lower cost than one enclosing the entire urban centre. The importance of such economic considerations is also underlined by the frequent reuse of stone from earlier buildings (*spolia*). This has sometimes been taken as a sign of hurried construction, in circumstances where cities were under direct threat of attack, or had already suffered an assault resulting in the demolition of some of their buildings. Yet many late antique circuits, although employing *spolia* for their foundations, were nevertheless very carefully built.[44] This suggests that recycled stone was actually used because it was cheaper than newly quarried stone, rather than for reasons of time.

Another practical reason for building reduced walled circuits in late antiquity was the ability of the community to defend them successfully if a city did come under attack. Elton has argued that Roman military force generally remained effective in Gaul until the end of the 450s,[45] and that field armies could be expected to relieve besieged cities. Until such relief arrived, however, it was important for the population of a city to be able to hold off their attackers, and this might prove impossible along an extensive walled circuit. Trier, which retained its 6 km-long second-century defences, appears to have experienced this problem in the fifth century, when it suffered violent Frankish attacks.[46] Reduced circuits, then, may actually have been better able to safeguard the local population. Finally, building defensive circuits around already depopulated areas of a former urban centre would have been futile. Work at both Saintes and Amiens has shown that the construction of reduced circuits in these cities took place after large sectors of their original urban centres had already been abandoned.[47] The new walls did enclose most of the monuments and houses still in use, excluding only unwanted ruins.

The course chosen for a defensive wall in a late antique city can also be an important indicator of its intended function and of local priorities. Defensive circuits could be built in a variety of different shapes, as well as different positions in relation to the existing urban centre. Perhaps the most common design was a roughly oval shape, usually enclosing the middle portion of the old urban centre.[48] This shape offers a higher ratio of area protected to length of wall than a square or rectangle, and could therefore enclose the largest possible area for the smallest amount of expenditure. At Bourges (Avaricum), it also clearly reflected the shape of a raised area of land in the centre of the city.[49] Such concerns, however, did not prevent some cities, such as

Bordeaux, building more or less regular rectangular circuits (figure 6.3, p. 218).[50] In these cases, the walls probably fulfilled a monumental, as well as a defensive, function, demonstrating continued order and control within the urban landscape, and recalling the appearance of earlier Roman *coloniae*, such as Aosta.[51]

Elsewhere, more irregular courses were chosen, responding to particular monuments within the existing urban fabric. The walls at Amiens[52] and Tours[53] (figure 6.2, p. 215) both incorporated existing amphitheatres into their circuits, converting them into fortresses. At Amiens, the unusual position of the amphitheatre near to the city's forum meant that the circuit could still be located in the middle of the old orthogonal grid. At Tours, however, the amphitheatre was on the perimeter of the old urban centre, and the walls seem to have been shifted away from the middle of the city in order to make use of its defensive potential. Similarly, at Périgueux, the city's amphitheatre was included in the defensive circuit,[54] but the forum and the Tour de Vésone were left outside it (figure 6.1).[55] These decisions indicate fundamental changes in local priorities, suggesting that the defensive qualities of the amphitheatres were now valued above the former political or religious significance of the monuments excluded from the circuits.

The location of a late defensive wall could also depend on natural geographical features. At Saint-Bertrand-de-Comminges, a new circuit was built at the start of the fifth century to the south-west of the existing urban centre, around a steep-sided hill apparently unoccupied before this time (figure 6.4, p. 226).[56] Such arrangements were fairly common in late antique Novempopulania, and usually did not mean that the former urban centre was completely abandoned.[57] Instead, life continued in the lower town, with the nearby fortified area acting as a defended retreat when necessary. Similar situations can also be observed elsewhere in Gaul. At Paris, a defensive circuit was built round the Île de la Cité around the end of the third century,[58] yet occupation appears to have continued within the former urban centre on the left bank of the Seine.[59] Along with Tours and Périgueux, however, these examples demonstrate a willingness on the part of late antique urban communities to shift the focal centres of their cities for the sake of more effective defences.

One city which experienced such a shift rather earlier than most is Lyon (figure 4.15, p. 120). There, occupation on the Fourvière plateau was slowly abandoned over the course of the third century in favour of the lower ground along the valleys of the Rhône and the Saône, and especially the Saint-Jean area at the foot of Fourvière.[60] The relatively early date of this change, and the rejection of an easily defended plateau in favour of low-lying riverside land, suggest that it was not prompted by defensive concerns. Instead, the economic draw of the rivers and the solution of earlier flooding problems in the area are likely to have caused the shift. In late antiquity, however, it is known that Lyon was walled,[61] and Gregory of Tours' reference to walls

GAUL IN LATE ANTIQUITY

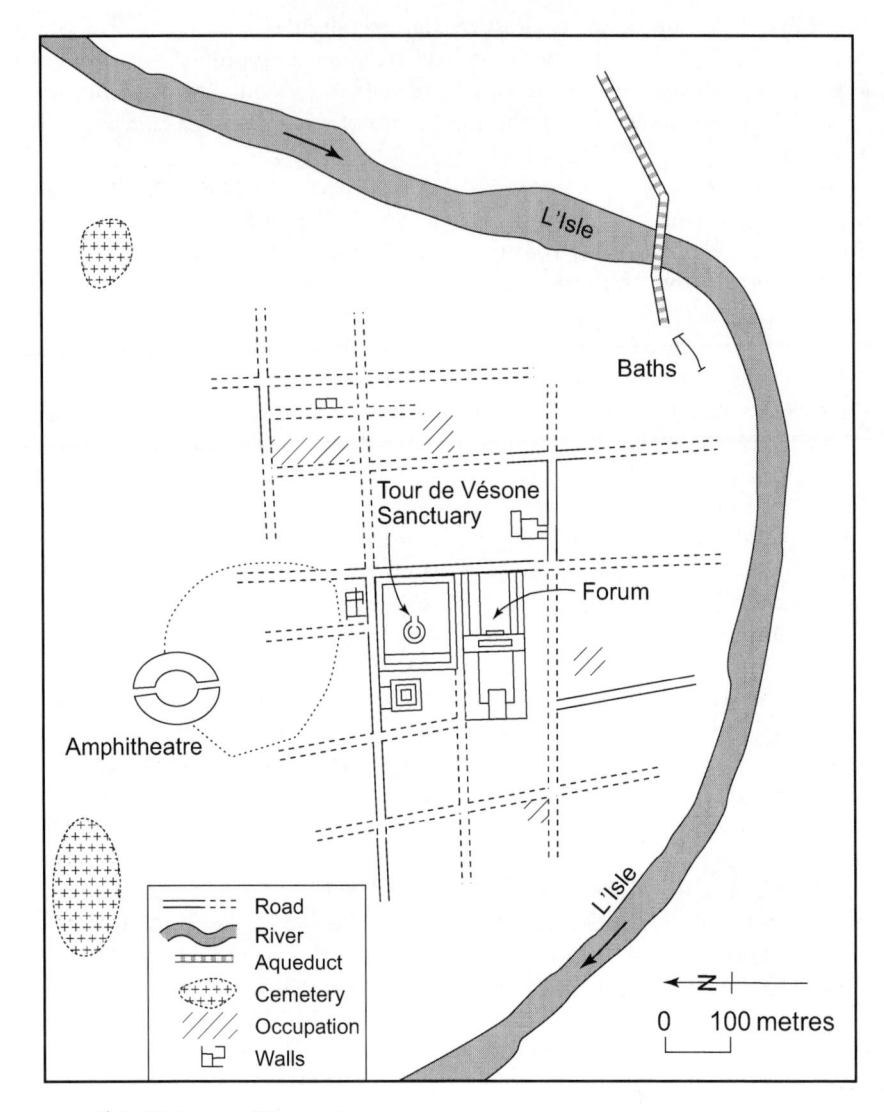

Figure 6.1 Périgueux (Vesunna).

undermined by flooding from the Rhône and Saône suggests that they ran close to the rivers.[62] A section of early fourth-century wall excavated on the right bank of the Saône was initially interpreted as part of a riverside circuit enclosing the new Saint-Jean district.[63] However, Reynaud, one of the original excavators, now argues that it is more likely to have been an enclosure wall for the nearby episcopal complex or a quay.[64] He believes that the puzzling course of Lyon's medieval walls along the south-west side of the Fourvière plateau and down to the bank of the Saône on each side arose because they were following the course of late antique walls enclosing the plateau, themselves possibly making use of an early imperial circuit. If this suggestion is correct, then the former urban centre at Fourvière was defended in late antiquity despite being largely abandoned. That is not to say, however, that it still functioned as Lyon's primary urban centre during late antiquity. The abandonment of the plateau and the construction of the fourth-century episcopal complex in the Saint-Jean quarter[65] clearly indicate that this area was now functioning as the city's urban centre, whatever course the late defences took.

Final comment should be made on the status of cities building walled circuits in this period. Autun excepted, defensive circuits of the high imperial era had been limited to cities of colonial rank. The practical defensive needs of late antiquity, however, completely changed this situation. Most *civitas*-capitals in what had been the Three Gauls eventually received defensive circuits, including those promoted from the status of secondary agglomerations. Bazas in Novempopulania, for example, became a *civitas*-capital around the turn of the fourth century, and Paulinus of Pella reveals that it was walled by AD 414.[66] Excavations there suggest that its walls were probably built in the second half of the fourth century, a date typical of other, longer-established, *civitas*-capitals in the region.[67] In the north and north-east of Gaul some of the larger secondary agglomerations also erected defensive walls.[68] This phenomenon, however, was not universal even here, and elsewhere walls remained associated primarily with the *civitas*-capitals. In Narbonensis, the issue was less pressing, since most major cities were already walled in the early imperial period, while the region experienced little military threat until the fifth century. However, even in the Three Gauls, some *civitas*-capitals were not walled until long after the region had passed out of Roman control. Thus Cahors (Divona), in the former province of Aquitania, was walled only at the initiative of its bishop, Didier, in the mid-seventh century.[69]

Churches and cemeteries

The emergence of Christianity in Gaul was associated with striking changes in urban topography. Starting in the fourth century AD and escalating in the fifth, churches, cathedrals and monasteries began to appear in cities across Gaul, and quickly came to dominate the urban landscape.[70] This proliferation of Christian buildings occurred at a time when traditional public monuments had been severely affected by social changes. From the end of the third century, the private euergetism which had until then financed most public buildings declined sharply. On a practical level, this probably meant that they did not receive the repairs or embellishments undertaken in earlier centuries, and became less able to function effectively. More importantly, it reflects a shift of interest away from monumental buildings as a means of expressing personal or civic status: a shift also apparent in the widespread willingness to demolish classical monuments to provide *spolia* for defensive walls. This shift is unlikely to have been the direct result of a growing interest in Christianity, since church-building did not begin in earnest until around a century later. Rather, the popularity of Christian buildings probably lay partly in their ability to provide services which had been dropping away with the decline of traditional monuments.

Beside their obvious religious function, churches could offer the kind of social contact previously sought in buildings such as bath-complexes. They hosted special ceremonies on local saints' days and festivals such as Christmas,[71] and might also be the focus of processions through the city streets.[72] These occasions would draw crowds with the same interest in entertainment as those attending games or religious processions in the high empire. They would also help to reinforce a feeling of communal identity by promoting a knowledge of local Christian traditions, and a sense of belonging to a wider Christian world. This function, too, had been performed in a different way by classical monuments, which had served both as an expression of local urban identity and as a sign of participation in the wider Roman empire.

The churches themselves also seem to have taken over some of the traditional function of buildings as a means of displaying personal status. Much of the money to pay for churches was raised through the personal influence of bishops, with contributors including members of the clergy, wealthy laymen and in one case a prefect of the Gauls.[73] The motivations of these contributors probably differed from benefactors in the high empire, with a greater emphasis on religious piety and salvation in the next life. However, for the bishops in particular, the relationship between the strength of the local church and their own personal influence must have meant that display remained an important factor. Church-building made a visible statement about the size of a Christian community, while reinforcing the faith of the converted and potentially adding to their numbers. It could thus increase a bishop's power-base, and perhaps open up new sources of church patronage. Finally, many churches also housed the relics of local and foreign saints and martyrs, and this gave them a protective function. Burial *'ad sanctos'* – in or around a church containing powerful relics – was thought to offer protection for the souls of the deceased,[74] and is comparable to the desire for remembrance sought through funerary monuments in the high empire. Meanwhile, the city as a whole would turn to its saints and martyrs for divine protection against disasters such as plagues or attacks.[75]

Churches, then, clearly played a major role in the life of late antique urban communities. Their positioning within the urban fabric is therefore of great importance for our understanding of different sectors of the city. At most cities, churches began to appear after late defensive walls had been constructed, although this was not always the case, especially in the south.[76]

Where churches do post-date reduced defensive circuits, however, their constructors will have been responding to the courses of these circuits when choosing the locations of the churches. It may therefore be possible to identify differences in the character and function of the areas inside and outside the new defences by observing the distribution of churches between the two.

Of particular interest in this context is the cathedral. Cathedrals performed many of the same functions as ordinary churches, but were unique in serving as the residence of the city's bishop. This in turn meant that they were the focus of special episcopal functions, such as baptisms, the local church administration, and, increasingly, the accumulation of public funds used to provide poor relief or buy up food in times of shortage.[77] Annexes connected with these activities, such as a baptistery or bishop's *domus*, usually created an episcopal 'complex' around the cathedral, while the building itself was generally larger than an ordinary church.[78] The cathedral also of course enjoyed a special identity as the symbolic centre of the local church and a link with the wider Christian community.

In Gaul, most cathedrals were located within the defended centre of the city. There are exceptions, however, and recent debate has raised the question of whether the earliest cathedrals were more usually located outside the walls, moving inside only at a later date.[79] The *Life* of the fourth-century bishop Amator reveals that in his day, the cathedral of Auxerre (Autessiodurum) lay just outside one of the city gates.[80] However, Amator himself was able to secure a new, intra-mural site by persuading a wealthy local citizen to give up part of his house for the purpose. One of the reasons given for Amator's relocation was the lack of room available around the existing cathedral, suggesting that it had been constructed in an area of extra-mural living occupation, rather than a necropolis.[81] Similar transfers are attested elsewhere. Gregory of Tours reveals that, although a cathedral had been built in the centre of Clermont-Ferrand (Augustonemetum) in the mid-fifth century, an extra-mural baptistery was still in use in the late sixth century[82] – probably a sign that the cathedral itself had also originally been extra-mural.[83] Much later, an early twelfth-century text records the transfer of the extra-mural cathedral at Dax to a site within the walls in the mid-eleventh century.[84] These examples suggest that where cathedrals were built outside defensive walls, it was a compromise position. A location within the defended centre was preferred, and moved to when possible. They are, in any case, in the minority, and the current scholarly consensus holds that most cathedrals were built within defended circuits from the beginning.[85]

Within the circuit, the exact placement of the cathedral might lie beyond the bishop's control. Land within the urban centre was limited and usually already occupied, while its defensive advantages must have made competition for it intense. Bishops relied largely on private patronage or state donations to provide the land they needed.[86] Thus at Trier the discovery of palace remains beneath the fourth-century cathedral confirms the literary tradition that the empress Helena, mother of Constantine, donated imperial property to allow its construction.[87] In such circumstances, bishops had little choice but to accept the site offered, and it is notable that cathedrals were often located only just inside the walls, rather than in the middle of the defended area.[88] Nevertheless, the importance of securing a cathedral site *somewhere* inside the defended centre is very clear. On a practical level, the walls would protect the cathedral, the bishop, the public wealth he controlled and, symbolically, the local Christian community from attack.[89] Yet the strength of the preference for intra-mural cathedral locations may also suggest that this part of the city was considered to enjoy a special ideological status not shared by the quarters outside the walls.

The urban distribution of non-cathedral churches is markedly different from that of the cathedrals, and emphasises the special efforts made to secure intra-mural positions for the latter. Le Mans at the end of the seventh century is typical. The cathedral and two churches were located within the reduced defensive circuit, but the other nine churches erected by this period all lay outside the walls.[90] Most early churches were extra-mural, and it was not generally until the late fifth century or after that non-cathedral churches began to appear within defensive circuits.[91] This has been interpreted by Harries as the result of the progressive establishment of Christianity as the dominant religion, and the increasing influence of the bishops doubtless did mean that it became easier to secure intra-mural space for churches. However, other factors may also have been at work, positively encouraging the construction of early churches outside defensive circuits. The continued custom of burying the dead outside the walls of cities, coupled with the new practice of burial in or around churches, is likely to have been particularly significant.

Extra-mural burial remained the norm in Gaul until at least the sixth century,[92] and is one of the strongest indications of differences in status between the defended and undefended parts of the old urban centre. Burials commonly encroached on abandoned sectors of old urban centres in the late antique period, indicating that the boundaries defining them had become obsolete, at least in the context of burial practices. They did not, however, appear within contemporary walled circuits. At Amiens, reduced city walls were built in the late third century, and new cemeteries grew up immediately outside them in the early fourth century.[93] These cemeteries occupied abandoned parts of the old urban centre, especially close to the amphitheatre. Thus, these areas clearly had taken on a new identity, changing from central areas where burial was forbidden to peripheral areas where it was not. Exceptions, as ever, do exist. At Poitiers, around forty skeletons were found in an intra-mural cemetery used during the third quarter of the fourth century.[94] However, the date of the walls at Poitiers is uncertain, and the cemetery's excavators have suggested that it may actually predate them. Even here, then, the burials may simply belong to a period of encroachments which took place before new urban boundaries had been clearly defined. In general, the evidence of cemetery distributions indicates that the differences between the extra-mural sectors of the former urban centre and the periurban districts beyond had been eroded. Both could now be used for burials as well as living occupation, while neither enjoyed the special status which drew cathedrals to the defended centre.

The distribution of late antique cemeteries would in its turn have encouraged the construction of extra-mural churches for two main reasons. First, many churches developed in existing cemeteries from cult structures built around the tombs of local saints and martyrs. The church of Saint-Martin at Tours is a well-documented example (figure 6.2). It began life as a modest structure over the saint's tomb in the second quarter of the fifth century, and was rebuilt on a more lavish scale shortly afterwards.[95] Other examples include Saint-Alyre at Clermont-Ferrand, Saint-Martial at Limoges, Saint-Hilaire at Poitiers[96] and Saint-Just at Lyon.[97] Such churches usually became the focus of further burials because of the protection they were believed to offer,[98] but this function was able to develop *because* of their extra-mural location, and was not its cause. Second, some churches were built specifically to receive the relics of saints and martyrs brought from elsewhere. These relics in themselves do not appear to have been subject to the usual customs or taboos regarding the dead: in fact, many central cathedrals housed imported relics.[99] However, given the popularity of burial '*ad sanctos*', it surely made good sense to locate some relic churches outside the city walls.

These positive factors doubtless do explain the extra-mural locations of many early churches. However, not all extra-mural churches had a funerary function. At Clermont-Ferrand, several churches were concentrated between the walled city and the curve of the river Tiretaine, but the cemeteries remained much further out, even in late antiquity.[100] These churches are most likely, therefore, to have been built for people living between the walled city and the river. Similarly, at Saint-Bertrand-de-Comminges in the first half of the fifth century, a church was built near the centre of the old high imperial city, but outside the contemporary defences on the hill to the south-west (figure 6.4, p. 226).[101] The church was constructed over earlier private houses, but fitted carefully amongst the surrounding buildings, apparently still in use.[102] It, too, was not initially associated with burials, although sarcophagi did appear within it from the late sixth century onwards: significantly, the same period when burials first began to appear within the defended circuits of cities in Gaul.

Seemingly, then, churches were sometimes built outside late antique city walls for the convenience of residents living in these areas. The presence of these churches and their congregations also refines the identification of extra-mural sectors of old urban centres as 'peripheral', made above on the basis of cemetery distributions. In some cities at least, a distinction appears to have been made between *abandoned* areas of the old urban centre, which were used for burial, and *occupied* areas which were not. Thus, occupied extra-mural quarters seem to have retained an identity closer to that of a high empire urban centre than an urban periphery, becoming used for burials only at the same time as land within the defended urban centre.

A number of positive factors, then, could encourage the construction of extra-mural churches, and the phenomenon need not be attributed simply to lack of space within the walls. In fact, even where walled circuits enclosed large areas, churches consistently arose outside them. Thus, the *TCCG* recognises five churches built by the eighth century outside the Augustan walls at Autun,[103] four outside the second-century walls at Trier[104] and twenty-nine outside the late third-century walls at Metz.[105] What, then, was the character of the landscape which these churches occupied, and what contribution were they making to the life of the city as a whole? In particular, can they be understood as part of a late antique urban periphery?

Certainly, extra-mural churches – whether located within the former urban centre or in areas that had always belonged to the urban periphery – did have close functional and ideological links with the defended urban centres. This is demonstrated in particular by literary descriptions of regular processions between the two. A vivid example is the Rogations, an extended ceremony of public parades and prayers instituted by Mamertus of Vienne, and taken up by other Gallic cities for performance at mid-Lent or in times of crisis. At Vienne, Mamertus had led processions between the defended urban centre and the church of Saint-Ferréol, just north of the old periurban quarter of Saint-Romain-en-Gal.[106] Similarly, when Tours was threatened by Roccolen, *dux* of Chilperic, during the episcopate of Gregory, he led a procession from the city's cathedral to the church of Saint Martin in an extra-mural sector of the old urban centre.[107] Ceremonies such as these would have created a living link between the centre of a late antique city and its extra-mural churches. They caused crowds of worshippers to pass back and forth between the two, visibly demonstrating the links between them and the interest of the centrally based bishop in the churches outside the city walls. Such behaviour may be compared with the frequent journeys between the city of Rome and its suburban villas performed by the high imperial elite, and is a clear sign that the churches were functioning as periurban monuments.

We have already seen that some of these periurban churches sprang up to serve existing populations outside the city walls. They could also become the focus of new occupation in themselves. One such example is the church which developed over the tomb of Saint Martin to the west of Tours (figure 6.2). At least two further churches and two monasteries, as well as an extensive area of domestic occupation, had developed around it by the sixth century.[108] The result was an important cluster of periurban settlement. Gregory of Tours referred to it as a *'vicus christianorum'*, suggesting that

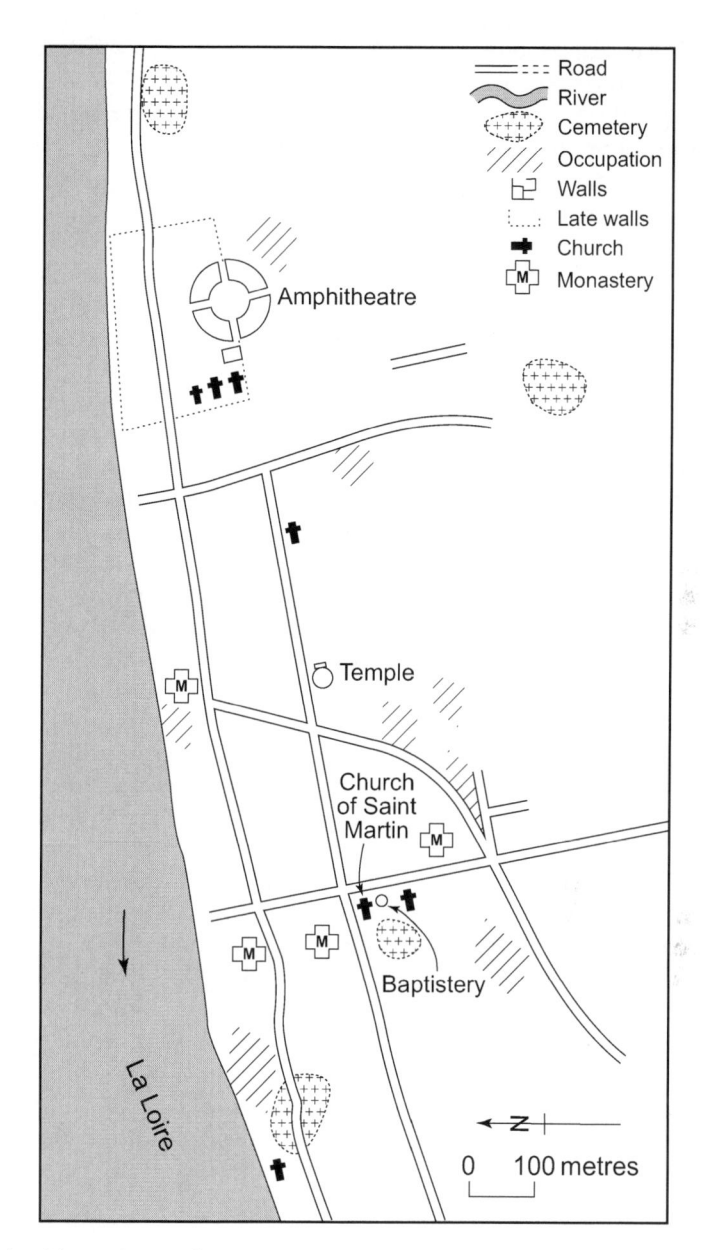

Figure 6.2 Tours (Caesarodunum).

its religious origins gave it a special, distinct identity,[109] and by the tenth century it had even been partially enclosed by a defensive wall.[110] Similarly, at Clermont-Ferrand, the tomb of Saint Alyre was transformed into a basilica by the end of the fourth century, and had become the centre of a small village by the sixth.[111] Such churches, then, had a distinct influence on the development of the periurban landscape. It is indicative of both their own importance and the continuing importance of the urban periphery in the life of the late antique city.

Periurban churches, then, were used by all city-dwellers for secure burial and regular religious festivals. They provided an accessible focus for regular worship and social contact for extra-mural populations, and could also give rise to new occupation in the periphery. This in turn affected the topography of the city as a whole by creating clusters of periurban settlement. Finally, the saints and martyrs whose relics some of them sheltered brought status for both the local bishop and the community as a whole.[112] In short, they made a crucial contribution to late antique urban life, and urban identity. Although not located within the urban centre, they were still very much a part of the fabric of the city, and helped to express its local character, its religious faith and its status in comparison with neighbouring communities. In all these respects, they bear strong similarities to the periurban public buildings of the high empire. Thus, Février's comment on the contribution of churches to the identity of the late urban periphery is accurate except in its underestimation of the importance of this zone during the high empire: *'Jusqu'alors, l'exterieur de la ville avait été exclusivement ou presque le lieu des nécropoles, l'espace des morts. Il devint – dans la communauté chrétienne – un espace privilégié.'*[113]

One more type of Christian building requires comment here: the monastery or convent. Monasteries first appeared in Gaul in the late fourth century, and were often located in a rural setting, where peace and seclusion could readily be attained.[114] In one sense, they constituted a conscious rejection of urbanism in preference for seclusion and isolation.[115] However, urban monasteries also developed, and may be found in both centre and periphery. Their chapels and cemeteries were usually reserved for their inhabitants, and so did not play a direct role in daily urban life. Nevertheless, the monasteries were an important constituent of the local church. Several bishops of Arles in particular had been monks before they were ordained, while Caesarius, the city's bishop in the early sixth century, founded monasteries for both sexes on its outskirts.[116] Meanwhile at Tours, the late fourth-century bishop Martin showed how a periurban monastery could successfully bridge the gap between city and countryside. Tiring of interruptions to his preferred lifestyle of seclusion, Martin retreated to a monastery at Marmoutier, 3 km from the walled urban centre and on the opposite bank of the Loire.[117] This move secured his isolation, and yet kept him close enough to continue functioning as the city's bishop. Sulpicius Severus comments that the monastery 'lacked none of the solitude of the desert',[118] but this is unlikely at a site so near to Tours. Rather, the description echoes the enthusiastic praise of earlier writers for their suburban villas, able to offer similar isolation without compromising access to the city.

Abandonment, demolition and destruction

The discussion so far has concentrated on new structures which appeared in late antiquity. Yet it has also touched upon changes affecting the existing urban fabric: the demolition of older buildings to obtain *spolia*, for instance, or the abandonment of parts of the former urban centre. It is now time to explore these changes in greater detail. The issue is of course problematic, since the fabric of any city alters and adapts continually to meet the changing needs of its inhabitants. Thus it can be difficult to distinguish between regular, small-scale urban change and the effects of the widespread transformations associated with late antiquity. None the less, with sufficient evidence, signs of serious urban change can be identified. The observation of similar transformations at several sites in the same area of a city and over the same period is one likely indicator. This applies particularly when the transformations represent a major break in the history of each site; for instance, its abandonment after several centuries of continuous occupation.

We begin by looking at those buildings which ceased to be used altogether, either because they were abandoned or because they were deliberately destroyed by their former owners or external attackers. Evidence for such abandonment or destruction has in the past often been attributed either to massive economic decline and urban depopulation or to barbarian invasions. Such analyses have found support in literary sources; for instance, Ammianus Marcellinus' description of the town of Avenches (Aventicum), in ruins by the second half of the fourth century.[119] However, the context of Ammianus' description is a catalogue of key cities in the still very lively Gallic dioceses, amongst which Avenches is an unusual exception.[120] Meanwhile, it must be remembered that abandonment and even fires regularly affected individual sites in antiquity, so that evidence of a localised disaster need not mean that whole quarters of a city were similarly affected. As archaeological evidence from the late antique period increases, scholars are now more cautious about identifying widespread abandonment and destruction or about explaining it with reference to a single event such as a barbarian invasion.[121]

It would be illuminating to compare changes affecting existing urban structures within and without the walls of late antique cities, in order to discover whether the two zones typically experienced different patterns of development. The task is made difficult by the continuous occupation of most walled urban centres, which has rendered many of them poorly documented in comparison with the areas outside their walls.[122] Yet valuable exceptions are available; for example, the Îlot Saint-Christoly at Bordeaux (figure 6.3). Here, excavations in an area of around 8,000m² have revealed well-preserved occupation dating from the first to sixth centuries AD.[123] The site lay at the confluence of two local streams, the Peugue and the Devèze, the latter of which had marked the approximate southern limit of the high imperial city. When Bordeaux's near-rectangular walled circuit was built

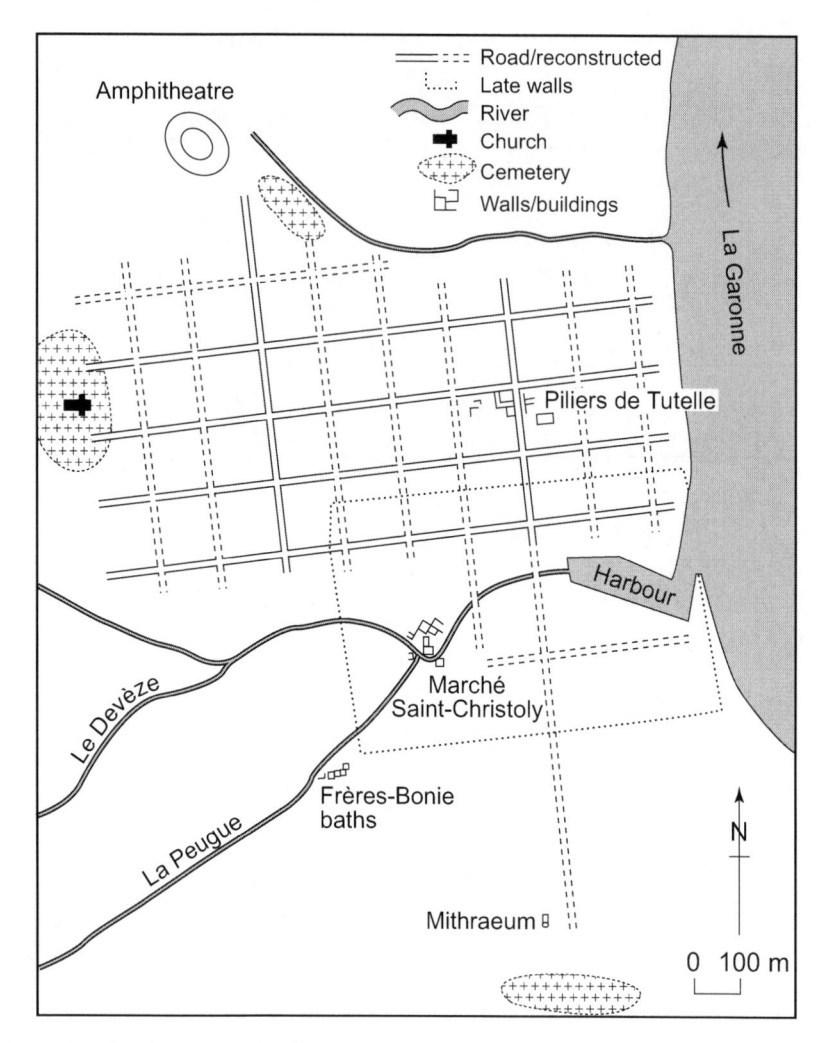

Figure 6.3 Bordeaux (Burdigala).

around the end of the third century, however, it was firmly incorporated into the new urban centre. Seemingly consisting of very loose domestic and artisanal settlement in the first century, the occupation at Saint-Christoly became denser in the second century, with the addition of new commercial and public buildings. Rising water-tables appear to have discouraged further construction during the third century, but when the city walls were built, the Peugue was diverted to pass away from the site, and the Devèze was canalised. This allowed further densification on the site in the fourth century, and life continued to flourish there throughout the fifth and sixth centuries. The overall picture, then, is one of healthy urban development, which continued unchecked throughout the late antique period, and intensified after the construction of the defences. However, the commercial importance of Bordeaux during late antiquity may mean that this is an atypical case.

Beyond the city walls, those buildings that had belonged to the urban peripheries of the high empire were almost universally abandoned during late antiquity. The only real exceptions are sites such as the right bank of the Saône at Lyon or the Île de la Cité at Paris, which continued to be occupied because they had become a part of a relocated urban centre. The character and circumstances of abandonment could vary, however. At Vienne (figure 4.4, p. 90), certain buildings at Saint-Romain-en-Gal were already falling into ruin at the end of the Severan period,[124] and complete abandonment of the area seems to have occurred by the end of the third century. The only activity after this time consisted of demolition for the recovery of building materials, and the development of a cemetery around the Thermes des Lutteurs. At Sainte-Colombe, a similar pattern is visible, with domestic buildings abandoned in the early third century, and a cemetery appearing in the fourth.[125] Similarly, south of the Augustan walls on the left bank of the Rhône, abandonment began in the early third century, and a cemetery appeared over an earlier warehouse site in the second half of the fourth.[126] The establishment of cemeteries in all three areas suggests that they had become devoid of living occupation. Yet the cemeteries were themselves a periurban feature, serving the needs of the intra-mural population, while the recovery of materials at Saint-Romain-en-Gal is an example of the exploitation of periurban resources. Vienne's high imperial periphery, then, was still in some senses acting as a periurban zone, despite the profound changes undergone by its built fabric.

At Arles (figure 4.9, p. 100), the periurban quarters at Trinquetaille and south of the remaining sections of the city walls seem to have been as active as ever during the first half of the third century. In the mid-third century, however, they experienced a sudden and dramatic change. Excavations on both sides of the river have revealed widespread signs of violent destruction involving fire, all datable to this period.[127] The disaster does not seem to have affected the occupied urban centre, and Heijmans has suggested that it was genuinely the result of an external attack, rather than a natural fire which would have stopped at the river. In any event, none of the periurban quarters were reoccupied after the disaster, indicating a changed level of interest in this type of occupation. Finally, at Metz (figure 4.16, p. 124), we have already encountered the sporadic abandonments affecting the periurban agglomeration of Pontiffroy: perhaps caused by political disturbances, perhaps by economic vicissitudes.[128] Schlemaire states that the final abandonment of this site took place in the early fourth century, but in fact three churches were built at Pontiffroy between the sixth and eighth centuries, probably serving an area of domestic occupation.[129] The fourth-century abandonment, then, may have been just another instance of the temporary desertions which the site had experienced since the first century AD.

These three cities demonstrate a range of different changes affecting former urban peripheries: gradual abandonment at Vienne, sudden destruction at Arles and a series of temporary desertions at Metz. The cemeteries at Vienne also reveal that the abandonment of periurban buildings did not necessarily mean the end of a periurban function for the area. They are all, however, cities which did not see significant reductions in the size of their related urban centres. Arles and Vienne appear to have retained their early imperial fortifications, while Metz saw the construction of new walls enclosing most of the existing urban centre.[130] It is therefore not possible in these cases to compare the fortunes of buildings in the old urban periphery with those in formerly central areas now excluded by reduced defensive walls. At Saintes, however, where a wall enclosing approximately one quarter of the old urban centre was built in the last quarter of the third century, such a comparison can be made. Here, excavations of a large *domus* on the rue Grelaud, in the old urban periphery across the Charente from the high imperial urban centre, revealed that this house was still in normal use until around AD 300.[131] The *domus* was then abandoned and its materials recovered, but occupation of a different kind arose. A small medium-quality construction was built nearby in the early fourth century and occupied for a short time, during which a hypocaust from the old house was used as a rubbish-dump. Finally, three burials appeared in the area after around 350, probably associated with a larger nearby necropolis.

The evidence of the rue Grelaud site can be instructively compared with another *domus* on the opposite side of the river, outside the late walls but well within the old urban centre. This house, part of the 'Ma Maison' site, was demolished in the second half of the second century,[132] a time when the rue Grelaud house was just being rebuilt in a grander style. Soon after, the standing walls and floors of the 'Ma Maison' *domus* were patched, and occupation of some kind then continued until the last quarter of the third century, when burials appeared on the site. Thus both sites passed through similar phases of abandonment, partial reoccupation and finally funerary usage. However, the 'Ma Maison' *domus*, despite being part of the old imperial urban centre, passed through them around half a century earlier than the rue Grelaud site. Most importantly, the initial demolition of the 'Ma Maison' *domus* took place well before Saintes' reduced defensive walls were built, meaning that it cannot be understood as a simple side-effect of their construction.[133] Instead, evidence from other parts of the old urban centre at Saintes suggests increasingly widespread decline from the late second century onwards, culminating in the almost complete abandonment of the areas outside the walled circuit *before* it was actually built.[134] Thus the areas excluded by the walled circuit at Saintes had already experienced a significant change of character before it was built. By contrast, the rue Grelaud *domus* continued to function for a short time after the reduced walls had been constructed on the other side of the Charente. This may merely reflect the personal circumstances of its owners, but it does demonstrate that those sites closest to the new, reduced urban centres were not always last to be abandoned.

The appearance of burials in the final phases of the rue Grelaud and 'Ma Maison' sites again indicates that both retained a periurban function even after the abandonment and demolition of their buildings. Thus the distinction between the former urban centre and urban periphery at Saintes was eroded, with the extra-mural sectors of the old urban centre coming to be used in much the same manner as places which had always formed part of the urban periphery. This underlines the changing identity of such areas already noted in the context of cathedral and cemetery distribution. The relationship between the construction of the walls at Saintes and the beginnings of change on the 'Ma Maison' site also reveals that such change did not always begin as a *result* of wall-building. This last point can be further illustrated through developments at Amiens between the mid-third century and the construction of its walls in the last quarter of that century.[135] Excavations have revealed that *insulae* around the edges of the Amiens' old urban centre began to be abandoned during the mid-third century, and that some were covered over by cemeteries. This was the beginning of a progressive decline which reduced the occupied area of the city from an initial extent of around 140 ha to only about 30–40 ha during the 260s. By the time the walled circuit was built, most of the *insulae* outside it had already been abandoned for around a decade, and no more than 20 ha were enclosed. Only sporadic pockets of occupation in semi-ruined buildings now remained outside the new walls.[136] Like Saintes, then, the construction of the walls was only the culmination of major changes in land-use which had begun up to fifty years previously. The two examples demonstrate that late antique walls could in fact be an expression of existing differences between the defended and excluded areas of the former urban centre, rather than a cause of those differences.

Continuity and adaptation

At Saintes and Amiens, there seems to have been virtually no living occupation outside the late antique walls by the mid-fourth century. Yet this situation was by no means universal. In many cities, existing extra-mural buildings remained occupied well into the late antique period, or were adapted and enjoyed continued use in a new form. Such continuity and adaptation are not always entirely separable from the abandonment of buildings described in the last section. Frequently, buildings adapted to new purposes had passed through a period of abandonment beforehand. It was also common for elite *domus* to go through a phase of occupation in a semi-ruined or poorly maintained state before being completely abandoned, as for the 'Ma Maison' and rue Grelaud houses at Saintes (above). The precise character of such occupation is not always clear, but it often seems to represent the opportunistic use of abandoned property by agriculturalists, artisans or those engaged in recovering building materials. It cannot really be regarded as a continuation of the original function of the *domus*, since the occupation was no longer connected with the elite lifestyles for which the building was designed. Rather, this type of 'squatting' is best considered a form of adaptation of an existing building.

At some cities, a more stable form of urban continuity is observable in the extra-mural sectors of the old urban centre. The church built on the plain at Saint-Bertrand-de-Comminges in the first half of the fifth century has been mentioned. It was established over the ruins of an existing building, either abandoned before this date or acquired intact and demolished to allow the construction of the church. Around it, however, other occupation continued. The church itself was relatively small,[137] and fitted closely into the existing urban fabric, suggesting that it was surrounded by buildings still in active use. A new pi-shaped portico had also been built in the same sector of the city, south of the macellum, in the fourth century.[138] Meanwhile, a nearby hostel or luxurious *domus* had its south wing lavishly restored in the early fourth century, a mosaic installed in the fifth, and was maintained carefully until at least the sixth century.[139] Such continuity did not apply to the whole of the old urban centre at Saint-Bertrand-de-Comminges, with a number of monuments apparently being systematically demolished at around the same time that the new defences were built.[140] Even so, some buildings in the old urban centre clearly did continue to function much as they had always done.

Such continuity is typical of Novempopulania, where occupation in former urban centres often persisted well after adjoining areas of high ground had been defended.[141] Similar areas of continuing occupation also seem likely elsewhere in Gaul; for example, outside the defences at Paris, Tours or Clermont-Ferrand. At each of these cities, the late antique cemeteries remained at a distance from the former urban centres, suggesting that living occupation continued between them and the new city walls.[142] It is noteworthy, though, that both Paris and Tours, like Saint-Bertrand-de-Comminges, had experienced a significant shift in the location of their urban centres in late antiquity. This makes them quite different cases from cities like Saintes or Amiens, where the existing urban centre shrank and was then defended. Continuity in the former urban centres at Paris, Tours and Saint-Bertrand perhaps reflects the special character of their defensive circuits. Rather than sheltering the last remains of a former urban centre, as at Saintes or Amiens, they may instead have acted somewhat like fortresses, capable of sheltering the local population when necessary, but not normally enclosing all of it.

Where continuity did not apply to extended quarters, individual buildings – especially public buildings – could nevertheless remain in use. Literary evidence indicates that games and spectacles continued to be held at certain cities in late antique Gaul,[143] although this will have depended greatly on local circumstances and resources. Often, games were celebrated in buildings which had belonged to the periphery of the earlier city. The circus at Arles, for instance, saw games held by the Franks in the mid-sixth century, even though domestic occupation had begun between its outer buttresses in the early fifth century.[144] Thus, it continued to make an important contribution to urban life and public display, despite the abandonment of the rest of Arles' former urban periphery. At Lyon, late fourth-century coin finds from the theatre at Fourvière show that this was one of the last features of the old urban centre to remain in use: now, of course, in the periphery of the new centre at St-Jean.[145] Other public buildings, however, were demolished and used as stone quarries. The amphitheatre to the south-east of Metz, apparently demolished at the end of the third century to provide *spolia* for the new city walls,[146] is such an example, as are the many public buildings used in the defensive circuit at Saintes.

Where not required either for their original purpose or as quarries, classical public buildings offered well-constructed walls and foundations which were too good to waste. Thus, they were often adapted to new purposes. This was certainly common in the centres of late antique cities, perhaps partly because it constituted a lesser risk to surrounding occupation than demolition and rebuilding. The old forum and a podium on its north side were used as the foundations for the cathedral at Aix-en-Provence soon after their abandonment.[147] At Cimiez (Cemenelum), an unwalled city in Alpes Maritimae, a set of public baths abandoned in the second half of the fourth century were transformed into a cathedral in the fifth.[148] Meanwhile, the Temple of Livia and Augustus near the forum at Vienne had become the church of Notre-Dame-de-la-Vie by the eleventh century: possibly earlier.[149] This last building is unusual, since the conversion of classical temples into churches was normally avoided.[150] Doubtless the reason was partly one of religious scruple, but there were also practical factors to consider. The small *cella* of a classical temple would provide little room for the gatherings of a Christian congregation.

Beyond the late antique centres, similar adaptations can be observed. Although partially demolished, the amphitheatre to the south-east of Metz became the focus for a Christian structure in the fourth century,[151] while at Saintes a church was installed in the abandoned Thermes de Saint-Saloine in an extra-mural sector of the old urban centre.[152] The circumstances were different from the central examples above, however, since these structures were not surrounded by other occupied buildings. The amphitheatre at Metz may have been of special interest because it had been a place of martyrdom, while the church at Saint-Saloine appears to have been established because the area had already become a focus for burials, and the nearby baths provided an embryonic structure. Meanwhile, as mentioned above, the circus at Arles saw lean-to domestic structures developing between its outer buttresses in the early fifth century.[153] Again, the circus does not seem to have been adapted because it was in the centre of a heavily occupied area, but rather used opportunistically because it offered niches where cheap shelters could be built. Nevertheless, the fact that people of apparently poor means were so keen to live in the periphery of Arles in the fifth and sixth centuries is of interest, since it suggests that the city offered opportunities for trade or employment which might make this worthwhile.

New buildings

Urban defences and Christian buildings were of course not the only new structures which could be erected in late antiquity. We shall now consider some of the other types of buildings constructed in Gallic cities at this time. One such, the domestic house, must have been a frequent creation, but late houses are generally little known except through their mosaics.[154] The Îlot Saint-Christoly excavations at Bordeaux revealed one house built on newly drained land in the late third century, and two constructed over earlier examples in the fourth.[155] All were of good-quality construction, and one was equipped with both hypocaust heating and at least two polychrome mosaics. Unfortunately, such finds are rare. New elite housing usually arose within late antique urban centres, and has thus been destroyed by later constructions. Outside the defences, meanwhile, domestic occupation was found mainly in continuously occupied older structures, rather than new buildings. Nevertheless, the Christian *'vici'* which grew up around the tombs of Saint-Martin at Tours and Saint-Alyre at Clermont-Ferrand featured houses as well as supplementary churches.[156] Thus, new domestic occupation could grow up in the urban periphery given the correct stimulus.

Urban public monuments were occasionally constructed during the late antique era, despite the decline of euergetism. At Trier, Arles and Lyon, for instance, sets of public baths were constructed during or after the fourth century: respectively, the Kaiserthermen in the early fourth (figure 4.14, p. 116),[157] the 'Baths of Constantine' in the fourth or fifth (figure 4.9, p. 100)[158] and baths in the Saint-Jean quarter in the late fourth (figure 4.15, p. 120).[159] Two important points of context must be noted, however. First, Trier and Arles were extremely prosperous cities during late antiquity, and Lyon relatively so, and second, all of these baths were built within the contemporary urban centres. Those at Lyon lay in the Saint-Jean quarter, which had become the new urban centre after the desertion of Fourvière. Those at Arles and Trier were both built on the perimeter of the occupied centre. However, the baths at Arles lay only 150m north of the forum, while those at Trier were on the edge of the orthogonal grid, but well within the second-century walls. Both, then, should probably be regarded as central monuments, located on the fringes of the urban centre because of the density of occupation further in, and perhaps also for the sake of visibility from the rivers at Arles and Trier.[160] Gregory of Tours also informs us that the Frankish king Chilperic had circuses built at Soissons and Paris in the mid-fifth century.[161] No remains have been found, perhaps because the circuses were temporary constructions of wood or earth, and Gregory does not divulge their locations. However, neither city's reduced defences could have accommodated a horse-racing circuit. Possibly, then, Chilperic embellished Soissons and Paris with monumental periurban structures.

One final type of new building was the fort: hitherto unknown in the Gallic interior since its conquest by Rome. Forts do not occur in any urban centre, but two periurban examples are known. One, at Jublains, was originally built in the early third century, not far from the south-west corner of the orthogonal grid (figure 4.18, p. 138).[162] It consisted of a rectangular defended hall, embellished with an earthen and later stone outer wall. Abandoned early in the fourth century, its purpose is far from clear. However, the provision of wells, cisterns, a small bath-suite and a probable kitchen suggest that it was intended to function independently of the urban centre.[163] This, Naveau believes, points to an imperial, rather than a municipal, construction.[164] No less mysterious is the 'Camp of Tranquistan', a square fortified enclosure to the east of the original urban centre at Saint-Bertrand-de-Comminges (figure 6.4).[165] This complex was built in the first half of the third century, destroyed at the end of that century, and then reoccupied during the late fourth and early fifth centuries. It was certainly military in origin, although its late reoccupation may not have been. Its imperial connections are also made clear by a fragmentary inscription from its west gate, facing the city.[166] Once again, though, its exact purpose is unknown, although May suggests that it could have policed the marble quarries at nearby Saint-Béat.[167]

With only two documented examples, these complexes are difficult to interpret. Yet they remain of interest, since they constitute a rare example of new structures other than churches being built specifically in the peripheries of late antique cities. Their apparent construction by the imperial administration rather than local urban authorities makes them very different from the other monuments discussed here. None the less, some comments about their relationship with the nearby urban centres may be offered. At both cities, practical concerns would have favoured a periurban location over a central one. Space was not readily available in either urban centre at the time of the forts' construction, while if the fort was attacked, surrounding buildings would in any case have provided platforms for besiegers to launch assaults. If the forts were intended partly to help protect the nearby cities, a periurban location may also have helped to divide the attentions of attackers between fort and urban centre, thus allowing the occupants of the forts to defend both more efficiently. But it is not clear that this was their primary function, and they are perhaps better interpreted as surviving elements in a province-wide defence network. In this case, a location in the periphery of a city would provide access to resources not available in the countryside, such as goods for sale in the urban centre

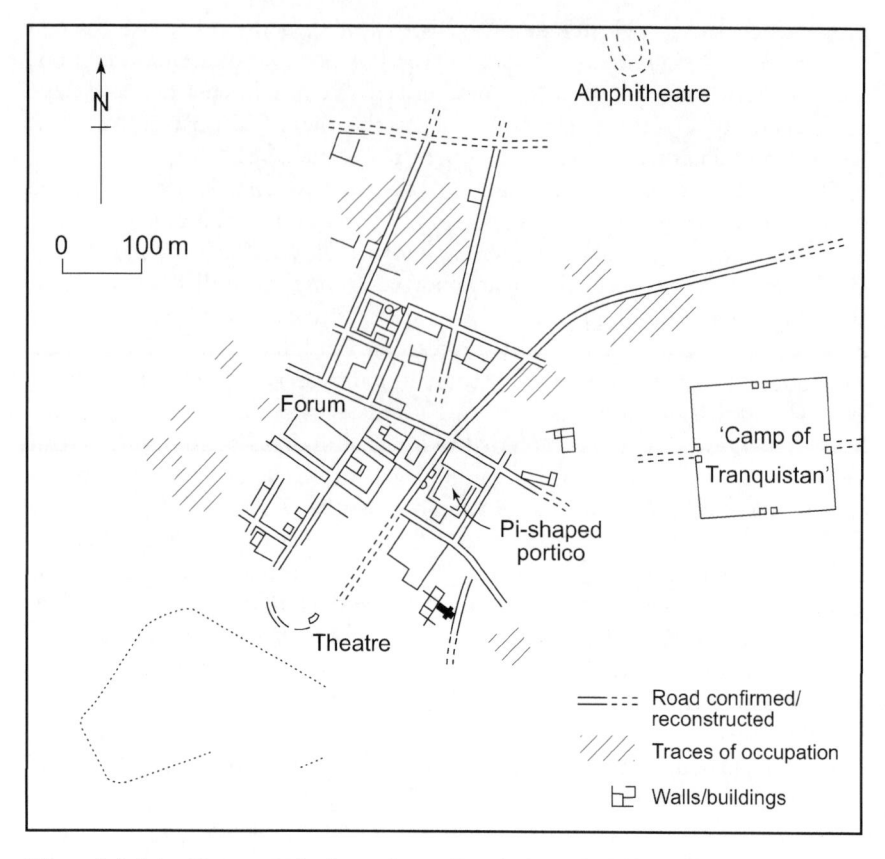

Figure 6.4 Saint-Bertrand-de-Comminges (Lugdunum Convenarum).

and roads converging upon it, while still allowing the fort to function independently from the city.

Villas

Chapter 4 concluded that, during the high empire, some Gallo-Roman villas may have been considered suburban by their owners, or at least used in a comparable fashion, but that it is difficult to detect this now from their archaeological remains. It is now time to consider whether any kind of suburban villa culture existed in late antique Gaul, and, if so, what contribution it may have made to the life of a late antique city. First, however, a general review of changes affecting villas of all kinds during this period is needed.

Archaeological evidence suggests that most Gallo-Roman villas were abandoned during the fourth and fifth centuries, with some experiencing a period of partial occupation before they fell into complete ruin.[168] Some sites, though, saw major modifications or embellishments in the fourth century or later. Sondages have revealed that the most splendid villa seen by Agache in his Somme valley survey, at Vieux-Rouen-sur-Bresle, reached its fullest and most lavish extent in the late fourth century.[169] Meanwhile, Balmelle's work in southern Aquitania has shown that elite villa culture in this region persisted well into late antiquity, with many properties continuing to function as aristocratic residences in the fifth century, and some, such as Plassac, into the sixth.[170] Late antiquity also saw new villas being built. Some resemble those of the high empire,[171] but more often they were fortified sites: perhaps best understood as a step towards the evolution of noblemen's castles. They make their appearance in literature during the fifth and sixth centuries, but at least one earlier example is known through archaeology: Pfalzel, near Trier, where construction began in the mid-fourth century.[172] As in the high empire, though, late antique villas often fell far from any city. Plassac lay around 35 km north of Bordeaux, and Vieux-Rouen around 40 km west-south-west of Amiens.

Percival has pointed out that availability of any villa site for excavation today is a function of its desertion at some point.[173] Many late antique villa sites, then, may be unavailable for excavation because they lie beneath later structures. He also draws attention to the survival of local toponyms derived from estate-names ending in '-*acum*'; for example, '-y', '-ac' or '-eux', depending on region.[174] These imply the continuing presence of some kind of feature within the landscape, and a group of people to whom it was significant. This does not, however, mean that the site was continuing to function as a villa in the classical sense. Rather, Percival proposes two main ways in which modern villages may have acquired such toponyms. First, the villa site could become the focus of a nucleated group of buildings, which eventually developed into a village and engulfed it.[175] Second, an abandoned villa may have been used for burials, later developing an associated church which in turn became the centre of a new village.[176] If, as Percival suggests, this type of evolution happened at a high proportion of villa sites, then it may frequently have obscured late antique occupation. Between such sites and the examples which are known through excavation, then, it is reasonable to say that some kind of villa system persisted into late antiquity. Yet the scale of known abandonment also indicates that the pool of people able or willing to participate in this lifestyle was steadily shrinking.

Archaeological and literary evidence both suggest that those who did own villa estates in late antiquity continued to divide their time between city and country. Studies of fifth-century Aquitania have revealed that very similar geometric and floral designs occur in mosaics and on marble sarcophagi found on rural estates and in the city of Bordeaux.[177] Thus, the same group of people appear to have been commissioning the works in each setting. Villas also feature heavily in the letters and poems of Ausonius in the fourth century and Sidonius Apollinaris in the fifth. Both men owned several estates of their own,[178] and refer frequently to those of others.[179] They also led active lives in an urban context: Ausonius as *rhetor* at Bordeaux and, later, imperial tutor at Trier, and Sidonius, amongst other things, as bishop at Clermont-Ferrand. Many of the villas they describe are rich rural estates, but others do seem to fit the mould of the classical suburban villa. We must note, though, that their authors were clearly well aware of the literary *topos*, and may have set out to depict themselves enjoying a Ciceronian lifestyle which did not reflect the reality of late antique Gaul.

The most explicitly 'suburban' villa description comes from Ausonius' '*De Herediolo*'. The poem, about an estate inherited from his father, closes by describing its relationship with Bordeaux:

> This estate of mine is neither far away from the city nor right beside it,
> lest I suffer its crowds and so that I possess its advantages.
> And whenever dislikes compel me to change place,
> I pass over and enjoy country and town by turns.[180]

Ausonius also reveals that he travels back and forth from the villa by boat, presumably to the port at Bordeaux.[181] Thus the familiar themes of the villa as both escape from and extension to the life of the city, and of regular journeys between the two are in place, at least on a literary level. Yet the very correspondence between Ausonius' writings and those of the classical period raises the question of whether they reflect actual behaviour, or are above all a poetic construction. Perhaps more revealing of real patterns of villa use is a letter written by Sidonius from Lyon to decline a fishing invitation. He explains that his daughter is sick, and continues, 'on account of this [illness] she desires to go out into our suburban estate. When we at last received your letter, we were already preparing to go to the little villa'.[182] Here the idea of the suburban villa crops up as a passing reference, rather than being the focus of an extensive literary exercise. Of course, the letter is still a literary construct, and classical antecedents are never far away: as Cicero's recovery from a stomach problem on his Tusculan estate, and Catullus' from a cough on his *suburbana villa*, remind us.[183] Yet a villa to which Sidonius might take a daughter with a worsening cough and fever is not likely to have been very far removed from Lyon, and he clearly is using it here as a supplement to his normal urban residence.

The writings of Ausonius and Sidonius certainly reveal that fourth- and fifth-century Gallic aristocrats were capable of *portraying* themselves as pursuing a suburban lifestyle, and this portrayal may have extended to real behaviour. In one sense, this is enough to classify their villas as 'suburban', since the concept had always rested as much on subjective interpretation and the mind-set of the villa owner as on the physical characteristics or location of the property concerned. Further questions, however, remain. Archaeological evidence for late antique villa occupation is, as shown above, scanty, but it has already been noted that those villas most obviously designed with impressive display in mind are not generally located within an easy day's journey of any urban centre. Regular city–villa journeys are difficult to imagine for any of them, and a picture of luxury rural villas as a more definitive place of retreat from the city than they had been during the high empire seems plausible.[184]

We may also ask whether the villa culture evoked by Ausonius and Sidonius, literary conceit or not, was widely subscribed to by other members of the Gallic elite. Notably, all the properties they mention, whether their own or other people's, are in the territories of important southern or eastern cities: Lyon, Arles, Narbonne, Saintes, Bordeaux and Clermont-Ferrand. At cities which were less prosperous, less influential or less distant from the Rhine frontier, the same culture may not have applied. As far as the contribution that these villas made to the life of the nearby city is concerned, the letters and poems contain some indications of an economic role. Ausonius details the proportions of arable land, pasture and vineyards on his inherited estate, as well as noting that he keeps two years' worth of food supplies in store.[185] Again, these details echo elements in classical villa descriptions, but, if a real reflection of Ausonius' property, would mean that the villa had economic connections with Bordeaux.

Finally, a mid-sixth century poem by Venantius Fortunatus reveals that villa estates could be conceived of as 'suburban' even in this period, and draws attention to a new group of elite landowners. The poem is the first in a series of three on estates belonging to Leontius, bishop of Bordeaux, and concerns a formerly dilapidated property at Bissonnum which he has renovated.[186] It seems to have been a classical-style villa, and Fortunatus states that it is seven miles from Bordeaux. This is the only one of the bishop's three estates which Fortunatus locates by reference to a city. The others are situated in an exclusively rural landscape, punctuated only by the Garonne and its tributaries.[187] Although no further indication is given, the suggestion is that Leontius used Bissonnum in a different manner from his other estates, travelling regularly between it and Bordeaux. As bishop, he would often have needed to visit Bordeaux, and only a villa within easy reach of that city would have allowed him to perform his episcopal duties while still spending significant amounts of time on his estate.

Certainly, Leontius was by no means alone as an estate-owning bishop in this period. By the sixth and seventh centuries, testaments to the church had bestowed upon many episcopal sees land not only within their own territory, but often in far-distant parts of Gaul.[188] Such testaments acted as a source of income for the church, but also allowed bishops like Leontius to build or rebuild their own personal residences.[189] The bishops did not have full control over the locations of the properties they inherited. But where they fell close to a city, it is quite plausible that many bishops chose to use them in a manner reminiscent of classical suburban villas. Just as the church had encouraged the persistence of administrative systems based on the city, then, it may also have been responsible for the survival at some level of a suburban villa culture.

Conclusion

This chapter set out to examine changes in the character and function of the urban periphery in late antiquity. Perhaps most important, though, is the simple survival of both the concept and the reality of periurban land-use in this period, despite the changes which it saw. Certainly, late antique and early medieval texts refer to extra-mural features, and especially churches, using phrases such as '*in suburbio*'.[190] This suggests that *an* idea of the suburban was current in this period, even if it was not identical to the classical concept. The archaeological evidence, too, makes it clear that the distinction between 'urban centre' and 'urban periphery' was still important, even if the areas considered to belong to each had been modified. The clear preference for locating cathedrals within new defensive circuits and the appearance of cemeteries in extra-mural parts of many old urban centres make it clear that the walled areas alone now enjoyed the special status of an urban centre, while the undefended parts of the city had acquired a periurban function. Meanwhile, the same function could still be performed by land which had lain beyond the old urban centre in the high imperial period; for example, in its use for burials. But former periurban occupation was more often abandoned, as the extent of the urban periphery at most cities shrank to match the contraction of their centres.

The relationship between centre and periphery in the late antique era is likely to have differed in some respects from that of the high empire. For one thing, urban boundaries had often been conceptual, rather than concrete, in the high empire. The edges of an orthogonal grid or a change in the direction of a major road indicated the limits of an urban centre, but did not impede passage across them. A defensive wall, however, generally offered only a few points of entry, and this is likely to have emphasised the division between centre and periphery. The beginnings of real problems with barbarian invaders and bands of brigands must also have affected the relationship. Periurban buildings had become much more liable than their central counterparts to attack and destruction. These factors doubtless lent a special attraction to the urban centre, encouraging those who could afford it to live within the walls. However, there is no reason to assume that they were any stronger than the ideological pull which the urban centre had exercised during the high empire as an arena for displays of wealth and status.

The actual functions of the late antique urban periphery, though, had changed little since the high empire. The periphery was still used for living occupation, cemeteries, elite villas and public monuments: although these were now churches, rather than baths, temples or amphitheatres. The churches in particular played an important role in urban life, offering religious protection, social contact, festivities, and a means of expressing status. Yet these same functions had been fulfilled by the public buildings of the high empire, themselves often in the urban periphery. It would thus seem an exaggeration to claim, like Février (above), that periurban churches gave the late antique urban periphery a special role which it had not been capable of playing before. Rather, they are evidence for the continuing importance of periurban activity at cities whose centres were restricted by static boundaries. Less prominent in this chapter has been periurban commerce and industry of the type known in the high empire. Economic activity, however, was not absent from the late antique urban periphery. Artisanal installations of the fourth century, for instance, have been identified amongst occupation west of the reduced circuit at Tours.[191] Equally, pottery workshops in the Saint-Rémi district, around 1.3 km south of the late antique circuit at Reims, continued production of grey coarse ware for a local market until late in the third century.[192] Such workshops were almost certainly a feature of surviving extra-mural occupation at other cities, but, like the domestic occupation in these areas, are rarely known in detail.

The persistence of the centre–periphery divide and the little-altered character of periurban land-use says much for continuity between the high imperial and late antique Gallo-Roman city. Certainly, the practice of marking out a distinct urban centre and imbuing it with special status was common to both eras. The reasons for doing so may have changed in late antiquity, when defence became as important as display. But the result was much as it had been in earlier centuries, with the only exception being that the boundaries used were generally less flexible and less permeable than those of the high empire. As in the classical period, any urban activity which could not be fitted within this static boundary, or was not considered compatible with its ideology, had to take place instead in its immediate periphery. Thus, in each period, the desire to mark out an urban centre and differentiate it from what lay beyond gave rise to a special form of development and occupation in its immediate periphery. Meanwhile, defensive walls remained one of the most important features of the medieval French city, and continued to have the same effect, distinguishing now between *ville* and *faubourgs*. It is only in the modern era, with the obsolescence of defensive walls and the absence of any new equivalent boundary, that this very sharp distinction between centre and suburbs has been left behind.

7

SOME WIDER QUESTIONS

Introduction

Recognisable periurban development was clearly a widespread feature of Gallo-Roman urbanism. It has already been stated in chapter 4 that more than half of the administrative cities of high empire Gaul have yielded evidence for periurban occupation, despite the imperfect nature of the archaeological record. Chapter 5 found that the most urban secondary agglomerations often generated very similar development, although different methods of spatial organisation were preferred in less urbanised settlements. Finally, chapter 6 was able to trace the continuation of periurban development into late antique Gaul, despite the political, social and economic changes which occurred in this period.

Only systematic investigation in other provinces can determine for certain whether the same patterns applied in other parts of the western empire. But the many other similarities between Gallo-Roman urbanism and that which occurred in other provinces — particularly the practice of marking out distinct urban centres — makes it highly likely. Certainly, chapter 3 was able to draw on plenty of known examples, all very much like those observed in Gaul. Meanwhile, although Esmonde Cleary did not explicitly state what proportion of Romano-British towns had generated known extra-mural development in his 1987 monograph, the evidence he presents speaks for itself. Of the sixty large and small Romano-British towns that he discusses, he is able to present positive evidence for extra-mural occupation (discounting cemeteries and villas) from all but ten.[1] Most of those are settlements at which there has either been very little excavation or the dating of the defences is poorly understood.

If the phenomenon of periurban development was part of the empire-wide model of Roman urbanism, then, we may ask what the study of it can contribute to our understanding of that model, and of the society that produced it. This question is explored here in relation to three key issues: the character and function of a Roman city, its relationship with the countryside, and the relationship between provincial elites and Rome

SOME WIDER QUESTIONS

Tensions and resolutions in Roman urbanism

Roman cities were many things to many people. To the Roman state, they were key components in an empire-wide administrative system. To local elites, they were showpieces for wealth, sophistication and cosmopolitanism: both their own and that of the communities they represented. To farmers, traders, artisans and their customers, they were centres of economic exchange. And to all these groups, they were arenas for social interaction, where the complex hierarchical relationships between them could be expressed, enacted and explored. The study of the urban periphery draws attention to all of these functions, and also demonstrates how conflicts of interest between some of them could be resolved.

One particular facet of the Roman city – its role in elite display – had the potential to create a number of problems. Chapter 2 showed that the display function of a city was greatly enhanced by the use of distinct boundaries to mark out a special, explicitly urban space. Boundaries demonstrated the local elite's understanding of the distinction between city and country, and the special role of the city in a civilised lifestyle. They could function as impressive display monuments in themselves, and also ensured that the impact of other buildings erected within them was enhanced by their context in a self-evidently urban – and therefore sophisticated – environment. The empire's elite, then, worked hard to ensure that their cities were suitably well defined. They created distinct physical boundaries around them, explored the antithesis between city and country in literature, and subscribed to the notion of an *urbs* or *oppidum* which ended at the urban boundaries.

This behaviour may have helped to create distinct showpieces of *urbanitas*. But it also had its drawbacks: both for the elite who drove it and for other city-dwellers. The main problem was that it created inflexible limits on the amount of space available in the city, not only for the very displays which the elite were so keen to make, but also for other urban-based activities. Competition for that space will therefore have developed, driving up land prices in the urban centre. And this is likely to have had a particular effect on its ability to function as a locus for economic exchange. It will have meant that people of small means found it more difficult to buy or rent space there, either to live in or to use for economic activities such as retail, storage or production. This, in turn, would also have had an impact on the lives of the elite, whose lifestyles depended on an ability to buy goods produced and retailed by the non-elite, use the buildings which they constructed and maintained, and court their votes in elections.

The urban periphery, however, offered a solution to these problems. The capacity for periurban development to be recognised as something different from the urban centre, and yet still inherently connected with it, lent great flexibility to Roman urbanism. It meant that an urban centre *could* be distinguished clearly from what lay beyond it, without this needing to constrict the development of the city as a socio-economic entity, or indeed the activities of its elite. Thus the potters who lived and worked across the river from the centre of Sens were able to sell their wares within the city and throughout the surrounding rural territory, without having to pay a premium for land in the actual urban centre. Similarly, the owners of wealthy *domus* such as those at Saint-Romain-en-Gal and Trinquetaille, or the Maison aux Xenia at Lyon, could enjoy easy access to the amenities of the city, but also build larger houses than they are likely to have been able to in the urban centre.

The very display function of the city was also extended by the phenomenon of the urban periphery. Urban public monuments may, in most cases, have been considered most effective as displays of local status if erected within the urban centre. But widespread recognition of the urban periphery as a part of the urban agglomeration meant that it, too, could be used as a successful setting for monumental public buildings. In some circumstances, it might even be more effective than the urban centre in showing those buildings off to best effect. Amphitheatres and circuses in particular seem often to have been built in the urban periphery partly to ensure that they were clearly visible to anybody approaching the city from outside.

The urban periphery, then, allowed the elite city and the socio-economic city to occupy the same space without having a negative impact on one another. It both arose from and resolved the tensions between the two. This observation may also go some way to resolving a tension in scholarly conceptions of the Roman city. Some scholars have emphasised the political and cultural role of the city over its economic function, seeing it as an 'artificial' elite creation, designed primarily for administration and to allow participation in privileged urban lifestyle. This view is particularly prevalent among those who see a loss of interest in this lifestyle as a major reason for the decline of cities in late antiquity. Liebeschuetz, for example, in an article entitled 'The end of the ancient city', stressed the political and administrative origins of ancient urbanism, and stated that 'classical cities were above all a means to living a particular kind of good life'.[2] Others argue that the city *was* a 'genuine' economic entity, which originated out of prosperity, and played a significant role in economic exchange. Hopkins, discussing economic development in the Bronze Age and Iron Age Mediterranean, stated that 'it was this increase in agricultural productivity which made the growth of towns possible',[3] while chapter 3 noted several scholars who have detected the influence of central place interactions behind the development of Roman settlement patterns. The truth, of course, is that the Roman city was both simultaneously: and the urban periphery is a vivid testimony to this.

City and country

Scholarly approaches to the Roman city have also long been concerned with another tension: that between city and country. The issue is by no means unique to the field of Roman history. Braudel, in his analysis of early modern Europe, insisted on the essential division between urban and rural, and followed in the footsteps of Adam Smith, Marx, Weber and Hoselitz when he did.[4] Indeed, all of them were in accord with ancient writers like Varro, Cicero and Quintilian (see chapter 2). Amongst Roman historians, the division has found its most vivid expression in economic debates over whether the city was or was not 'parasitical' on the countryside: usually known as the 'consumer city' debate. This was generated above all by Moses Finley, who saw urban manufacture as restricted to 'petty commodity production' destined for local consumption, and believed that the main role of the city in the ancient economy was to act as an efficient collector of rural wealth through the medium of rent and taxes.[5] The idea has generated numerous responses and counter-arguments, but both sides of the debate are generally characterised by an assumption that the city and the countryside were indeed separate, and meaningful as economic entities.[6]

Urban historians and sociologists, though, have long questioned whether the physical differences between city and country necessarily equate to any meaningful socio-economic divide.[7] As Abrams put it in 1978, 'The material and especially the visual presence of towns seem to have impelled a reification in which the town as a physical object is turned into a taken-for-granted social object.'[8] He argued that we should instead consider the place of towns within a wider social context, and especially hierarchical power-structures.[9]

Scholars of the ancient world, too, are now seeking to leave both the 'consumer city' and the urban–rural antithesis which it requires behind.[10] Even Whittaker, who defended the 'consumer city' theory in 1995, recognised 'the indifference of a specifically economic relationship between urban and rural' and noted that 'the study of cities is only an imperfect way of studying the operations of power in society'.[11] Horden and Purcell speak of 'the absence of clear *political* and *cultural* separation between city and countryside during much of Antiquity', while for Gaul, Woolf argues that 'Gallic economies and societies revolved much more around differences of wealth and power, than around any distinction between urban and rural.'[12] The preference is shifting towards studies of socio-economic interactions between different groups within ancient communities, without attempting to tie those groups to specific and exclusive physical locations. Meanwhile, analyses of the urban fabric as a distinct form of space continue to offer one way of exploring those interactions.[13]

The study of the urban periphery draws attention to the fact that even the physical distinction between city and country in the ancient world was not really as stark as a focus on literary texts or defensive walls might suggest. This much was clear to ancient commentators, who were as aware of the reality of the urban periphery as they were fond of the ideology of a neatly defined urban centre, and indeed celebrated the urban–rural divide as much by breaching it as by maintaining it. We are dealing with a world in which cows were kept within the walls of Pompeii, grandiose monuments were raised outside the *urbs* at Rome and villas everywhere were designed to evoke the public architecture of the city. And we must also allow for a wide range of secondary settlements, from those which were urban in all but title to the tiniest of rustic hamlets. Despite the best attempts of the ancients to divide city from country on a physical level, then, they were never as sharply polarised as the illustrations of the *Corpus Agrimensorum* might suggest (see figure 2.1, p. 30). It is better to think in terms of a spectrum, with the truly urban at one end and the truly rural at the other, but many indistinctly defined stages, including the urban periphery, in between.

The character of periurban development also supports the suggestion that the physical boundaries between city and country did not correspond directly with any particular socio-economic distinction. The case of the workshops at Autun, encountered in chapter 4, suggests that urban boundaries had little specific effect on economic activity. Although workshops were often located just outside the urban centre, at Autun they fell just *within* an unusually extensive walled circuit. This strongly suggests that their location – and that of other workshops which do fall outside urban boundaries – was being determined by free market economics, rather than any social or political attempts to keep industrial production out of urban space. There also do not seem to have been any restrictions on the movement of individuals between centre and periphery in Gaul, apart from the practical time constraints involved in passing through gates or across rivers.[14] Social exclusion was only applied to individuals such as the contractors for burials, punishments and executions at Puteoli (chapter 2): clearly an exceptional case connected with Roman fears about death pollution and the related exclusion of the dead. Any other evidence for the concentration of lower-class individuals in the urban periphery, such as the areas of poor-quality housing outside Amiens and Metz, can, like the workshops of Autun, be explained by independent economic factors rather than conscious attempts to keep 'undesirables' out of the city: and is anyway tempered by the presence of wealthy *domus* in the urban periphery. In socio-economic terms, then, we should envisage a gradual continuum between city and country, within which the actual urban boundaries had relatively little impact.

Rome and the provincial elites

Finally, what contribution can the study of the urban periphery make to debates surrounding the relationship between provincial elites and the power that was Rome? Were any correspondences between the character of periurban development in Gaul and the type of urbanism which had developed in the Roman empire before Gaul became part of it the result of a conscious, imperialising policy from the Roman state, of the kind described by Tacitus in Agricola's Britain?[15] Were they driven by local elites seeking to display their loyalty to Rome in the hope of direct reward?[16] Or were those elites instead 'borrowing' Roman tools as one means of expressing and maintaining their personal status within their own communities?[17] And what do any deviations from the established model mean? A rejection of Roman culture, or the creation of a new, local culture?[18]

Certainly, the Gallo-Roman elite had taken on board the Roman emphasis on the city–country divide, and applied it by marking out distinct urban centres in their administrative cities. The importance of urban boundaries in Gaul cannot be attributed solely to Roman imperative. Boundaries established at the foundation of Gallo-Roman cities were carefully maintained by their inhabitants, and sometimes reinforced through the establishment of new markers; for example, the four monumental arches at Reims.[19] New boundaries, like the second-century walled circuit at Trier, were also established, while secondary agglomerations aspiring towards a form of urban status might create a closely defined urban centre where none had existed before: the orthogonal grid established at Dalheim in the AD 70s, for instance.[20] Clearly, then, the boundaries were of interest to the Gauls themselves. It is also clear that they carried real significance throughout the Roman period and on into late antiquity. Across Gaul, considerable and consistent differences in the use of space can be observed within and without them.

Arguably, the defining characteristic of the urban centre, and that which marked it off most clearly from the urban periphery, was the amount of effort put into expressing *romanitas* within its boundaries. The very idea of having a city, and using it as a community showpiece, had essentially been presented to the Gauls by Rome. And the model which Rome offered carried with it the message that *urbanitas* and *romanitas* went hand in hand. *Romanitas* was demonstrated by *urbanitas*, while the best and most effective way to convey *urbanitas* was through *romanitas*: chiefly, principles of planning and architecture which had been honed and refined in a Roman context. The reasons why the Gallic elite – or indeed other provincials – chose to take on this model at all have been discussed elsewhere, but are likely to have included an interest in developing a profitable relationship with Rome, as well as a desire to demonstrate their membership of a civilised, up-to-date, sophisticated and even cosmopolitan world: to themselves, to their own communities and to others.[21] We should not, then, be too surprised if the Gauls showed the greatest eagerness to adhere to 'Roman' architectural principles in the space which the model would have taught them was best-suited to displays of status: the urban centre. By demonstrating their *romanitas* within the city boundaries, they were simultaneously making a more effective statement of their *urbanitas*: and, hence, their sophistication.

The closest adherence to the established Roman model of *urbanitas* can usually be observed in the forum area. The Gallic elite would have learnt from Rome that a forum constituted the proper social and political heart of a city.[22] It lay topographically at the centre of the urban grid, and hosted buildings and activities which were metaphorically central to the life of the community as a whole, and its relationship with Rome. Here would be found a *curia*, used for council meetings, and a *basilica*, for legal hearings, business and administration. This configuration was explicitly recommended by Vitruvius, who states that the basilica, treasury, prison and curia should all adjoin the forum, as should the temple of Mercury.[23] In *coloniae*, the complex would usually be dominated by a Capitolium: a temple to the chief gods of the Roman state, Jupiter, Juno and Minerva. Meanwhile, the paved space of the forum, often surrounded by porticoes and shops, was used as a social and commercial space. A forum, then, was a gathering-space for the community itself, but was also the part of the city most likely to be viewed in detail by visitors: including representatives of the Roman state. Of all the places to make statements about a community's identity, this was the greatest.

The forum complex did evolve over time, both before and after Gaul's incorporation into the empire.[24] But examples in Gaul always follow the contemporary model closely.[25] The forum of Feurs (Forum Segusiavorum) in Lugdunensis is a particularly well-documented case.[26] Rectangular in shape, it was flanked at one end by a *basilica* and *curia*, and dominated at the other by a large temple. The central space was paved, and surrounded by porticoes and shops. Meanwhile, at Narbonne a probable Capitolium faced on to the forum complex from the north,[27] and even outside the *coloniae* van Andringa has argued that the forum was above all the preserve of Jupiter and that other cornerstone of the community's politico-religious relationship with Rome: the imperial cult.[28] The architectural language used is consistently in keeping with that developed in Rome and Italy, and seen all over the empire. Thus it constituted a powerful demonstration of the *urbanitas* and the *romanitas* of the Gallic communities, in the very space which most united them with the rest of the civilised world. If this display was at its peak in the forum, though, the rest of the urban centre also helped to reinforce it: especially along the major roads. The orthogonally arranged street grid was a vivid expression of *romanitas–urbanitas* in itself, while an array of monumental public buildings could also make the same point. Again, most of these would have been instantly recognisable as 'Roman', in both architecture and function. They might include other temples of the imperial cult, such as the municipal sanctuary of the Verbe Incarné site at Lyon,[29] monumental bath-houses like the Thermes du Forum at Saint-Bertrand-de-Comminges,[30] and, as we have seen, classical theatres.

Having an urban periphery was 'Roman' too, of course. But the rules about how it might be used were rather more flexible than those which applied in the urban centre, while it did not carry the same intense connotations of *urbanitas* and *romanitas* as the central space. The evidence of Gaul shows that it certainly *could* function as an effective setting for Roman-style public monuments: classical amphitheatres and circuses are the obvious examples, but the same applies to lavish public baths. Yet the most urban and the most Roman building-types never appear here: *curiae* and *basilicae* were naturally kept to the forum, the only known periurban sanctuaries of the imperial cult are the exceptional examples at Lyon and Narbonne,[31] and even classical theatres were restricted to the urban centre as much as possible.

The urban periphery does, however, seem to have offered a suitable location for other forms of architecture, absent from the model of Roman urbanism to which the Gauls had been exposed. Prime among these were Romano-Celtic temples and the local forms of spectacle building: Gallic theatres and mixed edifices. Although not part of the classical architectural tradition, the very positioning of these monuments arguably demonstrates the extent to which Gauls had absorbed the Roman urban model. Their absence from the urban centre can be viewed in part as the effect of a desire to avoid diluting its *romanitas–urbanitas* with 'un-Roman' building types. But their presence in the urban periphery also demonstrates their understanding of what this zone meant in Roman thought. Epigraphy from the Lenus Mars precinct at Trier and the commanding positions of other periurban temples – the group at la Genetoye opposite Autun, for instance, or the north sanctuary at Jublains – make it obvious that these religious complexes in particular, and the theatres associated with them, played a major role in local civic life. That the Gallo-Roman elite realised these important monuments could be associated with their cities without compromising the special ideologies of the urban centre is eloquent testimony to their recognition of the ambiguous, urban-but-not-urban status of the urban periphery (see chapter 2). It can then be seen as a sign of Gallo-Roman culture working successfully with the Roman urban tradition, developing new uses for urban space which both maintained Roman principles and met local needs. Indeed, the development of distinct periurban satellite settlements at administrative cities and at the most urban secondary agglomerations can be seen in a similar light. It was fully compatible with the Roman urban model, but also accorded well with the polynuclear settlement structure already in use in pre-Roman Gaul.

Some of the ways in which periurban space was used in Gaul may be interpreted as direct emulations of the city of Rome itself, or other specific examples of the Roman urban model in action. Gauls who had visited Rome or read descriptions of the city by authors such as Strabo would have been well aware of the monumental complexes in the Campus Martius. Those who had not could, after 12 BC, observe a more accessible example in the form of the provincial sanctuary at Lyon. Indeed, the idea of the monumental urban periphery seems to have been particularly prominent in the Roman consciousness at the very time when most Gallo-Roman cities were being founded or monumentalised: the Augustan era, characterised by a slough of projects on the Campus Martius and, in the east, the celebration of Augustus' greatest victory through the foundation of Nicopolis, complete with peri-urban stadium, theatre, victory-monument, temple and festival.[32] This type of model may well have encouraged the construction of monumental squares at Saint-Romain-en-Gal opposite Vienne and Trinquetaille opposite Arles, as well as circuses to the south of the same two cities. Less directly, it might also be related to the practice of building monumentalising Romano-Celtic sanctuaries in the urban periphery. Although the architecture of these structures was not drawn directly from the Roman tradition, the idea of the monumental periurban sanctuary was.

Other characteristics of Gallo-Roman periurban development though, while similar to those seen at Rome and other western Roman cities in Italy and western Europe, are likely to have arisen through a much less self-conscious process. The construction of shops, workshops, warehouses, modest baths and all kinds of houses in the urban periphery, for instance, was matched at Rome, but in Gaul was probably driven mainly by local economic and social factors, rather than deliberate attempts at emulation. Although some of the circumstances at work were created by the interest of Gauls in the Roman urban model – particularly their use of urban boundaries – the actual use of the space is probably best understood as an example of independent parallel development, guided by simple common sense and human self-interest. It was, after all, the local elites who had the greatest vested interest in making public displays of their commitment to the cultural world of Rome. Thus it is in their use of the urban periphery as a place for constructing monumental public buildings that the relationship with Rome can best be traced.

NOTES

1 EXPLORING THE EDGES OF A ROMAN CITY

1 Grahame 1997.
2 Frézouls 1984; Duncan-Jones 1985; Laurence 1994: 20–37; Patterson 2000d: 31–8.
3 Wallace-Hadrill 1995: 43–4.
4 Essentially the theory of Structuration, outlined in Giddens 1984.
5 Vega also defines a periurban area as 'a space of transition between the country and the city which unites characteristics of both but which is difficult to ascribe to one or the other' (Vega 1994: 143).
6 For example Champlin 1982; Morley 1996; Pergola *et al.* 2003.
7 Braudel 1981: 503. Cf. also Keene 1976 on medieval suburbs in England.
8 Carter 1983: 137–45.
9 Carter 1983: 145–6.
10 Finley 1977 and see also Chapter 7.
11 Esmonde Cleary 1985: 74.
12 For example Lugli 1923; Ashby 1927; Jones 1962; Jones 1963; Quilici 1974; Champlin 1982; Purcell 1987a; Morley 1996, ch. 4; Patterson 2000a; Pergola *et al.* 2003. Quilici 1979, however, points out that even at Rome, the tendency has been for archaeologists to concentrate on the area within the wall of Aurelian.
13 La Regina *et al.* 2001, 2004 and 2005.
14 Lincoln – Jones 1981; Bologna – Scagliarini 1991.
15 Esmonde Cleary 1987.
16 Bedon 1998a and 1998b.
17 A more general survey was also undertaken in an article by Vega 1994. However, his evidence was drawn mainly from literary and documentary sources, supplemented by some archaeological syntheses, meaning that in practice his work focused on Rome.

2 THE URBAN PERIPHERY IN ROMAN THOUGHT

1 Existing studies of this evidence include Champlin 1982, Agusta-Boularot 1998, Arnaud 1998 and Chevallier 1998. Champlin and Agusta-Boularot, however, focus exclusively on Rome, while Chevallier examines only a small selection of visual sources.
2 For some exceptions, see Corbier 1991: 212–13.
3 Reynolds 1988: 22–3; Hanson 1988: 55.
4 Reynolds 1988: 24–5.

5 Crawford 1995.
6 Reynolds 1988: 26–7.
7 Wacher 1995: 22–3 (on Britain); Bedon 1999: 78 (on Gaul).
8 Reynolds 1988: 15–16.
9 *Lex Irnitana*, ch. 93 (González 1986).
10 Iul. Front., *Contr.* (Campbell 2000: 6–7): *'unam urbani soli, alteram agrestis . . .'.*
11 Varro, *Rust.* 3.1.1.
12 *'neque solum antiquior cultura agri, sed etiam melior'* (*Rust.* 3.1.4).
13 For example Braund 1989 on satire and Ramage 1973 on the developing *topos* from Plautus to late antiquity.
14 Quint., *Inst.* 2.4.24.
15 Cic., *Rosc. Am.* 74–5.
16 *'nullas Germanorum populis urbes habitari satis notum est, ne pati quidem inter se iunctas sedes'* (Tac., *Germ.* 16).
17 Tac., *Hist.* 4.64.
18 Pausanias, 10.4.1.
19 Strabo, *Geog.* 3.4.13.
20 For example *ILS* 6090, granting promotion to Tymandus in Pisidia.
21 Zanker 2000: 32; Tac., *Hist.* 4.64 (above). Cassiodorus on the *colonia* of Scylacium is also of interest, though from a sixth-century context – *'hoc quia modo non habet muros, civitatem credis ruralem'* (because the place has no walls, you might believe it to be merely a country town – *Var.* 12.15).
22 *Digesta* 1.8.9.4 (Ulpian) and 50.10.6 (Modestinus).
23 Hanson 1997: 75–6.
24 Woolf 1998: 119–20.
25 Gros 1992: 214–15. For anthropological approaches to boundaries – Parker Pearson and Richards 1994.
26 On public euergetism in general: Brunt 1976; Frézouls 1984; Duncan-Jones 1985; Mackie 1990.
27 Frere 1985.
28 Garnsey 1979: 10
29 Laurence 1994: 64–7; Greene 1986: 94–6. NB Greene's comment, 'The distinction between town and country is therefore truly blurred' (p. 96).
30 Purcell 1987b.
31 Purcell 1987b: 198–203.
32 Horace, *Satires* 2.6.80ff.
33 'Cabbage grown in dry fields is sweeter than that from a suburban estate; nothing is more washed out than the produce of an irrigated garden', *Satires* 2.4.15.
34 Robinson 1992: 7–8.
35 *'Ut Alfenus ait, "urbs" est "Roma", quae muro cingeretur, "Roma" est etiam, qua continentia aedificia essent: nam Romam non muro tenus existimari ex consuetudine cotidiana posse intellegi, cum diceremus Romam nos ire, etiamsi extra urbem habitaremus'* (*Digesta* 50.16.87).
36 See also the very similar definition by the Severan-period jurist, Iulius Paulus at *Digesta* 50.16.2.
37 Crawford 1996: I.24.
38 Line 20: *'in urbe Roma propiusve urbem Romam passus mille ubei continente habitabitur'*.
39 *Digesta* 50.16.139 and 50.16.147. The laws referred to here are probably the *lex Iulia de maritandis ordinis* and the related *lex Papia Poppaea*, regulating marriage and citizenship – Arnaud 1998: 70.
40 *Digesta* 3.3.6, Iulius Paulus.
41 Agusta-Boularot 1998: 51–3.

NOTES

42 Ch. 62: '*in oppido municipi Flavi Irnitani quaeque ei oppido continentia aedificia erunt*' (González 1986).
43 The municipal *lex Tarentina* forbids the same actions to be carried out '*in oppido quod eius municipi e*[*r*]*it*' (in the town which shall be of that municipium), without extending the law to the *continentia aedificia* – Crawford 1996: I.15.32–3.
44 Arnaud 1998: 71–2.
45 For example the Caesarian *lex Iulia repetundarum*, ll. 13 and 17, regulating against extortion in relation to public building works (Crawford 1996, vol. I: 86–7) or the *lex Valeria Aurelia*, l. 57 (AD 20) on reorganising the *comitia centuriata* in honour of Germanicus (*ibid.*: 521).
46 '*in urbe Roma vel intra primum urbis Romae miliarium*' (Gaius, *Inst.* 4.104).
47 '*mille passus non a miliario urbis sed a continentibus aedificiis numerandi sunt*' (*Digesta* 50.16.154).
48 Line 20: see n. 39, above.
49 Lines 26, 50, 64, 67–9 and 77.
50 Arnaud 1998: 70–1.
51 '*in . . . oppido propiusve it oppidum p*(*assus*) *m*(*ille*)' (*lex Coloniae Genetivae Iuliae*, ch. 91: Crawford 1996: I.25). As in the *lex Irnitana*, '*oppidum*' is used to mean the urban centre only.
52 Explicitly stated at *Digesta* 32.1.84 and 33.9.4.4–6 (both Iulius Paulus). The definitions by Alfenus and Iulius Paulus (50.16.2 and 50.16.87), which equate *Roma* with the *continentia aedificia* were probably formulated under similar circumstances.
53 *Digest* 32.1.41.6 (citing Scaevola, late second century AD).
54 '*prohibiti sunt tutores et curatores praedia rustica vel suburbana distrahere*' (*Digesta* 27.9.1, AD 195).
55 *Codex Iust.* 5.71.4 (AD 258), 5.71.5 (AD 260), 5.71.16 (AD 294), 5.72.3 (AD 295) and 5.73.3 (AD 294).
56 '*sine decreto praesidis provinciae in qua situm est*' (*Codex Iust.* 5.71.16).
57 '*hominem mortuum in urbe ne sepelito neve urito*' (he is not to bury or burn a dead man within the city) – Cic., *Leg.* 2.22.45 and 58 = Twelve Tables X.1 (Crawford 1996, vol. II: 704–5).
58 '*intra fines oppidi colon*(*iae*)*ve, qua aratro circumductum erit . . .*' (within the boundaries of the town or of the colony, where [a line] shall have been drawn around by a plough) – *lex Coloniae Genetivae Iuliae*, ch. 73 (Crawford 1996: I. 25).
59 *Lex Coloniae Genetivae Iuliae*, ch. 76, ll. 25–8 – Crawford 1996: I.25.
60 *AnnEp* 1971, no. 88. Similar laws include *AnnEp* 1971, no. 89 from Cumae, which is less complete than the Puteoli law, and *ILS* 6726 from Bergomum in N. Italy.
61 '*intra turrem ubi hodie lucus est Libit*(*inae*)' – II.3–7; Bodel 1994: 95–6, n. 61.
62 At Rome, burials were registered in the grove of Libitina on the Esquiline: Dion. Hal 4.15.5.
63 On Roman ideas about death-pollution, Lindsay 2000, esp. 157–60 on funeral professions.
64 Rome: *CIL* I² 838, 839 and 2931 (edicts of the praetor L. Sentius) and *CIL* I² 591 (senatusconsultum on the pagus Montanus); Luceria: *CIL* I² 401 = IX.782. See Bodel 1994, *passim* on the *lex Lucerina* (but with Purcell 1997), and 38–54 on the Esquiline burial grounds.
65 Bodel 1994: 32–8; Bodel 2000. The Puteolan *lex de munere publico libitinario* also appears to have specified fines if a corpse was left unburied – I.32–II.1 (fragmentary).

NOTES

66 *Lex de munere publico libitinario* III.1–4 (fragmentary); Bodel 1994: 16.
67 Purcell 1997: 342.
68 Packard Humanities Institute CD-ROM 5.3 (Latin Literature). *TLG* database: http://www.tlg.uci.edu/.
69 Dion. Hal. 4.13.3–5. Pliny also mentions the *'multas urbes'* (many cities) which have been added to the *'exspatiantia tecta'* (spreading roofs) of Rome (*NH* 3.5.67), while Strabo refers in passing to the extensive growth of the city at *Geog.* 5.3.7.
70 Livy, 1.44.
71 Strabo, *Geog.* 5.3.8; Purcell 1987a: 27.
72 Champlin 1982; Agusta-Boularot 1998.
73 Champlin 1982: 97. *'Suburbium'* occurs at Cic., *Phil.* 12.24.2.
74 Shrines – e.g. Ovid, *Fasti* 6.785. Funerary features – e.g. Ovid, *Fasti* 2.550. Towns/villages – e.g. Florus, 1.5.21 (Tibur and Praeneste), Ovid, *Fasti* 3.667 (Bovillae) and 6.58–64 (Aricia, Laurentum and Lanuvium).
75 For example Martial, *Epig.* 1.85 (*solum*); Ovid, *Trist.* 3.6.38 (*terra*); Cic., *Har. Resp.* 20.7 (*ager*).
76 Agusta-Boularot 1998: 42.
77 *'Rus suburbanus'* – Cic., *Rosc. Am.* 133.2; Ovid, *Ars Am.* 2.265; Martial, *Epig.* 8.61.9; Tac., *Ann.* 15.60.19.
78 Plaut., *Trin.* 508; Cato *Agr.* 8.2; Agusta-Boularot 1998: 38.
79 Champlin 1982: 97; Agusta-Boularot 1998: 43.
80 Agusta-Boularot 1998: 46.
81 Agusta-Boularot 1998: 37–9.
82 Champlin 1982: 98; Agusta-Boularot 1998: 49–50.
83 Champlin 1982, *passim* and esp. 99.
84 *'O funde noster, seu Sabine seu Tiburs (nam te esse Tiburtem autumant, quibus non est cordi Catullum laedere: at quibus cordist, quovis Sabinum pignore esse contendunt) ...'* (Catull., *Carm.* 44.1–4).
85 For example Florus, 1.5.21, Ovid, *Fasti* 6.56–61.
86 *'praedium ... suburbanum, quod ab urbanis non loco sed qualitate secernitur'* (5.71.16).
87 Sets of properties – *Rosc. Am.* 133; *Verr.* 2.1 54 and 2.4.121; *Att.* 8.2.3. Advice to Quintus – *Q. Fr.* 3.1.23–4 and 3.4.5. Cornelius Nepos illustrates the restraint of Cicero's friend, Atticus, by stating that he did *not* own the usual set of lavish suburban properties (Nep., *Att.* 14.3).
88 Champlin 1982: 102–3.
89 Martial, *Ep.* 8.61. Similar themes are treated in 3.47, 3.58, 10.58 and 12.72.
90 Pliny, *Ep.* 2.17
91 Clarke 1991: 12–19.
92 Tifernum – *Ep.* 4.1, 5.6, 9.36 and 10.8; Comum – *Ep.* 7.18 and 9.7.
93 Pliny, *Ep.* 4.6.
94 Champlin 1982: 107.
95 Columella, *Rust.* 1.1.19; Pliny, *Ep.* 2.17.2.
96 Laurence 1994: 122–9.
97 For example Cic., *Att.* 12.34.1; Pliny, *Ep.* 1.12; Fronto, *Ep.* 1.6. See Champlin 1982: 104–5.
98 Pliny, *Ep.* 1.24.
99 Seneca – Tac., *Ann.* 15.60.19; Phaon – Suet., *Nero* 48.1; Phyllis – Suet., *Dom.* 17; Remmius Palaemon – Pliny, *NH* 14.50. These villas may not have been directly adjacent to the major roads: they are more likely to have lain a slight distance away, and been connected by private side roads (Laurence 1999: 103–5).

NOTES

100 On the diffusion of urban culture into the suburban districts – Champlin 1982: 106–10.
101 *'tunc demum adiecta spe dignitatis ad otium concessit, modo in hortis et suburbana domo, modo in Campaniae secessu delitescens'* (Suet., *Claud.* 5.1). Di Matteo has tentatively linked this *suburbana domus* with a property on the eighth mile of the via Tiburtina, find-spot of a lead pipe stamped with Claudius' name (Di Matteo and Granino Cercere 2004).
102 Pliny, *Ep.* 3.11.
103 Suet., *Nero* 48.1 and *Dom.* 17.3.
104 Macr., *Sat* 3.13.13 – see Champlin 1982: 108 and Purcell 1987a: 155.
105 Pliny, *NH* 14.48–51.
106 Pliny, *Ep.* 2.17.15 and 28.
107 Seneca, *Ben.* 4.12.3–4.
108 Cato, *Agr.* 7–8.
109 Varro, *Rust.* 1.16.3; Columella, *Rust.* 3.2.1, 7.3.13, 7.3.22, 7.9.4, 8.5.9 and 8.8.2.
110 Morley 1996: 86–90.
111 Agusta-Boularot 1998: 43–4.
112 Pliny, *Ep.* 1.3.
113 *'modicis . . . aedibus nec multo laxiore suburbano . . .'* (Suet., *Tib.* 11.1).
114 Curt. 4.1.19 (*hortus* outside Sidon in Syria); Pliny, *NH* 35.105 (*hortulus* outside Ialysos on Rhodes); Martial, *Ep.* 5.35 (*suburbanum* at Corinth); SHA, *Op. Macr.* 15.1 (execution of Macrinus in a *suburbanum* outside a Bithynian city).
115 Gell. *NA* 1.2 and 18.10.1–2. The debates occur *'in villas ei urbi proximas'* (in his villas close to the city). For archaeological remains of Herodes' villas in the area, Tobin 1997: 211–39 (Kephisia) and 241–83 (Marathon).
116 Apul., *Apol.* 87–8 (*villa suburbana*) and *Flor.* 19 (*suburbanum*).
117 *Apol.* 23.
118 *CIL* II.4332.
119 Armies – e.g. Livy, 22.22.10 (*extra urbem*); sieges – e.g. Livy, 6.31.8 (*extra moenia*); attacks on citizens – e.g. Front., *Strat.* 4.4.1 (*extra murum*).
120 Tac. *Hist.* 2.21; Front., *Strat.* 3.2.5.
121 For example *amoenissima extra urbem aedificia* at Cremona (Tac., *Hist.* 3.30), *extra urbem tecta* at Mazagas (later Caesarea) in Asia Minor (Curt., 8.10.30), *aedificia extra urbem* at an Aetolian city (Livy, 36.24). Perhaps closest to the Roman *continentia aedificia* is a *'pars extra muros, quae frequentius prope quam in urbe habitabitur'* (region outside the walls, inhabited almost in larger numbers than the city) at Heraclea in Greece – Livy, 36.22.
122 For example Cic., *Att.* 7.1.5 or Livy, 40.43.4 (both *extra urbem*).
123 For example Livy, 33.24, 34.43 and 45.22.
124 Particularly clear at Florus, 1.5 – *'Tibur, nunc suburbanum, et aestivae Praeneste deliciae nuncupatis in Capitolio votis petebantur'* (Tibur, now suburban, and delightful summer-time Praeneste, were attacked after vows had been pronounced in the Capitol). See also Ovid, *Fasti* 6.361 and Prop., *Elegiae* 4.1a.33.
125 The spelling varied, but the 'e' will henceforth be included for consistency.
126 For example Thuc., 3.102.2 (Aetolian attack on Naupactis) or Xen., *Hell.* 7.1.25 (Arcadian attack on Asine).
127 Thucydides 2.34 describes this area as 'the most beautiful suburb of the city'.
128 Thuc., 4.69.1–2.
129 Cic. *Att.* 1.4 and 1.9 (Academy); *Att.* 1.10: *'Cum essem in Tusculano (erit hoc tibi pro illo tuo "cum essem in Ceramico")'*. See also Champlin 1982: 104–5 for Cicero's use of the suburban villa as a setting for philosophical dialogues.

NOTES

130 Attacks, military manoeuvres – Diod. Sic., 11.68.3–4, Joseph. *Bell. Jud.* 5.264 and Polyb. 5.60.5–8. Ambushes, trickery – Polyaenus, *Strat.* 5.10.1, Plut., *De mul. vir.* 255c. Triumphs – Appian, *Bell. Civ.* 2.2.8.
131 Julian mentions that he lived in the *proasteion* of Milan before being declared Caesar (*Athenaion* . . . 6).
132 For example Polybius' description of Seleucia (*Hist.* 5.59.7) or Strabo's of Amaseia (*Geog.* 12.3.39).
133 Plut., *Crassus* 1.2.
134 Flav. Phil., *Vit. Soph.* 2.606.
135 Strabo, *Geog.* 17.1.10.
136 Strabo, *Geog.* 12.3.11.
137 Flav. Phil. *Vit. Ap.* 1.7.47.
138 Plut., *Sulla* 12.3, Julian, *Themistioi Philosophoi* 5.46; Flav. Phil., *Vit. Soph.* 2.579. Note that Philostratus refers to a villa of Herodes Atticus, also described in suburban terms by Aulus Gellius (*NA* 1.2 and above).
139 Herodian, 2.1.2 (Commodus), 3.4.6 (Niger) and 5.4.11 (Macrinus). Also Joseph., *Bell. Jud.* 4.493 (Nero).
140 Cass. Dio, 56.1.1
141 Plut., *Apophth. Lac.* 241c.
142 Philo, *De Cong.* 10; Lucian, *Hermot.* 24.
143 Dilke 1985: 103–6.
144 Price and Trell 1977.
145 Carder 1978: 4–8; Campbell 2000: xxiii–vi.
146 Carder 1978: 189–95.
147 Levi and Levi 1967; Bosio 1983.
148 Variously interpreted as city gates, *mansiones* or extremely abbreviated city walls – Levi and Levi 1967: 66–82; Bosio 1983: 101–10; Dilke 1985: 115–16.
149 Blanckenhagen 1968, nos. 2, 5, 6 and 10.
150 Blanckenhagen 1968: 132; Ling 1991: 114–16.
151 For example Stern 1953: 124–44.
152 Carder 1978: 190.
153 Especially common in Vitruvius (e.g. *Arch.* 1.4.1; 1.6.6; 1.7.1; 5.3.1; 8.5.1), but see also Cic., *Cat.* 2.1.1; Virgil, *Aen.* 6.549; Florus, 1.4.2.
154 Lepper and Frere 1988; *CIL* VI.960.
155 Lepper and Frere 1988: 50.
156 Lepper and Frere 1988: 47–9.
157 Geffroy 1878.
158 Geffroy 1878: 10–11.
159 Geffroy 1878: 3–4.
160 Koeppel 1969.
161 Cass. Dio, 56.1.1.
162 Rodríguez Almeida 1981; Dilke 1985: 103–6.
163 Rodríguez Almeida 1981: 35–53; Stanford Digital Forma Urbis Romae Project 2002–3.
164 Rodríguez Almeida 1981: 39–43.
165 Rodríguez Almeida 1981, groups 27, 28, 33, 34 and 37a: 108, 119–21 and 140–3.
166 Van der Meer 1998; La Rocca 2000.
167 Van der Meer 1998: 63; La Rocca 2000: 59.
168 Ling 1991: 142–9.
169 Van der Meer 1998: 64–5.
170 La Rocca 2000.

171 La Rocca 2000: 59.
172 Illustration – Carder 1978: 141–2. Related text – Campbell 2000: 42–3.
173 Illustration – Carder 1978: 154–7. Related text – Campbell 2000: 220–1.
174 Bosio 1983: 83–9.
175 Lighthouse – Levi and Levi 1967: 151–9; Porphyry column – Bosio 1983: 87–8.
176 Bosio 1983: 89.
177 Catull., *Carm.* 44.1–4 (see above).

3 THE ARCHAEOLOGY OF THE URBAN PERIPHERY

1 See for example King 1984 for an introduction and overview.
2 See for example collected articles in Smith 1976 and Grant 1986.
3 Morley 1996: 166–74; Woolf 1998: 126–35.
4 Woolf 1998: 126–35 and 139–41; Millet 1986. For the pre-industrial Mediterranean world in general, see also the concerns of Horden and Purcell 2000: 102–3 (especially their fourth objection).
5 Hall 1966; Chisholm 1968: 20–32.
6 Grimal 1959; Ross Holloway 1994: 91–101; Andreussi 1996.
7 Livy 1.44; Dion. Hal. 3.13.5.
8 Le Gall 1991: 62.
9 Cass. Dio 74.1; Le Gall 1991: 59.
10 Patterson 2000a: 96–7.
11 SHA, *Aurel.* 21.10–11.
12 Pisani Sartorio 1996a.
13 Despite occasional proposals by figures such as Julius Caesar (Plut., *Caes.* 58.8) or Nero (Tac., *Ann.* 15.42) to do so.
14 Maischberger 2000.
15 SHA, *Sev.* 19.5.
16 Cic. *Att.* 12.19.1; *CIL* IV.9847.
17 Juvenal 14.201–205; Martial 1.41.
18 Certainly, Patterson 2000b argues that the prestige and significance of the area around the porta Capena and the via Appia prompted Augustus to make this his *regio* I.
19 Labrousse 1937; Price 1996; Andreussi 1999; Patterson 2000a: 88–9.
20 Le Gall rejects possible extensions by Sulla and Julius Caesar on the grounds that Dionysius of Halicarnassus does not recognise them (Le Gall 1991: 63; Dion. Hal. 4.13.3).
21 Aul. Gell., *Noct. Att.* 13.14.5–6; Patterson 2000a: 88.
22 Auspices – Varro, *Ling.* 5.143; Aul. Gell., *Noct. Att.* 13.14.1–2. Burial – Twelve Tables X.1 (Crawford 1996: II.40). Military *imperium* – e.g. Cicero, *Att.* 7.1.5; Caesar, *Bell. Civ.* 1.6.1; Livy, 34.52.3. Ambassadors – e.g. Livy, 30.21.12 and 33.24.5.
23 Augustus was given permanent proconsular *imperium* in 23 BC, and was no longer required to lay down his power every time he entered the *pomerium* (Cass. Dio 53.32.5).
24 Intra-pomerial burials appear in the fifth century AD (Meneghini and Santangeli Valenzani 1993).
25 *Cippi* of Claudius, Vespasian and Hadrian are at *CIL* VI.31537–9.
26 For some of the debates – Labrousse 1937, Poe 1984 and Andreussi 1999.
27 Palmer 1980.
28 Patterson 2000a: 94.

NOTES

29 Suet., *Aug.* 30; Cass. Dio 55.8; Robinson 1992: 9–13; Fraschetti 1999; Palombi 1999.
30 Robinson argues that the *regiones* must have been extended as Rome grew, while Patterson suggests that the customs boundary may also have coincided with them (Robinson 1992: 10; Patterson 2000a: 90).
31 Robinson 1992: 9–13; Lott 2004: 89.
32 Favro 1996: 136–7; Palombi 1999: 199.
33 Agusta-Boularot 1998: 53.
34 *CIL* VI.975 (the '*Basis Capitolina*') – '*magistri vicorum urbis regionum xiii*'.
35 *Digesta*, 50.16.87 (Ulpius Marcellus) and 50.16.2 (Iulius Paulus) – see chapter 2.
36 De Maria 1988.
37 Rodríguez Almeida 1993.
38 Patterson 2000b: 132; Pisani Sartorio 1993.
39 Vespasian spent the night outside the *pomerium* before his triumph over the Jews (Joseph., *BJ* 7.123).
40 Tac., *Ann.* 12.24. Lupercalia – Rykwert 1976: 91–6. Walls of the eighth to sixth centuries BC found on the Palatine may also have marked an early ritual boundary around the hill (Ross Holloway 1994: 101–2).
41 Terminus on the via Laurentina, Fortuna Muliebris on the via Latina and Dea Dia on the via Campana – Patterson 2000a: 89; Strabo *Geog.* 5.3.2.
42 Rodríguez Almeida 1981: group 37a, pp. 140–3.
43 Patterson 2000c.
44 Pages 51–88 in vol. III of Steinby's *LTUR* describe 64 sets of *horti*, most extramural.
45 Purcell 1996a: 127–5.
46 For example the *horti Lolliani* – Papi 1996.
47 Purcell 1987b: 203.
48 Transtiberim – Maischberger 2000; Rodríguez Almeida 1981: fragments 33 and 34, pp. 119–21. Emporium area – Rodríguez Almeida 1981: fragments 23–5, pp. 102–7.
49 It is still uncertain whether the Servian wall extended as far as the banks of the Tiber between the Aventine and Capitoline hills.
50 Patterson 2000a: 94.
51 Coarelli 1986: 42–3; Pisani Sartorio 1996b.
52 Patterson 2000a: 94–5.
53 Juv., *Sat.* 14.201–205; Mart., *Epig.* 6.93. Mills – Wilson 2001.
54 Wiseman 1993.
55 Cic. *Ad Att.* 12.38.4.
56 Purcell 1987a: 27. The first mile of the via Appia appears similarly to have become a monumental focus because it constituted a major route into the city from the south (Patterson 2000b).
57 Purcell 1987a: 26–7.
58 Pliny *NH* 29.16; Cass. Dio 53.2.4 (30 BC) and 54.6.6 (21 BC).
59 Cass. Dio 42.26.2.
60 Vitr., *Arch.* 1.7.
61 See further chapter 4.
62 Ross Holloway 1994: 20–50 and 97–9. For example Julius Caesar – Cass. Dio 44.7.1.
63 Purcell 1987a.
64 Purcell 1987a: 30–2; Patterson 2000b.
65 Known as *cepotaphia* – Toynbee 1971: 94–100; Purcell 1987a: 35–6; Purcell 1996a: 123–5.

NOTES

66 Bodel 2000: 131–2.
67 Bodel 2000: 133–4.
68 Cass. Dio 48.43.3.
69 Livy 7.23.3.
70 Bellona – e.g. Livy 26.21; Apollo – e.g. Livy 34.43.2.
71 Patterson 2000a: 91–2.
72 Suet. *Aug.* 29; Cass. Dio 54.8.3.
73 Patterson 2000a: 91; Pisani Sartorio 1996c.
74 For an imaginative reconstruction of the transition, Purcell 1987b.
75 Lugli 1923; Jones 1962; Jones 1963; Quilici 1974; Quilici 1979; Potter 1979; Morley 1996: 95–103.
76 Esp. Columella, *Rust.* 1.1.19 and Pliny, *Ep.* 2.17.2. See chapter 2.
77 Champlin 1982: 98 and n. 9; Laurence 1999: 82.
78 Champlin 1982: 111, n. 6.
79 Morley 1996: 97–101.
80 Quilici 1974 and 1979; Arnaud 1998: 80–1.
81 Ashby 1909.
82 *Ep.* 2.17.4.
83 Lugli 1930.
84 Vitr. *De Arch.* 6.5.
85 McKay 1975: 131; Barton 1996: 101–2.
86 MacDonald and Pinto 1995; Adembri 2000.
87 Pisani Sartorio and Calza 1976.
88 Oliver 1989, no. 74 *bis*. Domitian used his Alban villa in the same manner: *FIRA* I.75 and Pliny, *Ep.* 4.11.6.
89 Tobin 1997: 32 (consulship and marriage), 355–71 (estate).
90 Potter 1979: 130–1; Bodel 1997: 26–32.
91 Bodel 1997: 30.
92 Seneca, *Ben.* 4.12.3–4; Cato, *Agr.* 7–8; Varro, *Rust.* 1.16.3; Columella, *Rust.* 3.2.1, etc. See chapter 2.
93 Carandini 1985; Kolendo 1994; Purcell 1995a; Morley 1996, ch. 4.
94 Champlin 1982: 104.
95 Champlin *ibid.* For example Suet., *Aug.* 6.1 – 'in his grandfather's suburban villa near Velitrae' (*in avito suburbano iuxta Velitras*).
96 Potter 1979: 123 (on the south Etruria area).
97 Cotton and Métraux 1985.
98 Cato, *De Agr.* 1.2–7, Col., *Rust.* 1.3.3.
99 Bergmann 2002: 107–8.
100 D'Arms 2003: 121–6.
101 Franciscis 1975: 15–6.
102 Vitruvius is quite clear that this was standard practice (6.5.2–3). He recommends that elite town-houses should have '*publicorum operum magnificentia*' (the magnificence of public works), and discusses the characteristics of houses in the country which are *pseudourbana* (built in town-fashion). Cf. also Wallace-Hadrill 1994: 17–37.
103 Morley 1996: 99–101.
104 Jones 1962: 162–3.
105 Jones 1963: 147–58.
106 Morley 1996: 101–2.
107 Champlin 1982: 98 and 111, n. 6.
108 Zonaras 8.18.
109 Potter 1979: 93; Morley 1996: 180.

NOTES

110 Morley 1996: 179–80.
111 Quilici 1974: 426–30; Potter 1979: 109–20.
112 *Coloniae* include Lucus Feroniae, Praeneste (first a *municipium*) and Ostia. *Municipia* include Tusculum, Veii, Bovillae and Gabii.
113 Potter 1979: 117.
114 Cic., *Planc.* 23, with Morley 1996: 180.
115 Meiggs 1973: 298–310. Such officials include a *quaestor Ostiensis* from the third century BC, a *procurator annonae Ostiensis* from the Claudian period onwards, and a *procurator Portus Ostiensis* (later *procurator Portus Utriusque*) from the time of the construction of the harbours.
116 Purcell 1996b: 276; Rickman 1996: 290–1.
117 *Fasti* 6.771–90.
118 Cic., *Phil.* 12.24.
119 *CIL* VI.2023–2119 and 32338–32398.
120 Champeaux 1982: 3–147.
121 Quaestors (games) – Cic., *Planc.* 63. Praetor (games) – Cic., *Att.* 12.2.2. Consul (oracle) – Val. Max. 1.3.2. Emperors (oracle) – Suet., *Dom.* 15.2; SHA, *Alex. Sev.* 4.6. Cf. also Champeaux 1982: 55–9 and 78–84.
122 Wallace-Hadrill 2003 and personal communication.
123 Livy 5.17, 21.63, 22.1 and 25.12.
124 Ovid, *Met.* 15.479–551.
125 Potter 1979: 135–7, DeLaine 2000: 133–5.
126 DeLaine 2000.
127 Purcell 1987a: 35.
128 Catull., *Carm.* 44.1–4 (and ch. 2).
129 Horace, *Sat.* 2.4.15; Pliny, *NH* 31.24; Front., *Aq.* 75 and 78–86; Wilson 1999a: 315–17.
130 Arnaud 1998: 80–1.
131 *Exc. Val.* 6.35 – '*in suburbano Constantinopolitano villa publica iuxta Nicomediam*'.
132 Imposed demolition was usually reserved for bitter enemies such as Carthage and Corinth (Purcell 1995b: 137–8). Even Capua's 'unoffending houses and walls' (*tecta innoxia murosque*) were left intact (Livy 26.16).
133 Boatwright 1993.
134 Collis 1984: 107–9.
135 '*et quidem urbes fere omnes muro tenus finiri, Romam continentibus*' – *Digesta* 33.9.4.4–5.
136 Zanker 2000 on the development of the basic elements.
137 Richmond 1969; Corni 1989.
138 Strabo, *Geog.* 4.206; Cass. Dio, 53.25.
139 *CIL* IX.02443.
140 Gros 1992: 221–2. Cf. also Tergeste (*CIL* V.525).
141 Zanker 2000: 32; Tac., *Hist.* 4.64; discussion in chapter 2.
142 Richmond 1969: 253–4; Corni 1989: 44–7.
143 Richmond 1969: 253; Corni 1989: 44–5.
144 For example Celsa (*RPC* 261), Caesaraugusta (*RPC* 371), and eastern examples at Levick 1967: 35–7.
145 *Lex Coloniae Genetivae Iuliae*, ch. 73 (Crawford 1996: I.25), discussed in chapter 2.
146 Livy 1.44; Plut., *Rom.* 11.3; Ovid, *Fasti* 4.825; Dion. Hal., *Ant. Rom.* 1.88.2.
147 Labrousse 1937: 172–3 on frequent imperial iterations of the law, aimed mainly at the provinces.
148 *Digesta* 33.9.4.4–5 and discussion above.

NOTES

149 *'iussu Imp. Caesaris qua aratrum ductum est' (ILS* 6308).
150 Scagliarini 1991.
151 Plut. *C. Gracch.* 7 and Purcell 1990: 16.
152 Recommended by the surveyor Hyginus Gromaticus (Campbell 2000: 148–51).
153 On conscious Roman manipulation of the landscape in this region, including roads – Purcell 1990.
154 Cloppet 1998 and introductory article in Bedon 1998b: 11.
155 Scagliarini 1991: 88–90.
156 Potter 1979: 60–1.
157 Collis 1984.
158 Ward-Perkins 1982: 30–4.
159 MacDonald 1986: 75–86.
160 De Maria 1988: 53–4, 84 and 162–3.
161 De Maria 1988: 78; Gros 1992: 221.
162 MacDonald 1986: 13–14.
163 However, the courses, or even the existence, of walls may not be well known, whilst rivers may have shifted course since antiquity.
164 Wacher 1995: 214–41.
165 Wacher 1995: 219–23.
166 Frere 1962: 156.
167 Wacher 1995: 230–3.
168 Wacher 1995: 233; Frere 1962.
169 Wacher 1995: 233.
170 Jones 1992; Jones 1999.
171 Jones 1980.
172 Colyer 1975; Jones 1999: 106–7.
173 *Lex Irnitana* ch. 62 (González 1986), *Lex Coloniae Genetivae Iuliae* ch. 91 (Crawford 1996: I.25) and discussion in chapter 2.
174 For example *Lex Irnitana* ch. 62 (González 1986); Livy, 36.22.
175 Perhaps dating to Cicero's consulship of 63 BC: Zevi 1997.
176 Ward-Perkins 1981: 140–5; MacDonald 1986: 263–6; Internet Group Ostia 1996–2006.
177 Ward-Perkins 1981: 399–407.
178 Capitolium – Ballu 1897: 189 and 1903: 79; Courtois 1951: 30; Lassus 1969: 65; *CIL* VIII.2388.
179 Structures 3.7.2 and 4.9.2 (Cartilius Poplicola). MacDonald 1986: 265; van der Meer *et al.* 2005.
180 For example the Great North baths, built in the style of imperial *thermae* at Rome (Ballu 1903: 38–48).
181 Ward-Perkins 1981: 404.
182 Hesse and Renimel 1979.
183 Hesse and Renimel 1979: 643–4.
184 Hesse and Renimel 1979: 644.
185 Frézouls 1990: 81–2.
186 Golvin 1988: 166–7.
187 Golvin 1988: 412.
188 Frézouls 1990: 82–3.
189 Golvin 1988: 409.
190 Pliny, *Ep.* 1.3; Hoffer 1999: 29–43.
191 See chapter 2.
192 Britain – Rivet 1955 and Hodder and Millett 1980. Béziers in Gaul – Clavel 1970: 296–307. Caesarea in Mauretania – Leveau 1984: 483.

NOTES

193 Brothers 1996: 59–61.
194 Dunbabin 1978: 65–87 (amphitheatres) and 88–108 (circuses); Humphrey 1986: 208–46 (circuses); Kondoleon 1999 (relation to yearly cycles).
195 Dunbabin 1978: 85 and 88–9; Kondoleon 1999.
196 Mattingly 1988; Mattingly 1995: 140–4.
197 Merrony 2005; Wendowski and Ziegert 2005; Wendowski personal communication.
198 Mahjub 1983; Humphrey 1986: 211–6.
199 Aurigemma 1926; Dunbabin 1978: 66 and 235–7.
200 Villa dell'Odeon Marittimo – Salza Prina Ricotti 1970–71: 140–54. Villa del Piccolo Circo – Salza Prina Ricotti 1970–1: 154–61.
201 Mattingly 1995: 119–20; Humphrey 1986: 25–56.
202 Salza Prina Ricotti 1970–71: 137; Picard 1986 143–4; Mattingly 1988: 27; Mattingly 1995: 141.
203 Guidi 1933; Bianchi Bandinelli, *et al.* 1966: 105–6 and 116; Floriani Squarciapino 1966: 126–9.
204 Apul., *Apol.* 87–8.
205 Beschaouch 1966.
206 Mattingly 1995: 140–1.
207 Mattingly 1988: 37.
208 Esmonde Cleary 1987: 144–6.
209 Esmonde Cleary 1987: 146.
210 Garnsey 1979: 10; Greene 1986: 94–6; Purcell 1987b.
211 Own properties – e.g. summers spent on the Bay of Naples (D'Arms 2003). Properties of others – e.g. Cic. *Att.* 5.2, 16.6.1 and others.
212 Pliny, *Ep.* 5.6 and 9.36.5.
213 Cf. Henderson's argument that Pliny crafted a highly stylised self-portrait not only in his letters, but in his lifestyle too – Henderson 2003: 117.
214 Via Appia – Tobin 1997: 355–71 and discussion above. Kephisia – Tobin 1997: 211–39; Gell., *NA* 1.2; Flav. Phil., *Vit. Soph.* 2.579 and chapter 2.

4 GAUL IN THE HIGH EMPIRE: ADMINISTRATIVE CITIES

1 Bedon 1999: 201–38 on the Three Gauls.
2 Collis 1984; Bedon 1999: 27–53; Ferdière 2005: 101–4.
3 Goudineau 1980b; Ferdière 2005: 33–8.
4 Woolf 1998: 106–12.
5 Woolf 2000.
6 Figures for all of Gaul – Bedon *et al.* 1988 (eighty-one); Ferdière 2005: 134–5 (eighty-seven). Figures for the Three Gauls only – Drinkwater 1983: 228–31 and 137 (sixty-one); Bedon 1999: 343–6 (sixty-six). Figures for Narbonensis only – Rivet 1988 (twenty-six).
7 Clavel 1970: 245–6. Clavel's opening words on the subject typify the problem; *'Il resterait à évoquer le problème des quartiers suburbains, mais nous ignorons pratiquement tout de leur localisation et de leur importance'*.
8 Esmonde Cleary 1985: 74; Quilici 1979: 309.
9 Woolf 1998: 50–2.
10 Drinkwater 1983: 93–5.
11 Though the foundation dates of both *colonia* and the formal province of Transalpina are still debated – Rivet 1988: 44 and 47–8; Woolf 1998: 29; Ferdière 2005: 61.
12 Drinkwater 1983: 17–18; Rivet 1988: 74–9; Ferdière 2005: 123–6.
13 Drinkwater 1983: 17–18; Rivet 1988: 74–83.

NOTES

14 Drinkwater 1983: 18. The phenomenon is attested epigraphically at the contemporary north Italian foundation of Aosta – *ILS* 6753.
15 Drinkwater 1983: 54–71.
16 Drinkwater 1983: 67.
17 Rivet 1988: 80 provides a list of administrative cities in Narbonensis and their status.
18 Ferdière 2005: 64.
19 Drinkwater 1983: 18–19.
20 Drinkwater 1983: 95–6.
21 Goodman 2002.
22 Nîmes – Rivet 1988: 163. Marseille – Bedon *et al.* 1988: 168–9.
23 Bedon 1999: 119–29; Woolf 1998: 114–16.
24 Bedon *et al.* 1988: 33.
25 Bedon 1999: 268–70; Woolf 1998: 116–17. Cf. Vitruvius 1.6; Hyginus Gromaticus, *Constitutio* [*limitum*], etc.
26 Ward-Perkins 1981: 219–22; Drinkwater 1983: 143–9; Bedon *et al.* 1988: 14–18. Cf. Vitruvius 1.7 and books 3–5.
27 Ward-Perkins 1981: 166 and 232–3.
28 Ward-Perkins 1981: 72–3, 84–5, 129–32 and 442.
29 Ward-Perkins 1981: 222. Further on this theme, Ward-Perkins 1970.
30 Bedon 1999: 329–32; Woolf 1998: 116; 2000: 121.
31 Woolf 2000.
32 Tac., *Ann.* 3.43; Chardron-Picault 1996: 41–4.
33 Suet., *Gaius* 20; Pliny, *Ep.* 9.11.
34 Goudineau 1980b: 244–61; Bedon 1999: 303–5.
35 Ferdière 2005: 59–66.
36 Gruen 1990: 404–9.
37 Narbonensis: circuits known at Nîmes, Arles, Fréjus, Orange, Toulouse and Vienne and likely at Narbonne, Béziers and Aix-en-Provence, besides the Hellenistic circuit retained at Marseille. Three Gauls: known at Autun and Trier, probable at Lyon (Goudineau 1980b: 244).
38 Wacher 1995: 71–81.
39 Goudineau 1980b: 246–7.
40 Cloppet 1998 on Lugdunensis and the Two Germanies.
41 For example Bourges (Pinon 1981), Sens (Perrugot 1996: 267) or Amiens (Bayard and Massy 1983: 173–4).
42 Picard 1974; Fouqueray and Neiss 1976; Neiss 1984: 182. On arches as urban boundary markers in Gaul in general – Bedon 1999: 306–7.
43 Bedon 1999: 274–6.
44 An amphitheatre at Arles and an aqueduct at Fréjus – Goudineau 1980b: 247.
45 Bedon *et al.* 1988: 40.
46 Goudineau 1980b: 260–1; Bedon *et al.* 1988: 40; Woolf 1998: 120.
47 Bedon *et al.* 1988: 75–7.
48 Rodríguez Hidalgo 1995: 405.
49 Ward-Perkins 1981: 236–7; Küpper-Böhm 1996.
50 Bedon *et al.* 1988: 30.
51 Le Bot-Helly 1987.
52 Prisset 1999: 12.
53 Pelletier *et al.* 1981: 17–103.
54 Delaval *et al.* 1995: 18; Pelletier 1996: 169–71.
55 Presqu'île – Turcan 1980; Verot *et al.* 1989; Arlaud *et al.* 2000. Saint-Jean quarter – Villedieu 1990; Arlaud *et al.* 1994.

NOTES

56 Arlaud *et al.* 2000: 265–6.
57 Villedieu 1990: 21 and 105–6.
58 Arlaud *et al.* 1994: 40–1.
59 Desbat 1998: 417.
60 Villedieu 1990: 21; Arlaud *et al.* 1994: 37–9.
61 Audin 1956: 161–4; Villedieu 1990: 108–9.
62 Audin 1956: 162–3.
63 Villedieu 1990: 108–9.
64 Laws governing building on public land are at *Digesta* 43.8.2.1–19.
65 For example Sens – Perrugot 1996: 264; Lisieux – Lemaitre 1996: 138–41.
66 For example Autun – Rebourg 1999: 162–3.
67 Goudineau 1980b: 267; Bedon *et al.* 1988: 31–2; Bedon 1999: 287–8.
68 Roman civil law certainly allowed for this: *Digesta* 43.7 and 43.8.2.20–45 on public roads and Front., *Aq.* 126–7 on aqueducts.
69 See for example Heinen 1984: 336–7 on the contemporaneity of the first wooden bridge across the Mosel at Trier and city's orthogonal street-grid.
70 Urso, Spain – *Lex Coloniae Genetivae Iuliae* ch. 77 (Crawford 1996: I.25). Tarentum, Italy – *Lex Tarentina* ll. 39–42 (Crawford 1996: I.15).
71 Mignon *et al.* 1997. For an alternative interpretation of the *domus* – Bouet 1998: 52–7.
72 Guyard 1998b.
73 Baccrabère 1988.
74 Baccrabère 1990.
75 Baccrabère 1988: 481–6.
76 Baccrabère 1988: 484–5.
77 Baccrabère 1988: 21–57; Domergue, Fincker and Pailler 1990.
78 Dumasy and collaborators 1989: 45.
79 Baccrabère 1988: 433–49 and fig. 57.
80 Desbat 1998: 412–16.
81 Goudineau 1980b: 270.
82 Rebourg 1999: 158–60. This feature was labelled '*longs murs*' by Roidot-Deléage on his nineteenth-century plan of Roman Autun, but is now interpreted by Rebourg as a road.
83 Roidot-Deléage's plan of two buildings south of the temples shows an area of paving which may have been part of a road (Rebourg 1999: 159 and fig. 11).
84 Saint-Romain-en-Gal – Prisset 1999. Sainte-Colombe – Le Bot 1981, Musée de la Civilisation Gallo-Romaine de Lyon 1983–84: 146–51.
85 Prisset 1999: 10–19.
86 Jospin 1982; Le Bot-Helly 1991; Le Bot-Helly and Helly 1999: 77.
87 For example north of the Seine, Paris (Guyard 1996, 1998a and 1998b); Rue du Chapeau Rouge at Vaise, Lyon (Pelletier 1996: 173); Vieux-Lisieux, Lisieux (Lemaitre 1998a and 1998b).
88 Paillard in Musées de la ville de Lisieux 1994: 22–45; Lemaitre 1996: 142 and 149; Paillard 1998a and 1998b.
89 Heijmans and Sintès 1994: 149.
90 Bouet 1998: 69–103; Savay-Guerraz and Prisset 1992; Prisset 1999: 105.
91 Savay-Guerraz and Prisset 1992: 121; Prisset 1999: 105.
92 Sintès 1990: 137; Heijmans and Sintès 1994: 149; Bouet 1998: 87–8.
93 Bedon 1999: 145–7.
94 Frézouls 1982: 79–80; Bayard and Massy 1983: 109–13.
95 Roffin *et al.* 1966; Roffin and Vasselle 1966; Frézouls 1982: 75–6 and 93; Bayard and Massy 1983: 66–7 and 350.

NOTES

 96 Roffin *et al.* 1966: 200–2.
 97 Roffin *et al.* 1966: 203.
 98 Water pipes – Prisset 1999: 28–9. Public fountain – *ibid.*: 49. Supplies to baths – *ibid.*: 42–3 and 96–9; Bouet 1998: 83–6.
 99 Prisset 1999: 72–3.
100 Pelletier 1982b: 131–7 (aqueducts), 142–5 (water-supply pipes) and 165–7 (sewers).
101 Prisset 1999: 26–7.
102 Pelletier 1982b: 113–18.
103 Heijmans and Sintès 1994: 147; Arcelin *et al.* 1999: 128–9.
104 Woolf 1998: 116–19.
105 Raper 1977; Wallace-Hadrill 1991; Kaiser 2000.
106 Béraud *et al.* 1998: 75–9.
107 Olivier and Rebourg 1989; Rebourg 1999: 158–61.
108 Wightman 1970: 215–18; Scheid 1995. The Altbachtal sanctuary existed from at least the end of the first century BC, and lay outside the orthogonal grid which defined the urban centre at that time. The walled circuit which later surrounded both was not built until the second century AD.
109 Perrugot 1990.
110 Paillard 1998a: 54–5; 1998b: 154–5.
111 Rebourg 1999: 159 & 209–11.
112 Perrugot 1990: 30.
113 Paillard 1998a: 54.
114 Pelletier 1993: 126–7.
115 Wilson 2000: 288–9 on some of the problems in the context of the African textile industry.
116 For example pottery kilns – Peacock 1982: 90–9 and 103–13.
117 Mangin 1985; Whittaker 1990.
118 Woolf 2001a.
119 Peacock 1982: 119–20; Whittaker and Goody 2001: 231–3.
120 Goudineau 1980b: 271.
121 Maurin 1988: 41–4; Vernou and Buisson 1992: 160.
122 Rebourg 1999: 207–9.
123 Ferdière 1975a. For equivalents outside Gaul – Peacock 1982: 99–101.
124 Maurin 1988: 41–2 – 'The new [Gallo-Roman] urbanism would no longer tolerate polluting industries such as potters' kilns in the interior of the town'. Also Ferdière 2005: 201.
125 Woolf 1998: 117 – 'perhaps to remove it from the most public zones of the city, its thoroughfares, monuments and open spaces'.
126 For example Arnaud 1998: 68–9.
127 '*Figlinas teglarias maior<e>s tegularum (trecentarum) tegulariumq(ue) in oppido colon(iae) Iul(iae) ne quis habeto*' (*lex Coloniae Genetivae* 76.24–5; Crawford 1996: I.25).
128 Juv., *Sat.* 14. 202. For example Vega 1994: 145–6.
129 '*Qui habuerit, it5a} aedificium isque locus publicus colon(iae) Iul(iae) esto, eiusq(ue) aedficii quicumque in c(olonia) G(enetiva) Iul(ia) i(ure) d(icundo) p(raerit), s(ine) d(olo) m(alo) eam pecuniam in publicum redigito*' (*lex Coloniae Genetivae* 76.25–8; Crawford 1996: I.25).
130 Crawford 1996, vol. I: 438.
131 For example multiple industries in Pompeii (Laurence 1994), fish-salting vats at Sabratha (Wilson 1999b), fullers or dyers at Timgad (Wilson 2000).
132 *Digesta* 8.5.8.5 (Ulpian – on smoke from a cheese-shop affecting properties

NOTES

above it in Minturnae); *Digesta* 43.10.3–4 (Papinian – responsibilities of domestic and artisanal tenants for maintaining the streets in front of their properties).
133 Juvenal's Umbricius (*Sat.* 3.223–5) claims that a freehold country house can be bought for a year's rent on a gloomy garret in Rome. But this is a distinction between city and country, not centre and periphery, and must be seen in the context of a satirical tirade against urban living.
134 Chardron-Picault 1996: 38–40; Rebourg 1999: 164–70.
135 Brentchaloff 1980; Rivet *et al.* 2000: 434–7.
136 Perrugot 1990.
137 Perrugot 1990: 1.
138 Clisson *et al.* 1982; Billard *et al.* 1983a: 25–7; Vernou 1988; Vernou *et al.* 1990: 10; Vernou and Buisson 1992: 160.
139 Perrugot 1990.
140 Perrugot 1990: 30.
141 Deru and Grasset 1997.
142 Tranoy and Ayala 1994: 179 (and 18, n. 21 for the amphitheatre and houses).
143 Delaval *et al.* 1995: 94–6 and 130–60.
144 For example at the rue de la Muette and la Butte – Pelletier 1999: 85–6; Bertrand 2000.
145 Canal and Tourrenc 1979.
146 Bedon 1984.
147 Fiches and Veyrac 1996: nos. 534, 536, 542, 588, 594, 596 and 597; Bessac 1996.
148 Leveau 1996; Wilson 1999a: 325–7 and contribution from Leveau at pp. 331–2.
149 Frayn 1979.
150 Hopkins 1980.
151 MacMullen 1970; Frayn 1993; de Ligt 1993.
152 Peacock 1982: 156.
153 Peacock 1982: 158–9.
154 Known at Amiens (Bayard and Massy 1983: 81–2), Arles (Heijmans 1991), Bavay (Will 1973), Château-Roussillon (Bedon *et al.* 1988: 121), Paris (Musée Carnavalet 1984: 154–60), Saint-Bertrand-de-Comminges (Bedon 2001: 277) and possibly Autun (Rebourg 1999: 180–6).
155 Woolf 1998: 117.
156 Desbat 1998: 416–17.
157 For example two found in the Rue des Farges excavations at Lyon – Desbat 1984: 28.
158 *CIL* XII.4248 – Severan inscription mentioning a '[*po*]*rticum macel*[*l.* .]' (Clavel 1970: 261).
159 Guyon and contributors 1991: 102–6; Guyon 1992: 142.
160 Rickman 1971: 144–7.
161 De Ligt 1993: 155–98. A panegyric delivered to Constantius in AD 297 by a land-owner from Autun seems to refer to markets held on his own land ('*nundinas meas*' – *Paneg. Lat.* 8.9.3).
162 Not directly attested in Gaul, but known elsewhere – e.g. Pausanias 10.32.14–16.
163 De Ligt 1993: 117–18 discusses *nundinae* mentioned in an inscription from Aix-les-Bains in the territory of Vienne and a *mercatus* in a graffito from La Graufesenque in the territory of Rodez.
164 Frayn 1993: 133–44; De Ligt 1993: 35–9 and 56–105. Again not directly

NOTES

attested for Gaul, but known for Italy and North Africa, and almost certainly applicable all over the empire (see esp. de Ligt 1993: 75–7).

165 Paillard in Musées de la ville de Lisieux 1994: 37; Paillard 1998a: 54–5; 1998b: 154–5.
166 For example 'Maison aux Colonnes', 'Maison au Portique Peint' – Prisset 1999: 40–1 and 52–3.
167 Laroche and Savay-Guerraz 1984: 78–84; Prisset 1999: 50–9.
168 Laroche and Savay-Guerraz 1984: 91; Prisset 1999: 74–6.
169 Laroche and Savay-Guerraz 1984: 85–90; Prisset 1999: 60–3.
170 Savay-Guerraz *et al.* 1995: 393–9; Prisset 1999: 77–81.
171 Strabo 4.1.2 and 4.1.14.
172 For example Peacock 1982, figs. 80 and 84.
173 Bedon 1999: 144. Exceptions include Marseille, Antibes and Boulogne.
174 For example Bordeaux, Fréjus, Arles, Narbonne, Avranches, Lillebonne, Rouen.
175 Halbout-Bertin 1979: 42–3.
176 Nympheas II site – Tourrenc 1979; Godard 1995: 291–4. Quai Riondet site – Godard 1995: 288–9. Rue Laurent Florentin – Godard 1995: 285–8.
177 Le Bot-Helly and Helly 1999: 77; Tourrenc 1979: 47–55.
178 Delaval *et al.* 1995: 188–202.
179 Rickman 1971: 180–3.
180 For Rome, the Emporium district – see chapter 3.
181 Baccrabère 1988 and above.
182 Baccrabère 1988: 231–92 and 307–431.
183 Baccrabère 1988: 288–92 and personal communication.
184 Baccrabère 1996.
185 Stambaugh 1988: 166–7; Pelletier 1982a: 149.
186 For example the Maison au Dauphin at Vaison-la-Romaine – Pelletier 1982a: 155–7.
187 Woolf 1998: 123–4.
188 Bedon *et al.* 1988: 33–4.
189 Examples at Autun – Rebourg 1999: 203–4.
190 Desbat 1984.
191 Mandy 1983; Desbat 1998: 413–17; Pelletier 1999: 66–7 and 112–14.
192 Desbat 1984, *passim*, but esp. 45–9 and 54.
193 Desbat 1984, *passim*, but esp. 50–2.
194 Condate – Tranoy and Ayala 1994: 174–7. St-Jean quarter – Villedieu 1990: 139–44. Fourvière plateau outside area of *colonia* – Pelletier 1993: 119. Presqu'île (Canabae) – Audin 1956: 131–5; Turcan 1980: 73–80. Vaise – Delaval *et al.* 1995: 34.
195 Musée de la Civilisation Gallo-Romaine de Lyon 1983–84: 122–7.
196 Musée de la Civilisation Gallo-Romaine de Lyon 1983–84: 122.
197 Pelletier 1993: 118–21; Gruyer 1967.
198 Gruyer 1967: 44. Pompeian examples include the house of Neptune and Amphitrite (Clarke 1991: 255–7).
199 Delaval *et al.* 1995: 71–129.
200 Maison aux Masques – Desbat 1984: 39–41, 45 and 48. Maison aux Xenia – Delaval *et al.* 1995: 97–115.
201 Delaval *et al.* 1995: 88–9, 94 and 278.
202 Burdy 1993, 1996 and 2000.
203 Delaval *et al.* 1995: 129.
204 Crawford 1996: I.25.91.
205 Delaval *et al.* 1995: 94–6 and 130–60.

206 Delaval *et al.* 1995: 94–5.
207 Le Clos – Barruol 1968: 154–6; Rolland 1958; Rolland 1960.
208 For example Pierre Brossolette and La Verrerie sites at Trinquetaille – Rouquette and Sintès 1989: 89 and 92; Sintès 1987b.
209 Rue du Cursol – Gaidon-Bunuel *et al.* 1991; Parunis – Gaidon 1986a and 1986b: 26; Rue des Frères-Bonie – Barraud 1984 and Barraud and Gaidon 1985.
210 La Brunette – Mignon *et al.* 1997.
211 Rue Grelaud – Vernou *et al.* 1990.
212 Saint-Romain-en-Gal – Le Glay and Tourrenc 1971, Le Glay 1981 and Prisset 1999. Sainte-Colombe – Le Bot 1981, Musée de la Civilisation Gallo-Romaine de Lyon 1983–84: 146–51.
213 On Saint-Romain-en-Gal, see above. Trinquetaille – porticoed square (Heijmans and Sintès 1994: 149), docks at La Pointe (Heijmans and Sintès 1994: 150).
214 Roffin *et al.* 1966; Roffin and Vasselle 1966; Frézouls 1982: 75–6 and 93; Bayard and Massy 1983: 66–7 and 350.
215 Schlemaire 1974, 1976 and 1978; Vigneron 1986: 111–13.
216 Site S3 (Schlemaire 1976: 45–55).
217 Possibly a temple – Schlemaire 1978: 52 and 6.
218 Although there are possible traces of third-century potters' kilns at Pontiffroy – Schlemaire 1976: 45.
219 Garnsey 1979: 10.
220 Brunt 1980; Treggiari 1980.
221 Whittaker 1980.
222 Schlemaire 1978: 61.
223 Fauduet 1993: 32; van Andringa 2002: 112–14.
224 Bouet 2003: I.293–9.
225 On this basic distinction in Roman baths generally – Nielsen 1990: 119–20.
226 Barraud 1984; Barraud and Gaidon 1985.
227 Villedieu 1990: 21–5.
228 Conges *et al.* 1992: 125–6.
229 Laroche and Savay-Guerraz 1984: 63; Prisset 1999: 42–5.
230 Barraud and Gaidon 1985: 5.
231 Villedieu 1990: 21 and 105–6.
232 Conges *et al.* 1992: 123–6; Bouet 2003: II.37–40.
233 Thermes des Lutteurs, Saint-Romain (Prisset 1999: 96–104; Bouet 1998: 83–4), Palais du Miroir, Saint-Romain (Laroche and Savay-Guerraz 1984: 20–1; Bouet 1998: 85–6), Place de l'Égalité, Sainte-Colombe (Bouet 2003: II.278–83), Thermes du Sud, Sainte-Colombe? (Bouet 2003: II.283–4).
234 Baccrabère 1988: 57–148 (North baths), 149–202 (Central baths) and 203–19 (South baths).
235 Bouet and Carponsin-Martin 1999.
236 Béraud *et al.* 1998: 77–9; Bouet 2003: II.103–7.
237 Gayraud 1981: 279–80.
238 Prisset 1999; Baccrabère 1988: 219–27.
239 Bouet 1998: 69–83; Prisset 1999: 88–9.
240 Bouet 1998: 75–8.
241 Bouet 1998: 85–6.
242 Baccrabère 1988: 11–19 (temple) and 293–305 (fountain).
243 Bouet 2003: 293–6.
244 Baccrabère 1988: 201.
245 Bouet and Carponsin-Martin 1999.
246 Bouet 2003: II.283.

NOTES

247 Fauduet 1993; Fauduet and Bertin 1993. These structures are generally called *'fana'* or *'sanctuaires Romano-Celtiques'* by French scholars.
248 Ward-Perkins 1981: 227–30; Fauduet and Bertin 1993.
249 Woolf 1998: 235.
250 Fauduet 1993: 29–35.
251 For a classical temple in a rural context, the Temple of Vaugrenier, 4.5 km north of Antibes (Rivet 1988: 240–1). For a Romano-Celtic temple in an urban context, the sanctuary of the Tour de Vésone adjoining the forum at Périgueux (Bedon 2001: 253).
252 Goudineau 1980b: 280–2.
253 Baccrabère 1977: 70–1.
254 Herrenbrünnchen – Wightman 1970: 88; Scheid 1991: 48. Saint-Michel-du-Touch – Baccrabère 1988: 11–19.
255 Goodman 2002.
256 Fishwick 1987–92.
257 Drinkwater 1979.
258 Fishwick 1987–92: 137 and 268.
259 Strabo 4.3.2. Coins – *RIC* Augustus 229–30, Tiberius 31–2 and Claudius 1. Role of Drusus – Suet., *Claud.* 2.1; Cass. Dio 54.32.1; Livy, *Per.* 138–9.
260 *AnnEp* 1959, nos. 78 and 81.
261 Fishwick 1987–92: 308–16.
262 Audin 1979b.
263 *CIL* XIII.1667a–e.
264 Based on natural terracing and scattered finds probably originating from the sanctuary – Audin 1956: 149–56; Tranoy and Ayala 1994: 182–5.
265 Gayraud 1981: 279–80.
266 *CIL* XII.6038; Williamson 1987.
267 *CIL* XII.4342.
268 Gayraud 1981: 384–93.
269 Gayraud 1981: 296–300.
270 Gayraud 1981: 388–90.
271 Goodman 2002: 92.
272 *CIL* XII.4333.
273 Pelletier 1999: 66–7 and 112–14.
274 Council of the Three Gauls – *CIL* XIII.1686, 1688 and 1707–9. Narbonensis – *CIL* XII.6038, l. 26; Williamson 1987: 189.
275 Fauduet 1993.
276 Scheid 1995.
277 Langouët and Goulpeau 1984; Provost 2000.
278 Vigneron 1986: 115–25 and 152–7; Frézouls 1982: 324–5.
279 Lemaitre 1998a; Lemaitre 1998b.
280 Olivier and Rebourg 1989; Rebourg 1999: 158–61.
281 Harmand 1958.
282 Wightman 1970: 211–15; Scheid 1991.
283 Boissel and Lavoquer 1943; Naveau and Pivette 1994; Naveau 1996: 115–16 and 120–2.
284 Magnan 1988: 80–3.
285 Maurin and Vienne 1977; Billard *et al.* 1983b: 34–7; Buisson 1989.
286 Bedon 2001: 258.
287 Bedon 1999: 178.
288 For the history of this interpretation, Scheid 1995: 227–8 and Woolf 1998: 206–7.

NOTES

289 Woolf 1998: 209–11; van Andringa 2002: 99–101; Ferdière 2005: 42 and 118–19.
290 Scheid 1995; Woolf 1998: 230–7.
291 For example at the source of the Clitumnus in Umbria – Pliny, *Ep.* 8.8.
292 Vitr. *Arch.* 1.7; Woolf 2001b: 604.
293 Van Andringa 2002: 144–5.
294 The festival and sanctuary of the imperial cult at Lyon have sometimes been viewed as a 'Romanisation' of an indigenous cult of the god Lug (e.g. Audin 1979a: 100–1). If correct, this association may have governed the location of the new sanctuary, but the theory is now largely discredited – Ferdière 2005: 118.
295 Bedon 1999: 311; 2001: 253 and 309–10; van Andringa 2002: 65–6 and 78–9.
296 Chamiers – Bouet and Carponsin-Martin 1999.
297 Lenus Mars, Trier – Wightman 1970: 211–15. La Bauve, Meaux – Magnan 1988: 80–3; Laporte 1996: 203–6. North sanctuary, Jublains – Boissel and Lavoquer 1943: 272. Vieux-Lisieux, Lisieux – Lemaitre 1998b: 130.
298 Bedon 1999: 311.
299 Woolf 2003 questioned whether all Romano-Celtic temples should be considered together as a single category on similar grounds.
300 Saint-Vigor – Bedon 1999: 178.
301 Boissel and Lavoquer 1943; Naveau and Pivette 1994; Naveau 1996: 115–6 and 120–2.
302 Naveau 1996: 121.
303 Orientation, roads – Naveau 1986: 113–14. Burials – Barbe 1865: 89–91; Naveau 1996: 119.
304 Bedon 1999: 177–83.
305 Usually described by French scholars as a '*théâtre du plan gaulois*' – Dumasy 1975 and Dumasy and collaborators 1989.
306 Dumasy and collaborators 1989: 56–65.
307 Picard 1970: 185 (citing 40 examples); Fauduet 1993: 32 (citing 60 examples); van Andringa 2002: 115 (citing a round hundred both outside administrative cities and in their peripheries).
308 Classical examples include Autun (Rebourg 1999: 188–90), Lyon (Pelletier 1999: 59–60), Nîmes (Bedon 2001: 238), Orange (Bedon 2001: 244), Vaison-la-Romaine (Bedon 2001: 314), Valence (Bedon 2001: 317) and Vienne (Pelletier 1982b: 211–16 and 415–16).
309 It is known only through modern land-parcels and partial remains (Bedon 2001: 110), but must have been of classical type, since Gallic theatres do not occur in Narbonensis.
310 Saint-Bertrand-de-Comminges – Guyon and contributors 1991: 108–12; Sablayrolles *et al.* 2001–12: 46–51. Soissons – Bedon 2001: 299.
311 The exceptions, Évreux, Lillebonne and Orléans, are poorly known, and the same may have applied.
312 Wightman 1970: 211–18.
313 Lemaitre 1998a: 62; 1998b: 134–5.
314 Rebourg 1999: 159–60; Bedon 2001: 90.
315 Naveau 1996: 116.
316 Naveau 1986: 110–11.
317 Sanctuary – Langouët and Goulpeau 1984: 86. Theatre – Naveau 1991: 108–11, nos 12–14.
318 Fauduet 1993: 32; Picard 1970: 185.
319 Examples include Lyon (sanctuary of Cybele(?), Pelletier 1999: 61), Nîmes (spring sanctuary/Augusteum) – Bedon 2001: 238), Orange (cult complex on

NOTES

colline Saint-Eutrope, Bedon 2001: 244) and Vienne (temple of Bacchus(?), Pelletier 1982b: 211–16 and 415–16).
320 Hanson 1959: 43–55 (theatre of Pompey), 9–26 (cultural precedents) and 29–9 (architectural precedents).
321 Van Andringa 2002: 115.
322 Bouley 1983.
323 Bouley 1983: 570–1.
324 Often described by French scholars as an *'amphithéâtre à scene'* or *'édifice mixte'* (Golvin 1988: 225–36). Golvin divides his *'édifices mixtes'* into two sub-categories: the semi-amphitheatre and the theatre-amphitheatre. But Dumasy challenged the latter on the basis that these buildings did not have an enclosed arena suitable for fighting. They are now usually categorised as Gallic theatres.
325 Dumasy and collaborators 1989: 45.
326 Golvin 1988: 226–30 and own research (see table 4.2).
327 Golvin 1988: 408–9.
328 Frézouls 1990: 79.
329 Goudineau 1980b: 294; Golvin 1988: 410–11; Frézouls 1990: 84.
330 Nîmes – Bedon 2001: 238. Autun – Rebourg 1999: 189–90 and 207–9.
331 Rebourg 1999: 184–6.
332 Goudineau 1980b: 247.
333 Frézouls 1982: 84–7; Bayard and Massy 1983: 86–94.
334 Walthew 1981: 300.
335 Bedon 2001: 113.
336 Frézouls 1990: 81–2; Golvin 1988: 409.
337 Doreau *et al.* 1982.
338 Woolf 2000: 126–31.
339 Vega 1994: 148.
340 Catull., *Carm.* 55.4; Juv. *Sat.* 6.582–3 and 588–91; *CIL* VI.9822.
341 Baccrabère 1988: 21–54.
342 Cited as a commonly held opinion at Frézouls 1990: 79 and Bedon 1999: 320.
343 Valerius Maximus, 2.4.7
344 Ville 1981: 9, 42–51 and 57–72; Clavel-Lévêque 1984: 29–30.
345 Le Glay 1990: 217.
346 Clavel-Lévêque 1984: 65; Futrell 1997: esp. 205–10. Counter-arguments – Ville 1981: 9–19.
347 Kyle 1998: 155–9.
348 Le Glay 1990: 221–2.
349 For example Cic., *Sest.* 124–47; Plut., *C. Gracch.* 33.5–6; Ville 1981: 44–5. See ch. 71 of the Urso charter for gladiatorial games in provincial fora (Crawford 1996: I.25).
350 Ville 1981: 9–19; Clavel-Lévêque 1984: 63–77; Vismara 1990.
351 Wiedemann 1992: 46.
352 Le Glay 1990: 218–21.
353 Crawford 1996: I.25.
354 Ville 1981: 175–6.
355 Kolendo 1981, Clavel-Lévêque 1984: 153–61.
356 Golvin 1988: 386.
357 Dumasy and Fincker 1992: 301; Bedon 1999: 320.
358 Musée Carnavalet 1984: 166.
359 Futrell 1997: 69–71; Drinkwater 1983: 149–50.
360 For example Grimal in Woloch 1983: 67.
361 Futrell 1997: 71.

NOTES

362 Drinkwater 1983: 149–50.
363 Futrell 1997: 71.
364 Theatre – late first or early second century, mixed edifice – course of second century (Musée Carnavalet 1984: 166–71).
365 Lyon – *CIL* XIII.1805 and 1919. Trier – *Pan. Constantin.* 22.4–5; Augustine, *Conf.* 8.14.
366 Arles – Benoit 1927: 60–1; Hallier and Sintès 1987. Vienne – Pelletier 1982b: 221–2.
367 Le Bot-Helly and Helly 1999.
368 Hallier and Sintès 1987: 64.
369 Hallier and Sintès 1987: 63.
370 Sintès 1987a.
371 Varro, *Ling.* 5.154; *CIL* VI.32323.153–6.
372 Suet. *Iul.* 39.4.
373 Eusebius, *HE* 5.1.47.
374 Scheid 1991: 51.
375 Fiches 1989: 267–8.
376 Collis 1977: 8–9.
377 Collis 1977: 8–9; Woolf 1998: 18.
378 Cic., *Leg.* 2.24.61
379 *Lex Coloniae Genetivae Iuliae*, ch. 74 (Crawford 1996: I.25).
380 Hope 2000.
381 Lindsay 2000.
382 Toynbee 1971: 61–4; Ovid, *Fasti* 2.533–70.
383 Hope 2000: 105.
384 Pelletier 1993: 126–7.
385 Italian benefactions of land for burial include *CIL* I^2 2123 (Horatius Balbus at Sarsina) and *ILS* 7847 (a freedman at Tolentinum).
386 Gayraud 1981: 306–13.
387 Gayraud 1981: 313, 485 (metal-working), 489 (pottery) and 543 (oysters).
388 On this kind of development around Rome – Purcell 1987a: 36.
389 Béraud *et al.* 1998: 70–2.
390 Pre-Roman Gaul – Woolf 1998: 166; Ferdière 2005: 115–16. Rome – Purcell 1987a: 32–40.
391 Pelletier 1993: 126–7.
392 *CIL* XIII.1941.
393 Via Appia – Patterson 2000a: 97–101; 2000b. Pompeii – Toynbee 1971: 119–26.
394 Orange – Mignon 2000. Autun – Pinette and Rebourg 1986: 76–7; Rebourg 1999: 209–12.
395 Petr., *Sat.* 61–2; Hor., *Sat.* 1.8.
396 Pinette and Rebourg 1986: 40.
397 Pinette and Rebourg 1986: 40; Rebourg 1999: 209–12. On cenotaphs – Toynbee 1971: 54.
398 *AnnÉp* 1979, no. 407.
399 Luck 1985: 18 and 165.
400 For example Agache 1973 and 1978 or Leday 1980 on specific regions; Percival 1976: 67–82 on a province-wide level.
401 Woolf 1998: 152–3.
402 Garmy and Leveau 2002.
403 Percival 1976: 67–8.
404 Walker 1981: 300–1.

405 Vasselle 1978.
406 Agache 1973: 43.
407 Agache 1973; Wightman 1985: 105–4.
408 Rebourg 1993: 132–3, no. 333; Rebourg 1999: 213.
409 Rebourg 1999: 213.
410 Comparable examples include La Plaine near Alba (Musée de la Civilisation Gallo-Romaine de Lyon 1983–84: 106–8), Brachaud near Limoges (Loustaud 1981, 1982 and 1983–88), Lazenay near Bourges (Ferdière 1975b; 1977; Holmgren and Leday 1980) and Newel near Trier (Wightman 1970).
411 Joulin 1901. Note, however, Balmelle's suggestion that Chiragan's great phase of extension should be redated from the latter half of the second century to the late antique period (Balmelle 2001: 367–70).
412 Fouet 1969.
413 For example 'Maison des Athlètes', Vienne (Lancha 1981: 58–70, no. 264), Circus mosaic from the Presqu'île, Lyon (Stern 1967: 63–9, no. 73), Gladiator mosaic, Reims (Stern 1957: 33–5, no. 38).
414 Stern and Blanchard-Lemée 1975: 110–2 (no. 302).
415 For example Les Baumelles (40 km from Aix-en-Provence and 30 km from Marseille), St-Ulrich-Dolving (c. 50 km each from Metz and Strasbourg) and St-Émilion (34 km from Bordeaux). Percival 1976: 67–82.
416 Clavel 1970: 296–307; Woolf 1998: 158–60. For examples of more modest agricultural buildings close to cities – Mont Saint-Vaast, 2 km north-west of Arras (Hosdez et al. 1992; Delmaire 1994: 153–5), Cours Gambetta buildings, 600m south-east of Aix-en-Provence (Gauthier 1986c; Nin et al. 1987).
417 Woolf 1998: 160.
418 Wilson 1999a: 323–5 (Nîmes); Gazenbeek 2000 (Nîmes and Arles).
419 Agache 1973: 46–50.
420 Pliny, *Ep.* 9.11.
421 Rebourg 1993: 134, no. 342; Rebourg 1999: 213.
422 Ziegert 2001–02: 91–2.
423 Bouet and Carponsin-Martin 1999: 225–9.
424 The exceptions, shown on the tables, are mixed edifices at Bourges (Aquitania) and Senlis (Belgica), and the two theatres connected with religious sites at Trier (Belgica).
425 Pliny, *NH* 3.35.
426 Béraud et al. 1998.
427 Kérébel 1996; Kérébel 2000.
428 Goudineau 1982.
429 Brentchaloff 1980.
430 Seneca, *Ep.* 91.10, comments on it with some surprise.
431 Goudineau 1980b: 247
432 Audin 1956: 161–4; Villedieu 1990: 108–9.

5 GAUL IN THE HIGH EMPIRE: SECONDARY AGGLOMERATIONS

1 This term, an English equivalent of the French '*agglomérations secondaires*', is favoured here because, unlike alternatives such as 'small towns' or '*vici*', it implies no assumptions about the status of these settlements other than that they are secondary to the local administrative centre.
2 Petit et al. 1994b: 91–3.
3 Langouët 1985, with site plan.

NOTES

4   Petit *et al.* 1994b: 91.
5   Pausanias, 10.4.1.
6   Woolf 1998: 119–20.
7   Drinkwater 1979; Woolf 1998: 133–4; Rorison 2001: 55–7.
8   Mangin and Tassaux 1992: 475–6; Rorison 2001: 84.
9   Leveau 1994: 185–6.
10 Woolf 1998: 133–5.
11 Bedon *et al.* 1988: 33.
12 For example Glanum (Goudineau 1980a: 178–81); Alesia (Bénard and Mangin 1985: 104–7).
13 Kruta 1980: 227–9
14 '*Vicus*': Wightman 1976: 60. '*Conciliabulum*': Jacques 1991.
15 Wightman 1976: 60–1.
16 Leveau 1994: 182–3.
17 Picard 1970, 1975 and 1976.
18 Jacques 1991; Woolf 1998: 135, n. 98.
19 Aeberhardt 1985: 49–50; Desbordes 1985: 146; Aupert 1992: 166.
20 This is likely to have been especially true in the early Roman period. Ambrussum (near modern Villetelle), for instance, minted its own coins in the 40s BC, and was probably given Latin rights by Caesar, but was soon afterwards demoted and attributed to the territory of Nîmes (Fiches 1989: 269).
21 Leveau 1994: 182; Rivet 1988: 100 and 136–40.
22 Rorison 2001: 51–9.
23 For example Sanxay (Aupert 1992). Only detailed dating evidence, however, can show whether a settlement grew up around a temple, or a temple was built to serve the needs of a settlement (Galliou 1984: 224).
24 Commerce: e.g. Talmont l'Antique (Dassié 1975: 40; Tassaux 1994: 206). Industry: Mangin and Tassaux 1992: 472–3. Mangin 1985 for Gaul and Whittaker 1990 for the west in general have argued that industrial activity in secondary agglomerations was a significant factor in the Roman economy.
25 Mangin and Tassaux 1992: 467.
26 Woolf 1998:126–35.
27 Rorison 2001: 17–28.
28 Desbordes 1985; Mangin and Tassaux 1992: 465–7; Galliou 1984: 223.
29 Woolf 1998: 130–1; Rorison 2001: 28–32.
30 Mangin and Tassaux 1992: 467–8.
31 Woolf 1998: 130–1.
32 Woolf 1998: 135.
33 Mangin and Tassaux 1992: 463–5.
34 Leveau 1993; 1994: 187–91.
35 Tarpin 1991.
36 Tassaux 1994: 200–1.
37 Burnham and Wacher 1990.
38 Mangin and Tassaux 1992: 162; Leveau 1994 for a representative description of the situation in Gallia Narbonensis.
39 For example Aeberhardt 1985 on the settlements of the Charente.
40 Mangin and Tassaux 1992.
41 Petit *et al.* 1994a and 1994b; Bénard *et al.* 1994.
42 Mangin *et al.* 1986.
43 Fiches 2002.
44 Mangin and Tassaux 1992: 463–4.
45 'It should be noted here that the immediate surroundings of the agglomerations

NOTES

are not at all well known: no suburbs, no cemeteries have been identified' (Aupert *et al.* 1998: 53).
46 Also known as Vieux-Poitiers.
47 Also known as Gué de Sciaux.
48 Also known as Brion.
49 Between the modern villages of Argenton-sur-Creuse and Saint-Marcel.
50 Beaumont-sur-Oise was on the border between two *civitates*, one in Belgica and one in Lugdunensis, leading to debate over which community, and which province, it belonged to (Petit *et al.* 1994b: 243).
51 Near modern Saint-Rémy-de-Provence.
52 Vendeuvre-du-Poitou belonged to the same group, but has yet to yield any significant periurban occupation.
53 Aupert *et al.* 1998: 61.
54 Saint-Germain – Romano-Celtic temple, theatre and at least two other public buildings (Garmy *et al.* 1992). Argentomagus – monumental fountain, several temples, theatre, amphitheatre, baths (Dumasy 1992a). Ambrussum – portico, urban-style *domus* (Fiches 1989: 269 and 272). Glanum – forum, basilica, temples, monumental fountain, baths, etc. (Rivet 1988: 198–200).
55 Fiches 1989: 269.
56 *CIL* XII.1005; Leveau 1994: 183
57 Agusta-Boularot *et al.* 1998; Gazenbeek 1998; Fontan and Roth Congès 1999.
58 Fiches 1989: 267.
59 Dumasy 1992a: 25.
60 Petit *et al.* 1994b: 266.
61 Petit *et al.* 1994b: 243.
62 Coulon 1996: 151; Fauduet 1982: 77–84; Allain *et al.* 1992.
63 Gazenbeek 1998: 93.
64 Gazenbeek 1998: 93–4.
65 Rolland 1977: 43–6.
66 Rorison 2001: 34–8.
67 Petit *et al.* 1994b: 267.
68 Petit *et al.* 1994b: 213; Frézouls 1973, 1975 and 1977.
69 See chapter 3.
70 Argentomagus: Coulon 1996. Ambrussum: Fiches 1989: 267–9. Glanum: Rivet 1988; Fontan and Roth Congès 1999.
71 Petit *et al.* 1994b: 267.
72 Petit *et al.* 1994b: 93; Frézouls 1988: 479.
73 Ollivier and Fritsch 1982: 55.
74 Petit *et al.* 1994b: 212.
75 Beaumont-sur-Oise – Petit *et al.* 1994b: 244–5. Dalheim – *ibid.*: 267. Mandeure – *ibid.*: 93. Antigny – Richard 1989: 199–200. Naintré – Ollivier and Fritsch 1982: 55–6. Saint-Germain-d'Esteuil – Garmy *et al.* 1992: 148. Sanxay – Aupert 1992: 164.
76 Dumasy 1992b; Coulon 1996: 108–12.
77 Petit *et al.* 1994b: 94.
78 Petit *et al.* 1994b: 266–7.
79 Dumasy and Fincker 1992: 302.
80 Aupert 1992.
81 Coulon 1996: 107–12.
82 Petit *et al.* 1994b: 91–3; Frézouls 1988: 485–6.
83 Dumasy 1992a: 29; Coulon 1996: 59.
84 Dumasy 1992a: 25 and 29; Coulon 1996: 59.

NOTES

85 Baths – Coulon 1996: 112. Further occupation – Dumasy 1992a: 26.
86 Petit *et al.* 1994b: 91–4; Frézouls 1988: 423–505.
87 Frézouls 1988: 466.
88 Petit *et al.* 1994b: 94.
89 Richard 1989: 19.
90 Fiches 1989.
91 Petit *et al.* 1994b: 212.
92 Richard 1992: 22.
93 Aupert 1992: 166.
94 Petit *et al.* 1994b, entries 73, 224 and 349; Ollivier and Fritsch 1982; Fauduet 1982: 55.
95 Ollivier and Fritsch 1982: 55.
96 Papinot *et al.* 1989: 295.
97 Frézouls 1988: 486; Petit *et al.* 1994b: 93–4.
98 Navigability of the Doubs to Mandeure: Petit *et al.* 1994b: 92.
99 Fiches 1989: 64–143.
100 Fiches 1989: 271.
101 Gazenbeek 1998: 94.
102 Agusta-Boularot *et al.* 1998: 24–5.
103 Richard 1989: 15–21.
104 Frézouls 1988: 488–9.
105 Petit *et al.* 1994b: 94.
106 Some also argue for a theatre at Glanum – Bedon 2001: 291.
107 Petit *et al.* 1994b: 243. Chapter 4 showed that theatres of Gallic type built at administrative cities were always located in the urban periphery.
108 Dumasy 1995: 204; Coulon 1996: 107–12.
109 Fontan and Roth Congès 1999: 44.
110 Richard 1992: 24; 1989.
111 Richard 1992: 22; 1989: 20.
112 Petit *et al.* 1994b: 212.
113 Frézouls 1988: 485–6. *CIL* XIII.5416 and 5417, found *in situ*, also record that these baths were paved with marble using money left in the will of one Flavius Catullus.
114 Frézouls 1988: 472–4; Petit *et al.* 1994b: 92.
115 In Petit *et al.* 1994b: 92.
116 Dense occupation in centre by end of first century – Fauduet 1982: 53–65; Coulon 1996: 86–7.
117 Fauduet 1982: 58–9; Coulon 1996: 69–73.
118 Dumasy 1992a: 25.
119 Antigny – Richard 1989: 13. Beaumont – Petit *et al.* 1994b: 243. Château-Porcien – Petit *et al.* 1994b: 213. Dalheim – Petit *et al.* 1994b: 266. Mandeure – Petit *et al.* 1994b: 93; Frézouls 1988: 474. Naintré – Ollivier and Fritsch 1982: 59–61.
120 Ollivier and Fristch 1982: 59–61.
121 Ollivier and Fritsch 1982: 59–61.
122 Petit *et al.* 1994b: 93; Frézouls 1988: 474.
123 For example sanctuaries in centre of Antigny (Richard 1992: 23–4), cult area in centre of Argentomagus (Dumasy 1992b: 28), *fanum* site in centre of Château-Porcien (Frézouls 1975).
124 Richard 1989.
125 See chapter 4.
126 Lintz 1992.

127 Lintz 1992: 92.
128 Lintz 1992: 96.
129 Lintz 1984–86.
130 Lintz 1984–86: 290.
131 Galliou 1984: 76
132 Galliou 1989: 159–62; 1984: 79.
133 Lémant 1991a and 1991b; Petit *et al.* 1994b: 211.
134 Aoste – Rémy and Jospin 1998. Roanne – Blin 1991; Lavendhomme and Guichard 1997.
135 Petit *et al.* 1994b: 211.
136 Petit *et al.* 1994b: 264.
137 Petit *et al.* 1994b: 230–1; Bedon 2001: 321–2.
138 Rémy and Jospin 1998; Bedon 2001: 77–8. A temple built for the *Salus* of Marcus Aurelius is also attested epigraphically, but unlocated (*CIL* XII.2391–2).
139 Petit *et al.* 1994b: 254.
140 Galliou 1984: 79; 1989: 159–62; Bedon 2001: 260–1.
141 Petit *et al.* 1994b: 230–1; Bedon 2001: 321–2.
142 Pape 1978: 82–8 and 185–6.
143 Laborde 1957–59.
144 Galliou 1989: 164.
145 Petit in Petit *et al.* 1994a: 24–6; Petit and Schaub 1995.
146 Petit and Schaub 1995: 84–93.
147 Rorison 2001: 43–6.
148 See introduction to this chapter; also Leveau 1994: 185–6 and Woolf 1998: 134.

6 GAUL IN LATE ANTIQUITY

1 Gros 1998.
2 For example Février 1980: 434.
3 Drinkwater 1983: 214.
4 Pelletier 1999: 23–4.
5 Drinkwater 1987.
6 Février 1980: 460–2.
7 Clear above all from Sidonius Apollinaris; see e.g. Harries 1992b.
8 Février 1980: 462.
9 Pelletier 1999: 126–7.
10 Biarne 1987: 45–8.
11 Février 1980: 451–2.
12 Février 1980: 454–5.
13 Gregory of Tours, *HF* 2.38
14 Février 1980: 455–6.
15 Meeks 1983.
16 Eusebius, *HE* 5.1; Reynaud 1998: 19.
17 Février 1980: 423–4.
18 Meeks 1983: 16–23.
19 Loseby 1992: 144–9.
20 Février 1980: 424.
21 Harries 1992a; Février 1980: 458–60.
22 Février 1980: 424; Loseby 1992: 147.
23 Second-century walls – Bedon *et al.* 1988: 40.
24 Maurin and Thauré 1994: 58.
25 Garmy and Maurin 1996: 10–11.

NOTES

26 Février 1980: 408.
27 For example Dax (mid-fourth century) or Bazas (second half fourth century) – Garmy and Maurin 1996.
28 Février 1980: 410.
29 Heijmans and Sintès 1994: 160; Février 1980: 462.
30 Guyon 1986: 22–3; Benoit 1954.
31 Perrugot 1996.
32 Frézouls 1982: 314–15; Vigneron 1986: 257–69.
33 Maurin and Watier in Garmy and Maurin 1996: 81–125.
34 Février 1980: 409.
35 As at Saint-Bertrand-de-Comminges.
36 De Filippo 1993; Baccrabère 1977: 43–58.
37 Baccrabère 1974; 1977: 58–62.
38 Pietri and Picard 1986: 41.
39 Février 1980: 400.
40 The exception is Autun.
41 *CIL* XII.3151.
42 Though they may still have provided incentives or labour from the army – Johnson 1983: 10.
43 Ward-Perkins 1984: 14–37 (on Italy); Liebeschuetz 1992.
44 For example Février 1980: 402–5; Barraud, Linères and Maurin in Garmy and Maurin 1996: 62–9.
45 Elton 1992.
46 Salvian, *De Gub. Dei* 6.82–4.
47 Maurin 1988: 44–9; Bayard and Massy 1983: 214–21.
48 For example Angers, Bourges, Gap, Limoges, Reims, Rennes, Senlis and Sens.
49 Février 1980: 405.
50 Barraud, Linères and Maurin in Garmy and Maurin 1996: 35–49. Similar circuits are known at Bayeux, Clermont-Ferrand, Lisieux, Orléans, Rouen and Soissons.
51 See Ausonius' approving description of the '*quadrua murorum species*' (fourfold shape of the walls) at Bordeaux (Aus., *Ordo nob. urb.* 20).
52 Frézouls 1982: 68–72; Bayard and Massy 1983: 221–2.
53 Pietri 1983: 343–4.
54 Girardy-Caillat in Garmy and Maurin 1996: 149–50.
55 Girardy-Caillat in Garmy and Maurin 1996: 127–54.
56 May 1996: 56–7; Sablayrolles and collaborators 2001–02: 65–74.
57 Garmy and Maurin 1996: 192.
58 Musée Carnavalet 1984: 373–6.
59 Février 1980: 411.
60 Desbat 1981; Reynaud 1998: 186.
61 Amm. Marc., *Hist.* 16.15.4; Sid. Apoll., *Ep.* 1.5.2.
62 Greg. of Tours, *HF* 5.33.
63 Audin and Reynaud 1981; Reynaud 1998: 57–8.
64 Reynaud 1998: 186–7.
65 Reynaud 1998: 43–86.
66 Maurin and Pichonneau in Garmy and Maurin 1996: 159; Paulinus of Pella, *Euch.* 383–9.
67 Maurin and Pichonneau in Garmy and Maurin 1996: 81–125.
68 Février 1980: 411.
69 Février 1980: 458.
70 Février 1980: 440.

NOTES

71 Gregory of Tours lists sixteen annual vigils performed in the churches of Tours (*HF* 10.31).
72 For example the three days of parades and public prayers which made up the Rogations – Février 1980: 449; Sid. Apoll., *Ep.* 5.14 and 7.1.
73 Février 1980: 429.
74 Harries 1992a: 85.
75 Février 1980: 448–50.
76 For example Aix-en-Provence – Guyon 1986.
77 Février 1980: 456–62.
78 Loseby 1992: 149–50.
79 Loseby 1992: 150.
80 *Vita Amatori* 18–21; Loseby 1992: 151; Février 1980: 411–12.
81 Février argues that this was the norm for extra-mural cathedrals (1980: 424).
82 Greg. of Tours, *HF* 2.16 and 5.11.
83 Loseby 1992: 150.
84 Guyon *et al.* 1992: 395.
85 Loseby 1992; Guyon *et al.* 1992.
86 Loseby 1992.
87 Gauthier 1986b: 21–5.
88 Février 1980: 428; Guyon *et al.* 1992: 395. Compare S. Giovanni in Laterano at Rome (Lançon 2000: 27).
89 Loseby 1992: 151; Brühl 1988.
90 Biarne 1987.
91 Harries 1992a: 86. Gregory of Tours believed that the cathedral of Clermont-Ferrand was older than any of the other intra-mural churches (*HF* 2.16).
92 Guyon *et al.* 1992: 398.
93 Bayard and Massy 1983: 243–4.
94 Le Masne de Chermont 1987.
95 Pietri 1983: 372–81.
96 Guyon *et al.* 1992: 400
97 Reynaud 1998: 87–135.
98 For example a large Christian necropolis developed around the church of Saint-Just at Lyon, itself established in an existing cemetery during the fourth century (Reynaud 1998: 96–108).
99 The cathedral at Bourges contained relics of the martyr Saint Stephen (Greg. of Tours, *HF* 1.31), while that at Clermont-Ferrand housed relics of the Italian saints Agricola and Vitalis (Harries 1992a: 94–5; Greg. of Tours, *HF* 2.16).
100 Février 1980: 412.
101 Guyon and Paillet in Février and Leyge 1986: 86; Guyon and contributors 1991: 118–22.
102 Guyon and contributors 1991: 94.
103 Pietri and Picard 1986: 43–4
104 Gauthier 1986b: 26–30.
105 Gauthier 1986a: 42 and 48–53.
106 Sid. Apoll., *Ep.* 5.14 and 7.1; Reynaud 1978.
107 Greg. of Tours, *HF* 5.4.
108 Pietri 1983: 372–420.
109 Greg. of Tours, *HF* 10.31.1. Gregory's reference actually occurs in his description of the burial of Tours' first bishop around AD 300. However, Pietri suggests that the word '*vicus*' is likely to be based on his own observances in the sixth century (Pietri 1983: 348, n. 37).
110 Pietri 1983: 415–16.

NOTES

111 Guyon *et al.* 1992: 402.
112 Harries 1992a: 83–9.
113 'Until now, the exterior of the city had been exclusively, or almost, the place of necropoleis, the space of the dead. It became – in the Christian community – a privileged space' (Février 1980: 434).
114 Février 1980: 440–3.
115 Brown 1981: 8.
116 Février 1980: 442–3; Heijmans and Sintès 1994: 161–2.
117 Pietri 1983: 421–30.
118 Sulp. Sev., *Vita Sancti Martini* 10.3.
119 Amm. Marc. 15.11.12 – '*Aventicam, desertam quidem civitatem sed non ignobilem quondam, ut aedificia semiruta nunc quoque demonstrant*' ('Aventicum, indeed a deserted city but formerly not unimportant, as even now its half-collapsed buildings show').
120 In fact, Ammianus singles out Avenches as the most notable city of Alpes Graiae et Poeninae despite its semi-ruined state, and it appeared in the *Notitia Galliarum* at the same time. Harries has questioned whether it could really have been as deserted as Ammianus suggests (Harries 1992a: 80).
121 Février 1980: 410.
122 For example Pietri, in his 853-page work on Tours between the fourth and sixth centuries is able to offer only eighteen pages on the defended centre (Pietri 1983: 350–67).
123 Gauthier and Debord 1982; Sivan 1992.
124 Leblanc and Savay-Guerraz 1996.
125 Le Bot 1981.
126 Godard 1995.
127 Heijmans 1996.
128 Schlemaire 1978: 61 and discussion in chapter 4.
129 Gauthier 1986a: 50–1.
130 There is unresolved debate concerning late antique walls at Vienne, however – Pelletier 1974; Février and Leyge 1986: 53.
131 Vernou *et al.* 1990.
132 Maurin 1988: 44–5.
133 Maurin 1988: 46–9.
134 Maurin 1988: 45–8.
135 Bayard and Massy 1983: 217–21.
136 For example the baths of the rue de Beauvais and some *domus* (Bayard and Massy 1983: 243).
137 45m × 13.6m (Février and Leyge 1986: 86).
138 Guyon and contributors 1991: 106–7; Sablayrolles and collaborators 2001–02: 42–3.
139 Guyon 1992: 144.
140 Sablayrolles and collaborators 2001–02: 70–4.
141 Garmy and Maurin 1996: 192.
142 Paris – Février 1980: 411; Tours – Pietri 1983: 348–9; Clermont-Ferrand – Février 1980: 412.
143 For example Salvian, *De Gub. Dei.* 6.82–9, Sid. Apoll., *Ep.* 1.11.10.
144 Hallier and Sintès 1987.
145 Pelletier 1999: 130–5.
146 Vigneron 1986: 231–42.
147 Loseby 1992: 152–3; Guyon 1986: 26.
148 Benoit 1977: 137–53.

NOTES

149 Descombes *et al.* 1986: 34.
150 Brühl 1988: 44–5.
151 Gauthier 1986a: 42.
152 Maurin and Thauré 1994: 53–5.
153 Hallier and Sintès 1987: 64–5.
154 Février 1980: 417.
155 Gauthier and Debord 1982: 45–55.
156 Pietri 1983: 372–420; Guyon *et al.* 1992: 402.
157 Wightman 1970: 98–102 and 113–14.
158 Heijmans and Sintès 1994: 151.
159 Succeeding early third-century baths on the same site, destroyed by fire – Villedieu 1990: 26–8.
160 Bouet 2003: I.311.
161 Greg. of Tours, *HF* 5.17.
162 Barbe 1865: 35–60 and 113–14; Naveau 1996: 114–15 and 123–4.
163 Barbe 1865: 40–1 and 113–14.
164 Naveau 1996: 123–4.
165 Guyon and contributors 1991: 116–18; Schaad and Soukiassian 1990.
166 Schaad and Soukiassian 1990: 116–17.
167 May 1996: 28–9
168 Percival 1976: 169–70.
169 Agache 1978: 296–9.
170 Balmelle 2001: 118–19 and 393–5; Coupry 1973, 1975, 1977 and 1979.
171 For example Palat, east of Bordeaux, built over the fourth and fifth centuries (Sivan 1992: 140–1).
172 Percival 1976: 175–6 and 1992: 159.
173 Percival 1976: 177–8.
174 Percival 1976: 172; Percival 1992: 164.
175 Percival 1976: 178–99; Percival 1992.
176 Percival 1976: 183–99; Percival 1992. Cf. also Balmelle 2001: 122–3.
177 Février 1980: 471–3; Sivan 1992.
178 Ausonius – Lucaniacus nr Saintes (*Eps.* 2, 4, 11, 15 and 20 (Green)), Pauliacus nr Bordeaux (*Ep.* 15 (Green)), inherited estate nr Bordeaux, prob. at Bazas (*De Herediolo*). Cf. also Paulinus of Nola *c.* 10, lines 248 (Bazas) and 256–9 (Lucan(iac)us). Sidonius – Avitacum nr Clermont-Ferrand (*Ep.* 2.2), '*villula*' nr Lyon (*Ep.* 2.12).
179 Ausonius – villas along the Moselle (*Mosella* 318–48). Sidonius – 'burgus' of Pontius Leontius nr Bordeaux (*Carm.* 22), villas of Tonantius Ferreolus and his cousin(?), Apollinaris (*Ep.* 2.9), estate of Pastor nr Arles (*Ep.* 5.20), estate of Consentius nr Narbonne (*Ep.* 8.4).
180 '*Haec mihi nec procul urbe sita est, nec prorsus ad urbem, ne patiar turbas utque bonis potiar. Et quotiens mutare locum fastidia cogunt, transeo et alternis rure vel urbe fruor*' (Aus., *Hered.*, 29–32). Sidonius (*Ep.* 8.4) also describes the villa of his friend Consentius at Narbonne as '*civitati fluvio mari proximus*' (very near to the city, the river and the sea).
181 Itself treated at Aus. *Ordo nob. urb.* 20.18–20.
182 *Ep.* 2.12 – '*propter quod optat exire in suburbanum; litteras tuas denique cum sumeremus, egredi ad villulam iam parabamus*'.
183 Cic. *Fam.* 7.26; Cat., *Carm.* 44.
184 Ward-Perkins 1984: 17 and esp. n. 12 (for Italy).
185 Aus., *Hered.* 21–6.
186 *Carm.* 2.18.

187 *Carm.* 1.19 (the Garonne and the Vérégine); *Carm.* 1.20 (the Garonne).
188 Février 1980: 474–6; Percival 1992: 160 (on Plassac)
189 Venantius Fortunatus also describes a new, fortified villa built by bishop Nicetius of Trier (*Carm.* 3.12).
190 For example the *'ecclesia sancti Martini in suburbio Augustodonensi'* at Autun, mentioned in a letter of Gregory the Great in 602 (Pietri and Picard 1986: 44).
191 Pietri 1983: 348.
192 Deru and Grasset 1997.

7 SOME WIDER QUESTIONS

1 The exceptions are Bitterne, Canterbury, Corbridge, Dorchester-on-Thames, Dorn, Hardham, Iping, Penkridge, Rochester and Wroxeter – Esmonde Cleary 1987.
2 Liebeschuetz 1992: 1–2. *Cf.* also Perring 1991.
3 Hopkins 1978: 35.
4 Braudel 1981: 479–81; Abrams 1978: 9; Wrigley 1991: 107–8 and 111; Whittaker 1995: 9–12.
5 Finley 1977; Finley 1985: 123–49 and 191–6.
6 For example Moeller 1976; Fulford 1982; Jongman 1988; Whittaker 1995; papers in Parkins 1997.
7 Adams 1977: 267–8; Abrams 1978; Wrigley 1991.
8 Abrams 1978: 9.
9 Abrams 1978: 31.
10 Most explicitly, Parkins 1997.
11 Whittaker 1995: 22; Horden and Purcell 2000: 108.
12 Horden and Purcell 2000: 102; Woolf 1998: 144.
13 Laurence 1994; Grahame 1997; Kaiser 2000.
14 Vega 1994: 142 on the general inability of walls to perform such a function.
15 Tac., *Agr.* 21.
16 Brunt 1976.
17 Woolf 2000.
18 Woolf 1997; Webster 2003.
19 Picard 1974; Fouqueray and Neiss 1976; Neiss 1984: 182.
20 Petit *et al.* 1994b: 267.
21 Woolf 1998: 124–6.
22 Pelletier 1982a: 58–68; Zanker 2000: 33–7.
23 Vitruvius, 1.7 and 5.1–2.
24 Perring 1991: 280.
25 Bedon 1999: 307–10.
26 Valette 1996: 87–9; Valette and Guichard 1991.
27 Bedon 2001: 230.
28 Van Andringa 2002: 45–64.
29 Mandy 1983; Bedon 1999: 317.
30 Guyon and contributors 1991: 97–100.
31 A plaque inscribed in honour of Jupiter Optimus Maximus and Tiberius inspired Bouet and Carponsin-Martin 1999 to propose that the sanctuary at Chamiers outside Périgueux was dedicated to the imperial cult. But it does not prove conclusively that this was its primary function.
32 Purcell 1987a: 26; Purcell 1987c: 78.

BIBLIOGRAPHY

Abrams, P. (1978), 'Towns and economic growth: some theories and problems', in Abrams, P. and Wrigley, E.A. (eds), *Towns in Societies*, Cambridge: Cambridge University Press, pp. 9–33.

Adams, R. McC. (1977), 'World picture, anthropological frame', *American Anthropologist* 79: 265–79.

Adembri, B. (2000), *Hadrian's Villa*, Milan: Electa.

Aeberhardt, A. (1985), 'Sanctuaires ruraux et pré-urbanisation en Charente', *Caesarodunum* 20 ('Les débuts de l'urbanisation en Gaule et dans les provinces voisines'): 47–59.

Agache, R. (1973), 'La villa gallo-romaine dans les grandes plaines du nord de la France', *Archéologia* 55: 37–52.

Agache, R. (1978), *La Somme pre-romaine et romaine d'après les prospections aériennes à basse altitude* (Mémoires de la Société des Antiquaires de Picardie 24), Amiens: Société des Antiquaires de Picardie.

Agusta-Boularot, S. (1998), 'Banlieue et faubourgs de Rome: approche linguistique et définition spatiale', *Caesarodunum* 32 (*'Suburbia*: Les Faubourgs en Gaule Romaine et dans les Régions Voisines'): 35–62.

Agusta-Boularot, S., Gazenbeek, M., Marcadal, Y. and Paillet, J.-L. (1998), '*Glanum*, l'extension de la ville et sa périphérie', *DossArch* 237: 20–5.

Allain, J., Fauduet, I. and Tuffreau-Libre, M. (1992), *La nécropole du Champ de l'Image à Argentomagus (Saint-Marcel, Indre)*, Saint-Marcel: Musée d'Argentomagus.

Andreussi, M. (1996), ' "Murus Servii Tullii"; Mura Repubblicane', in Steinby, E.M. (ed.), *Lexicon Topographicum Urbis Romae, vol. Terzo, H-O*, Roma: Edizioni Quasar, pp. 319–24.

Andreussi, M. (1999), 'Pomerium', in Steinby, E.M. (ed.), *Lexicon Topographicum Urbis Romae, vol. Quarto, P-S*, Roma: Edizioni Quasar, pp. 96–105.

Andringa, W. van (2002), *La religion en Gaule romaine. Piété et politique*, Paris: Éditions Errance.

Arcelin, P., Arnaud-Fassetta, G., Heijmans, M. and Valentin, F. (1999), 'Le Rhône à Arles. Données archéologiques et sédimentologiques', *Gallia* 56: 121–9.

Arlaud, C., Burnouf, J., Bravard, J.-P., Lurol, J.-M. and Vérot-Bourrély, A. (1994), *Lyon Saint-Jean. Les Fouilles de l'Îlot Tramassac* (Documents d'Archéologie en Rhône-Alpes, no. 10), Lyon: Service régional de l'archéologie de Rhône-Alpes.

Arlaud, C., Lurol, J.-M., Savay-Guerraz, S. and Vérot-Bourrély, A. (2000), *Lyon, les*

BIBLIOGRAPHY

Dessous de la Presqu'île. Bourse – République – Célestins – Terraux. Sites Lyon Parc Auto, (Documents d'Archéologie en Rhône-Alpes, no. 20), Lyon: Service régional de l'archéologie de Rhône-Alpes.

Arnaud, P. (1998), 'Vers une définition géodynamique des *suburbia*: Éléments pour une zonation des zones péri-urbaines', *Caesarodunum* 32 ('*Suburbia*: Les Faubourgs en Gaule Romaine et dans les Régions Voisines'): 63–81.

Ashby, T. (1909), 'La villa dei Quintilii', *Ausonia* 4: 48–88.

Ashby, T. (1927), *The Roman Campagna in Classical Times*, London: E. Benn.

Audin, A. (1956), *Essai sur la Topographie de Lyon*, Lyon: Publication hors série de la Revue du Géographie de Lyon.

Audin, A. (1979a), *Lyon, Miroir de Rome*, Paris: Fayard.

Audin, A. (1979b), 'L'amphithéâtre des Trois Gaules à Lyon. Nouvelles campagnes de fouilles (1971–1972, 1976–1978)', *Gallia* 37: 85–100.

Audin, A, and Reynaud, J.-F. (1981), 'Le mur des bords de Saône et ses inscriptions antiques', *BMML* 6.2: 457–79.

Aupert, P. (1992), 'Sanxay (Vienne)', in Maurin, L. (ed.), *Villes et Agglomérations Urbaines Antiques du Sud-Ouest de la Gaule. Histoire et Archéologie* (Sixième supplément à *Aquitania*), Bordeaux: La Nef, pp. 163–6.

Aupert, P., Fincker, M. and Tassaux, F. (1998), 'Agglomérations secondaires de l'Aquitaine atlantique', in Gros, P. (ed.), *Villes et campagnes en Gaule romaine*, Paris: Éditions du CTHS, pp. 45–70.

Aurigemma, S. (1926), *I mosaici di Zliten*, Rome and Milan: Societa Editrice d'Arte Illustrata.

Baccrabère, G. (1974), *Le Rempart Antique de l'Institut Catholique de Toulouse* (Supplément au Bulletin de Littérature Ecclésiastique), Toulouse: Institut Catholique de Toulouse.

Baccrabère, G. (1977), *Étude de Toulouse Romaine* (Supplément au Bulletin de Littérature Ecclésiastique), Toulouse: Institut Catholique de Toulouse.

Baccrabère, G. (1988), *Le Sanctuaire Rural Antique d'Ancely, Commune de Toulouse* (Supplément au Bulletin de Littérature Ecclésiastique), Toulouse: Institut Catholique de Toulouse.

Baccrabère, G. (1990), 'La protohistorique à Ancely, et remarques sur les autres sites toulousains', *MSAM* 50: 6–83.

Baccrabère, G. (1996), 'Les fours de potiers du Ier siècle av. J.-C. à Ancely (Commune de Toulouse)', *MSAM* 56: 11–30.

Ballu, A. (1897), *Les ruines de Timgad (antique Thamugadi)*, Paris: Ernest Leroux.

Ballu, A. (1903), *Les ruines de Timgad (antique Thamugadi): nouvelles découvertes*, Paris: Ernest Leroux.

Ballu, A. (1911), *Les ruines de Timgad (antique Thamugadi): Sept années de découvertes 1903–1910*, Paris: Neurdein Frères.

Balmelle, C. (2001), *Les Demeures Aristocratiques d'Aquitaine. Société et culture de l'Antiquité tardive dans le Sud-Ouest de la Gaule* (Dixième supplément à *Aquitania*), Bordeaux and Paris: Éditions de Boccard.

Barbe, H. (1865), *Jublains (Mayenne). Note sur ses antiquités, époque gallo-romaine*, Le Mans: Monnoyer Frères.

Barraud, D. (1984), 'Rue des Frères-Bonie (Chronique d'archéologie bordelaise)', *BMSAB* 75: 6–7.

Barraud, D. and Gaidon, M.-A. (1985), 'Rue des Frères-Bonie (Chronique d'archéologie bordelaise)', *BMSAB* 76: 5.
Barraud, D. and Régaldo-Saint Blancard, P. (2000), 'Recherches récentes de Burdigala à Bordeaux', *Archéologia* 367: 56–65.
Barruol, G. (1968), 'Essai sur la topographie d'Apta Iulia', *RAN* 1: 101–58.
Barton, I.M. (1996), 'Palaces', in Barton, I. (ed.), *Roman Domestic Buildings*, Exeter: University of Exeter Press, pp. 91–120.
Bayard, D. and Massy, J.-L. (1983), *Amiens Romain. Samarobriva Ambianorum*, Picardie: Revue Archéologique de Picardie.
Bedon, R. (1984), *Les Carrières et les Carriers de la Gaule Romaine*, Paris: Picard.
Bedon, R. (ed.) (1998a), *Les Villes et Leurs Faubourgs en Gaule Romaine* (*Dossiers de l'Archéologie* 237), Dijon: Éditions Faton.
Bedon, R. (ed.) (1998b), *Suburbia: Les Faubourgs en Gaule Romaine et dans les Régions Voisines* (*Caesarodunum* 32), Limoges: PULIM.
Bedon, R. (1999), *Les Villes des Trois Gaules de César à Néron, dans leur contexte historique, territorial et politique*, Paris: Éditions Picard.
Bedon, R. (2001), *Atlas des Villes, Bourgs, Villages de France au Passé Romain*, Paris: Éditions Picard.
Bedon, R., Chevallier, R. and Pinon, P. (1988), *Architecture et Urbanisme en Gaule Romaine. Tome 2 – L'urbanisme (52 av. J.-C. – 486 ap. J.-C.)*, Paris: Éditions Errance.
Bénard, J. and Mangin, M. (1985), 'Les étapes de la romanisation d'une agglomération indigène du centre-est des Gaules: l'exemple d'Alésia', *Caesarodunum* 20: 103–15.
Bénard, J., Mangin, M., Goguey, R. and Roussel, L. (eds) (1994), *Les agglomérations antiques de Côte d'Or*, Paris: Les Belles Lettres.
Benoit, F. (1927), *Arles*, Lyon: Imprimerie A. Rey.
Benoit, F. (1954), 'Recherches archéologiques dans la région d'Aix-en-Provence', *Gallia* 12: 285–300.
Benoit, F. (1977), *Cimiez, la ville antique. Fouilles de Cemenelum I*, Paris: Éditions de Boccard.
Béraud, I., Gébara, C. and Rivet, L. (1998), *Fréjus Antique* (Guides Archéologiques de la France, no. 36), Paris: Imprimerie Nationale.
Bergmann, B. (2002), 'Art and nature in the villa at Oplontis', in McGinn, T. *et al.* (eds), *Pompeian Brothels . . .* (*JRA* supplement no. 47), Portsmouth, RI: Journal of Roman Archaeology, pp. 87–120.
Bergonzoni, F. and Bonova, G. (1976), *Bologna Romana*, Bologna: Istituto per la Storia di Bologna.
Bertrand, E. (2000), 'Les audacieux potiers gallo-romains de la Butte', *Archéologia* 371: 60–5.
Beschaouch, A. (1966), 'La mosaïque de chasse à l'amphithéâtre découverte à Smirat en Tunisie', *CRAI*: 134–57.
Bessac, J.-C. (1996), *La pierre en Gaule narbonnaise et les carrières du Bois de Lens (Nîmes). Histoire, archéologie, ethnographie et techniques* (*JRA* supplement no. 16), Ann Arbor, MI: Journal of Roman Archaeology.
Bianchi Bandinelli, R., et al. (1966), *The Buried City: Excavations at Leptis Magna*, London: Weidenfeld and Nicolson.
Biarne, J. (1987), 'Le Mans (annexe: Jublains)', in Pietri, L. and Biarne, J. (eds), *TCCG V – Province Ecclésiastique de Tours (Lugdunensis Tertia)*, Paris: Éditions de Boccard, pp. 41–56.

Billard, M., Clisson, J.-F., Henriet, J.-L., Lauranceau, N., Michaud, A., Trochut, J.-M., Vernou, C. and Vienne, G. (1983a), 'Fouille de sauvetage urgent de Champ Cloux, dans la prairie de la Palue', *BSAHCM* 10: 25–7.

Billard, M., Clisson, J.-F., Henriet, J.-L., Lauranceau, N., Michaud, A., Trochut, J.-M., Vernou, C. and Vienne, G. (1983b), 'Fouille de sauvetage urgent des ateliers municipaux, rue Daniel Massiou', *BSAHCM* 10: 34–7.

Blanckenhagen, P.H. von (1968), 'Daedalus and Icarus on Pompeian Walls', *MDAIR* 75: 106–145.

Blin, O. (1991), 'Roanne (Loire): les fouilles de la rue Charlieu en 1990. Lecture d'une occupation péri-urbaine du Ier au IIIe siècle ap. J.-C.', *RAC* 30: 163–74.

Boatwright, M. (1993), 'The city gate of Plancia Magna in Perge', in d'Ambra, E. (ed.), *Roman Art in Context: an Anthology*, New Jersey: Prentice Hall, pp. 189–207.

Bodel, J. (1994), *Graveyards and Groves. A Study of the Lex Lucerina* (=*AJAH* 11 (1986 [1994])), Cambridge, MA: American Journal of Ancient History.

Bodel, J. (1997) 'Monumental villas and villa monuments', *JRA* 10: 5–35.

Bodel, J. (2000), 'Dealing with the dead: undertakers, executioners and potters' fields in ancient Rome', in Hope, V.M. and Marshall, E. (eds), *Death and Disease in the Ancient City*, London and New York: Routledge, pp. 128–51.

Boissel, R. and Lavoquer, Y. (1943), 'Les fouilles du temple de Jublains (Mayenne) en 1942', *Gallia* 2: 266–73.

Bosio, L. (1983), *La Tabula Peutingeriana. Una descrizione pittorica del mondo antico*, Rimini: Maggioli Editore.

Bouet, A. (1998), 'Complexes sportifs et centres monumentaux en occident romain: les exemples d'Orange et Vienne', *RevArch* n.s. 1: 33–105.

Bouet, A. (2003), *Les thermes privés et publics en Gaule Narbonnaise*, Rome: École Française de Rome.

Bouet, A. and Carponsin-Martin, C. (1999), 'Enfin un sanctuaire "rural" chez les Pétrucores: Chamiers (Dordogne)', *Aquitania* 16: 183–249.

Bouley, E. (1983), 'Les théâtres cultuels de Belgique et des Germanies. Réflexions sur les ensembles architecturaux théâtres-temples', *Latomus* 42: 546–71.

Braudel, F. (1981), *Civilization and Capitalism, 15th–18th century. Volume I. The Structures of Everyday Life*, London: Collins.

Braund, S.H. (1989), 'City and country in Roman satire', in Braund, S.H. (ed.), *Satire and Society in Ancient Rome*, Exeter: Exeter University Press, pp. 23–47.

Brentchaloff, D. (1980), 'L'atelier de Pauvadou, une officine de potiers flaviens à Fréjus', *RAN* 13: 73–114.

Brothers, A.J. (1996), 'Urban housing', in Barton, I.M. (ed.), *Roman Domestic Buildings*, Exeter: University of Exeter Press, pp. 33–63.

Brown, P. (1981), *The Cult of the Saints: its rise and function in Latin Christianity*, Chicago, IL: University of Chicago Press.

Brühl, C.R. (1988), 'Problems of the continuity of Roman civitates in Gaul, as illustrated by the interrelation of cathedral and palatium', in Hodges, R. and Hobley, B. (eds), *The Rebirth of Towns in the West* (CBA Research Report 69), London: Council for British Archaeology: 43–6.

Brunt, P.A. (1976), 'The Romanisation of the local ruling classes in the Roman empire', in Pippidi, D.M. (ed.), *Assimilation et Résistance à la Culture Greco-Romaine dans le Monde Ancien*, Bucarest and Paris: Editura Academiei and Les Belles Lettres, pp. 161–73.

Brunt, P.A. (1980), 'Free labour and public works at Rome', *JRS* 70: 81–100.
Buisson, J.-F. (1989), 'Ateliers municipaux', *BSAHCM* 16: 20–1.
Burdy, J. (1993), 'L'eau à Lugdunum', in Pelletier, A. and Roussiaud, J. (eds), *Histoire de Lyon des origines à nos jours, vol. I*, Le Couteau: Éditions Horvath, pp. 133–61.
Burdy, J. (1996), *Lyon. L'Aqueduc Romain du Gier* (Preinventaire des Monuments et Richesses Artistiques, IV), Oullins: Bosc Frères.
Burdy, J. (2000), 'La protection antique des aqueducs', *Archéologia* 368: 54–7.
Burnham, B.C. and Wacher, J. (1990), *The 'Small Towns' of Roman Britain*, London: Batsford.
Campbell, J.B. (2000), *The Writings of the Roman Land Surveyors* (*JRS* monographs no. 9), London: Society for the Promotion of Roman Studies.
Canal, A. and Tourrenc, S. (1979), 'Les ateliers trouvés à Saint-Romain-en-Gal (Rhône)', *Figlina* 4: 85–94.
Carandini, A. (1985), 'Orti e fruttetti intorno a Roma', in *Misurare la terra: centurazione e coloni nel mondo romano. Città, agricoltura, commercio: materiali da Roma e dal suburbio*, Modena: Edizioni Panini, pp. 66–74.
Carder, J.N. (1978), *Art Historical Problems of a Roman Land Surveying Manuscript: The Codex Arcerianus A, Wolfenbüttel*, New York: Garland Publishing.
Carter, H. (1983), *An Introduction to Urban Historical Geography*, London: Edward Arnold.
Champeaux, J. (1982), *Fortuna. Recherches sur le culte de la Fortune à Rome et dans le monde romain des origines à la mort de César*, Rome: École Française de Rome.
Champlin, E. (1982), 'The suburbium of Rome', *AJAH* 7: 97–117.
Chardron-Picault, P. (1996), 'Autun-*Augustodunum*. Bilan des dernières découvertes', *Caesarodunum* 30 ('Les Villes de la Gaule Lyonnaise'): 35–57.
Chardron-Picault, P. and Pernot, M. (eds) (1999), *Un quartier d'artisanat métallurgique à Autun. Le site du Lycée militaire* (Documents d'Archéologie Française, no. 76), Paris: Éditions de la Maison des Sciences de l'Homme.
Chevallier, R. (1998), 'L'iconographie antique des faubourgs', *DossArch* 237: 84–7.
Chisholm, M. (1968), *Rural Settlement and Land Use: an essay in location*, London: Hutchinson.
Clarke, J.R. (1991), *The Houses of Roman Italy, 100 BC–AD 250: Ritual, Space and Decoration*, Berkeley and Los Angeles: University of California Press.
Clavel, M. (1970), *Béziers et son territoire dans l'Antiquité*, Paris, Les Belles Lettres.
Clavel-Lévêque, M. (1984), *L'Empire en Jeux. Espace Symbolique et Pratique Sociales dans le Monde Romain*, Paris: Éditions du CNRS.
Clisson, J.-F., Michaud, A., Surmely, M., Vernou, C. and Vienne, G. (1982), 'Fouille de sauvetage urgent du Champ Cloux, dans la prairie de la Palue', *BSAHCM* 9: 20–1.
Cloppet, C. (1998), 'Rapports ville-routes dans les *suburbia*', *DossArch* 237: 14–19.
Coarelli, F. (1986), 'L'urbs e il suburbio', in Giardina, A. (ed.), *Società Romana e Impero Tardoantico II. Roma Politica Economia Paesaggio Urbano*, Roma: Editori Laterza, pp. 1–58.
Collis, J.R. (1977), 'Pre-Roman burial rites in north-western Europe', in Reece, R. (ed.), *Burial in the Roman World* (CBA Research Report 22), London: Council for British Archaeology, pp. 1–13.
Collis, J.R. (1984), *Oppida: Earliest Towns North of the Alps*, Sheffield: Department of Prehistory and Archaeology.

Colyer, C. (1975), 'Excavations at Lincoln: First interim report, 1970–1972: The western defences of the lower town', *Antiquaries Journal* 55.2: 227–66.

Conges, G., Brun, J.-P., Roth-Conges, A., Bertucchi, G., Bremond, J. and Piton, J. (1992), 'L'Évolution d'un quartier suburbain d'Arles: l'Esplanade', *PH* 42: 119–33.

Corbier, M. (1991), 'City, territory and taxation', in Rich, J. and Wallace-Hadrill, A. (eds), *City and Country in the Ancient World*, London and New York: Routledge, pp. 211–39.

Corni, F. (1989), *Aosta Antica. La Città Romana*, Aosta: Tipografia Valdostana.

Cotton, M.A. and Métraux, G.P.R. (1985), *The San Rocco Villa at Francolise*, Hertford: British School at Rome.

Coulon, G. (1996), *Argentomagus. Du site gaulois à la ville gallo-romaine*, Paris: Éditions Errance.

Coupry, J. (1973), 'Informations Archéologiques (Plassac)', *Gallia* 31: 455–6.

Coupry, J. (1975), 'Informations Archéologiques (Plassac)', *Gallia* 33: 468–9.

Coupry, J. (1977), 'Informations Archéologiques (Plassac)', *Gallia* 35: 452.

Coupry, J. (1979), 'Informations Archéologiques (Plassac)', *Gallia* 37: 496–7.

Courtois (1951), *Timgad, antique Thamugadi*, Alger: Direction de l'Intérieur et des Beaux-Arts (Service des Antiquités).

Crawford, M.H. (1995), 'Roman towns and their charters: legislation and experience', in Cunliffe, B. and Keay, S. (eds), *Social Complexity and the Development of Towns in Iberia: From the Copper Age to the Second Century A.D.* (Proceedings of the British Academy, no. 86), Oxford: Oxford University Press, pp. 423–31.

Crawford, M.H. (1996), *Roman Statutes* (Bulletin of the Institute of Classical Studies Supplement no. 64), London: Institute of Classical Studies.

D'Arms, J.H. (2003), *Romans on the Bay of Naples and other essays on Roman Campania*, Bari: Edipuglia.

Dassié, J. (1975), 'Talmont l'antique, ville et port des saintongeois', *Archéologia* 89: 36–45.

DeLaine, J. (2000), 'Building the Eternal City: the construction industry of imperial Rome', in Coulston, J. and Dodge, H. (eds), *Ancient Rome: the Archaeology of the Eternal City*, Oxford: Oxford University School of Archaeology, pp. 119–41.

Delaval, E., Bellon, C., Chastel, J., Plassot, E. and Tranoy, L. (1995), *Vaise. Un Quartier de Lyon Antique* (Documents d'Archéologie en Rhône-Alpes, no. 11), Lyon: Service régional de l'archéologie de Rhône-Alpes.

Delmaire, R. (ed.) (1994), *Le Pas-de-Calais* (CAG 62/1), Paris: Académie des Inscriptions et Belles-Lettres.

De Maria, S. (1988), *Gli archi onorari di Roma e dell'Italia romana*, Roma: 'L'Erma' di Bretschneider.

Deru, X. and Grasset, L. (1997), 'The Roman pottery workshop in the Saint-Rémi district (Reims, Marne). Preliminary report', *RCRF* 35: 151–7.

Desbat, A. (1981), 'Note sur l'abandon de la ville haute de Lyon', in Walker, S. (ed.), *Récentes recherches en archéologie gallo-romaine et paléochrétienne sur Lyon et sa région* (BAR Int. Series no. 108), Oxford: BAR Publications.

Desbat, A. (1984), *Les Fouilles de la Rue des Farges à Lyon, 1974–1980*, Lyon: Groupe Lyonnais de Recherche en Archéologie Gallo-romaine.

Desbat, A. (1998), 'Colonia Copia Claudia Augusta Lugdunum – Lyon à l'époque claudienne', in Burnand, Y., Le Bohec, Y. and Martin, J.-P. (eds), *Claude de Lyon,*

Empereur Romain (Actes de Colloque Paris-Nancy-Lyon, novembre 1992), Paris: Presses de l'Université de Paris-Sorbonne, pp. 407–31.

Desbordes, J.-M. (1985), 'La typologie des sites urbains dans la cité des Lémovices', *Caesarodunum* 20 ('Les débuts de l'urbanisation en Gaule et dans les provinces voisines'): 145–56.

Descombes, F., Février, P.-A. and Gauthier, N. (1986), 'Vienne', in Gauthier, N. and Picard, J.-C. (eds), *TCCG III – Provinces Ecclésiastiques de Vienne et d'Arles (Viennensis et Alpes Graiae et Poeninae)*, Paris: Éditions de Boccard, pp. 17–35.

Dilke, O.A.W. (1985), *Greek and Roman Maps*, London: Thames & Hudson.

Di Matteo, F. and Granino Cercere, M.G. (2004), 'Ti. Claudii Suburbana Domus', in La Regina, A. (ed.), *Lexicon Topographicum Urbis Romae: Suburbium, Volume Secondo C-F*, Roma: Edizioni Quasar, pp. 108.

Domergue, C., Fincker, M. and Pailler, J.-M. (1990), 'L'amphithéâtre de Purpan. Esquisse d'étude architecturale et problèmes de chronologie', in Domergue, C., Landes, C. and Pailler, J.-M. (eds), *Spectacula I. Gladiateurs et Amphithéâtres* (Actes du colloque tenu à Toulouse et à Lattes les 25, 27, 28 et 29 mai 1987), Lattes: Éditions Imago, pp. 63–6.

Domergue, C., Landes, C. and Pailler, J.-M. (eds) (1990), *Spectacula I. Gladiateurs et Amphithéâtres* (Actes du colloque tenu à Toulouse et à Lattes les 25, 27, 28 et 29 mai 1987), Lattes: Éditions Imago.

Doreau, J., Golvin, J.-C. and Maurin, L. (1982), *L'Amphithéâtre Gallo-Romain de Saintes*, Paris: Éditions du CNRS.

Drinkwater, J.F. (1979) 'A note on local careers in the three Gauls under the early empire', *Britannia* 10: 89–100.

Drinkwater, J. (1983), *Roman Gaul. The Three Provinces, 58 BC–AD 260*, London and Canberra: Croom Helm.

Drinkwater, J. (1987), *The Gallic Empire: Separatism and Continuity in the Northwestern Provinces of the Roman Empire, AD 260–274* (Historia Einzelschrift 52), Stuttgart: Steiner-Verlag.

Drinkwater, J. and Elton, H. (eds) (1992), *Fifth-century Gaul: a crisis of identity?*, Cambridge: Cambridge University Press.

Dumasy, F. (1975), 'Les édifices théâtraux de type gallo-romain. Essai d'une définition', *Latomus* 34: 1010–19.

Dumasy, F. (1992a), 'Argenton-Saint-Marcel (Indre), Argentomagus', in Maurin, L. (ed.), *Villes et Agglomérations Urbaines Antiques du Sud-Ouest de la Gaule. Histoire et Archéologie* (Sixième supplément à *Aquitania*), Bordeaux: La Nef, pp. 24–30.

Dumasy, F. (1992b), '*Argentomagus*: d'un théâtre à l'autre', in Landes, C. (ed.), *Spectacula II. Le théâtre antique et ses spectacles* (Actes du colloque tenu au Musée archéologique Henri Prades de Lattes les 27, 28, 29 et 30 avril 1989), Lattes: Imago, pp. 21–7.

Dumasy, F. (1995), 'Recherches récentes à *Argentomagus*-Saint-Marcel (Indre)', *RevArch* n.s. 95.1: 199–205.

Dumasy, F. and collaborators (1989), 'Petit atlas des édifices de spectacles en Gaule Romaine', in Landes, C. (ed.), *Le Goût du théâtre à Rome et en Gaule Romaine*, Lattes: Imago, pp. 43–75.

Dumasy, F. and Fincker, M. (1992), 'Les édifices de spectacle', in Maurin, L. (ed.), *Villes et Agglomérations Urbaines Antiques du Sud-Ouest de la Gaule. Histoire et Archéologie* (Sixième supplément à *Aquitania*), Bordeaux: La Nef, pp. 293–321.

BIBLIOGRAPHY

Dunbabin, K.M.D. (1978), *The Mosaics of Roman North Africa: Studies in Iconography and Patronage*, Oxford: Clarendon Press.

Duncan-Jones, R.P. (1985), 'Who paid for public buildings in Roman cities?', in Grew F. and Hobley, B. (eds), *Roman Urban Topography in Britain and the Western Empire*, London: Council for British Archaeology, pp. 28–33.

Elton, H. (1992), 'Defence in fifth-century Gaul', in Drinkwater, J. and Elton, H. (eds), *Fifth-century Gaul: a crisis of identity?*, Cambridge: Cambridge University Press, pp. 167–76.

Esmonde Cleary, S. (1985), 'The quick and the dead: suburbs, cemeteries, and the town', in Grew, F. and Hobley, B. (eds), *Roman Urban Topography in Britain and the Western Empire*, London: Council for British Archaeology.

Esmonde Cleary, S. (1987), *Extra-Mural Areas of Romano-British Towns* (BAR British Series 169), Oxford: BAR publications.

Fauduet, I. (1982), *Argentomagus (Saint-Marcel). 20 ans de recherches archéologiques (1962–1982)*, Chauvigny: Association des Publications Chauvinoises.

Fauduet, I. (1993), *Les Temples de la Tradition Celtique en Gaule Romaine*, Paris: Éditions Errance.

Fauduet, I. and Bertin, D. (1993), *Atlas des Sanctuaires Romano-Celtiques de Gaule*, Paris: Éditions Errance.

Favro, D. (1996), *The urban image of Augustan Rome*, Cambridge: Cambridge University Press.

Ferdière, A. (1975a), 'Notes de la céramologie de la région centre VII. Les ateliers de potiers gallo-romains de la région centre', *RAC* 14: 85–111.

Ferdière, A. (1975b), 'Compte rendu de fouilles préliminaires (septembre-octobre 1974) à Bourges-Lazenay', *CAHB* 40: 11–8.

Ferdière, A. (1977), 'Découverte d'un quai romain à Bourges, "Lazenay" (Cher)', *Caesarodunum* 12 ('Géographie commerciale de la Gaule'): 326–32.

Ferdière, A. (2005), *Les Gaules. IIe s. av. J.-C. – Ve s. ap. J.-C.*, Paris: Armand Colin.

Février, P.-A. (1980), 'Vetera et nova', in Duby, G. (ed.), *Histoire de la France Urbaine I. La ville antique*, Paris: Éditions du Seuil, pp. 393–494

Février, P.-A. and Leyge, F. (eds) (1986), *Premiers Temps Chrétiennes en Gaule Méridionale: Antiquité Tardive et Haut Moyen Ages, IIIeme – VIIIeme siècles*, Lyon: Association Lyonnaise de Sauvetage des Sites Archéologiques Medievaux.

Fiches, J.-L. (ed.) (1989), *L'oppidum d'Ambrussum et son territoire. Fouilles au quartier du Sablas (Villetelle, Hérault): 1979–1985* (Monographie du CRA no. 2), Paris: Éditions du CNRS.

Fiches, J.-L. (ed.) (2002), *Les agglomerations gallo-romaines en Languedoc-Roussillon: projet collectif de recherche (1993–1999)*, Lattes: Association pour le développement de l'archéologie en Languedoc-Roussillon.

Fiches, J.-L. and Veyrac, A. (eds) (1996), *Nîmes* (CAG 30/1), Paris: Académie des Inscriptions et Belles-Lettres.

Filippo, R. de (1993), 'Nouvelle définition de l'enceinte romaine de Toulouse', *Gallia* 50: 183–204.

Finley, M.I. (1977), 'The ancient city: from Fustel de Coulanges to Max Weber and beyond', *Comparative Studies in Society and History* 19: 305–27.

Finley, M.I. (1985), *The Ancient Economy* (2nd edn), Harmondsworth: Penguin.

Fishwick, D. (1987–92), *The Imperial Cult in the Latin West*, Leiden: E.J. Brill.

Floriani Squarciapino, M. (1966), *Leptis Magna*, Basel: Raggi.

Fontan, J.-C. and Roth Congès, A. (1999), 'Mise en valeur et études récentes à Glanum', *Archéologia* 359: 36–47.
Fouet, G. (1969), *La villa Gallo-romaine de Montmaurin*, Paris: Éditions du CNRS.
Fouqueray, B. and Neiss, R. (1976), 'La Porte Bazée à Reims, premier essai de reconstitution', *Études Champenoises* 2: 5–26.
Franciscis, A. de (1975), 'La villa Romana di Oplontis', in Andreae, A. and Kyrieleis, H. (eds), *Neue Forschungen in Pompeji*, Recklinghausen: Aurel Bongers, pp. 9–17.
Fraschetti, A. (1999), 'Regiones Quattuordecim (Storia)', in Steinby, E.M. (ed.), *Lexicon Topographicum Urbis Romae, vol. Quarto, P-S*, Roma: Edizioni Quasar, pp. 197–9.
Frayn, J.M. (1979), *Subsistence Farming in Roman Italy*, London: Centaur Press.
Frayn, J.M. (1993), *Markets and Fairs in Roman Italy*, Oxford: Clarendon Press.
Frere, S.S. (1962), 'Excavations at Verulamium, 1961. Sixth and final interim report', *Antiquaries Journal* 42: 148–59.
Frere, S.S. (1985), 'Civic pride: a factor in Roman town planning', in Grew F. and Hobley, B. (eds), *Roman Urban Topography in Britain and the Western Empire*, London: Council for British Archaeology, pp. 34–6.
Frézouls, E. (1973), 'Informations: Château-Porcien', *Gallia* 31.2: 394–8.
Frézouls, E. (1975), 'Informations: Château-Porcien', *Gallia* 33.2: 387.
Frézouls, E. (1977), 'Informations: Château-Porcien', *Gallia* 35.2: 391–2.
Frézouls, E. (ed.) (1982), *Les Villes Antiques de la France I. Belgique 1. Amiens – Beauvais – Grand – Metz*, Strasbourg: AECR, pp. 7–106.
Frézouls, E. (1984), 'Évergétisme et construction urbaine dans les Trois Gaules et les Germanies', *RdN* 66: 27–54.
Frézouls, E. (ed.) (1988), *Les villes antiques de la France II.1. Germanie Supérieure. Besançon, Dijon, Langres, Mandeure*, Strasbourg: AECR.
Frézouls, E. (1990), 'Les monuments des spectacles dans la ville: théâtre et amphithéâtre', Domergue, C., Landes, C. and Pailler, J.-M. (eds), *Spectacula – I. Gladiateurs et Amphithéâtres* (Actes du colloque tenu à Toulouse et à Lattes, les 26, 27, 28, et 29 mai 1987), Lattes: Éditions Imago, pp. 77–92.
Fulford, M.G. (1982), 'Town and country in Roman Britain – a parasitical relationship', in Miles, D. (ed.), *The Romano-British Countryside* (BAR British Series 103), Oxford: BAR Publications, pp. 403–19.
Futrell, A. (1997), *Blood in the Arena: The Spectacle of Roman Power*, Austin, TX: University of Texas Press.
Gaidon, M.-A. (1986a), 'Bordeaux, Parunis. Sauvetage programmé', *ArchAqui* 5: 23–7.
Gaidon, M.-A. (1986b), 'Bordeaux, Parunis (Chronique d'Archéologie Bordelaise)', *BMSAB* 77: 7–20.
Gaidon-Bunuel, M.-A., Barraud, D. and Lerat-Hardy, M.-C. (1991), 'U.A.S.O.: 12, rue de Cursol (Chronique d'archéologie bordelaise)', *BMSAB* 82: 8–11.
Galliou, P. (1984), *L'Armorique romaine*, Braspars: Bibliophiles de Bretagne.
Galliou, P. (1989), *Finistère* (CAG 29), Paris: Academie des Inscriptions et Belles-Lettres.
Garmy, P., Faravel, S. and Pichonneau, J.-F. (1992), 'Saint-Germain-d'Esteuil (Gironde); Brion', in Maurin, L. (ed.), *Villes et Agglomérations Urbaines Antiques du Sud-Ouest de la Gaule. Histoire et Archéologie* (Sixième supplément à *Aquitania*), Bordeaux: La Nef, pp. 145–9.

BIBLIOGRAPHY

Garmy, P. and Leveau, P. (2002), 'Présentation du dossier: *villa* et *vicus* en Narbonnaise, un débat', *RAN* 35: 1–3.

Garmy, P. and Maurin, L. (eds) (1996), *Enceintes romaines d'Aquitaine. Bordeaux, Dax, Périgueux, Bazas* (Documents d'Archéologie Française, no. 53), Paris: Éditions de la Maison des Sciences de l'Homme.

Garnsey, P.D.A. (1979), 'Where did Italian peasants live?', *PCPS* n.s. 25: 1–25.

Gauthier, N. (1986a), 'Metz', in Gauthier, N. and Picard, J.-C. (eds), *TCCG I – Province Ecclésiastique de Trèves (Belgica Prima)*, Paris: Éditions de Boccard, pp. 13–32.

Gauthier, N. (1986b), 'Trèves', in Gauthier, N. and Picard, J.-C. (eds), *TCCG I – Province Ecclésiastique de Trèves (Belgica Prima)*, Paris: Éditions de Boccard, pp. 33–53.

Gauthier, M. (1986c), 'Informations Archéologique', *Gallia* 44: 388.

Gauthier, M. and Debord, P. (1982), *Bordeaux Saint-Christoly. Sauvetage Archéologique et Histoire Urbaine*, Bordeaux: Direction des Antiquités Historiques d'Aquitaine.

Gayraud, M. (1981), *Narbonne antique des origines à la fin du IIIe siècle* (Revue Archéologique de Narbonnaise, suppl. 8), Paris: Diffusion de Boccard.

Gazenbeek, M. (1998), 'Prospections systématiques autour de *Glanum* (Bouches-du-Rhône): l'extension de l'agglomération', *Caesarodunum* 32 ('*Suburbia*: les faubourgs en Gaule romaine et dans les regions voisines'): 83–103.

Gazenbeek, M. (2000) 'Interaction entre aqueduc et habitat rural: deux cas d'étude en France méditerranéenne: Nîmes et Arles', in Jansen, G.C.M. (ed.), *Cura aquarum in Sicilia* (Proceedings of the Tenth International Congress on the History of Water Management and Hydraulic Engineering in the Mediterranean Region, Syracuse May 1998), Leiden: Stichting Babesch.

Geffroy, A. (1878), 'L'archéologie du lac Fucin', *Revue Archéologique* 1878.2: 1–11.

Giddens, A. (1984), *The Constitution of Society: Outline of the Theory of Structuration*, Oxford: Polity Press.

Godard, C. (1995), 'Quatre niveaux d'abandon de la ville de Vienne (Isère): éléments pour la chronologie des céramiques de la fin du IIe et du IIIe siècle après J.-C.', in Rivet, L. (ed.), *Société Française d'Étude de la Céramique Antique en Gaule* (Actes du Congrès de Rouen, 25–28 mai 1995), Marseille: SFECAG, pp. 285–322.

Golvin, J.-C. (1988), *L'amphithéâtre romain. Essai sur la théorisation de sa forme et de ses functions*, Paris: Diffusion de Boccard.

González, J. (1986), 'The Lex Irnitana: a new copy of the Flavian municipal law', *JRS* 76: 147–243.

Goodman, P.J. (2002), 'The provincial sanctuaries of the imperial cult at Lyon and Narbonne: examples of urban exclusion or social inclusion?', in Muskett, G., Koltsida, A. and Georgiadis, M. (eds), *Symposium on Mediterranean Archaeology 2001, Proceedings* (BAR Int. Series 1040), Oxford: Archaeopress, pp. 91–104.

Goudineau, C. (1980a), 'Les antécedents: y a-t-il une ville protohistorique? La Gaule méridionale', in Duby, G. (ed.), *Histoire de la France Urbaine I. La ville antique*, Paris: Éditions du Seuil, pp. 141–93.

Goudineau, C. (1980b), 'Les villes de la paix romaine', in Duby, G. (ed.), *Histoire de la France Urbaine I. La ville antique*, Paris: Éditions du Seuil, pp. 233–391.

Goudineau, C. (1982), 'Une fouille récente à la périphérie de Forum Julii: le chantier des Aiguières', *CRAI*: 279–92.

Grahame, M. (1997), 'Towards a theory of Roman urbanism: beyond economics and ideal-types', in Meadows, K., Lemke, C. and Heron, J. (eds), *Proceedings of the Sixth Annual Theoretical Roman Archaeology Conference*, Oxford: Oxbow Books, pp. 151–62.

Grant, E. (ed.) (1986), *Central Places, Archaeology and History*, Sheffield: Sheffield University Print Unit.

Greene, K. (1986), *The Archaeology of the Roman Economy*, London: Batsford.

Grenier, A. (1958), *Manuel d'archéologie gallo-romaine. Troisième partie: L'Architecture*, Paris: Picard.

Grimal, M.P. (1959), 'L'enceinte servienne dans l'histoire urbaine de Rome', *Mélanges d'Archéologie et d'Histoire* 71: 43–64.

Gros, P. (1992), 'Moenia: aspects défensif et aspects représentatifs des fortifications', in Van de Maele, S. and Forsse, J.M. (eds), *Fortificationes antiquae*, Amsterdam: Gieben, pp. 211–25.

Gros, P. (1998), 'Villes et "non-villes": les ambiguïtés de la hiérarchie juridique et de l'aménagement urbain', in Gros, P. (ed.), *Villes et campagnes en Gaule romaine*, Paris: Éditions du CTHS, pp. 11–25.

Gruen, E. (1990), 'The imperial policy of Augustus', in Raaflaub, K.A. and Toher, K. (eds), *Between Republic and Empire: interpretations of Augustus and his principate*, Berkeley and Los Angeles: University of California Press.

Gruyer, J. (1967), 'Le nymphée de la Solitude à Lyon', *BMML* 4.3: 43–54.

Guidi, G. (1933), 'La Villa del Nilo', *Africa Italiana* 5: 1–56.

Guyard, L. (1996), 'Lutece: la période proto-urbaine et l'installation du cardo', *Caesarodunum* 30 ('Les villes de la Gaule Lyonnaise'): 237–40.

Guyard, L. (1998a), 'Le faubourg nord de Lutèce', *DossArch* 237: 42–51.

Guyard, L. (1998b), 'Paris: le faubourg nord de Lutèce', *Caesarodunum* 32 ('*Suburbia*. Les faubourgs en Gaul Romaine et dans les Régions Voisines'): 163–80.

Guyon, J. (1986), 'Aix-en-Provence', in Gauthier, N. and Picard, J.-C. (eds), *TCCG II – Provinces Ecclésiastiques d'Aix et d'Embrun* (*Narbonensis Secunda et Alpes Maritimae*), Paris: Éditions de Boccard, pp. 17–28.

Guyon, J. (1992), 'Saint-Bertrand-de-Comminges, Valcabrère (Haute-Garonne). Lugdunum, Civitas Convenarum', in Maurin, L. (ed.), *Villes et Agglomérations Urbaines Antiques du Sud-Ouest de la Gaule. Histoire et Archéologie* (Sixième supplément à *Aquitania*), Bordeaux: La Nef, pp. 140–5.

Guyon, J. and contributors (1991), 'From *Lugdunum* to *Convenae*: recent work on Saint-Bertrand-de-Comminges (Haute-Garonne)', *JRA* 4: 89–122.

Guyon, J., Boissairt-Camus, B. and Souilhac, V. (1992), 'Topographie chrétienne des agglomérations', in Maurin, L. (ed.), *Villes et Agglomérations Urbaines Antiques du Sud-Ouest de la Gaule. Histoire et Archéologie* (Sixième supplément à *Aquitania*), Bordeaux: La Nef, pp. 391–430.

Halbout-Bertin, D. (1979), 'Place de la Haute Vieille-Tour', *Archéologia* 136: 34–43.

Hall, P. (ed.) (1966), *Von Thünen's Isolated State: an English Translation of 'Der isolierte Staat' by C.M. Wartenberg*, Oxford: Pergamon Press.

Hallier, G. and Sintès, C. (1987), 'Le cirque romain', in Sintès, C. (ed.), *Du Nouveau Sur l'Arles Antique* (Catalogue d'Exposition), Arles, Hommage des Musées d'Arles, pp. 56–65.

Hanson, J.A. (1959), *Roman Theater-Temples*, Princeton, NJ: Princeton University Press.

Hanson, W.S. (1988), 'Administration, urbanisation and acculturation in the Roman

West', in Braund, D.C. (ed.), *The Administration of the Roman Empire, 241 BC–AD 193*, Exeter: University of Exeter Press, pp. 53–68.

Hanson, W.S. (1997), 'Forces of change and methods of control', in Mattingly, D. (ed.), *Dialogues in Roman Imperialism* (*JRA* supplement no. 23), Portsmouth, RI: Journal of Roman Archaeology, pp. 76–90.

Harmand (1958), 'Le sanctuaire gallo-romaine de la Motte du Ciar à Sens', *RAE* 9: 43–73.

Harries, J. (1992a), 'Christianity and the city in Late Roman Gaul', in Rich, J. (ed.), *The City in Late Antiquity*, London: Routledge, pp. 77–98.

Harries, J. (1992b), 'Sidonius Apollinaris, Rome and the barbarians: a climate of treason?', in Drinkwater, J. and Elton, H. (eds), *Fifth-century Gaul: a crisis of identity?*, Cambridge: Cambridge University Press, pp. 298–308.

Heijmans, M. (1991), 'Nouvelles recherches sur les cryptoportiques d'Arles et la topographie du centre de la colonie', *RAN* 24: 161–99.

Heijmans, M. (1996), 'L'abandon des quartiers périphériques d'Arles', in Fiches, J.-L. (ed.), *Le IIIe siècle en Gaule Narbonnaise. Données régionales sur la crise de l'Empire* (Actes de la table ronde du GDR954), Sophia Antipolis: Éditions APDCA, pp. 121–33.

Heijmans, M. and Sintès, C. (1994), 'L'évolution de la topographie de l'Arles antique. Un état de la question', *Gallia* 51: 135–70.

Heinen, H. (1984), 'Auguste en Gaule et les origines de la ville romaine de Trèves', in Walter, H. (ed.), *Hommages à Lucien Lerat*, Paris: Les Belles Lettres, pp. 329–48.

Heinen, H. (1985), *Trier und das Trevererland in Römischer Zeit*, Trier: Spee-Verlag.

Henderson, J. (2003), 'Portrait of the Artist as a Figure of Style: P.L.I.N.Y's Letters', in Morello, R. and Gibson, R. (eds), *Arethusa Special Issue: Re-Imagining Pliny the Younger* (Volume 36, Number 2), Baltimore, MD and London: Johns Hopkins University Press, pp. 115–25.

Hesse, A. and Renimel, S. (1979), 'Can we survey the limits of an archaeological site? The example of Saint-Romain-en-Gal (France)', in *Archaeo-Physiko 10* (Proceedings of the 18th International Symposium on Archaeometry and Archaeological Prospection, Bonn, 14–17 March, 1978), Bonn: Rheinisches Landesmuseum, pp. 638–46.

Hillier, B. and Hanson, J. (1984), *The Social Logic of Space*, Cambridge: Cambridge University Press.

Hodder, I. and Millett, M. (1980), 'Romano-British villas and towns: a systematic analysis', *World Archaeology* 12: 69–76.

Hoffer, S. (1999), *The Anxieties of Pliny the Younger* (American Classical Studies, no. 43), Atlanta: American Philological Association.

Holmgren, J. and Leday, A. (1980), 'Château de Lazenay', *CAHB* 60: 7, 15 and 17.

Hope, V.M. (2000), 'Contempt and respect: the treatment of the corpse in ancient Rome', in Hope, V.M. and Marshall, E. (eds), *Death and Disease in the Ancient City*, London: Routledge, pp. 104–27.

Hopkins, K. (1978), 'Economic growth and towns in classical antiquity', in Abrams, P. and Wrigely, E.A. (eds), *Towns in Societies*, Cambridge: Cambridge University Press, pp. 35–77.

Hopkins, K. (1980), 'Taxes and trade in the Roman empire (200 BC–AD 400)', *JRS* 70: 101–25.

BIBLIOGRAPHY

Horden, P. and Purcell, N. (2000), *The Corrupting Sea: A study of Mediterranean history*, Oxford: Blackwell.

Hosdez, C., Jacques, A. and Tuffreau-Libre, M. (1992), 'La villa suburbaine du Mont Saint-Vaast à Arras', *BCPdC* 13.2: 305–48.

Humphrey, J.H. (1986), *Roman Circuses: Arenas for Chariot Racing*, London: Batsford.

Internet Group Ostia (1996–2006), *Ostia – Harbour City of Ancient Rome*: <http://www.ostia-antica.org/> (accessed 30 March 2006).

Jacques, F. (1991), 'Statut et fonction des conciliabula d'après les sources latines', in Brunaux, J.-L. (ed.), *Les sanctuaires celtiques et le monde méditerranéen*, Paris: Éditions Errance, pp. 58–65.

Johnson, S. (1983), *Late Roman Fortifications*, London: Batsford.

Jones, G.D.B. (1962), 'Capena and the Ager Capenas', *PBSR* 30: 116–207.

Jones, G.D.B. (1963), 'Capena and the Ager Capenas Part II', *PBSR* 31: 100–58.

Jones, M.J. (1980), *The Defences of the Upper Roman Enclosure* (Lincoln Archaeological Trust Monograph Series VII–1), London: Lincoln Archaeological Trust.

Jones, M.J. (ed.) (1981), 'Excavations at Lincoln: Third interim report: Sites outside the walled city', *Antiquaries Journal* 61.1: 83–114.

Jones, M.J. (1992), 'Roman Lincoln', in Whitwell, J.B. (ed.), *Roman Lincolnshire* (2nd edn), Lincoln: History of Lincolnshire Committee, pp. xvii–xxiv.

Jones, M.J. (1999), 'Roman Lincoln: changing perspectives', in Hurst, H. (ed.), *The Coloniae of Roman Britain: New Studies and a Review* (*JRA* supplement no. 36), Portsmouth, RI: Journal of Roman Archaeology, pp. 101–12.

Jongman, W. (1988), *The Economy and Society of Pompeii*, Amsterdam: Gieben.

Jospin, J.-P. (1982), 'Quelques aspects du quartier sud de Vienne dans l'antiquité', *BSAV* 77.1: 5–22.

Joulin, L. (1901), *Les etablissements gallo-romaines de la plaine de Martres-Tolosanes*, Paris: Imprimerie Nationale.

Kaiser, A. (2000), *The Urban Dialogue. An Analysis of the Use of Space in the Roman City of Empúries, Spain* (BAR Int. Series 901), Oxford: Archaeopress.

Keene, D.J. (1976), 'Suburban growth', in Barley, M.W. (ed.), *The Plans and Topography of Medieval Towns in England and Wales* (Council for British Archaeology Research Report no. 14), Leamington: Council for British Archaeology, pp. 71–82.

Kérébel, H. (1996), 'Évolution d'un chef-lieu de cité au cours de la première moitié du Ier siècle: Corseul (Fanum Martis), capitale de la cité des Coriosolites', *Caesarodunum* 30 ('Les Villes de la Gaule Lyonnaise'): 59–78.

Kérébel, H. (2000), 'Corseul, capitale gallo-romain', *Archéologia* 364: 28–9.

King, L.J. (1984), *Central Place Theory*, Beverly Hills: Sage Publications.

Koeppel, G. (1969), '*Profectio* und *adventus*', *Bonner Jahrbücher* 169: 130–94.

Kolendo, J. (1981), 'La répartition des places aux spectacles et la stratification sociale dans l'Empire Romain', *Ktéma* 6: 301–15.

Kolendo, J. (1994), 'Praedia suburbana e loro reddività', in Carlsen, J. Ørsted, P. and Skydsgaard, J.E. (eds), *Landuse in the Roman Empire*, Roma: 'L'Erma' di Bretschneider, pp. 59–71.

Kondoleon, C. (1999), 'Timing spectacles: Roman domestic art and performance', in Bergmann, B. and Kondoleon, C. (eds), *The Art of Spectacle*, New Haven, CT and London: Yale University Press, pp. 321–41.

Kruta, V. (1980), 'Les antécedents: y a-t-il une ville protohistorique? La Gaule

intérieure', in Duby, G. (ed.), *Histoire de la France Urbaine I. La ville antique*, Paris: Éditions du Seuil, pp. 195–229.
Küpper-Böhm, A. (1996), *Die Römischen Bogenmonumente der Gallia Narbonensis in ihrem Urbanen Kontext*, Espelkamp: Verlag Marie Leidorf GmbH.
Kyle, D.G. (1998), *Spectacles of Death in Ancient Rome*, London: Routledge.
Laborde, A. (1957–59), 'Villa gallo-romaine d'Evaux', *MSSNAC* 33: 504–7.
Labrousse, M. (1937), 'Le *pomerium* de la Rome impériale', *Mélanges d'Archéologie et d'Histoire* 54: 165–99.
Lancha, J. (1981), *Recueil Général des Mosaïques de la Gaule III. Province de Narbonnaise 2 – Vienne*, Paris: Éditions du CNRS.
Lançon, B. (2000), *Rome in Late Antiquity*, Edinburgh: Edinburgh University Press.
Landes, C. (ed.) (1989), *Le Goût du théâtre à Rome et en Gaule Romaines*, Lattes: Imago.
Langouët, L. (1985), 'Un *vicus* routier et portuaire à Taden (Côtes-du-Nord), sur les bords de la Rance', *RAO* 2: 73–82.
Langouët, L. and Goulpeau, L. (1984), 'La datation archéomagnetique du temple du Haut-Bécherel à Corseul', *RAO* 1: 85–8.
Laporte, J.-P. (1996), 'Meaux gallo-romain', *Caesarodunum* 30 ('Les Villes de la Gaule Lyonnaise'): 179–224.
La Regina, A. *et al.* (eds) (2001), *Lexicon Topographicum Urbis Romae: Suburbium, Volume Primo A-B*, Roma: Edizioni Quasar.
La Regina, A. *et al.* (eds) (2004), *Lexicon Topographicum Urbis Romae: Suburbium, Volume Secondo C-F*, Roma: Edizioni Quasar.
La Regina, A. *et al.* (eds) (2005), *Lexicon Topographicum Urbis Romae: Suburbium, Volume Terzo G-L*, Roma: Edizioni Quasar.
La Rocca, E. (2000), 'L'affresco con veduta di città dal colle Oppio', in Fentress, E. (ed.), *Romanisation and the City: Creation, Dynamics and Failures* (*JRA* supplement no. 38), Portsmouth, RI: Journal of Roman Archaeology, pp. 57–72.
Laroche, C. and Savay-Guerraz, H. (1984), *Saint-Romain-en-Gal: Un quartier de Vienne antique sur la rive droite du Rhône* (Guides Archéologique de la France, no. 2), Paris: Imprimerie Nationale.
Lassus, L. (1969), *Visite à Timgad*, Alger: Ministere de l'Éducation Nationale.
Laurence, R. (1994), *Roman Pompeii: Space and Society*, London: Routledge.
Laurence, R. (1999) *The Roads of Roman Italy: Mobility and Cultural Change*, London: Routledge.
Lavendhomme, M.-O. and Guichard, V. (1997), *Rodumna (Roanne, Loire), le village gaulois* (Documents d'Archéologie Française, no. 62), Paris: Éditions de la Maison des Sciences de l'Homme.
Leblanc, O. and Savay-Guerraz, H. (1996), 'Chronologie de l'abandon du site de Saint-Romain-en-Gal (Rhône)', in Fiches, J.-L. (ed.), *Le IIIe siècle en Gaule Narbonnaise. Données régionales sur la crise de l'Empire* (Actes de la table ronde du GDR954), Sophia Antipolis: Éditions APDCA, pp. 103–19.
Le Bot, A. (1981), 'Sainte-Colombe: fouilles de sauvetage programmé et intégration des vestiges', *BSAV* 76.4: 53–64.
Le Bot-Helly, A. (1987), 'L'Enceinte de Vienne', *BEAN* 18: 51–61.
Le Bot-Helly, A. (1991), 'Vienne, cours Brillier. Sauvetage urgent', in Direction Régionale des Affaires Culturelles Rhône-Alpes. Service Régional de l'Archéologie, *Bilan Scientifique*: 75–6.
Le Bot-Helly, A. and Helly, B. (1999), 'Vienne, contraintes hydrologiques et

BIBLIOGRAPHY

aménagements des rives du Rhône. De la *komè* allobroge à la ville du Haut-Empire', *Gallia* 56: 73–9.

Leday, A. (1980), *La campagne à l'époque romaine dans le centre de la Gaule* (BAR Int. Series no. 73), Oxford: BAR Publications.

Lefebvre, C. and Wagner, P. (1984), 'Metz antique. Remarques sur le connaissance de l'organisation spatiale du fait urbain', *RAP* 3–4: 149–69.

Le Gall, J. (1991), 'La muraille servienne sous le Haut-Empire', in Hinard, F. and Royo, M. (eds), *Rome. L'Espace Urbaine et ses Représentations*, Paris, Presses de l'Université Paris-Sorbonne, pp. 55–63.

Le Glay, M. (1981), 'Les jardins à Vienne', in MacDougall, E.B. and Jashemski, W.F. (eds), *Ancient Roman Gardens* (Seventh Dumbarton Oaks Colloquium on the History of Landscape Architecture), Washington: Dumbarton Oaks, pp. 51–65.

Le Glay, M. (1990), 'Les amphithéâtres: *Loci religiosi?*', in Domergue, C., Landes, C. and Pailler, J.-M. (eds), *Spectacula I. Gladiateurs et Amphithéâtres* (Actes du colloque tenu à Toulouse et à Lattes les 25, 27, 28 et 29 mai 1987), Lattes: Éditions Imago, pp. 217–30.

Le Glay, M. and Tourrenc, S. (1971), 'L'originalité de l'architecture domestique à Vienne d'après les découvertes récentes de Saint-Romain-en-Gal (Rhône)', *CRAI*: 764–73.

Lemaitre, C. (1996), 'Noviomagus Lexoviorum. Réflexion sur les origines de Lisieux', *Caesarodunum* 30 ('Les Villes de la Gaule Lyonnaise'): 133–65.

Lemaitre, C. (1998a), 'Le Vieux-Lisieux, ville ou sanctuaire suburbain?', *DossArch* 237: 58–63.

Lemaitre, C. (1998b), 'Le Vieux-Lisieux: ville ou sanctuaire suburbain? Premières réflexions', *Caesarodunum* 32 ('*Suburbia*. Les Faubourgs en Gaule Romaine et dans les Régions Voisines'): 125–45.

Lémant, J.-P. (1991a), *Charleville-Mézières, l'apport de l'archéologie*, Paris: Éditions Bonneton.

Lémant, J.-P. (1991b), *Archéologie Ardenne, vestiges romains dans la région de Charleville-Mézières*, Bruxelles: Crédit communal.

Le Masne de Chermont, N. (1987), 'Les fouilles de l'ancien évêché de Poitiers', *Aquitania* 5: 149–75.

Lepper, F. and Frere, S.S. (1988), *Trajan's Column: A new edition of the Cichorius plates. Introduction, commentary and notes*, Gloucester: Alan Sutton.

Leveau, P. (1984), *Caesarea de Maurétanie: une ville romaine et ses campagnes* (Collection de l'École Francaise de Rome 70), Rome: École Francaise de Rome.

Leveau, P. (1993), 'Agglomérations secondaires et territoires en Gaule Narbonnaise', *RAN* 26: 277–99.

Leveau, P. (1994), 'La recherche sur les agglomérations secondaires en Gaule Narbonnaise', in Petit, J.-P., Mangin, M. and Brunella, P. (eds), *Les agglomérations secondaires. La Gaule Belgique, les Germanies et l'Occident romain*, Paris: Éditions Errance, pp. 181–93.

Leveau, P. (1996), 'The Barbegal water mill and its environment: archaeology and the economic and social history of antiquity', *JRA* 9: 137–53.

Levi, A.C. and Levi, M. (1967), *Itineraria Picta. Contributo allo studio della Tabula Peutingeriana*, Roma: 'L'Erma' di Bretschneider.

Levick, B.M. (1967), *Roman Colonies in Southern Asia Minor*, Oxford: Clarendon Press.

Liebeschuetz, W. (1992), 'The end of the ancient city', in Rich, J. (ed.), *The City in Late Antiquity*, London and New York: Routledge.

Ligt, L. de (1993), *Fairs and Markets in the Roman Empire*, Amsterdam: J.C. Gieben.

Lindsay, H. (2000), 'Death-pollution and funerals in the city of Rome', in Hope, V.M. and Marshall, E. (eds), *Death and Disease in the Ancient City*, London: Routledge, pp. 152–73.

Ling, R. (1991), *Roman Painting*, Cambridge: Cambridge University Press.

Lintz, G. (1984–86), 'Evaux gallo-romain. La galerie d'accès aux thermes', *MSSNAC* 42: 277–93.

Lintz, G. (1992), 'Evaux (Creuse) – Ivanum (?), Vicus Evaunensis', in Maurin, L. (ed.), *Villes et Agglomérations Urbaines Antiques du Sud-Ouest de la Gaule. Histoire et Archéologie* (Sixième supplément à *Aquitania*), Bordeaux: La Nef, pp. 90–6.

Loseby, S.T. (1992), 'Bishops and cathedrals: order and diversity in the fifth-century urban landscape of southern Gaul', in Drinkwater, J. and Elton, H. (eds), *Fifth-century Gaul: a crisis of identity?*, Cambridge: Cambridge University Press, pp. 144–55.

Lott, J.B. (2004), *The Neighbourhoods of Augustan Rome*, Cambridge: Cambridge University Press.

Loustaud, J.-P. (1981), 'Limoges, Brachaud. Villa gallo-romaine', *TAL* 2: 162–4.

Loustaud, J.-P. (1982), 'Les thermes de la villa gallo-romaine de Brachaud. Synthèse d'une évolution', *TAL* 3: 31–52.

Loustaud, J.-P. (1983–88), Yearly reports on the villa at Brachaud in *TAL*.

Luck, G. (1985), *Arcana Mundi: Magic and Occult in the Greek and Roman Worlds*, Baltimore, MD and London: Johns Hopkins University Press.

Lugli, G. (1923), 'Il suburbio di Roma', *BCAR* 51: 3–62.

Lugli, G. (1930), 'Scavo di una villa di età repubblicana in località S. Basilio', *NS*: 529–35.

MacDonald, W.L. (1986), *The Architecture of the Roman Empire Volume II: an urban appraisal*, New Haven, CT and London: Yale University Press.

MacDonald, W.L. and Pinto, J.A. (1995), *Hadrian's Villa and its Legacy*, New Haven, CT: Yale University Press.

Mackie, N. (1990), 'Urban munificence and the growth of urban consciousness in Roman Spain', in Blagg, T. and Millett, M. (eds), *The Early Roman Empire in the West*, Oxford: Oxbow Books, pp. 179–92.

MacMullen, R. (1970) 'Market-days in the Roman empire', *Phoenix* 24: 333–41.

Magnan, D. (ed.) (1988), *Meaux Gallo-Romain et la Bauve*, Meaux: Association Meldoise d'Archéologie.

Mahjub, O. al (1983), 'I mosaici della villa Romana di Silin', in Campanati, R.F. (ed.), *III Colloquio Internazionale Sul Mosaico Antico*, Ravenna: Edizioni del Girasole, pp. 299–306.

Maischberger, M. (2000), 'Transtiberim', in Steinby, E.M. (ed.), *Lexicon Topographicum Urbis Romae, vol. Quinto, T-Z*, Roma: Edizioni Quasar, pp. 77–83.

Mandy, B. (1983), 'Le quartier antique du Verbe Incarné', *DossArch* 78: 23–6.

Mangin, M. (1985), 'Artisanat et commerce dans les agglomérations secondaires du Centre-Est de la Gaule sous l'empire', in Leveau, P. (ed.), *Les origines des richesses dépensées dans la ville antique* (Actes de colloque d'Aix-en-Provence, mai 1984), Aix: Université de Provence, pp. 113–31.

Mangin, M. (1994), 'Les agglomérations secondaires dans les régions de Franche-

Comté et de Bourgogne', in Petit J.-P., Mangin, M. and Brunella, P. (eds), *Les agglomérations secondaires. La Gaule Belgique, les Germanies et l'Occident romain*, Paris: Éditions Errance, pp. 45–79.

Mangin, M., Jacquet, B. and Jacob, J.-P. (eds) (1986), *Les agglomérations secondaires en Franche Comté romain*, Paris: Belles Lettres.

Mangin, M. and Tassaux, F. (1992), 'Les agglomérations secondaires de l'Aquitaine romaine', in Maurin, L. (ed.), *Villes et Agglomérations urbaines antiques du sud-ouest de la Gaule* (Sixième supplément à *Aquitania*), Bordeaux: La Nef, pp. 461–96.

Mattingly, D.J. (1988), 'The Olive Boom: Oil surpluses, wealth and power in Roman Tripolitania', *Libyan Studies* 19: 21–41.

Mattingly, D.J. (1995), *Tripolitania*, London: Batsford.

Maurin, L. (ed.) (1988), *Les fouilles de 'Ma Maison'. Études sur Saintes Antique* (*Aquitania* supplément no. 3), Bordeaux: Fédération Aquitania.

Maurin, L. and Thauré, M. (1994), *Saintes antique* (Guides Archéologiques de la France, no. 29), Paris: Imprimerie Nationale.

Maurin, L. and Vienne, G. (1977), 'Ateliers Municipaux', *BSAHCM* 4: 31–4.

May, R. (1996), *Lugdunum Convenarum. Saint-Bertrand-de-Comminges* (Collection Galliae Civitates), Lyon: Presses Universitaires de Lyon.

McKay, A.G. (1975), *Houses, Villas and Palaces in the Roman World*, Baltimore, MD and London: Johns Hopkins Press.

Meeks, W.A. (1983), *The First Urban Christians: The Social World of the Apostle Paul*, New Haven, CT and London: Yale University Press.

Meer, L.B. van der (1998), 'L'affresco sotto le terme di Traiano del Colle Oppio, Roma. Neropolis: realtà e progetto', *OMRL* 78: 63–73.

Meer, L.B. van der, Stevens, N.L.C. and Stöger, H. (2005), 'Domus Fulminata: The House of the Thunderbolt at Ostia (III, vii, 3–5)', *Babesch* 80: 91–111.

Meiggs, R. (1973), *Roman Ostia*, Oxford: Clarendon Press.

Meneghini, R. and Santangeli Valenzani, R. (1993), 'Sepolture intramuranee e paesaggio urbano a Roma tra V e VII secolo', in Paroli, L. and Delogu, P. (eds), *La storia economica di Roma nell'alto medioevo all luce dei recenti scavi archeologici. Atti del Seminario, Roma, 2–3 Aprile 1992*, Firenze: Biblioteca di Archeologia Medievale, pp. 89–112.

Merrony, M. (2005), 'Sensational mosaic from the wadi Lebda Roman villa, Libya', *Minerva* 16.4 (July/August): 4.

Mignon, J.-M. (2000), 'Les mausolées antiques d'Orange', *Archéologia* 364: 48–57.

Mignon, J.-M., Doray, I., Faure, C. and Bouet, A. (1997), 'La *domus* suburbaine de "La Brunette" à Orange', *RAN* 30: 173–202.

Millet, M. (1986), 'Central places in a decentralised Roman Britain', in Grant, E. (ed.), *Central Places, Archaeology and History*, Sheffield: Sheffield University Print Unit, pp. 45–7.

Moeller, W.O. (1976), *The Wool Trade of Ancient Pompeii*, Leiden: E.J. Brill.

Morley, N. (1996), *Metropolis and Hinterland: The City of Rome and the Italian Economy, 200 BC–AD 200*, London: Routledge.

Musée Carnavalet (1984), *Lutece, Paris de César à Clovis* (Exhibition catalogue; Musée Carnavalet et Musée national des Thermes et de l'Hôtel de Cluny. Paris, 3 mai 1984 – printemps 1985), Paris: Société des Amis du Musées Carnavalet.

Musée de la Civilisation Gallo-Romaine de Lyon (1983–84), *Archéologie en Rhône-Alpes. Protohistoire et monde gallo-romain, 10 ans de recherches*, Lyon: Ministère de la Culture.

Musées de la ville de Lisieux (1994), *Lisieux Avant l'An Mil. Essai de Reconstitution* (Exposition du 25 juin au 29 août 1994), Alençon: Imprimerie Alençonnaise.

Naveau, J. (1986), 'Le plan antique de Jublains (Mayenne)', *RAO* 3: 107–17.

Naveau, J. (1991), 'L'épigraphie du site de Jublains (Mayenne)', *RAO* 8: 103–16.

Naveau, J. (1996), '*Noviodunum*, Jublains. Un site urbain dans l'ouest de la Lyonnaise', *Caesarodunum* 30 ('Les Villes de la Gaule Lyonnaise'): 113–32.

Naveau, J. and Pivette, B. (1994), 'Le temple de Jublains (Mayenne) et la circulation de l'eau dans les sanctuaires gallo-romains', in Goudineau, C., Fauduet, I. and Coulon, G. (eds), *Les Sanctuaires de Tradition Indigène en Gaule Romaine* (Actes du Colloque d'Argentomagus), Paris: Éditions Errance, pp. 99–103.

Neiss, R. (1984), 'La structure urbaine de Reims antique et son évolution du Ier au IIIe siècle ap. J.-C.', *RAP* 3–4: 171–91.

Nielsen, I. (1990), *Thermae et Balnea: The Architecture and Cultural History of Roman Public Baths*, Aarhus: Aarhus University Press.

Nin, N., de Luca, B. and Charlet, J.-L. (1987), 'La voie aurélienne et ses abords à Aix-en-Provence. Nouvelles données sur un paysage périurbain', *RAN* 20: 191–280.

Oliver, J.H. (1989), *Greek Constitutions of Early Roman Emperors from Inscriptions and Papyri*, Philadelphia, PA: American Philosophical Society.

Olivier, A. and Fritsch, R. (1982), 'Le vicus de Vieux-Poitiers', *Archéologia* 163: 52–61.

Olivier, A. and Rebourg, A. (1989), 'Un nouveau temple gallo-romain à la Genetoye, Autun (Saône-et-Loire)', *RAE* 40: 111–14.

Packard Humanities Institute CD-ROM 5.3 (Latin Literature).

Paillard, D. (1998a), 'Un *suburbium* à Lisieux. L'apport du site archéologique Michelet', *DossArch* 237: 52–7.

Paillard, D. (1998b), 'Un *suburbium* à Lisieux (Calvados) et mouvance périphérique d'une cité. L'apport du site archéologique Michelet', *Caesarodunum* 32 ('*Suburbia*. Les Faubourgs en Gaule Romaine et dans les Régions Voisines'): 151–62.

Palmer, R.E.A. (1980), 'Customs on market goods imported into the city of Rome', in D'Arms, J.H. and Kopff, E.C. (eds), *The Seaborne Commerce of Ancient Rome: Studies in Archaeology and History* (*MAAR*, no. 36), Rome: American Academy in Rome, pp. 217–33.

Palombi, D. (1999), 'Regiones Quattuordecim (Topographia)', in Steinby, E.M. (ed.), *Lexicon Topographicum Urbis Romae, vol. Quarto, P-S*, Roma: Edizioni Quasar, pp. 199–204.

Pape, L. (1978), *La civitas des Osismes à l'époque gallo-romaine*, Paris: Klincksieck.

Papi, E. (1996), 'Horti Lolliani', in Steinby, E.M. (ed.), *Lexicon Topographicum Urbis Romae, vol. Terzo, H-O*, Roma: Edizioni Quasar, p. 67.

Papinot, J.-C., Fabioux, M., Lévêque, F. and Le Masne de Chermont, N. (1989), 'Naintré', in *Gallia Informations* 2: 294–5.

Parker Pearson, M. and Richards, C. (1994), 'Ordering the world: perceptions of architecture, space and time', in Parker Pearson, M. and Richards, C. (eds), *Architecture and Order: Approaches to Social Space*, London: Routledge, pp. 1–37.

Parkins, H. (ed.) (1997), *Roman Urbanism: Beyond the Consumer City*, London: Routledge.

Patterson, J.R. (2000a), 'On the margins of the city of Rome', in Hope, V.M. and

Marshall, E. (eds), *Death and Disease in the Ancient City*, London: Routledge, pp. 85–103.
Patterson, J.R. (2000b), 'Via Appia', in Steinby, E.M. (ed.), *Lexicon Topographicum Urbis Romae, vol. Quinto, T-Z*, Roma: Edizioni Quasar, pp. 130–3.
Patterson, J.R. (2000c), 'Living and dying in the city of Rome: houses and tombs', in Coulston, J. and Dodge, H. (eds), *Ancient Rome: the Archaeology of the Eternal City*, Oxford: Oxford University School of Archaeology, pp. 259–89.
Patterson, J.R. (2000d), *Political Life in the City of Rome*, London: Bristol Classical Press.
Peacock, D.P.S. (1982), *Pottery in the Roman World: An Ethnoarchaeological Approach*, London: Longman.
Pelletier, A. (1974), *Vienne gallo-romaine au Bas-Empire, 275–469 après J.C.*, Lyon: Bosc.
Pelletier, A. (1982a), *L'Urbanisme Romain Sous l'Empire*, Paris: Éditions Picard.
Pelletier, A. (1982b), *Vienne Antique*, Roanne: Éditions Horvath.
Pelletier, A. (1993), 'Topographie et Urbanisme', ch. IX in Pelletier, A. and Roussiaud, J. (eds), *Histoire de Lyon des origines à nos jours*, vol. I; Le Couteau: Éditions Horvath, pp. 101–32.
Pelletier, A. (1996), 'Pour une nouvelle histoire des origines de Lugdunum: l'enseignement de l'archéologie', *Caesarodunum* 30 ('Les Villes de la Gaule Lyonnaise'): 167–77.
Pelletier, A. (1999), *Lugdunum, Lyon* (Collection Galliae Civitates), Lyon: Presses Universitaires de Lyon.
Pelletier, A., Savay-Guerraz, H., Barbet, A., Lancha, J. and Canal, A. (1981), 'Découvertes archéologiques récentes à Vienne', *MMPiot* 64: 17–140.
Percival, J. (1976), *The Roman Villa*, London: Batsford.
Percival, J. (1992), 'The fifth-century villa: new life or death postponed?', in Drinkwater, J. and Elton, H. (eds), *Fifth-century Gaul: a crisis of identity?*, Cambridge: Cambridge University Press, pp. 156–64.
Pergola, P., Santangeli Valenzani, R. and Volpe, R. (eds) (2003), *Suburbium: Il Suburbio di Roma dalla crisi del sistema delle ville a Gregorio Magno*, Roma: École Française de Rome.
Perring, D. (1991), 'Spatial organisation and social change in Roman towns', in Rich, J. and Wallace-Hadrill, A. (eds), *City and Country in the Ancient World*, London: Routledge, pp. 273–93.
Perrugot, D. (1990), 'L'atelier de céramique gallo-romain de Sens', *BSAS* 32: 1–31.
Perrugot, D. (1996), 'Sens: Origine, développement et repli du Ier siècle au début du Vème siècle. Aux origines de la ville antique', *Caesarodunum* 30 ('Les Villes de la Gaule Lyonnaise'): 263–78.
Peters, W.J.T. (1963), *Landscape in Romano-Campanian Mural Painting*, Assen: Van Gorcum.
Petit, J.-P., Mangin, M. and Brunella, P. (eds) (1994a), *Les agglomérations secondaires. La Gaule Belgique, les Germanies et l'Occident romain*, Paris: Éditions Errance.
Petit, J.-P., Mangin, M. and Brunella, P. (eds) (1994b), *Atlas des agglomérations secondaires de la Gaule Belgique et des Germanies*, Paris: Éditions Errance.
Petit, J.P. and Schaub, J. (1995), *Bliesbruck-Reinheim. Parc archéologique européen* (Guides Archéologiques de la France, no. 32), Paris: Imprimerie Nationale.
Picard, G.C. (1970), 'Les théâtres ruraux de Gaule', *RevArch* 1: 185–92.

Picard, G.C. (1974), 'La "Porte de Mars" à Reims', in *Actes du 95e Congrès National des Sociétés Savantes (Reims, 1970)*, Paris: Bibliotheque Nationale, pp. 59–73.

Picard, G.C. (1975), 'Observations sur la condition des populations rurales dans l'Empire Romain, en Gaule et en Afrique', *ANRW* II.3: 98–111.

Picard, G.C. (1976), 'Vicus et conciliabulum', *Caesarodunum* 11 ('Le *vicus* gallo-romain'): 47–9.

Picard, G.C. (1986), 'Banlieues de villes dans l'Afrique romaine', in *Histoire et Archéologie de l'Afrique du Nord. Actes du IIIe Colloque International*, Paris: Comité des Travaux Historiques et Scientifiques.

Pietri, L. (1983), *La ville de Tours du IVe au VIe siècle: naissance d'une cité chrétienne*, Roma: École Française de Rome.

Pietri, C. and Picard, J.-C. (1986), 'Autun', in Février, P.-A. (ed.), *TCCG IV – Province Ecclésiastique de Lyon (Lugdunensis Prima)*, Paris, Éditions de Boccard, 37–45.

Pinette, M. and Rebourg, A. (1986), *Autun (Saône-et-Loire). Ville gallo-romaine, Musée Rolin et Musée Lapidaire* (Guides Archéologiques de la France, no. 12), Paris: Imprimerie Nationale.

Pinon, P. (1981), 'Le plan romain de Bourges', *Archéologia* 155: 38–45.

Pion, P. and Guichard, V. (1993), 'Tombes et nécropoles en France et au Luxembourg entre le IIIème et le Ier siècles avant J.-C. Essai d'inventaire', in Cliquet, D., Rémy-Watte, M., Guichard, V. and Vaginay, M. (eds), *Les Celtes en Normandie. Les rites funéraires en Gaule (IIIème – Ier s. av. J.-C.)* (RAO suppl. 6), Rennes: Pole Editorial Archéologique de l'Ouest, pp. 175–236.

Pisani Sartorio, G. (1993), 'Arcus Drusi (via Appia)', in Steinby, E.M. (ed.), *Lexicon Topographicum Urbis Romae, vol. Primo, A-C*, Roma: Edizioni Quasar, p. 93.

Pisani Sartorio, G. (1996a), 'Muri Aureliani', in Steinby, E.M. (ed.), *Lexicon Topographicum Urbis Romae, vol. Terzo, H-0*, Roma: Edizioni Quasar, pp. 290–4.

Pisani Sartorio, G. (1996b), 'Macellum Magnum', in Steinby, E.M. (ed.), *Lexicon Topographicum Urbis Romae, vol. Terzo, H-0*, Roma: Edizioni Quasar, pp. 204–6.

Pisani Sartorio, G. (1996c), 'Mutatorium Caesaris', in Steinby, E.M. (ed.), *Lexicon Topographicum Urbis Romae, vol. Terzo, H-0*, Roma: Edizioni Quasar, p. 335.

Pisani Sartorio, G. and Calza, R. (eds) (1976), *La Villa di Massenzio sulla via Appia. Il palazzo – le opere di arte*, Roma: Fratelli Palombi Editori.

Poe, J.P. (1984), 'The Secular Games, the Aventine and the *pomerium* in the Campus Martius', *Classical Antiquity* 3: 57–81.

Potter, T.W. (1979), *The Changing Landscape of South Etruria*, London: Paul Elek.

Price, M.J. and Trell, B.L. (1977), *Coins and their Cities: Architecture on the Ancient Coins of Greece, Rome and Palestine*, London: Friary Press.

Price, S. (1996), 'The place of religion: Rome in the early empire', in Bowman, A.K., Champlin, E. and Lintott, A.W. (eds), *Cambridge Ancient History* vol. X (2nd edn), Cambridge: Cambridge University Press, pp. 818–20.

Prisset, J.-L. (ed.) (1999), *Guide du site. Saint-Romain-en-Gal*, Paris: Réunion des Musées Nationaux.

Provost, A. (2000), 'Le sanctuaire du Haut-Bécherel', *Archéologia* 364: 30–1.

Purcell, N. (1987a), 'Tomb and suburb', in Hesberg, H. von and Zanker, P. (eds), *Römische Gräberstraßen. Selbstdarstellung – Status – Standard*, Munich: Bayerische Akademie des Wissenschaften, pp. 25–41.

Purcell, N. (1987b), 'Town in country and country in town', in MacDougall, E.B. (ed.), *Ancient Roman Villa Gardens* (Dumbarton Oaks Colloquium on the History of Landscape Architecture, 10), Washington, DC: Dumbarton Oaks Research Library and Collection, pp. 185–203.

Purcell, N. (1987c), 'The Nicopolitan synoecism and Roman urban policy', in Chrysos, E. (ed.), *Nicopolis I* (Proceedings of the first International Symposium on Nicopolis), Preveza: Municipality of Preveza, pp. 71–90.

Purcell, N. (1990), 'The creation of provincial landscape: the Roman impact on Cisalpine Gaul', in Blagg, T. and Millett, M. (eds), *The Early Roman Empire in the West*, Oxford: Oxbow Books, pp. 7–29.

Purcell, N. (1995a), 'The Roman villa and the landscape of production', in Cornell, T.J. and Lomas, K. (eds) *Urban Society in Roman Italy*, London: UCL Press, pp. 151–79.

Purcell, N. (1995b), 'On the sacking of Carthage and Corinth', in Innes, D., Hine, H. and Pelling, C. (eds), *Ethics and Rhetoric. Classical Essays for Donald Russell on his Seventy-Fifth Birthday*, Oxford: Clarendon, pp. 133–48.

Purcell, N. (1996a), 'The Roman garden as a domestic building', in Barton, I.M. (ed.), *Roman Domestic Buildings*, Exeter: University of Exeter Press, pp. 121–51.

Purcell, N. (1996b), 'The ports of Rome: evolution of a *"façade maritime"* ', in Zevi, A.G. and Claridge, A. (eds), *'Roman Ostia' Revisited*, London: British School at Rome, pp. 267–79.

Purcell, N. (1997), 'Regulating funerary space and groves at Luceria and Rome' (review of Bodel (1994)) *JRA* 10: 340–2.

Quilici, L. (1974), 'La Campagna romana come suburbio di Roma Antica', *La Pavola del Passato* 29: 410–38.

Quilici, L. (1979), 'La villa nel suburbio romano: problemi di studio e di inquadrimento storico-topografico', *ArchClass* 31: 309–17.

Ramage, E.S. (1973), *Urbanitas: Ancient Sophistication and Refinement*, Norman, OK: University of Oklahoma Press.

Raper, R.A. (1977), 'The analysis of the urban structure of Pompeii: a sociological examination of land use (semi-micro)', in Clarke, D.L. (ed.), *Spatial Archaeology*, London: Academic Press, pp. 189–221.

Rebourg, A. (1993), *Autun* (CAG 71/1), Paris: Académie des Inscriptions et Belles-Lettres.

Rebourg, A. (1999), *L'urbanisme d'Augustodunum (Autun, Saône-et-Loire)* (Extract from *Gallia* 55 (1998): 141–236), Paris: Éditions CNRS.

Rémy, B. and Jospin, J.-P. (1998), 'Recherches sur la société d'une agglomération de la cité de Vienne: Aoste (Isère)', *RAN* 31: 73–89.

Reynaud, J.-F. (1978), 'Saint-Ferréol, une de plus anciennes églises viennoises', *Archéologia* 122: 44–51.

Reynaud, J.-F. (1998), *Lugdunum Christianum* (Documents d'Archéologie Française, no. 69), Paris: Éditions de la Maison des Sciences de l'Homme.

Reynolds, J. (1988), 'Cities', in Braund, D.C. (ed.), *The Administration of the Roman Empire, 241 BC–AD 193*, Exeter: University of Exeter Press, 15–51.

Rich, J. (ed.) (1992), *The City in Late Antiquity*, London: Routledge.

Richard, C. (1989), *Gué de Sciaux; Antigny, Vienne. Une ville gallo-romain; fouilles d'un sanctuaire* (Société de Recherches Archéologiques de Chauvigny, Mémoire IV), Chauvigny: Association des Publications Chauvinoises.

Richard, C. (1992), 'Antigny (Vienne)', in Maurin, L. (ed.), *Villes et Agglomérations*

BIBLIOGRAPHY

Urbaines Antiques du Sud-Ouest de la Gaule. Histoire et Archéologie (Sixième supplément à *Aquitania*), Bordeaux: La Nef, pp. 22–4.
Richmond, I.A. (1969), 'Aosta', in Salway, P. (ed.), *Roman Archaeology and Art: essays and studies by Sir Ian Richmond*, London: Faber and Faber, pp. 249–59.
Rickman, G.E. (1971), *Roman Granaries and Store Buildings*, Cambridge: Cambridge University Press.
Rickman, G.E. (1996), 'Portus in perspective', in Zevi, A.G. and Claridge, A. (eds), *'Roman Ostia' Revisited*, London: British School at Rome, pp. 281–91.
Rivet, A.L.F. (1955), 'The distribution of villas in Roman Britain', *Archaeological Newsletter* 6: 29–34.
Rivet, A.L.F. (1988), *Gallia Narbonensis*, London: Batsford.
Rivet, L., Brentchaloff, D., Roucoule, S. and Saulnier, S. (2000), *Atlas Topographique des Villes de Gaule Méridionale 2: Fréjus* (*RAN* suppl. 32), Montpellier: Éditions de l'Association de la *RAN*.
Robinson, O.F. (1992), *Ancient Rome: City Planning and Administration*, London: Routledge.
Rodríguez Almeida, E. (1981), *Forma Urbis Marmorea. Aggiornamento Generale 1980*, Roma: Edizioni Quasar.
Rodríguez Almeida, E. (1993), 'Arcus Claudii (a. 43 d.C.)', in Steinby, E.M. (ed.), *Lexicon Topographicum Urbis Romae, vol. Primo, A-C*, Roma: Edizioni Quasar, pp. 85–6.
Rodríguez Hidalgo, J.M. (1995), 'Recent work at Itálica', in Cunliffe, B. and Keay, S. (eds), *Social Complexity and the Development of Towns in Iberia: From the Copper Age to the Second Century A.D.* (Proceedings of the British Academy, no. 86), Oxford: Oxford University Press, pp. 395–420.
Roffin, R. and Vasselle, F. (1966), 'Habitat gallo-romain au nord-ouest d'Amiens. Inventaire du matériel gallo-romain', *RdN* 48: 605–25.
Roffin, R., Roffin-Prégermain, F., Decottignies, N. and Vasselle, F. (1966), 'Habitat gallo-romain près de la citadelle d'Amiens (Somme)', *Celticum* 15: 185–205.
Rolland, H. (1958), 'Informations', *Gallia* 16: 405–6.
Rolland, H. (1960), 'Informations', *Gallia* 18: 273.
Rolland, H. (1977), *L'arc de Glanum* (31st suppl. to *Gallia*), Paris: Éditions du CNRS.
Rorison, M. (2001), *Vici in Roman Gaul* (BAR Int. Series 933), Oxford: Archaeopress.
Ross Holloway, R. (1994), *The Archaeology of Early Rome and Latium*, London: Routledge.
Rouquette, J.M. and Sintès, C. (1989), *Arles antique: monuments et sites* (Guides Archéologiques de la France, no. 17), Paris: Imprimerie Nationale.
Rykwert, J. (1976), *The Idea of a Town: The Anthropology of Urban Form in Rome, Italy and the Ancient World*, Cambridge, MA and London: MIT Press.
Sablayrolles, R. and collaborators (2001–02), 'Lugdunum des Convènes (Saint-Bertrand-de-Comminges/Valcabrère, Haute-Garonne): acquis récents de la recherche (1992–2002)', *Aquitania* 18: 29–77.
Salza Prina Ricotti, E. (1970–71), 'Le ville marittime di Silin (Leptis Magna)', *AttiPontAcc* 43: 136–63.
Savay-Guerraz, H. and Prisset, J.-L. (1992), 'Le portique de Saint-Romain-en-Gal (Rhone) et son contexte. Etat des recherches', *RAN* 25: 105–24.
Savay-Guerraz, H., Prisset, J.-L and Delaval, E. (1995), 'Le quartier viennois de Saint-Romain-en-Gal au milieu du Ier siècle', in Burnand, Y., Le Bohec, Y. and

Martin, J.-P. (eds), *Claude de Lyon. Empereur Romain* (Actes de Colloque Paris-Nancy-Lyon, novembre 1992), Paris: Presses de l'Université de Paris-Sorbonne, pp. 391–405.

Scagliarini, D. (1991), 'Bologna (*Bononia*) and its suburban territory' in Barker, G. and Lloyd, J. (eds), *Roman Landscapes* (Archaeological Monographs of the British School at Rome, no. 2), London: The British School at Rome, pp. 88–95.

Schaad, D. and Soukiassian, G. (1990), '*Encraustos*: un camp militaire romain à *Lugdunum civitas Convenarum* (Saint-Bertrand-de-Comminges)', *Aquitania* 8: 99–120.

Scheid, J. (1991), 'Sanctuaires et territoire dans la *colonia Augusta Treverorum*', in Brunaux, J.-L. (ed.), *Les Sanctuaires Celtiques et Leurs Rapports avec le Monde Méditerranéen*, Paris: Éditions Errance, pp. 42–57.

Scheid, J. (1995), 'Les temples de l'Altbachtal à Trèves: un "sanctuaire national"?', *CCGG* 6: 227–43.

Schlemaire, G. (1974), 'Fouilles de sauvetage au Pontiffroy à Metz en 1973. Cave S.1', *ASHAL* 74: 19–28.

Schlemaire, G. (1976), 'Fouilles de sauvetage au Pontiffroy à Metz en 1974. Bâtiments S.2 et S.3', *ASHAL* 76: 37–59.

Schlemaire, G. (1978), 'Fouilles de sauvetage au Pontiffroy à Metz en 1976. Sites S4 à S11', *ASHAL* 78: 41–63.

Sintès, C. (1987a), 'Les fouilles de l'Hôpital Van Gogh', in Sintès, C. (ed.), *Du Nouveau Sur l'Arles Antique* (Catalogue d'Exposition), Arles: Hommage des Musées d'Arles, pp. 44–9.

Sintès, C. (1987b), 'La Verrerie' in Sintès, C. (ed.), *Du Nouveau Sur l'Arles Antique* (Catalogue d'Exposition), Arles: Hommage des Musées d'Arles, pp. 80–8.

Sintès, C. (1990), 'L'évolution topographique de l'Arles antique du Haut-Empire à la lumière des fouilles récentes', *JRA* 5: 130–47.

Sivan, H. (1992), 'Town and country in late antique Gaul: the example of Bordeaux', in Drinkwater, J. and Elton, H. (eds), *Fifth-century Gaul: a crisis of identity?*, Cambridge: Cambridge University Press, pp. 132–43.

Smith, C.A. (ed.) (1976), *Regional Analysis* (2 vols), New York: Academic Press.

Stambaugh, J.E. (1988), *The Ancient Roman City*, Baltimore, MD and London: Johns Hopkins University Press.

Stanford Digital Forma Urbis Romae Project (2002–03), <http://formaurbis.stanford.edu/> (accessed 12 December 2005).

Steinby, E.M. et al. (eds) (1993–2000), *Lexicon Topographicum Urbis Roma* (6 vols), Roma: Edizioni Quasar.

Stern, H. (1953), *Le Calendrier de 354*, Paris: Geuthner.

Stern, H. (1957), *Recueil Général des Mosaïques de la Gaule I. Province de Belgiaue 1 – Partie Ouest*, Paris: Éditions du CNRS.

Stern, H. (1967), *Recueil Général des Mosaïques de la Gaule II. Province de Lyonnaise 1 – Lyon*, Paris: Éditions du CNRS.

Stern, H. and Blanchard-Lemée, M. (1975), *Recueil Général des Mosaïques de la Gaule II. Province de Lyonnaise 2 – Partie Sud-Est*, Paris: Éditions du CNRS.

Talbert, J.A. (ed.) (2000), *Barrington Atlas of the Greek and Roman World*, Princeton, NJ and Oxford: Princeton University Press.

Tarpin, M. (1991), '*Vici* et *pagi* chez les Voconces et les Allobroges', *Revue Drômoise* 89: 301–2.

Tassaux, F. (1994), 'Les agglomérations secondaires de l'Aquitaine romaine: morphologie et réseaux', in Petit J.-P., Mangin, M. and Brunella, P. (eds), *Les agglomérations secondaires. La Gaule Belgique, les Germanies et l'Occident romain*, Paris: Éditions Errance, pp. 197–214.

Thesaurus Linguae Graecae digital library of Greek literature (1972–present), <http://www.tlg.uci.edu/> (accessed 4 June 2005).

Tobin, J. (1997), *Herodes Attikos and the City of Athens: Patronage and conflict under the Antonines*, Amsterdam: Gieben.

Tourrenc, S. (1979), 'Fouille de sauvetage "Nympheas II", effectuée quai Riondet, à Vienne, en 1978', *BSAV* 74.1: 44–60.

Toynbee, J.M.C. (1971), *Death and Burial in the Roman World*, Baltimore, MD and London: Johns Hopkins University Press.

Tranoy, L. and Ayala, G. (1994), 'Les pentes de la Croix-Rousse à Lyon dans l'Antiquité. État des connaissances', *Gallia* 51: 171–89.

Treggiari, S.M. (1980), 'Urban labour in Rome: *mercennarii* and *tabernarii*', in Garnsey, P. (ed.), *Non-slave labour in the Greco-Roman world* (*PCPS*, suppl. no. 6), Cambridge: Cambridge Philological Society, pp. 48–64.

Turcan, R. (1980), 'La Presqu'île à l'époque romaine: problemes historiques et archéologiques', *RevLyon* 2.2: 65–91.

Valette, P. (1996), 'Un aspect de l'urbanisme antique de *Forum Segusiavorum* (Feurs): la mise en place de la trame urbaine', *Caesarodunum* 30 ('Les Villes de la Gaule Lyonnaise'): 79–112.

Valette, P. and Guichard, V. (1991), 'Le *forum* gallo-romain de Feurs (Loire)', *Gallia* 48: 109–64.

Vasselle, F. (1978), 'Compte-rendu de la découverte d'une villa romaine à Saint-Acheul, 1972–1976', *BTSAP* 57: 293–306.

Vega, P.A.F. (1994), 'Las áreas periurbanas de las ciudades altoimperiales romanas. Usos del suelo y zonas residenciales', *Hispania Antiqua* 18: 141–58.

Vernou, C. (1988), 'Une année de recherche archéologique à l'Abbaye aux Dames', *BSAHCM* 15: 18–19.

Vernou, C. and Buisson, J.-F. (1992), 'Saintes (Charente-Maritime) – Mediolanum, Civitas Santonum', in Maurin, L. (ed.), *Villes et Agglomérations Urbaines Antiques du Sud-Ouest de la Gaule. Histoire et Archéologie* (Sixième supplément à *Aquitania*), Bordeaux: La Nef, pp. 154–63.

Vernou, C., Tilhard, J.-L., Surmely, M., Baigl, J.-P. and Courtaud, P. (1990), 'Le site gallo-romain de la rue Grelaud, à Saintes', *RSaintonge* 16: 7–74.

Verot, A., Jacquet, C., Burnouf, J., Arnoros, C. and Bravard, J.-P. (1989), 'Le site gallo-romain de la Place Bellecour (Lyon 2e); reconstitution interdisciplinaire du paléoenvironnement', in Comité des Travaux Historiques et Scientifiques, *La Ville et le Fleuve*, Paris: Éditions du CTHS, pp. 147–55.

Vigneron, B. (1986), *Divodurum Mediomatricorum. Metz Antique*, Sainte-Ruffine: Maisonneuve.

Ville, G. (1981), *La Gladiature en Occident des Origines à la Mort de Domitien*, Roma: École Française de Rome.

Villedieu, F. (1990), *Lyon Saint-Jean. Les Fouilles de l'Avenue Adolphe-Max* (Documents d'Archéologie en Rhône-Alpes, no. 3), Lyon: Service régional de l'archéologie de Rhône-Alpes.

Vismara, C. (1990), 'L'amphithéâtre comme lieu de supplice', *Spectacula I. Gladiateurs et Amphithéâtres* (Actes du colloque tenu à Toulouse et à Lattes les 25, 27, 28 et 29 mai 1987), Lattes: Éditions Imago, pp. 253–8.

Wacher, J. (1995), *The Towns of Roman Britain* (2nd edn), London: Routledge.

Walker, S. (1981), 'La campagne lyonnaise du Ier siècle av. J.-C. jusqu'au 5e siècle ap. J.-C.', in Walker, S. (ed.), *Récentes recherches en archéologie gallo-romaine et paléochrétienne sur Lyon et sa région* (BAR Int. Series no. 108), Oxford: BAR Publications, pp. 279–329.

Wallace-Hadrill, A. (1991), 'Elites and trade in the Roman town', in Rich, J. and Wallace Hadrill, A. (eds), *City and Country in the Ancient World*, London: Routledge, pp. 241–72.

Wallace-Hadrill, A. (1994), *Houses and Society in Pompeii and Herculaneum*, Princeton, NJ: Princeton University Press.

Wallace-Hadrill, A. (1995), 'Public honour and private shame: the urban texture of Pompeii', in Cornell, T.J. and Lomas, K. (eds), *Urban Society in Roman Italy*, London: UCL Press, pp. 39–62.

Wallace-Hadrill, A. (2003), 'The cities of central Italy in the second century BC: Hellenization, Romanization and local identity': paper delivered at Oxford in November 2003 and kindly shared by its author in draft form.

Walthew, C.V. (1981), 'A note on the street-plan and early growth of Roman Amiens', *Britannia* 12: 298–302.

Ward-Perkins, B. (ed.) (1984), *From Classical Antiquity to the Middle Ages: Urban Public Building in Northern and Central Italy, AD 300–800*, Oxford: Oxford University Press.

Ward-Perkins, J.B. (1970), 'From Republic to Empire: Reflections on the early imperial provincial architecture of the Roman west', *JRS* 60: 1–19.

Ward-Perkins, J.B. (1981), *Roman Imperial Architecture*, Harmondsworth: Penguin.

Ward-Perkins, J.B. (1982), 'Town planning in North Africa', *MDAIR, Erganzungsheft* 25: 29–49.

Webster, J. (2003), 'Art as resistance and negotiation', in Scott, S. and Webster, J. (eds), *Roman Imperialism and Provincial Art*, Cambridge: Cambridge University Press, pp. 24–51.

Wendowski, M. and Ziegert, H. (2005), 'The wadi Lebda Roman villa, Libya', *Minerva* 16.6 (November/December): 33–4.

Whittaker, C.R. (1980), 'Rural labour in three Roman provinces', in Garnsey, P. (ed.), *Non-slave labour in the Greco-Roman world* (*PCPS* suppl. no. 6), Cambridge: Cambridge Philological Society, pp. 73–99.

Whittaker, C.R. (1990), 'The consumer city revisited: the vicus and the city', *JRA* 3: 110–18.

Whittaker, C.R. (1995), 'Do theories of the ancient city matter?', in Cornell, T.J. and Lomas, K. (eds), *Urban Society in Roman Italy*, London: UCL Press, pp. 9–26.

Whittaker, C.R. and Goody, J. (2001), 'Rural manufacturing in the Rouergue from antiquity to the present: the examples of pottery and cheese', *Comparative Studies in Society and History* 43.2: 225–43.

Wiedemann, T. (1992), *Emperors and Gladiators*, London: Routledge.

Wightman, E.M. (1970), *Roman Trier and the Treveri*, London: Rupert Hart-Davis Ltd.

Wightman, E.M. (1976), 'Le vicus dans le contexte de l'administration et de la société gallo-romaine: quelques réflexions', *Caesarodunum* 6 ('Le vicus Gallo-romain'): 59–64.

Wightman, E.M. (1985), *Gallia Belgica*, London: Batsford.
Will, E. (1973) 'Les cryptoportiques de forum de la Gaule', in *Les cryptoportiques dans l'architecture romaine* (Collection École Française de Rome no. 14), Rome: École Français de Rome, pp. 325–46.
Williamson, C.H. (1987), 'A Roman law from Narbonne', *Athenaeum* 65: 173–89.
Wilson, A.I. (1999a), 'Deliveries *extra urbem*: aqueducts and the countryside', *JRA* 12: 314–31.
Wilson, A.I. (1999b), 'Commerce and industry in Roman Sabratha', *Libyan Studies* 30: 29–52.
Wilson, A.I. (2000), 'Timgad and textile production', in Mattingly, D.J. and Salmon, J. (eds), *Economies Beyond Agriculture in the Classical World*, (London: Routledge), pp. 271–96.
Wilson, A.I. (2001), 'The water-mills on the Janiculum', *MAAR* 45: 219–46.
Wiseman, T.P. (1993), 'Campus Martius', in Steinby, E.M. (ed.), *Lexicon Topographicum Urbis Romae, vol. Primo, A-C*, Roma: Edizioni Quasar, pp. 220–4.
Woloch, G.M. (1983), *Roman Cities*, Wisconsin: University of Wisconsin Press.
Woolf, G. (1997), 'Beyond Romans and natives', *World Archaeology* 28.3: 339–50.
Woolf, G. (1998), *Becoming Roman: The Origins of Provincial Civilisation in Gaul*, Cambridge: Cambridge University Press.
Woolf, G. (2000), 'Urbanization and its discontents in early Roman Gaul', in Fentress, E. (ed.), *Romanisation and the City: Creation, Dynamics and Failures* (*JRA* supplement no. 38); Portsmouth, RI: Journal of Roman Archaeology, pp. 115–31.
Woolf, G. (2001a), 'Regional productions in early Roman Gaul', in Mattingly, D.J. and Salmon, J. (eds) *Economies Beyond Agriculture in the Classical World*, London: Routledge, pp. 49–65.
Woolf, G. (2001b), 'Two conferences on Gallo-Roman urbanism' (review article), *JRA* 14: 603–4.
Woolf, G. (2003), 'The temple habit': paper delivered at Oxford in March 2003.
Wrigley, E.A. (1991), 'City and country in the past – separate or part of a continuum?', *Historical Research* 64: 107–20.
Zanker, P. (2000), 'The city as symbol: Rome and the creation of an urban image', in Fentress, E. (ed.), *Romanisation and the City: Creation, Dynamics and Failures* (*JRA* supplement no. 38), Portsmouth, RI: Journal of Roman Archaeology, 25–41.
Zevi, F. (1997), 'Costruttori eccellenti per le mura di Ostia. Cicerone, Clodio e l'iscrizione della Porta Romana', *RivIstArch* 19–20: 61–112.
Ziegert, H. (2001–02), ' "Loess" over Ledba: a preliminary report of investigations 1999–2002', *Hephaistos* 19/20: 83–96.

INDEX

Page numbers in italics refer to plates, figures and tables.

abandonment, of standing structures 91, 201, 206–7, 217, 219–22, 226–7
Abrams, P. 235
adaptation, of standing structures 201, 221–4, 227
adventus see profectio and *adventus*
Aedui 150
Aegae, Vergina 27
Aesculapius 48
Africa *see* North Africa, Roman provinces of
Agache, R. 155–6, 227
ager suburbanus see Rome: *suburbium*
agriculture 24–5, 40–1, 47, 50–5, 72–3, 76–7, 92, 112–13, 123, 153–7, 189, 195–7, 222, 229, 233
agrimensores 9; *see also Corpus Agrimensorum*
Agusta-Boularot, S. 20
Aix-en-Provence (Aquae Sextiae) 205, 223
Alamanni 204
Alba, nr. Rome 51
Alba Fucens 33
Alexandria, Egypt 27
Allobroges 82
Ambrussum 150, 175–6, 179, 181, 183–5, 199, 264n20; Sablas 184–5
Amiens (Samarobriva Ambianorum) 64–5, 86, 101, *102*, 123–5, 144, 150–1, 155, 157, 159, 176, 183, 199, 206–7, 212, 221–2, 227, 236; Saint-Maurice 101–2, 123–5, 159, 236
Ammianus Marcellinus 217
amphitheatres 26, 47–8, 71–4, 85, *88*, 89, 93, 96, 111, 117, *130*, 131, 136, 142–8, *143*, *145*, 149–50, 158, 160–6, 181, 188, 190–1, 207, 212, 223, 230, 234; classical type 87–9, 93, 96, 129, 142–8, 161, 238; mixed edifices 87–9, 142, 147–8, 161, 239
Andringa, W. van 141, 238
Angers (Iuliomagus) 86, 147, 161
Antibes (Antipolis) 159, 162, 259n251
Antigny 175–6, 181, 183–7, 190, 199
Antioch, Syria 27, 35–7
Antium (Anzio) 20
Antoninus Pius (emperor) 131
Aosta (Augusta Praetoria) 60, *61*, 85–6, 142, 207
Aoste (Augusta/um) 193–5, 199
Apollo 36, 49
Apt (Apta) 122, 162
Apuleius of Madauros 25, 37, 73
aqueducts 47, 58, 91–2, 100–3, 112, 121, 123, 127, 156, 163, 192
arches, monumental 33, 45, 65–8, 86, 89, 178, 192, 237
Argentomagus (Argenton-sur-Creuse / Saint-Michel) *153*, 175–6, 178–82, *182*, 184–8, 191
Aricia (Ariccia) 55, 57
Aristotle 27
Arles (Arelate) 85–6, 98, *100*, 102–3, 112–3, 122, 125–6, 144, 147–9, 158, 160, 162–4, 176, 203, 205, 216, 219–20, 223–4, 229, 239; area south of the city walls 125–6, 219; Trinquetaille 98, 102–3, 122, 148, 158, 219, 234, 239
Arnaud, P. 58
Arretine ware *see terra sigillata*

INDEX

Arroux 96, 103, 116, 152
Artemidorus (philosopher) 24
artisans *see* industry
Arval brethren 56
Asia Minor 26–7, 48, 203
Athens 25, 27, 47, 72, 77
Audin, A. 91, 130
Augst (Augusta Raurica) 82, 85
Augustus (emperor) 28, 33, 43–9, 62, 65, 81, 85–6, 130–3, 163, 206, 223, 239
Aulerci Cenomanni 202
Aulerci Diablintes 137, 202
Aulus Gellius 25, 72, 77
Aurelian (emperor) 34, 36, 42–4, 202
Ausonius, D. Magnus 227–9
Autun (Augustodunum) 85, 96, 97, *101*, 103, 106, 108, 116, 134, 136, 141–2, 144, 152, *153*, 155–7, 162, 205, 209, 214, 236, 239; la Genetoye 96, 103, 134, 136, 141, 239
Auxerre (Autessiodurum) 211
Avenches (Aventicum) 86, 217
Avezzano relief *see* Fucine Lake reliefs

Baccrabère, L'Abbé G. 93, 117
Balmelle, C. 227
baths 43, 47, 56, 69, 73, 77, 83, 85, 93, 117, 119, 123, 125–9, 131, 136, 141, 155–6, 163, 165–7, 172, 176, 180–1, 188–9, 192, 195, 197, 210, 219, 223–5, 230, 238–9
Bavay (Bagacum) 113, 155
Bayeux (Augustodurum) 134, 137
Bazas (Cossio) 209
Beaumont-sur-Oise 175–6, 178, 184, 186–7, 265n50
Bedon, R. 5, 137
Bellona 49
benefactions *see* euergetism
Besançon (Vesontio) 183–4, 186
Béziers (Baeterrae) 80, 113, 139, 162
bishops 202–3, 210–12, 214, 216, 228–30
Blicquy 194–5, 199
Bliesbruck-Reinheim *196*, 197, 199
Bologna (Bononia) 5, 62–4, *63*, 86
Bordeaux (Burdigala) 82, 122, 125–6, 144, 207, 217–19, *218*, 224, 227–9
Bouet, A. 128, 159
Bouley, E. 141
Boulogne (Gesoriacum, Bononia) 171

boundaries *see* urban boundaries
Bourges (Avaricum) 147, 162, 183, 206
Bovillae 55–6
Braudel, F. 3, 235
bridges 32, 34, 45, 64, 66, 79, 93, 123, 128, 181, 189
Britain (Britannia), Roman province 5, 8, 41, 66–8, 72, 80, 86, 111, 155, 173, 201–2, 232, 236
Brunt, P. 123
building materials 16–17, 57
Burgundians 202–3
burial practices 2, 17–18, 43–5, 48–9, 60, 62, 65, 145–6, 150–3, 159, 210, 212–14, 216, 230, 236
burials *see* cemeteries, tombs
Burnham, B. and Wacher, J. 173

Caesar *see* Julius Caesar
Cahors (Divona) 209
Cales (Calvi) 53
Caligula (emperor) 85
Campagna (region around Rome) 20, 50
Capua 62
Caracalla (emperor) 65
Carcassonne (Carcasso) 171
Carhaix (Vorgium) 86, 147
Carthage 25, 146
Cassius Dio 28, 33, 48–9
cathedrals 201, 208–9, 211, 213, 221, 223, 230
Cato, M. Porcius 20, 24, 54
Catullus, C. Valerius 21, 38, 58, 228
cemeteries 48, 62, 65–6, 83, 86, 89–90, 103, 148, 150–3, 159–60, 178, 189, 204, 210, 212–13, 219–23, 227, 230
central place theory 40–1, 55, 74, 234
cepotaphia 48
ceramics *see* pottery production and distribution
Chalcedon 27
Châlon-sur-Saône 156
Champlin, E. 20, 50, 52
Charente 106, 109, 220
Charleville-Mezières 193–4, 199
Chartres (Autricum) 106
Château-Porcien 175–6, 179–81, 183, 185–7, 199
Château-Roussillon (Ruscino) 171
Chilperic (Frankish king) 214, 224–5
Christianity 149, 200–1, 203, 209–162, 219, 222–3, 229–30

300

INDEX

churches 36, 192, 200–1, 203, 209–16, 219, 222–5, 227, 230–1
Cicero, M. Tullius 10, 22, 25, 27, 47, 56, 72, 150, 157, 189, 228, 235
Cicero, Q. Tullius 22
Cimiez (Cemenelum) 223
circuses 72–3, 136, 148–50, 160, 164–6, 223–5, 234, 238–9
cities: as administrative centres 8–10, 56, 79, 82–3, 156, 189, 202–3, 211–12, 233–4, 237–8; as socio-economic centres 9, 13, 24–5, 40–1, 51–7, 72, 75, 79, 105–118, 123–5, 156, 158–9, 172, 184–5, 189–90, 203, 211–12, 224, 231, 233–6, 238, 240; as places for display 10–11, 18, 20, 56, 60, 68, 98, 106, 128, 135–6, 147, 149–50, 160, 170, 187, 210, 216, 223, 230–1, 233–4, 237–40; foundation and planning 55, 60–8, 83–6, 89–92, 98, 100, 132, 137, 141–2, 151, 158, 163–4, 170, 203–5, 237–9; visual representations of 28–37, 117, 236
city, Roman ideas about 8–13, 28–32, 34, 37–9, 59–60, 71, 75–6, 85, 108, 118, 137, 141–2, 150, 210, 216, 233–40
city--country relationship 2, 4, 8–15, 19–20, 22–3, 30, 39–41, 57–8, 69, 85–6, 133–7, 149–50, 156, 203, 216, 227, 233–7, 256n133
civic councils 8–9, 56, 82, 92, 98, 101–2, 106–8, 115, 158–9, 167–70, 202–3, 225; *see also* magistrates
Claudius (emperor) 23–4, 32–3, 44–5, 82
Clavel, M. 80
clergy, Christian 202, 210
Clermont Ferrand (Augustonemetum) 211, 213, 215, 222, 224, 228–9
Clodia 47
Clodius Albinus (usurper) 201
Clodius Pulcher, P. 56
Clovis (Frankish king) 203
Coarelli, F. 47
Codex Iustinianus 17, 21
coinage 29, 85, 130, 176, 203
collegia 48
Cologne *see* Köln
colonial charters *see* constitutional charters

columbaria 48
Columella, L. Iunius 23–4, 54
commerce 57, 69, 83, 80, 91–3, 103, 105–6, 109, 112–19, 121–2, 125–7, 144, 149, 151, 158–60, 163–6, 172, 183–4, 189, 201, 203, 218–19, 231, 233, 237, 240
Commodus (emperor) 27
commuting 4, 23
Comum (Como) 22, 24–5, 72
conciliabula 171
confluences 93, 127, 129, 134, 164, 217
'consumer city' debate 4, 234
Constantine I (emperor) 33, 35, 59, 202–3, 211
Constantinople 35, 59
constitutional charters 9, 15–17, 68, 106–8, 122; *see also* individual charters
continentia aedificia 14–16, 26, 39, 68–71, 76, 93, 111, 128, 155, 159
Corinth 47
Corpus Agrimensorum 29, 30, 35, 236
Corseul (Fanum Martis) 134, 136–7, 162–3
countryside, ancient ideas about 8–13, 39, 76
countryside, characteristics of *see* rural land-use
Crawford, M. 107
Creuse 181, 186, 188
cults *see* imperial cult, religion, temples
cultural interactions 2, 6, 11–12, 19, 25, 27–8, 37–8, 42, 59, 68, 72, 83–9, 98, 100, 117, 121, 128–39, 141–2, 147, 150, 160–2, 198–9, 236–40, 260n294
Curtius Rufus, Q. 25
Cybele 48

Dacia, Roman province 32
Dalheim 175–6, 178–9, 181, 184, 186, 237
Danube 201–2
Dax (Aquae Tarbellicae) 205, 211
Dea Dia 56
death and the dead *see* burials; burial practices
defences *see* walls, defensive
defixiones 146, 152–3
Delphic Amphictiony 51
De Maria, S. 65

301

INDEX

demolition, of standing structures 201, 204, 217, 219–23
Diana Nemorensis 57
Digesta of Justinian 12, 16, 42, 59, 62, 108
Diocletian 202
Dionysius of Halicarnassus 19, 42
Djemila (Cuicul) 65, 69
docks *see* quays
domestic occupation 56, 69, 83, 91, 93, 101, 103, 106, 117–126, 158–9, 165–6, 171, 181, 183, 185–7, 189, 193, 195–6, 213–16, 218–24, 230–1, 233
Domitian (emperor) 23–4, 51
domus (elite houses) 51, 72–3, 91, 93, 98, 103, 111, 113–4, 118–122, 127, 131, 155, 159–60, 163, 176, 211, 220–2, 224, 234, 236, 249n102
Doubs 176, 182–6
Drinkwater, J. 82, 147
Drusus (son of Livia) 130–1

eastern empire *see* Greek east
economic activity 17, 24–5, 40–1, 44, 47, 51–55, 57, 105–118, *114*, 123–7, 156, 158–9, 172, 184–6, 189, 195–7, 201–22, 224, 229, 231, 233–6, 240; *see also* agriculture; commerce; industry; trade
economic choices 24–5, 55, 92–3, 108–11, 113–5, 206–7, 224, 236, 240
education 85
Egeria 57
Egypt 48
elites: empire-wide 2, 9, 11–13, 18, 25, 37–8, 68, 72–5, 77–8, 108, 112, 158, 237; Gallo-Roman 7–8, 79–80, 85–7, 117–18, 129–30, 137, 141, 145, 151–2, 157, 160, 168–71, 189–90, 196–7, 199, 206, 226–30, 233–4, 236–40; metropolitan (Roman) 2, 7, 11, 18–26, 37–8, 46, 50–6, 58, 72, 74, 76–7, 157, 160, 214, 236–40
Elton, H. 206
emperors 11–12, 17, 24, 33, 43, 45, 47, 49, 56–7, 146, 206; *see also* individual emperors
Ephesus, Asia Minor 27
Ermine Street 75
Esmonde Cleary, S. 5, 80, 232

Etruscan urbanism 55, 64
euergetism 12, 125, 128, 141, 147, 151, 170–1, 203, 206, 209–10, 224
Eusebius of Caesarea 149, 203
Évaux (Evaunum) 192, 196
Évreux (Mediolanum) 159, 161–2
extra urbem 2–3, 19, 26, 37, 48
extra moenia 2–3, 19, 26
extra murum 2–3, 19, 26, 200

Falerii Veteres 55
fana see temples, Romano-Celtic
farms 54–5, 58, 153–7
Fauduet, I. 134, 137
Feronia 56
festivals 46, 56, 113, 117, 149–51, 184, 210, 214, 231, 239
Feurs (Forum Segusiavorum) 238
Février, P.-A. 216, 231
Finley, M.I. 235
Fishwick, D. 130
Flavius Philostratus, L. 72, 77
fora 85, 98, 103, 113, 131–3, 135, 137, 141, 144, 200, 204, 207, 223–4, 237–9
Forma Urbis 29, 33–4, 37, 46
Fors Fortuna 56
fortresses 207, 222, 225
Fortuna Primigenia 56–7
fountains, monumental 121, 127, 155, 188
France 5, 80
Franks 202–4, 206, 223
fratres arvales 56
Fréjus (Forum Iulii) 86, 93, 103, 109, *110*, 126–7, 139, 151, 160, 162–3, 185, 205
Frontinus, Sex. Iulius 26
Fucine Lake reliefs 32–33
funerary monuments *see* cemeteries, tombs
Futrell, A. 146–7

Gabii 55
Gades (Cádiz) 16
Gaius (emperor) *see* Caligula
Gaius (lawyer) 16
gardens 13, 23–5, 27, 46, 50, 54, 73
Garnsey, P. 123
Garonne 93, 127, 172, 205, 229
Gartempe 183, 185
gates (in city walls) 42, 45, 60, 65–6, 69,

INDEX

85, 129, 152, 158, 178, 211, 230, 236
Gaul (Gallia), Roman province 5–6, 8, 25, 41–2, 62, 64–5, 71–2, 79–240, 84; Aquitania 82, 147, 151–2, 161–2, 172–5, 192, 202, 209, 227; Armorica 192–3; Belgica 82, 111, 141, 161–2, 174–5, 193–4; 'Gallic empire' (AD 260–74) 201; late antique 200–31; Lugdunensis 82, 160–4, 167, 175, 193, 202, 238; Narbonensis 41, 81–3, 85–9, 118, 129–34, 149–51, 160–4, 170, 175, 179, 187, 193, 205, 209; Novempopulania 205, 207, 209, 222; pre-Roman 79, 83, 128, 134, 137, 150–1, 170–2, 176–81, 192–4, 198–9; provincial councils 81–3, 129–33; regional variation 80–1, 87–9, 147, 154, 160–2, 172, 204–5, 209–10, 229; Three Gauls 81–3, 85–9, 118, 129–37, 141, 149, 152, 202, 209; urbanism, special characteristics of 85–9, 141, 198–9
Geneva (Geneva) 171
Germanies, Roman provinces of 81–2, 86, 111, 117, 141, 167–71, 174–5
Glanum (St-Rémy-de-Provence) 175–9, 177, 184–7, 266n106
gods *see* individual gods, religion
governors *see* provincial administration
Greek east 9–11, 26–9, 35–8, 47, 51, 59–60, 72, 77, 168, 203, 239
Gregory of Tours 207, 211, 214, 224–5
Grenoble (Cularo, Gratianopolis) 171
grids *see* orthogonal grids

Hadrian (emperor) 44–5, 48, 51, 130
harbours 34, 93, 115, 163, 228; *see also* docks
Harries, J. 212
Heijmans, M. 219
Hercules 48
Herodes Atticus 25, 51, 77–8; villas of 77–8
Herodian 27
Herodotus 27
hills 64, 83, 86, 89, 117, 134–5, 152, 163–4, 172, 179, 193, 207
hill-sides *see* sloping land
Hispania *see* Spain
Historia Augusta 25
Hopkins, K. 234

Horace (Q. Horatius Flaccus) 13, 152
Hortensius (orator) 24
horti see Rome
hypocausts 119, 123, 195, 220, 224

Iberia *see* Spain
Illyricum, Roman province 28
imperial cult 81–2, 113, 119, 126, 129–33, 145–6, 160, 164, 187, 200, 223, 238–9
industry 17, 47, 57–8, 69, 75, 83, 90, 92–3, 103, 105–15, *114*, 117, 122, 151, 158–60, 163, 165–6, 172, 181, 183–6, 189, 193, 195–6, 218, 222, 231, 233–6, 240
Irni / Irnium, Spain 15–16
Isis 48
isolated state *see* Thünen, J.H. von
Itálica (Italica) 86
Italy (Italia) 17–18, 22, 25–6, 32–3, 41, 52–4, 59–65, 69–72, 74, 77, 82, 85–6, 93, 113, 118, 123, 134, 141–2, 157, 161, 163, 240
itineraries 171

Jerusalem 34
Jublains (Noviodunum) 134, 136–7, *138*, 141, 186, 202, 225–6, 239
Julian (author and emperor) 72
Julius Caesar (Republican politician) 81, 85, 149, 163
Juno 146, 238
Jupiter 146, 238; Latiaris 57
Juvenal (D. Iunius Iuvenalis) 43, 47, 106, 159

Kérilien 192–3
kilns *see* industry
Knossos, Crete 30
Köln (Colonia Agrippinensis) 10, 183

land alterations 91–3, 148, 164, 217–19, 224
land ownership 16, 22–4, 51, 54–5, 92, 113, 121–2, 151
land prices 22, 24, 46, 107–9, 122–3, 160, 233
land-surveyors *see agrimensores*
Laurence, R. 50
law, Roman 9, 13–18, 44, 49, 106–8, 202; *see also* constitutional charters; *Digesta* of Justinian, *Codex Iustinianus*

303

INDEX

Le Mans (Vindinum) 159, 202, 212
Lenus Mars *see* Mars Lenus
Leptiminus (Lamta) 74
Leptis Magna 64, 73–5, 78, 159
Leveau, P. 171
lex Coloniae Genetivae (Urso charter) 16–17, 60, 106–8, 122, 146, 150, 159
lex de flamonio provinciae Narbonensis 131
lex de munere publico libitinario (Puteoli) 17
lex Irnitana 15–16
lex Iulia municipalis see Tabula Heracleensis
lex Lucerina 18
Libitina 17
Liebeschuetz, W. 234
Ligt, L. de 113
Limoges (Augustoritum) 86, 135, 162, 213
Lincoln (Lindum) 5, 68, 76
Lindsay, H. 150
Lintz, G. 192
Lisieux (Noviomagus) 98, 99, 103, 111, 114, 134, 136, 141, 159, 163, 183, 199; site Michelet 98, 103, 111, 114; Vieux-Lisieux 134, 136, 141, 159
Livy (Titus Livius) 19, 42
local rivalry 149, 164, 175
Loire 162, 216
Lombards 202
London (Londinium) 34, 64, 72
Luceria (Lucera) 18
Lucian of Samosata 28
Lucius Verus (emperor) 51
Lucus Feroniae 51–2, *53*, 55–6, 197
ludi Saeculares 149
ludi Taurenses 149
Luni (Luna) 71
Lupercalia 46
Lyon (Lugdunum) 34, 81–3, 85, 89–93, 96, 103, 105, 109, 111, 113, 117, 119–122, *120*, 125–6, 129–33, *130*, *133*, 135–6, 144, 146–9, 151–2, 154, 157, 159–60, 162–4, 176, 181, 185, 199, 201–3, 207–9, 213, 219, 223–4, 228–9, 234, 238–9; Canabae (Presqu'île) 91; Condate 111, 129–33, *130*, 164; foundation 82, 89–90; Fourvière plateau 90–1, 93, 96, 113, 119–122, 131, *133*, 163, 207–9, 223–4; Saint-Jean quarter 91, 125–6,

207–9, 223–4; Trion 103, 119–20, 151–2, 269n98; Vaise 90–1, 111, 117, 121, 159

macella 113, 222
Mâcon 156
Macrinus, M. Opellius (emperor) 27
Maecenas, C. 48
magic 146, 152–3
magistrates: of the city of Rome 44–5; of the Roman state 51, 56–7, 203, 210, 238; urban 16, 56, 80, 93, 122, 152, 167–70, 202–3; *see also* civic councils
Magna Mater *see* Cybele
Mandeure (Epomanduorum) 167–71, *168*, 175–6, 179–89; Faubourg du Pont 182–3, 185; Mathay 180, 183–5
Mangin, M. and Tassaux, F. 170, 173, 175
mapping, ancient 29–30, 33–37, 45
marble, decorative 50, 54, 73, 155, 188–9
Marcus Aurelius (emperor) 33, 51, 201
markets *see* commerce
Mars 49; Lenus 134–6, 149, 239; Ultor 49
Marseille (Massilia) 79, 81, 83
Martial (M. Valerius Martialis) 22, 25, 43, 47, 159
Martin of Tours 213–4, 216
Maxentius (emperor) 51
May, R. 225
Meaux (Iatinum) 86, 87, 134, 136–7, 139, 162
Melun (Metlosedum) 110
Mercury 238
Mérida (Augusta Emerita) 64
Metz (Divodurum) 86, 123–5, *124*, 134, 159, 163, 183, 197, 199, 205, 214, 219–20, 223, 236; Pontiffroy 123–5, 159, 219, 236
Meuse 194
military activity 26–8, 32, 36–7, 49, 81, 163, 201–2, 206, 217, 219, 225–6, 230
military personnel 26–7, 33, 43, 49, 81, 206, 225
Millett, M. 41
Minerva 146, 187, 238
mixed land-use 69, 89, 103–5, 111, 114–15, 118–19, 122–3, 151, 158–9
monasteries 209, 214, 216
Mons Albanus 57

304

INDEX

Mont Afrique 171
Mont Beuvray (Bibracte) 150
Monte Canino 54
Monte Forco 54
monumental public buildings 10–11, 20, 48–9, 56, 60, 68–9, 71, 85, 87–9, 88, 93, 98, *101*, 103, 108, 111, 113–5, 119, 123, 125–50, *130*, *143*, *145*, 159–63, 167–71, 175, 178–81, *180*, 186–93, 200–1, 203–4, 207, 209–16, 218, 222–5, 230–1, 233–4, 236–40; orientation 71, 92, 128, 137, 144, 148, 159, 176, 181, 186, 189, 193; *see also* individual building types
Morley, N. 40–1, 54–5
mortuary practices *see* burial practices
mosaics 73–4, 85, 119, 127, 185, 188, 222, 224, 227
Moselle (Mosel) 86, 116, 123, 141
municipal charters *see* constitutional charters

Naintré 175–6, 179, 184–6, 189
Narbonne (Narbo Martius) 81–3, 113, 126, 129–33, *132*, 136, 144, 160, 229, 238–9
Naveau, J. 137, 225
Nero (emperor) 13, 23–4, 34, 54, 137, 141
Nicomedia (Izmit) 59
Nicopolis, Achaea 239
Nîmes (Nemausus) 83, 85, 112, 142, 144, 185, 206
Nisaea, port of Megara 27
North Africa, Roman provinces of 8, 25, 63–4, 69–70, 72, 80, 113, 155, 157
Nyon (Noviodunum) 82, 85

Oea (Tripoli) 73–5
oppida (pre-Roman settlements) 59, 64, 79, 83–4, 150, 179
oppidum (urban centre) 15, 68, 106, 233
Orange (Arausio) 93, 122, 152, 163
orientation *see* roads; monumental public buildings
Orléans (Cenabum) 161
orthogonal grids 12, 56, 62–3, 65–6, 69, 85–6, 92, 96, 98, 103, 131, 139, 141–2, 144, 150, 163, 167–71, 175, 178–9, 183–4, 186, 188–9, 191–2, 205, 224–5, 230, 237–8
Ostia 2, 34, 55–6, 83, 163

Ovid 56

pagi 149, 170–1
painted plaster 185, 196; *see also* wall paintings
palaces 203, 211
Pape, L. 195
Parentalia 151
Paris (Lutetia) 93, *94*, 110, 139, 147–8, 176, 203, 207, 219, 222, 224–5
passus mille 15–16, 44
Patterson, J.R. 43, 47
Paulinus of Pella 209
Pausanias (geographer) 10–11, 168
Peacock, D. 105
Percival, J. 227
Perge, Asia Minor 59
Périgueux (Vesunna) 126–8, 135–6, 159, 183, 199, 207, *208*; Chamiers 126–8, 136, 159, 272n31
personifications 31–2, 35–7
Pescennius Niger, C. (usurper) 27
Petronius (satirist) 152
Peutinger Table 29–30, 35–7, *36*, 171
Philo Judaeus 28
Philostratus *see* Flavius Philostratus, L.
Picard, G.C. 171
Pictones 175
Placentia (Piacenza) 26
Plato 27
Plautus, T. Maccius 20
Pliny the Elder 19, 25, 48, 171
Pliny the Younger 22–5, 50, 72, 77, 85, 157; Laurentine villa of 22–4, 50, 77
Plutarch (Mestrius Plutarchus) 27
Poitiers (Limonum) 82, 134, 175, 212–3
polynuclear settlement organisation 181–3, 189, 191, 193–5, 197–9, 232, 239
pomerial boundaries 42–4, 60, 62, 65–6, 150, 178; *see also* Rome: *pomerium*
Pompeii 30, 54, 118, 121, 147, 152, 236
porticoes, monumental 32, 55, 98, 113, 121, 127, 131, 139, 167, 222, 238
ports *see* harbours
Portus *see* Ostia
pottery production and distribution 105, 109–11, 115, 117, 151, 163, 184–5, 195, 231, 234; *see also terra sigillata*
praedia see villa properties

INDEX

Praeneste (Palestrina) 55–7
proast(e)ion 2, 19, 27–8, 33, 37, 47
profectio and *adventus* 33, 37, 49
property disputes 13–14, 59
provincial administration 17, 79, 82–3, 85, 119, 129–33, 154, 160, 170, 201–3, 225
Punic urbanism 59
Purcell, N. 13, 235
Puteoli (Pozzuoli) 17, 236

quarrying 111–12, 185, 225
quays 47, 79, 116, 208
Quilici, L. 80
Quimper 193–6
Quintilian, M. Fabius 10, 235

ramparts, earthen 66–8, 171, 178, 188, 194
Rance 167
Rebourg, A. 155
regionary catalogues 44
Reims (Durocortorum) 82, 86, 110, 113, 163, 231, 237
reliefs, sculptural 32–3, 36–7, 49
religion, polytheistic 9, 12, 42–4, 46, 48–9, 56–7, 61, 72, 82, 93, 96, 103, 113, 117, 119, 125, 127–38, 141, 145–6, 149–53, 172, 184, 187–8, 194–5, 207, 237–9; *see also* Christianity; festivals; imperial cult; temples
Remmius Palaemon (grammarian) 23–4
Reynaud, J.-F. 208
Rhine 85, 117, 201–3, 229
Rhodes 25
Rhône 71, 79, 89–91, 96, 98, 103, 105, 114–17, 121, 148–9, 163–4, 203, 207–8, 219
Ribemont-sur-Ancre 136
Rickman, G. 113, 117
rivers *see* watercourses, individual rivers
roads 23, 39, 55, 58–9, 62–3, 71, 75, 79, 81, 86, 91–3, 96, 98, *101*, 102–3, 105, 109, 111, 114, 123, 125, 137, 144, 148, 151, 154, 156–7, 159, 167, 172, 181–6, 189, 191, 196; in open country 23, 36, 134; in the urban centre 14–15, 96, 129, 135, 141, 144, 149, 204; orientation 62–3, 65–6, 86, 98, 137, 183, 192, 230
Roanne (Rodumna) 193–4, 199

Rodez (Segodunum) 162
Rogations 214
Roma (goddess) 187
Roman state 8–9, 12, 56, 60, 79–82, 112, 117, 129–33, 137, 150, 163, 201–2, 206, 211, 225, 233, 236–40
Roman urbanism, characteristics of 11–12, 59–75, 81, 85, 161–2, 192, 198, 200–1, 232–40
'Romanisation' *see* cultural interactions
romanitas, ancient conception of 10–11, 60, 142, 210, 237–9
Rome 13–28, *21*, 33–37, *36*, 39, 42–59, 66, 68–9, 71, 73–6, 80, 85, 98, 100, 106, 117, 123–5, 127, 130, 134, 136, 141, 146, 149–51, 154, 157, 159, 197–201, 236, 239–40; amphitheatres 47–8, 85, 146; Anio 57; aqueducts 47, 58; arches, monumental 33, 45, 65; Augustan *regiones* 43–6, 49; Aurelianic wall 34, 36, 42–5; Aventine hill 46; barracks 49; baths 43, 47, 85; Caelian hill 46–7; Campus Martius 20, 34, 37, 43–4, 47, 49, 76, 98, 117, 127, 149, 239; Capitoline hill 46–9; circuses 145; *continentia aedificia* 14–16, 34, 44–9, 57–8, 68; customs boundary 44, 47; domestic occupation 34, 46, 49; *Domus Aurea* (Golden House) 13, 34; Emporium district 47, 117; Esquiline hill 17–18, 46, 48, 152; Forum Romanum 47–8, 146; *horti* 46–7, 49; imperial *fora* 47, 49; industry 47; Janiculum 34, 43, 46; legal definitions of 14, 42, 44–5; *macella* 47; Mutatorium Caesaris 49; Oppian hill 34, 36; Palatine hill 45, 48; *pomerium* 17, 20, 26, 42–5, 48–9; St. Peter's 36; 'Servian' (Republican) wall 14–15, 19–20, 34, 42–9, 59; suburban settlements 51–2, 55–9, 75; suburban villas 19–25, 27, 33, 39, 46, 50–55, 72, 74–8, 197, 199, 214, 216; *suburbium*, the 2–5, 20–27, *21*, 33, 37, 46, 49–59, 72, 74–5; temples 46–9, 134, 136; *Templum Pacis* 33; theatres 48, 141; Tiber 20, 34, 36, 43, 46–7, 50, 57, 106, 117; Tiber island 48; tombs 48–9; Trajan's column 32, 36, 117; Transtiberim 34, 43, 46–7, 76, 106; *urbs* 14–17, 20, 34, 42–9, 57, 59,

306

68, 76, 233, 236; *vici* 44–5;
  warehouses 44, 47, 123
Romulus (legendary king) 46
Romulus Augustulus (emperor) 202
Rouen (Rotomagus) 116, 176
rural land-use 40–2, 74, 76–8, 89, 105,
  113, 124–5, 128, 134–7, 139, 153–7,
  203, 216, 226–9

Saepinum (Altilia) 60
Saint-Bertrand-de-Comminges
  (Lugdunum Convenarum) 113, 139,
  155, 186, 207, 213, 222, 225, *226*,
  238
Saint-Germain-d'Esteuil 175–6, 179,
  181, 186
Saint-Michel-du-Touch *see* Toulouse
Saint-Romain-en-Gal *see* Vienne
Saintes (Mediolanum Santonum) 81, 96,
  106, *107*, 109, 122, 130, 134, 144,
  145, 159, 163, 176, 185, 204, 206,
  220–3, 229
sanctuaries 82, 125, 128, 139, 158,
  162–4, 184, 186, 188, 195; *see also*
  temples
Sanxay 136, 175–6, 181, 184, 186–7
Saône 91, 111, 121, 163–4, 207–8, 219
satellite settlements 56, 68–9, 75, 93,
  95–6, 117, 128, 159, 183–5, 187,
  189, 191, 195, 197–9, 214–16, 224,
  239
Scheid, J. 149
Schlemaire, G. 125, 219
seasonal land-use 117, 144, 149
secondary agglomerations 8, 89, 105,
  125, 128, 136, 139, 142, 156, 159,
  167–99, 203, 209, 232, 236–7, 239
Seine 93, 116, 162, 207
Seneca, L. Annaeus (the Younger) 23–4,
  52
Senlis (Augustomagus) 147, 162
Sens (Agedincum) 103, *104*, 109–11,
  123, 134, 136, 160, 163, 185, 205,
  234
Septimius Severus (emperor) 17, 42–3,
  201
Sequani 81, 167
Serapis 48
settlement hierarchies 40–1, 83, 172,
  198
Severan marble map of Rome *see Forma
  Urbis*

sewers 92, 101–2, 123
Sidonius Apollinaris 227–9
Sinope 27
slave labour 123–4
sloping land 64–6, 69, 73, 89, 92–3,
  111, 130, 134–5, 139, 141, 144,
  147–8, 163–4, 176, 179, 186, 192–3
Soissons (Augusta Suessionum) 139,
  162, 224–5
soldiers *see* military personnel
Somme 64, 101, 123, 150–1, 227
Spain (Hispania, Iberia), Roman
  province 8, 11, 15–16, 25, 60, 64, 72,
  86, 93, 163, 201–2
Sparta 28
spectacles *see* amphitheatres, circuses,
  theatres
springs 93, 96, 100, 121, 125, 127, 129,
  134, 152, 172, 181, 192
Strabo (geographer) 11, 19, 37, 98, 115,
  130, 171, 239
streets *see* roads
stucco 54, 73, 188
suburban settlements, villas *see* Rome
suburbanus and cognates 2, 16–17,
  19–27, 37, 51–2, 56, 72–3, 77–8,
  228
suburbium (Latin noun) 2, 19–20, 200,
  230
suburbium, the *see* Rome
suburbs: connotations 2–4, 20; medieval
  3–4, 158–9, 231; modern 3, 118,
  122, 158–9, 231
Suetonius Tranquillus, C. 23–5
Sulpicius Severus 216
Switzerland 150

Tabula Heracleensis 15–16
Tacitus, Cornelius 10, 26, 46, 236
Taden 167–70, *169*, 191, 198
Tarpin, M. 173
Tarraco (Tarragona) 25
taxation 202, 234; customs duties 44,
  47, 60; provincial *tributum* 112
Teanum Sidicinum (Teano) 53
temples 26, 36, 46–9, 56–8, 69, 75, 83,
  88, 89, 93, 96, 103, 113, 117,
  128–38, 141, 149–50, 163, 165–7,
  172, 176, 180–1, 186–8, 190, 192,
  195, 207, 223, 230, 237, 239;
  classical 87–9, 128–33, 135–6, 187,
  190; Romano-Celtic 87–9, 103, 128,

INDEX

133–7, 142, 160, 167, 187, 190, 195, 239–40; *see also* individual deities, sanctuaries
tenancy 54–5, 92, 108, 113, 233, 234
Terminalia 46, 56
terra sigillata 105–6, 111–2
Thapsus 74
theatres 48, 69, 73, *88*, 96, 103, 119, 136, 139–42, *140*, 144–5, 148–50, 161–7, 176, 180–1, 186–8, 193, 223, 239; classical 87–9, 139–42, 161, 238–9; of Gallic type 87–9, 139–42, 161, *180*, 186–7, 239
Thucydides 27
Thünen, J.H. von 41, 50, 55, 72, 76, 156
Thysdrus (El Djem) 74
Tiberius (emperor) 23, 25, 28, 33, 35, 130, 133
Tibur (Tivoli) 21, 51, 55–8
Tifernum Tiberinum (Città di Castello) 22, 24, 77
Timgad (Thamugadi) 63, 69, *70*
Tiretaine 213
Titus (emperor) 44
tombs 33, 47–9, 57–8, 69, 83, 93, 96, 103, 137, 150–3, *153*, 160, 170, 178, 204, 210, 220–1
tomb-gardens *see cepotaphia*
Tongres (Atuatuca) 155
Toulouse (Tolosa) 86, 93, 117, 129, 135, 145, 155, 159, 176, 183, 199, 205; Saint-Michel-du-Touch 93, *95*, 96, 117, 123, 126–9, 135, 145, 149, 159
Tournai (Tornacum) 171
Tours (Caesarodunum) 106, 135–6, 207, 213–6, *215*, 222, 224, 231
trade *see* commerce
Treggiari, S. 123
Treveri 134, 149
Trier (Augusta Treverorum) 82, 85–6, 103, 105, *116*, 129, 134–6, 141, 146–9, 162, 197, 201–3, 205–6, 214, 224, 227–8, 237, 239, 255n108; Altbachtal sanctuary 103, 134, 136, 141
Troyes (Augustobona) 110
Turin (Augusta Taurinorum) 85–6
Tusculum 27
Twelve Tables 17

Ugernum 150

urban boundaries 3, 11–13, 15, 38–40, 42–6, 59–71, 73, 75–6, 83, 85–6, 89, 103, 108–9, 115–17, 131, 142, 144, 148, 150–2, 154, 158, 176–9, 192, 194, 203–9, 211–13, 217, 230–3, 236–7, 240; *see also* arches, monumental; roads: orientation; orthogonal grids; pomerial boundaries; watercourses; walls, defensive
urban centres 18, 39, 59–68, 72, 75–6, 80, 85–6, 91–2, 96, 101–3, 105–8, 113, 115–23, 125, 127–9, 131–7, 139, 141, 142, 144–6, 148, 150–1, 158–61, 163, 174, 176–81, 183–91, 198–200, 203–9, 211–14, 216–26, 230–7; shifts in location 91, 207–9, 219; *see also oppidum, urbs*
urban periphery: ambiguity 14, 16–18, 20–21, 37–40, 57–8, 69, 71, 76–8, 150–3, 228, 239; ancient ideas about 7–38, 227–30, 239; as a place of exclusion 17–18, 23–4, 37, 106–8, 134–5, 145–6, 150–3, 158–61, 184, 204, 231, 236; attempts to regulate 17–18, 37, 49; definitions 1, 4, 8, 74–5, 156, 174, 191, 241n5; identification from modern perspective 5, 38–78, 204; visual representations of 31–7
urban space, pressures on 46, 48–9, 69, 89, 91–2, 108, 122, 132, 136, 142, 148, 160, 163, 185, 188, 211–2, 214, 224–5, 233
urban status 8–13, 56, 60, 68, 81–2, 167–71, 174–6, 183–4, 187, 189–90, 193, 200, 202–5, 209–10, 216, 233–4, 236
urbanitas see city, Roman ideas about; Roman urbanism, characteristics of
urbs see Rome
Urso, Spain *see lex Coloniae Genetivae*

Valens 202
Valentinian I 202
Varro, M. Terentius 9, 24, 235
Veii 42, 55, 57, 64
Venantius Fortunatus 229
Ventimiglia 163
Vermand (Viromandis) 194–5
Verona 64, 85
Verulamium (St. Albans) 66–8, *67*, 76

INDEX

Vesle 111
Vespasian (emperor) 33, 44
via Aemilia 62–4
via Appia 45, 48–51, 53, 77, 152
via Campana 56
via Domitia 151, 183, 185
via Flaminia 33, 45, 47
via Latina 23, 53
via Nomentana 23, 51
via Salaria 23
via Tiburtina 23
vici 171
Vidourle 183, 185
Vienne (Vienna) 71, 80, 89, *90*, 96, 98, 101–3, 111, 114–16, 122, 125–8, 147–9, 158, 160, 162–4, 181, 185, 203, 214, 219–20, 223, 239, 270n130; area south of the city walls 117, 148–9; Sainte-Colombe-lès-Vienne 96, 126, 128, 219; Saint-Romain-en-Gal 96, 98, *101*, 102–3, 111, *114*, 115–17, 122, 125–8, 148, 158, 214, 219, 234, 239
Vieux (Aregenua) 147, 161
villa at Oplontis 54
villa at S. Basilio 50–1
villa landscapes 2, 20, 50, 52, 58, 73–4
villa of Magerius, Smirat 74
villa of San Rocco, Francolise 52–3, 74
villa of the Quintilii 50–1
villa of the Volusii 51–2, 197
villa properties 19–25, 27, 33, 39, 46, 50–55, 58, 68, 71–8, 105, 127–8, 153–7, 189, 191, 195–6, 199, 201, 226–30, 236, 244n99; journeys to and from 23, 39, 50–1, 56, 58, 77, 157, 214, 229; urbanising / monumentalising features in 22, 39, 50–4, 72–4, 77, 155–6, 189, 236
Villedieu, F. 91
visibility: of boundaries 45, 62, 65–6, 68, 71, 86, 89; of monuments 47–8, 58, 93, 131–2, 137, 147, 151–2, 154, 159, 186–7, 189, 224, 234
Visigoths 202–3
Vitruvius Pollio 48, 135, 237, 249n102
Vocontii 82
Vonne 187

Walker, S. 154
Wallace-Hadrill, A. 57
wall paintings 30, *31*, 34, 54, 73, 123, 127; *see also* painted plaster
walls, defensive 11–13, 26, 29–36, 38–9, 41–6, 59–60, 62, 65–71, 74, 83, 85–6, 89, 96, *101*, 103, 106, 108–9, 116–17, 129, 142, 144, 152, 163–4, 173, 176–9, 192, 201, 203–15, 217–21, 230–2, 235–7
warehouses *see* commerce
waste disposal 18
Water Newton (Durobrivae) 75
watercourses 53, 64–6, 71, 73–5, 86, 91–3, 96, 98, 100, 105, 109, 115–17, 123, 127, 134–5, 137, 148–9, 152, 162–4, 167, 171, 176, 179, 188, 191–2, 194, 207–9, 213, 217–19, 224, 234, 236
water-pipes 51, 101, 103, 188
wells 100–1, 117, 123, 152, 163, 225
Whittaker, C.R. 124, 235
Wiedemann, T. 146
Woolf, G. 12, 41, 150, 156, 170, 172, 235
workshops *see* industry

Xenophon 27

Yonne 103, 109, 111

Ziegert, H. 159
zoned land-use 4, 103, 119, 151, 158–9

eBooks – at www.eBookstore.tandf.co.uk

A library at your fingertips!

eBooks are electronic versions of printed books. You can store them on your PC/laptop or browse them online.

They have advantages for anyone needing rapid access to a wide variety of published, copyright information.

eBooks can help your research by enabling you to bookmark chapters, annotate text and use instant searches to find specific words or phrases. Several eBook files would fit on even a small laptop or PDA.

NEW: Save money by eSubscribing: cheap, online access to any eBook for as long as you need it.

Annual subscription packages

We now offer special low-cost bulk subscriptions to packages of eBooks in certain subject areas. These are available to libraries or to individuals.

For more information please contact webmaster.ebooks@tandf.co.uk

We're continually developing the eBook concept, so keep up to date by visiting the website.

www.eBookstore.tandf.co.uk

Related titles from Routledge

Globalizing Roman Culture
Unity, Diversity and Empire
Richard Hingley

What is Romanization?

Was Rome the first global culture?

Romanization has been represented as a simple progression from barbarism to civilization. Roman forms in architecture, coinage, language and literature came to dominate the world from Britain to Syria. Hingley argues for a more complex and nuanced view in which Roman models provided the means for provincial elites to articulate their own concerns. Inhabitants of the Roman provinces were able to develop identities they never knew they had until Rome gave them the language to express them.

Most work that has been done in this area has concentrated on specific areas or provinces. Hingley draws together the threads in a sophisticated theoretical framework that spans the whole Roman Empire, and provokes intriguing comparisons with modern discussions of 'Coca-colaization' and resistance to American cultural domination.

ISBN10: 0–415–35175–8 (hbk)
ISBN10: 0–415–35176–6 (pbk)

ISBN13: 978–0–415–35175–1 (hbk)
ISBN13: 978–0–415–35176–8 (pbk)

Available at all good bookshops
For ordering and further information please visit:
www.routledge.com

Related titles from Routledge

The Romans
An Introduction
Brian Campbell

The Romans provides students with an excellent introduction to all aspects of Roman culture. Antony Kamm focuses on literature, art and architecture, and includes discussion of major contemporary developments in the study of ancient Rome.

All the crucial elements of Roman history such as the reign of the Caesars and the role of the army are discussed. Again drawing on recent scholarship, the author examines important themes like imperialism, religion and everyday social life.

Incorporating maps, charts and pictures as well as a comprehensive bibliography and index, *The Romans* is a concise yet thorough introductory survey of Roman civilization. An indispensable textbook, *The Romans* will prove invaluable for students of disciplines such as ancient history, art, literature or history, who require a reliable, accessible guide to all aspects of Roman culture.

ISBN10: 0–415–12039–X (hbk)
ISBN10: 0–415–12040–3 (pbk)

ISBN13: 978–0–415–12039–5 (hbk)
ISBN13: 978–0–415–12040–1 (pbk)

Available at all good bookshops
For ordering and further information please visit:
www.routledge.com